D0049690

THE HERO AND THE GODDESS

ALSO BY JEAN HOUSTON

A Passion for the Possible: A Guide to Realizing Your Full Potential
The Mythic Path: Discovering the Guiding Stories of Your Past—Creating a Vision for Your Future (with Mary Catherine Bateson)
The Passion of Isis and Osiris: A Union of Two Souls
The Science of Mind
The Search for the Beloved: Journeys into Sacred Psychology
The Possible Human
Life Force: The Pyscho-Historical Recovery of the Self
Godseed: The Journey of Christ
A Feminine Myth of Creation (with Diana Vandenberg)

COAUTHORED WITH ROBERT MASTERS

Mind Games
Listening to the Body

BOOK 1: THE TRANSFORMING MYTHS SERIES

THE HERO AND THE GODDESS

The Odyssey as Mystery and Initiation

Jean Houston

BALLANTINE BOOKS
NEW YORK

Sale of this book without a front cover may be unauthorized. If this book is coverless, it may have been reported to the publisher as "unsold or destroyed" and neither the author nor the publisher may have received payment for it.

A Ballantine Book
Published by The Ballantine Publishing Group

Copyright © 1992 by Jean Houston

All rights reserved under International and Pan-American Copyright Conventions. Published in the United States by The Ballantine Publishing Group, a division of Random House, Inc., New York, and simultaneously distributed in Canada by Random House of Canada Limited, Toronto.

Grateful acknowledgment is made to the following for permission to reprint previously published material: BEACON PRESS: Excerpt from *Lost Goddesses of Early Greece* by Charlene Spretnak. Copyright © 1984 by Charlene Spretnak. Reprinted by permission of Beacon Press. HARPERCOLLINS PUBLISHERS INC.: Excerpts from *The Odyssey of Homer*, translated with an introduction by Richard Lattimore. Copyright © 1965, 1967 by Richard Lattimore. Reprinted by permission of HarperCollins Publishers Inc. THOMAS NELSON & SONS LTD.: Excerpts from *The Odyssey* by Homer, translated by William H.D. Rouse, published by Thomas Nelson & Sons Ltd. PENGUIN BOOKS LTD.: Excerpts from *The Odyssey* by Homer, translated by E.V. Rieu (Penguin Classics, 1946). Copyright © 1946 by the Estate of E.V. Rieu. Reprinted by permission of Penguin Books Ltd. PRINCETON UNIVERSITY PRESS: Excerpts from *The Hero with a Thousand Faces* by Joseph Campbell. Copyright © 1949 by Princeton University Press. Copyright renewed 1976 by Princeton University Press. "Ithaka" from *C.P. Cavafy: Collected Poems* translated by Edmund Keeley and Philip Sherrard. Copyright © 1975 by Princeton University Press. Reprinted by permission of Princeton University Press. RANDOM HOUSE, INC.: Excerpts from *The Odyssey* by Homer, translated by Robert Fitzgerald. Copyright © 1961, 1963 by Robert Fitzgerald. Copyright renewed 1989 by Benedict R.C. Fitzgerald. Reprinted by permission of Vintage Books, a division of Random House, Inc. VIKING PENGUIN: "The Song of a Man Who Has Come Through" from *The Complete Poems of D.H. Lawrence* by D.H. Lawrence. Copyright © 1964, 1971 by Angelo Ravagli and C.M. Weekley, Executors of the Estate of Frieda Lawrence Ravagli. Used by permission of Viking Penguin, a division of Penguin Books USA Inc.

http://www.randomhouse.com

Library of Congress Catalog Card Number: 91-92142

ISBN: 0-345-36567-4

Text design by Debby Jay
Cover painting: William Russell Flint, *Athene Helping Odysseus Store his Treasures.*
Photograph: Mary Evans Picture Library © Estate of William Russell Flint.

Manufactured in the United States of America

First Edition: February 1992

10 9 8 7 6 5 4 3

In Memoriam
Derek C. Lawley

Ἄνδρα μοι ἔννεπε, Μοῦσα, πολύτροπον . . .

Contents

Note on Translations and Spelling

I offer a variety of translations throughout the text so that the reader may enjoy many styles, both poetic and prose, of reading and interpreting *The Odyssey*. I maintain one spelling for names and places. Alternate spellings may occur within quotations from different translations.

Acknowledgments

The Odyssey is my favorite of all books, so my first acknowledgment goes to whoever Homer or Homers were. The book has provided me with years of delectation, of wonder and astonishment, a constant marvel of surprise and a mirror into my soul. Then I must acknowledge, too, my first encounter with Athena in the form of Mrs. Mabel Finnigan, my Latin teacher at Julia Richman High School. She introduced me to the world of classical scholarship and ancient languages from which I, *mirabile dictu,* will never recover.

In 1988 I took some seventy of my students on a sailing voyage from Troy to Ithaca, reliving the voyage of Odysseus and performing on various plausible islands some of the adventures and processes contained in this book. I am grateful to these students for going to their edges with me on this voyage and for their insights on living the life of the "man of many ways." Bill Lefakinis, president of Valef Yachts, and the captains of his boats were wonderfully helpful in allowing us to meander through the Aegean, Mediterranean, and Ionian seas as we wished and to stop on whatever island we thought Odysseus had visited. The citizens of Ithaca welcomed us with warmth and courtesy and took us to places still mythic to the memory of Odysseus and Penelope.

I want to thank my close associates in my seminar work, Margaret Rubin, Robin Van Doren, and Elisabeth Rothenberger, for having accompanied and encouraged our seminars on *The Odyssey*. With radical insight and classic wisdom, they have been my muses, my mainstays, my mentors of the Triple Goddess. Cheryl Woodruff, my editor at Ballantine, has offered an eye of blazing acuity to help me through the Scylla and Charybdis of mixed metaphors and questionable insights. Her skill is masterful, and if I have succumbed to the Sirens of excess and extravagance, the fault is entirely my own.

My literary agent, Rosyln Targ, could have been the Queen of the Phaeacians, so welcoming of one's talent is she, so full of humor and high games, setting one on one's journey with abundant gifts, and knowing who one really is.

To all of these, and finally to Herself, Pallas Athena, my guiding archetype, I offer my thanks and deepest gratitude.

Preface

Working with, and playing with, the world's great myths and stories can change our lives. Totally. One can argue, of course, and rightly, that our lives are changed any time we watch great drama, listen to great music chanted or sung or played on instruments, see great dance, fall with our eyes into great paintings and sculpture, or read great literature. Indeed, all works of art contain patterns, even secrets, about the nature of creativity and perhaps about the nature of life itself. All of this enhances the awareness and deepens the understanding of those willing to welcome such works into their hearts.

But the process of change that I invite you to embark upon through the use of this book is one that requires conscious participation, vigorous engagement, and a willingness to play a game with the universe.

My challenge to you is to work with, and play with, this book about *The Odyssey*—and Homer's *Odyssey* as well—as if it were the story of your own journey, your own initiation. As if the story held clues and codes to illumine your life and help enhance your human possibilities. Work with it as if you believed your life had meaning, or the capacity for deeper meaning, and much of that meaning could be brought into greater focus and more delight through a full-fledged encounter with this Hero and this Goddess. My goal in making this challenge is to invite you to create many new moments in your life that bring the reality of spiritual things more home to you.

I believe that all great stories have power coded in them that can help us change our lives, and by changing our lives, change the world—for the better, one hopes. There is no story in the world that has more of this transformative energy than *The Odyssey*. In fact, its power is so great that it very likely served as the beginning point for Greek civilization. Through that high culture it influenced, for good and bad, all that we in the West have subsequently become. And despite its great antiquity, *The Odyssey* remains a living work that can be read with fresh eyes for today's needs.

One of the most important lessons of *The Odyssey* comes through the relationship between the Hero and the Goddess. From their partnership we can learn patterns for creating or restoring a sense of the deep connections that are possible between our mortal selves and the immortal realities.

Another powerful reason for working with *The Odyssey* in dramatic and full-blooded ways is that great stories live in a realm outside the one we ordinarily inhabit. Such tales are citizens of a world they share with the laws of nature, with great music and art, with the High Self, with the Beloved Friend of the Soul, and with universal archetypes—the grand patterns of life, those constellations of energy we have often called goddesses and gods.

The realm of myth exists beyond time and space and daily reality. It is a symbolic world that dwells within us at levels deeper than our normal consciousness. And yet, it can be openly and vividly engaged in ways that expand the possibilities of every aspect of our lives. But to reach these depths and heights, we must pledge our commitment, our theatricality, our excitement. We must not bore the gods—or ourselves.

When we energetically and dramatically encounter this mythic realm and the beings who dwell there, we begin to understand that our individual lives—our personal stories—echo the events and truths of their lives and stories. We reflect these mythic beings and they reflect us. Experiencing this mutual recognition gives us access to more vigor and energy, a greater sense of joy and release, and an even deeper commitment to the unfolding planetary story. We begin living with the doors and windows of ordinary life wide open to the depth world.

At the very least this can renew our powers of creativity. But also, our loving participation in this realm as the wildly individual human beings we are—with all our unique stories, our creativity, our imagination, and our dreams—can inform and enrich, change and deepen the mythic realm itself. The challenge involves not only choosing to believe that our lives matter, but that they also matter to the gods themselves.

When we reenact the life of Francis of Assisi, we allow this patron saint of greenness to live again through us. When we go questing for the Grail as Percival, we learn how to ask the great questions of our lives as well as his. By embodying the divine presence of Jesus and the Sophia, we achieve new awareness of the miracle inherent in all life. By mourning with Isis and being torn apart and restored to union as Osiris, we feel the core realities of death and resurrection. And by journeying side by side with Odysseus, we undertake a soul journey from which we can emerge as did Odysseus' men after their interlude as pigs on Circe's isle, "taller and more beautiful than before."

And by adventuring with us, Odysseus, celebrated in the mythic realm of human experience and story, is changed also. He undergoes our rites of passage as we do his. He argues with us about his activities. He explains himself over and over. And he tricks us time and again. But when at last we come home to Ithaca with him, he and all his companions, his beloved Penelope, his son Telemachus, and above all, his Great Friend, the goddess Athena, live again. They, too, have experienced rich new ways of being because we have shared their great story and they have shared ours.

Please do not consider this work simply an interesting esoteric diversion, for it embraces the full context of human and world transformation. As we set sail with Odysseus, together we will endure wounding and betrayal, suffering and loss, shipwreck and disaster, yearning for and searching for the Divine Beloved of the Soul. When we deal truthfully and precisely with these themes, we discover ways to effect healing, movement, and resolution in those areas of our lives that have kept us immobilized and in anguish. By probing our own tragic dimension for its deeper story, and by raising it to a mythic level, our wounding can become an opening through which grace can pour its healing balm. We become spiritually charged and awakened to a larger, nobler life.

This is a book, then, to be done, not just read. It provides an experiential journey into a myth and mystery that has engaged the human spirit for some three thousand years. As it did when Odysseus first set sail, it requires courage and willingness to participate in a powerful adventure of the soul that is at once both universal and intensely personal. In pursuing the adventures of Odysseus, we meet ourselves writ large.

THE HERO AND THE GODDESS

Introduction

WHEN I was a young girl I read a book that primed the deepest knowings and imaginings of my childhood. It sent me off on quests and adventures more appropriate to myths and fairy tales than to the America of the early 1950s. When I was twenty I read the book again, and it seized the now abstracted and metaphysicalized focus of my mind and leavened it with the eternal stories of the human soul and the gruesome, gorgeous, awesome living patterns that can quicken, destroy, or transform the human endeavor at any time and any place along life's turnings.

Recently I read the book again, after many years of exploring the vastness of the human condition and its possibilities. My reading this time was impelled by what I have come to sense of the nature and nearness of the "possible human." By that I mean the one who comes to make actual that which is still, for most of us, only potential, the vast untapped possibilities of mind, body, and spirit that reside in every one of us. The wider use of the self has been the dream for millennia, but only in our time do we have access to the findings of many cultures as well as scientific studies concerning the nature and variety of this potential. The last several decades have witnessed a phenomenal growth in both ancient and modern methods and experiential processes to bring this potential forth into everyday life. I myself—with the help of my associates at The Foundation for Mind Research—have developed many ways to evoke the many levels of the possible human. But now there is also a quickening, an almost desperate sense of need for this possible human to help create the possible society and the possible world if we are to survive our own personal and planetary odyssey and come safely home to the sanctuary of the soul.

The title of the book that so inspired my life and work is *The Hero with a Thousand Faces*, by Joseph Campbell. In this and in many of his subsequent works, Campbell combed through the great inspired stories of the world's peoples to discover and illustrate the potent similarities of theme and event they contain. He was a pioneer in the study of the realm of human understanding and consciousness where mythology rules.

Today, Joseph Campbell has become a luminous spokesman for myth, ritual, and symbol, famed for evoking and writing about the timeless images and stories that form the loom upon which our humanity is woven. I was privileged to have known and worked with him over the course of the last twenty years of his life. His great genius was to discover that

> throughout the inhabited world, in all times and under every circumstance, the myths of man have flourished; and they have been the living inspiration of whatever else may have appeared out of the activities of the human body and mind. It would not be too much to say that the myth is the secret opening through which the inexhaustible energies of the cosmos pour into human cultural manifestation. Religions, philosophies, arts, the social forms of primitive and historic man, prime discoveries in science and technology, the very dreams that blister sleep, boil up from the basic magic ring of myth.
>
> The wonder is that the characteristic efficacy to touch and inspire deep creative centers dwells in the smallest nursery fairytale—as the flavor of the ocean is contained in a droplet

or the whole mystery of life within the egg of a flea. For the symbols of mythology are not manufactured, they cannot be ordered, invented, or permanently suppressed. They are spontaneous productions of the psyche, and each bears within it, undamaged, the germ power of its source.[1]

THE NATURE OF MYTH

Whenever a society is in a state of breakdown and breakthrough—what I see as whole system transition—it often requires a new social alignment that only the complex and comprehensive understandings of myth can bring. It is only the mythologically wise community that finds ways to mediate and so refocus the shadow sides of self and society. In its Jungian usage, "shadow" refers to the repressed and disacknowledged aspects of self. When these same shadow qualities are recognized and reconciled, there is often a movement to greater maturity and depth of personality. Since time immemorial, myth and mythic knowing have served to balance shadow and light in person and culture; in this way preventing the exaltation of certain archetypal themes that if played out unchecked and unorchestrated, could destroy the world. Never has this mythic knowing been more needed than today, when our shadows are lengthened by a nuclear sun that is threatening to lead us into a world of endless night. Thus, it is imperative that we understand the functions of mediation and integration that myth can provide for past, present, and future societies.

Joseph Campbell has observed how mythology serves four major psychological and social functions in any given civilization:

1. It provides a bridging between one's local consciousness and the *mysterium tremendum et fascinans* of the universe—the vast, overwhelming environment of Being. It reconciles local, historical space-time with the transcendent realms and the eternal forms.

2. Myth offers an interpretive all-encompassing image of this relationship. In artistic and religious form, it provides a "revelation to waking consciousness of the powers of its own sustaining source."

3. Myth empowers the moral order and brings about both a shaping and a conciliation between individuals and the requirements of their differing climates, geography, cultures, and social groups. Perhaps you follow certain ethical precepts because Moses received them on the tablets on Sinai millennia ago; or, you are a Navajo because many moons ago Spider Woman laid an egg and from it the Dine (Navajo) people emerged; or, perhaps you are an American because "four score and seven years ago . . ." Now, for those societies in which the local mythology still works, there is "the experience both of accord with the social order, and of harmony with the universe." However, those of us who are several times removed from that harmony—by virtue of the effects of industrialization on our lives, which includes the shattering of natural rhythms—find ourselves longing for that storied universe we were once so intimately a part of, that realm of Nature, that deep belonging.

Myth assures us that the universe fits together, even though we may live in towering glass houses and get our dogma from editorials in the media. But when the mythological symbols no longer work, there is a pervading sense of alienation from society, often followed by a desperate quest to replace the lost meaning of our once-powerful myths. The demonic, shadow side of this questing can be a willingness to comply with totalitarian regimes when all else fails. Or it can mean returning to a primitivizing fundamentalism that reduces consciousness to a limiting if comforting notion of the way things work.

4. The fourth and most important function of myth is to "foster the centering and unfolding of the individual in integrity," with himself (the microcosm); his culture (the mesocosm); the universe (the macrocosm); and finally with the pan-cosmic unity, the ultimate creative Mystery, which is "both beyond and within himself and all things."[2]

As Campbell also noted, much has happened in the last three hundred years to cause the timeless universe of symbols and archetypes to collapse in upon itself in just the way black holes swallow stars in the far reaches of the galaxies. Power-driven machines, instantaneous communication, the scientific method, economics, and politics have become the central and controlling power of most social units. Since the beginning of the Industrial Revolution, these fascinations have pulled our focus away from the mystery of life; in some cases they have even invited us to pretend there no longer is a mystery. This has severely limited our awareness of the world of spirit and drugged us into a coma of forgetfulness. We have lost our capacity to tap into the greening power of the symbolic and mythic resources of humankind. Gods, myths, and metaphors have been abandoned, then blamed for being dead.

And yet, myth still beckons to us like a strange and beautiful country seen through the mist, only to retreat again when we have approached too near. Myth remains closer than breathing, nearer than our hands and feet. I think it is built into our very being. It winds its way through the labyrinthine pathways of our brain, codes itself into our cells, plays games with our genes, incarnates with us in the womb, weaves through the roles and rituals of our lives, and finds dénouement with our death. Myth waters our every conscious act. It is the very sea of the unconscious.

Myths serve as source patterns originating in the ground of our being. While they appear to exist solely in the transpersonal realm, they are the keys to our personal and historical existence, the DNA of the human psyche. These primal patterns unfold in our daily lives as culture, mythology, religion, art, architecture, drama, ritual, epic, social customs, and even mental disorders.

As Joseph Campbell once wrote: "The last incarnation of Oedipus, the continuing romance of Beauty and the Beast, stand this afternoon on the corner of Forty-second Street and Fifth Avenue, waiting for the light to change."[3] Is it any wonder, then, that our most popular television shows and movies brim mythically with thinly disguised high-tech scenarios rooted in the oldest stories in the world.

Myths, however, are not the same as fairy tales or legends. Fairy tales are essentially narrative complexes that collapse many mythic archetypal structures into one story. Myth has a more universal formulation than fairy tales; it speaks to the codings of the deep unconscious. Embedded in the psyche itself, myth engages the depths because it expresses in its own imagery and on its own terms the symbolic figures and actions of both the realms of the unconscious and the superconscious—the mind of Creation.

Because of its affinity to the Creative Principle itself, myth not only excites our understanding, it evokes our own passionate creativity. How often in the midst of a creative moment have you felt your horizons expanding to mythic proportions? Suddenly, you know yourself to be a creator, a celebrant of the Mass of the World, a willing participant in the re-storying of life with all its possibilities.

A myth is something that never was but is always happening. And this continual happening declares its presence in the news of the world. Daily, we see the flow of current events coursing through the time-deepened runnels of mythic themes. For example, the continuing conflicts between Protestant and Catholic in Northern Ireland, between India and Pakistan, between the Israelis and the Palestinians, and the struggles of the South Africans—black and white—all recall the myths of many cultures about two battling brothers: Cain and Abel in the Old Testament; Osiris and Seth in ancient Egypt; and among the West African Dogons of Mali, the mythological warring siblings Nommo and Ogo from the star Sirius.

Mythic themes are rampant in modern life. In the Middle East we find Dragon Kings snorting fire from the latest unnatural weaponry to protect their black gold from pale corporate princes. Drugs seep into the veins of those who could be heroes, rendering them as pathetic and dysfunctional as those in ancient tales who were lured to sip the poisoned brew of mad magicians, or were frozen into immobility at the sight of the Gorgon's writhing snakes.

Then there are the money mad—individuals and countries alike—who are endlessly driven to seek the elusive Grail of material success because they have lost their inner spirit and can only look outward for identity and meaning. They resemble the mythic hero Percival, who, by remaining silent at the sight of the Grail when visiting the Fisher King at Grail Castle, failed in his spiritual task of asking the great question concerning the service of the Grail. As a result he spent years in brooding pursuit of the now elusive Grail, doing knightly things with no passion, and through his unconscious actions committing mayhem and adding to the Wasteland his realm had become.

In all the dramatic, soul-threatening, even world-threatening action of these present-day reflections of ancient myths, one thing becomes very clear—these modern participants have not studied and lived the myth deeply enough to understand its true purposes. They have not played it through to the end. They have not understood that in the myth a force of wisdom heals and restores the wounded ones. They have not learned that the fierce Seth willingly becomes the vehicle that allows the greening power of his brother Osiris to be felt through the "million years"; that while Percival endures his years of dreary toil in the Wasteland, he is also learning to listen to others, and when the time is right, he is given another chance to ask the appropriate question.

I do not mean to imply that myth's major reason for existence is our education—nothing so narrow. But suggestions, warnings, and genuine guidance are encoded there that we would be foolish to ignore. Sometimes modern sensibilities demand that we change the story, or add to it, or make substitutions as we enact our own versions of the world's many myths. But we deny much of life's juiciness when we fail to embrace as fully as possible the inexhaustible richness of the classic myth.

MYTHIC ARCHETYPES: IN THE NATURAL WORLD

Myths are filled with archetypes, and archetypes are about derivations. The word itself refers to the "first types" or "primal patterns" from which people derive their sense of essence and existence. Earlier peoples saw archetypes in Nature and in the starry Heavens—in the Sun, the Moon, the Earth, the vast oceans—implicitly realizing our descent from these primal entities.

Everyone and everything derives from the stars—those fiery solar generators of the primary elements of beingness. The sediments of Earth make up our cells, and the briny oceans flow through our veins and tissues. Our ancestors storied this deep knowing into tales of the community of Nature: the marriage of Heaven and Earth; the churning of the ocean to create the nectar of life; the action of the wind upon the waters to bring form out of chaos. In these mythic tellings, our forerunners located higher reality and its values in the larger community—in the things of this world, shining reflections of the community of archetypes. They clearly perceived that the pattern connecting both world and archetype was the essential weave that sustains all life. And they saw themselves as just slightly more conscious and self-reflective members of this larger community.

I once asked an Australian Aboriginal woman how humans differed from the animals—from wallaby and kangaroo and koala. She replied, with some astonishment at my naïveté, "Why, we are the ones who can tell the stories about all the others."

The many indigenous peoples all over this planet continuously remind us that Nature—the Earth and all her species—are entirely derived from, and dependent upon, the community of life. They understand clearly that, while "simpler" life-forms can survive the elimination of more complex forms, the more complex ones cannot survive without the simpler ones, and that the more "advanced" cultures have been living as if this were not true.

The biophysical assault made upon the planet by our plundering industrial economies is polluting and depleting the major life-giving archetypes and architects of our existence: air, water, soil. Mind declares war on Nature in the name of progress and, as a consequence, we lose our ability to tell Her stories. We have become autistic, as non-mythic, non-storied folk always do when they lose the ability to communicate with the inner life of the natural world, or with their own inner life.

What if the stories that our indigenous brothers and sisters have been telling us are true? What if the soul of Nature is indeed trying to commune with us like a valiant nurse with a patient no one else really wants? How do we learn to listen?

If words fail, perhaps we can see images with fresh eyes—images with the potential to remind us of Nature as a sustaining and refreshing spiritual source. For example, seeing the image of the whole Earth from space never fails to jolt us out of our stupor. As we look back at this living planet and see the immense power of the image of our Mother, the Earth, floating live and luminescent in the vast ocean of space, our feeling of partnership with Her is quickened. We say "Gaia"—the ancient Greek Earth goddess whose name has become synonymous with our planet—and we mean "Mama." In Gaia, a once and future archetype has risen among the Earth's peoples. She has become our Homeplace, in the sense that Ithaca was the archetypal homeplace for Odysseus.

Yet, rich and vivid as Gaia's archetypal dance is for us, we are now venturing out through space and time in the macrocosm of galaxies upon galaxies, investigating quantum fields and primal cosmic forces. At the same time, our imaginations and technologies are also allowing us to spiral into the microcosm, toward subatomic infinities where we see the universe in miniature. We marvel anew at the ancient alchemical dictum of Hermes Trismegistus: "As above, so below; as below, so above." We study and reflect upon these miracles and mysteries, hoping to fathom the vastness expanding in both directions, as well as the fragile balancing point between them where we find ourselves.

This awareness is a fabulous gift. But it comes with strings attached. For today, our vision of the possible human must include all present knowledge, plus all previous visions of time and space and natural phenomena, as well as tribe, race, and social class. What a responsibility! It requires us to reexamine and honor the archetypes, which contain all human possibilities, and which are emerging once again to be freshly considered, explored, played out, and transfigured.

MYTHIC ARCHETYPES: IN THE INNER SOUL

Quintessentially, archetypes are about relationship. They are the connectiveness for the way things evolve, grow, relate, and become more complex, until they are integrated into the essence of simplicity. It is easier perhaps to understand archetypes in psychological terms. Standard interpretations describe them as the primary forms and constellations of energy that govern the psyche or that inner self we sometimes call the soul.

Carl Jung, the great Swiss psychoanalyst, was fascinated by archetypes. He saw them as the essential structures of the psyche—at once universal and yet manifesting in unique ways in each of us. He believed that, in the psyche, archetypes perform very like non-material organs, conferring the formal patterns of connection. He also observed that when archetypes are repressed—whether within one person or in an entire society—all kinds of alienation occur, and we are cut off from Nature, self, society, and Spirit.

The consequences of this alienation can be seen wherever today's mechanistic view of the world has infected modern life with what American philosopher Lawrence Cahoone calls "the three pernicious dichotomies": the split between subject and object (mind and body, inner and outer); the split between individuals and their relationships; and the split between the world of human culture and the natural realm.[4] This split has thrust us out of an Eden of ever more proliferating life-forms into a new day when all life is desperately endangered.

Archetypal structures are always available; but when they are perceived through the lens of alienated cultures and consciousness, they appear as warped, even demonic versions of what they truly are, and their energy becomes brutalized. For example, we've seen how Hitler's Germany refashioned Teutonic and Scandinavian myths and archetypes for its own alienated purposes. And, in fact, Jung reported a remarkable increase in the appearance of these archaic myths and archetypes in the dreams of his German patients in the early 1920s. This certainly explains the valid fear throughout Europe and Russia today concerning a reunified and rearmed Germany. For the real question behind the prevailing fear is not about economics, politics, or even militarism—it's about archetypes. Has this warped archetypal energy finally played itself out in the twentieth century? Will the reunification of Germany activate it again? Or will the East Germans' yearning for a better life be joined to the success and affability of the West German experience and lead them all to a deeper and more coherent archetypal relationship of planetary cooperation?

Archetypes, in their finest sense, bridge spirit with nature, mind with body, and self with universe. They are always within us, essential elements within the structure of our psyches. Without them, we would live in a gray world, a two-dimensional "Flatland" with no art, no music, no poetry, no invention, and no imagination. We would not "live" at all. And that is why even when archetypes are repressed, they bleed through into other realms of human experience: dreams, religious knowings, visions, artwork, ritual, love—and madness.

Sometimes the archetypes come in the archaic forms of gods, demons, and rituals of earlier cultures. But always they ask to be seen in new and fresh ways. They ask to be regrown.

Sometimes they come as pulses and impulses from some hitherto unknown place, demanding that we receive their charge and their possibility. Then they seem to be new archetypes, bearing messages relevant to the turning of the times. But however come by, whenever they move into our awareness, both personally and collectively, mythic archetypes announce a time of change and deepening. And this is what I deeply believe is happening all over the globe.

SEEKING THE SOUL OF THE WORLD

In my depth probings of many different kinds of consciousness in many different styles of culture, what I find emerging today is what the ancient Neoplatonic philosophers referred to as the *anima mundi*, the Soul of the World. In this time of whole system transition, the Soul of the World seems to be communicating with us through all the things and events of the world. Speaking through myths, it enlarges our perceptions of the deeper story that is unfolding in our time. Myths do not ground our experience; rather, they open the questions of life to culturally imaginative reflection and movement.

When we work with a mythic figure—or a historical being who has through time and legend been rendered mythic—this figure allows us to see the experience of our own lives reflected and ennobled within the story of that great life. We actively "become" Isis and Osiris. We quest for the Grail with Percival. We experience the passion and the pathos of Psyche and Eros. We search for the Beloved of the Soul with Rumi, the great Persian mystic, poet, and teacher. And we go adventuring with Odysseus.

Gradually, we discover that these stories are our own stories, that they amplify the rhythms and cadences of our own lives. After becoming Percival, and Isis, and Odysseus, and Penelope, we come back to a life enhanced. We find ourselves saying, "I have the strength, the depth, the capacity, the wisdom, and the purpose. I will prevail."

SACRED PSYCHOLOGY: BECOMING THE MYTH

To be true to any myth, we must also speak of its autonomy—the great stories and actions of the soul as it functions within each of us seemingly quite apart from our own directives or even awareness. These stories emerge as spontaneous creations, full and richly detailed realities glimpsed in dreams, in visions, and in those moments when the walls between the worlds are let down. When myths are actively pursued—as they will be in our journey with Odysseus and his family—they can lead us from the personal-particular concerns and frustrations of our everyday lives to the personal-universal, with its capacity to broaden the context of our lives and our vision and to integrate these new understandings within us.

This is one of the basic practices of what I call "sacred psychology." In this most ancient and pervasive of all psychologies, the participant accesses and then participates in these mythic and symbolic dramas. In this journey of transformation, we form a powerful sense of identity with the mythic character, often called the hero or heroine. This mythic being then assumes an aspect of ourselves writ large, and symbolic happenings appear with undisguised relevance not only for our own lives and problems, but for the remaking of society as well.

Myth is always about soulmaking. It is always about the pathos that accompanies the journey of the heroic soul as it travels from outmoded forms of existence to the larger life of the Kingdom. In times of breakdown and breakthrough—such as the one we're living through now—myths arise telling of new heroes and heroines and of the new and noble journey they must take in search of the possible human, both within themselves and in others. For it is only when we have discovered this possibility that we can create the possible society and, in T. S. Eliot's great phrase from "Ash-Wednesday": "Redeem the time."

However, true action on behalf of the redeeming vision has never taken place in society until it has played out its work within the individual soul, especially the soul that allows itself the journey of *palingenesia*—the opportunity to experience new birth on all levels and in all forms of life. Such a journey invites a new and deeper reality to enter into time where it can be made into a vital part of our lives. Thus, *palingenesia* not only means our own rebirth, it also opens us up to the larger dimension of reality beyond the womb of time.

The soul is the place where the roles of the hero and heroine are reconsidered. Joseph Campbell tells us this role is traditionally taken by:

> The man or woman who has been able to battle past his or her personal and local historical limitations to new, emergent human forms. Such a one's visions, ideals, and inspirations come pristine from the primary springs of human life and thought. Hence they are eloquent, not of the present, disintegrating society and psyche, but of the unquenched source through which society is reborn.[5]

In becoming a hero or heroine, we undertake the extraordinary task of dying to our current, local selves and being reborn to our eternal selves. Through the soul's journey, we enter those archetypal realms where the patterns demand divestiture of the old self, and then we continue to travel deeper still until we reach the eternal place of sourcing and resourcing.

There are two great works for heroes and heroines to perform. The first is to withdraw from everyday life and to open ourselves to the causal zones through which lie our only means of reaching the Source. The second work is to return to everyday life, carrying the knowledge we have gained in the depths and putting it to use to redeem time and society.

For the first work, we journey within to seek the great patterns and stories, the forgotten magic and knowings of earlier or even deeper phases of our own existence, down to the seedings of evolution to come, to the structures within the self that remain unfulfilled and unfinished. These are our hidden heroic potentials, which in myth often appear as secret helpers. What a task this is, and what glory might come from its completion! As Joseph Campbell has promised:

> If only a portion of that lost totality could be dredged up into the light of day, we should experience a marvelous expansion of our powers, a vivid renewal of life, we should tower in stature. Moreover, if we could dredge up something forgotten not only by ourselves but by our whole generation or our entire civilization we should become indeed the boonbringer, the culture hero of the day, a personage of not only local but world historical moment.[6]

These forgotten or neglected potentials for living the larger life must not be thought of as dead and buried. Rather, we must view them more profoundly and accurately as deep codings of the Source—the Infinite within. By uncovering them, by having the courage to cleanse, purify, and prepare the soul for the difficult task of becoming an instrument through which the Source may play its great music, the hero or heroine becomes the inspiration for raising culture and consciousness to its next level of possibility. The hero's journey is always about the deepening of culture—the means through which the unfolding universe enters more fully into our local lives. We become agents of the entelechy—the Life Force itself—the great purposeful, potentiating agent of being.

THE THREE REALMS OF SACRED PSYCHOLOGY

Another way our new selves may express this revelation is to say: "I prevail because I become part of a larger life altogether, the life of the psyche." For it is not psyche that exists in us, but we who exist in psyche—just as the larger life of psyche exists within the realm of God. This tripartite view of existence—our local lives, the life of psyche, and the realm of God—is another essential tenet of sacred psychology.

The many traditions of sacred psychology tend to map three major realms of experience:

1. The realm of the historic and factual (This Is Me).
2. The realm of the mythic and symbolic (We Are).
3. The realm of the unitive, the source level of being (I Am).

Each realm seems to have its own reality. And while each is reflected within us, each exists independently of us as well. We are not the only center of reality. We do not singularly create all we behold and experience, as some psychologies have suggested. Neither, however, can we escape from any part of experience, existence, or reality, for all are woven together. Our challenge now is to become fully aware, fully conscious co-creators in all three realms—the historic, the mythic, and the unitive.

This Is Me

The first and certainly the most familiar realm, the This Is Me reality, refers to everyday, ordinary existence. It is bounded and limited by geographical space and calendrical time. When we operate in this realm, we are guided by habit, personal conditioning, and cultural patterns. Our joint reality is structured by the definitions of gender, physical characteristics, name, local identity, profession, family, and other relationships and affiliations, all of which cease to exist when we die. This Is Me is the mask we wear, the persona of our everyday existence, our biography.

However, many of us never quite accept the This Is Me as a final statement of who we are. We perpetually yearn for the self from "Someplace Else." For in a world limited solely to the objective, definable, and measurable, our lives would be what the seventeenth-century English philosopher Thomas Hobbes in another context described as "solitary, poor, nasty, brutish, and short."[7]

We Are

Beyond the realm of This Is Me lies the realm of the We Are, the residence of symbols, guiding archetypes, and myths. Durative and enduring in an eternal world outside of time and space, as well as thoroughly transhistorical, the We Are realm functions as the contact point for sacred time and space. As this is the realm the entire *Odyssey* dwells within, I will discuss it at greater length below.

I Am

However, first we must take note of the third realm, which exists both beyond and also within the other two. This is the I Am, the realm of Being itself, pure potency, love, the very stuff of reality. This is the realm many know as God. However, this does not mean "the gods," for they live in the We Are, but rather, God as the Unity of Being. This is the "I Am" in the "I Am That I Am," spoken by God in self-definition in the Old Testament book of Exodus. It is not to be confused with the "I" of the human ego.

It is precisely because sacred psychology includes the realm of I Am that it can be differentiated from many of the more secular psychologies, such as those of the Freudians or the behaviorists, which may tend to avoid, exclude, and even deny this dimension. Sacred psychology assumes that the inherent yearning in every human heart is to experience some form of union and communion with the ultimate reality.

THE WE ARE REALM: DANCING WITH THE GODS

Since the source of the archetypal We Are realm is complex, its coding is intense.

The archetypal image is a psycho-genetically and creatively loaded form, loaded because it is potent, bearing within itself worlds within worlds—multiple meanings, potentials, dimensions.

What we call "gods" are actually uncodings of particular energy patterns from this realm seen with certain qualities and moods to help us relate to them more readily. That is to say, this is the place where the self joins its larger possibilities—often perceived as gods and goddesses. Athena, Asclepius, Sophia, Shiva, Quetzalcoatl, and thousands of others, are actually potentiating forces that have been crystallized in human cultures and worshiped as personalized emanations of a greater and unnameable power that comes both from within and beyond the psyche. Sometimes they assume a humanized, semihistorical form, as with Jesus, Krishna, Buddha, Kwan Yin, and Zoroaster. We may feel a particularly loving resonance with such beings who have been elevated to godhood, identifying with both their numinous power and their storied humanity.

Myths and archetypes communicate from the poetic level of mind and thought, allowing Nature to speak to the imagining soul rather than just presenting us with scientific laws and probabilities. This poetic level of mind brings with it a higher order of coherence because it has color, aesthetic form, and rhythmic relation. Indeed, evidence exists that in certain states of consciousness, the mind-brain system appears to move into a larger wave resonance, which may itself be nested in a continuum of mind beyond the field of the experiencing body. In this state, mystics and highly creative people come back enriched and enlivened to do or think remarkable things. When we meet myths and archetypes in this state, we can speak directly to the inner imaginal realm where mind, nature, and spirit converge and our potentialities become available to us.

My studies of many creative thinkers and artists point directly to their capacity to delve into these depth levels of reality where the forms and creations of the existential life are conceived. Albert Einstein, for example, could be said to have drawn his insight into the nature of relativity and the quantum universe not only from the workings of his own capacious mind but also from the great creative archetypal realm—the storehouse of the principles that source the creation of new ideas and forms.

Psychologically, for us as individuals, a sense of relationship with an archetype—especially one that is experienced as a spiritual partner, the Beloved of the Soul—amplifies the deeper aspects of the self. This relationship disengages us for a while from the demands and demeanings of our local, ego-focused personalities and allows us to view our personal concerns from a universal perspective.

GROWING THE GODS

Today, what we call "the gods" come down to us as the imaginative products of earlier historical ages—Greek, Roman, Egyptian, Germanic, Native American, Middle Eastern. They are numinous borderline persons. Embedded in earlier myths and ways of being, they serve as vehicles through which we may come to understand our strengths as well as our shadows. They grant us perspective into the ways in which certain behavioral patterns dominate our lives.

This explains the success of the recent books that use the Greek gods as behavioral archetypes to help us identify the ways we relate to the world. We come to see our strengths and weaknesses in terms of theirs. However, although this has proved to be an immensely useful form of reflection, ultimately it sells the gods short. It forces them to become adjuncts to psychotherapy rather than honored for their autonomy. It also leaves them left back in the school of evolution.

For these great principles and meta-level patterners to be evolved in our consciousness, they must be allowed the fullness of their potentiality. Part of the emergence of an archetypal spirituality and mythology is our ongoing story of allowing the gods their growth. Only then can they be seen as the ones that transduce the imagery and energy of the cosmos to us in highly effective ways that allow us to rise to them as co-partners in Creation.

The Divine-Human partnership has thus become the leading archetypal image for our time. This archetype of partnership is a once and future image—mystics and poets seem always to have known it to be true. For example, the Jewish mystical tradition teaches that God made the human being because He needed a partner in creation.

In the words of poet Rainer Maria Rilke: "We are the bees of the invisible. We madly gather the honey of the visible to store it in the great golden hive of the invisible."[8]

Perhaps the whole purpose of evolution is to create co-creators who can help transform the potentialities existing in matter and ideas into new forms, richer meanings, and high art. The archetype of Divine-Human partnership arises to declare to us that our depths are structured for just such a relationship, that there is within us the capacity to be transparent to the Divine, that we contain a beingness that is diaphanous to and with Being itself. In such an all-encompassing relationship we have a feeling of participation in the totality and vigor, the creativity and generosity of Divine Life.

According to the great student of mysticism, Evelyn Underhill, the marks of this state of correspondence are:

> (1) A complete absorption in the interests of the Infinite, under whatever mode it is apprehended by the self; (2) a consciousness of sharing Its strength, acting by Its authority, which results in a complete sense of freedom, an invulnerable serenity, and usually urges the self to some form of heroic effort or creative activity; (3) the establishment of the self as a "power for life," a centre of energy, an actual parent of spiritual vitality in other men.[9]

These qualities illumine the correspondences and relationships of everything to everything else. They give us the ways of knowing and being that we need in order to embrace the unitive vision. Through them, our local personalities take on a wider consciousness, a deeper self that, in essence, becomes a significant mutation of our being. The seed within, which held and nurtured the divine spark, is now fully grown, and we find ourselves transplanted into the vast gardens of Universal Life.

When we who are traversing this path to mystic union stand in the presence of one who is firmly planted in this garden, we too become aware that everything is filled with light and meaning, that everything falls into place in the great pattern of connections. Why? Because we are living both here and in another order of Being, one in which the relationships between realities seem to be more important than the things themselves. Within the Eternal Order, everything is seen and known to be dynamically and creatively related to everything else. Perhaps that is why when we dwell there—and are aware of dwelling there—we can suddenly become so creative, able to do almost anything we want in service to all life.

This shift from the personal-particular to the personal-universal may well be a deep and essential requirement for an emerging planetary society. Otherwise, locked into our own experience and culture, we will have neither the passion for the possible nor the moral energy to co-create with others of different cultures and beliefs a world that works. We are now in the process of learning to see with our souls—combining our life's experience with our deepest archetypal knowings.

This movement into the greater life is what awaits us as we grow our partnership with the mythic hero Odysseus and with his Great Friend, the goddess Athena. By participating in their experience, and that of everyone else we shall meet in *The Odyssey*, human and divine, we will be expanding our perceptions, our understandings, our creativity—the very limits of our being. And we shall return from our journeys in the depth realms to our own Ithacas, renewed, reborn, rededicated to the full potentialities of life.

How to Use This Book

THE *Hero and the Goddess* is divided into working chapters that follow the major exploits of *The Odyssey*. Each of these adventures is followed by experiential processes that allow you to participate in the story, to interact with it, and even perhaps to change it.

How to proceed? Here are my recommendations for those who will be journeying alone as well as for those who will be part of a group experience. But whichever mode is appropriate to your situation, be sure to read both sets of suggestions and all the scripts for the guide. Many things can be adapted to your needs that will stretch your imagination and creativity, as well as add new kinds of insights to the processes.

IF YOU ARE VOYAGING SOLO

If you are working alone, the first thing you need to do is make the commitment to go all out in this journey of transformation. Then perform your own time-honored rituals of preparation, remembering that while the ancient parts of your brain are not fond of change, they do like and need rituals. Buy a new notebook for journaling. Make sure you have Crayons or colored pens and plenty of paper for drawing, pens and pencils for writing. Create a sacred space where you will do the work; it is best if this space has a boundary of some kind, so that you cross a threshold to enter it. This prevents the energies of everyday life from bleeding through and diverting your attention.

Make sure there is music available for you there—your favorites as well as some Greek music to dance yourself into that Mediterranean mind-body space. The musical selections listed at the end of the book are meant only as suggestions for the types of music you might want to use.

Set specific times for doing this work. Make an agreement with yourself about those times; try not to let more than a week go by between sessions. (It is also possible to perform it all in a long weekend if you prefer total immersion.) Dedicate that time to your game with the universe.

You may wish to decorate the front of your journal with images that seem appropriate for your Odyssey. If it seems helpful, you might even decorate your space and create some kind of costume or robe to wear especially for this time.

Write out a contract with yourself to embark upon this journey toward your soul's true home, your Ithaca, and to complete it, as Odysseus did. Perhaps set the time span for the entire voyage. Sign and date the contract. You might even wish to set a forfeit should you not comply with the terms of the contract. This could be the giving up of special foods or entertainments that you enjoy. Or, on the more constructive side, the giving of a service to friends or community, offering unexpected help to surprise and delight.

Then tell someone who cares about you and will support your inner work that you're making a transformational journey of the soul. Ask if you may call upon this person occasionally to ask for assistance or a second opinion or a shoulder to cry on. Have this friend witness and sign the contract you have made.

In my experience it has proven to be good practice to work

with at least one other person in making your Odyssey. Another voice, another life story, a companion for the road helps train us in that most valuable of human skills—working and playing together with mutual and equal honor. I also realize that, for most people, this is not easy or practicable. But at least tell someone what you're doing, and invite her or him to participate in the process, to see that you keep your side of the bargain and play this game with the universe fully.

MAKE a practice of reading and chanting, even singing, some portion of the chapter, the story itself, or the suggested process ALOUD. Choose several paragraphs that strike your fancy, rehearse them a number of times, then perform them in full voice as if you were Homer come to life again. At first you may feel foolish, but do it anyway. Moving beyond the fear of foolishness is one of the quickest ways to reach the realms where all things are recognized as sacred.

One of the potencies of *The Odyssey* lies in its origins: It is bardic. People spoke and sang this great poem on celebratory occasions over many centuries. Listeners heard every line and cadence over again many times. Thus, by reciting aloud, we can unlock one of its most important potencies. We charge and change the brain when we sing and chant. And using the energies of full speech not only vitalizes the mouth and throat, it reactivates our capacity for rich language. It also appears to attract the attention of those beings who live within the mythic realm. Our voices, raised in Homer's glorious speech, tell them we are present and ready to work together.

If you are voyaging solo, you will find it of critical importance to prerecord the scripts for the guide on tape. This will give you greater freedom and spontaneity in doing the exercises. A cautionary note here. Please don't use an overly dramatic or lugubrious voice when you make the tapes or you'll end up not trusting that person on the tape! Also, be sure to leave yourself pauses of sufficient length wherever they're called for so that you have enough time to do the exercises fully.

Where processes require working with other people, there

are detailed suggestions at appropriate places in the text for solo voyagers. But as a general rule, using your imagination is key. Wherever a partner or partners are needed you can always imagine or visualize them being present and then dialogue with them either by writing in your journal or by actually playing their parts. The lovely thing about imaginal partners is that you can ask for anyone you like—Odysseus himself and all his crew, or Athena, or Penelope, or Hermes, or your own Great Friend of the Soul.

Create an ongoing process of dialogue, interchange, and persuasion by devising new ways of working with your journal. Remember that one important way of looking at any great story is to experience ourselves as all the characters—sometimes all at once. For example, in your journal work you might want to write out the dialogue that takes place (offstage in *The Odyssey*) between Odysseus and his men as they set up their attack on the Ciconians—the blunder that sets *The Odyssey* in motion. Then switch about and write what the Ciconians must be feeling and saying as they are suddenly and mercilessly attacked by these seagoing marauders. Then, speak it out, all the parts, as if you were performing a Greek play. Suddenly, you may see with fresh vigor, and in a context that releases both laughter and tears, how your pirate self and your unsuspecting, peaceful self interact. As you experience the loss of parts of yourself that have been devastated in similar battles, do as Odysseus did: Call out the names of those lost parts in honor and in grief. In this process you may become more clearly aware of the presence of the gods in your personal battles, and the ensuing adventures you were sent upon in order to find new depths of compassion and understanding for yourself and others. You experience being the playwright, director, actor, and audience in the most important sacred drama there is—your own life.

Trust yourself to know your essential limits, but keep asking yourself to move out—slowly but surely—beyond your personality-imposed limitations. *The Odyssey* is an adventure of the soul. Embrace it. And be aware that a process that seems to bring up too much at one time can be lightened by doing what Odysseus and his modern soul brother Zorba would do: dance! Dance until your body is exhausted. Then write an invocation to the archetypal partner that you have selected—it may be Athena, Hermes, Aphrodite, even Odysseus himself, or perhaps the Friend in Court, whom you will meet shortly as we set out upon the journey. Speak this invocation aloud. It is also exciting to ask your archetypal companion what is happening from Her or His perspective. Write your questions in your journal to this "god" or archetype. And then, in response, allow the answers to be written through your hand from the archetype. Simply write down whatever enters your mind.

Later, if you like, consult your human ally. Then listen deeply to your own knowing about whether it is appropriate to go back to the issue that has been raised immediately, or to let it grow and develop in your unconscious and in your dream life until your next session.

GO to night school. On the nights before and after a session, ask your mind to take you to that place where *The Odyssey* and all its people and events are still alive and busy, so that you may be part of the action, as observer or participant, in these durative realms. Record your images, the wisps of knowing that may come, the dreams that have come in the night, and your feelings when you awake. Then dialogue with that person of *The Odyssey* whose story you feel you are sharing. Treat it gently, lightly—without attachment or feeling that something portentous depends on the outcome.

Create art with your learning and your feelings. Most especially, write poetry. But also draw and paint, make sculptures and collages. It makes no difference whether you think you have no special gift for writing or for painting—just let your imagination loose. Free your hand to move as it wants, directed by your inner knowing and seeing. You may be surprised and pleased with the results.

IF YOU ARE VOYAGING WITH A GROUP

Group work has been at the heart of my own development. And so one of the intentions of this book is to enable groups of people to share experiences as co-voyagers in this ancient, yet strangely modern, psycho-spiritual journey. Very often, the presence of others helps us go deeper on the journey.

There is another important consideration: We are living in a critical time in the history of Earth. Never has the ultimatum "Grow or Die" threatened us more. Working in groups creates a transformational synergy that allows us to travel faster and deeper together than often we can travel alone. Through the evocation of one another we expand the base of our concern, developing an enhanced relationship to our planet and intensifying our recognition of Her needs as well as our willingness to respond to those needs creatively.

Together, we will embark on each of the adventures of Odysseus, experience the night journey of his son Telemachus, and maintain the home center, physically and spiritually, as Penelope. Together, we will also undergo some of the initiations of humans and gods into deepening realities and larger frames of consciousness.

The community of voyagers you gather together may take any form: your family, friends, colleagues, students, clients, parishioners, and so forth. However, each participant should be clear as to his or her intentions. The effect of these experiences can run the gamut from trivial to profound depending upon the seriousness, dedication, and motivation of the group members. Therefore, the group should consist of only those who freely choose to participate and who feel deeply the call to do so. We should try to involve people who, in their faith in the future of humanity and the planet, are willing to work together with constancy and caring to develop and extend the Sacred in daily life. Galloping narcissists, psychic exhibitionists, and "poor me" whiners may offer more challenge and distraction than you need.

In general, the experiences should be undertaken by intelligent, resourceful people who are mature enough to have had sufficient life experience to appreciate the psychological and spiritual scope of the divine-human drama they will be invited to enact.

Working in groups helps eradicate one of the worst tyrannies that afflict *Homo sapiens*—the tyranny of the dominant perception. This is reflected in such smug statements as "If it's good enough for me, it's good enough for you" and "Why can't you respond like everyone else does?"

The members of your sacred voyaging community will stimulate, support, and evoke each other. In their diverse reactions, they will prime a diversity of responses in each voyager. While consensus and commonalities are quite important, our differences are equally enriching: "Thank God," we say to ourselves, "I need not be limited to my own experience but may share in yours." As we recognize the enormous richness of the realm of the Sacred in others, we can drop simplistic judgments and stand in awe before this wild abundance of creative variation.

By pursuing the adventures of Odysseus as part of a group, we also bypass one of the most insidious of human failings—the potential for sloth. Self-discipline and good intentions have a way of evaporating without some consistent external commitment. The practice of sacred psychology—which challenges the deeply entrenched patterns of the conscious mind, psyche, and body—needs allies. Resistance to change is natural, maybe even healthy, but one of the few ways to overcome it is through regular participation in the loving, celebrating company of co-journeyers. This is why solo voyagers need to tell at least one person close to them of their momentous undertaking.

Access to the Sacred is available to us all. Groups may be made up of people who may range in age from twelve to ninety-four, and in education from a few years of grade school to a superfluity of Ph.Ds. Their spiritual beliefs may also vary widely, from agnostic and private seeker to those devoted practitioners of religious orthodoxies. Such variety always enhances the experience, and it is fascinating to watch culturally determined labels and expectations fall away. Be aware also that, as myths have always told us, allies often come in disguise.

Your group of co-voyagers for the journey of *The Odyssey* should probably number not fewer than five nor more than twenty-five. It is also helpful to have an uneven number of participants since some of the experiences are performed by couples while one member of the group acts as guide.

Any group that meets together to experience these adventures and initiations must devote careful attention to preparing and conducting each session. The suggestions below are recommended as guidelines for taking this mythic journey.

AT its initial meeting, the group should assign members to take responsibility for obtaining and preparing the setting or settings (indoors or out) for each of the adventures. This includes providing appropriate music and record or tape players, art supplies, musical instruments and other materials, as well as bringing food for closing celebrations after each session. Special attention should be taken to preventing interruptions—whatever their form: wandering dogs, curious children, ringing telephones—during the sessions. The setting is to be created and treated as sacred space.

Because each session is built around a particular chapter and sequence from Homer's story, it is necessary that every member of the group read not only the relevant material from this book but also the relevant chapter from Homer prior to each meeting. Dialogue with the texts as you read them; take note of images and ideas that emerge so that these may feed the group discussion. And then begin each meeting with this group discussion, exploring the material and its content as they apply to the lives and understanding of the members of your group. The purpose of the texts is to evoke within you and your companions a depth reflection of psychological and spiritual patterns of transformation. The question you will continually ask is: How does *The Odyssey* speak to my life journey and the "long voyage home"?

My presentation of the story of *The Odyssey* is not to be viewed as a scholarly study of classical texts, although scholarly supportive evidence is presented in the notes. Rather, this book offers a series of opportunities for psychological and spiritual adventures to be done and danced and encountered in our depths, where each part of the ancient Homeric story becomes a living metaphor of transformation. Thus, the reader is gently warned not to become too preoccupied with issues concerning the present state of classical scholarship—that is not what this journey is about. In *The Hero and the Goddess,* Odysseus is our shipmate, not our professor. Some participants will agree with the perspectives I offer here, others will not. Simply remember that the metaphoric mode demands a symbolic and participative use of the materials that come down to us. When these are treated mythically and dramatically, they gain in usefulness and creative energy what they may lose in present orthodoxy with regard to Homeric studies.

AFTER the group's opening discussion has ended, there should be a break of at least fifteen minutes before it comes back together to share the mystery of the particular stage of the Odyssean journey that has been reached. A good way to do this is to leave the space in which the discussion was held, and then reenter it after a time as sacred space—silently, with full awareness of your commitment to making this journey meaningful. Members of the group may want to spend some time centering themselves and bringing consciousness to the experience about to be undertaken. Each should make an internal agreement to take responsibility for himself or herself, while at the same time remaining respectful of the needs of others and of the group as a whole.

The Guide

The role of the guide is critical. This role may be held by one person for the entire journey, or it may alternate among members of the community. In any case, the guide needs to be thoroughly familiar with the material, attentive to the amount of time the group needs to process the material, and respectful of the experience of everyone in the group. The guide is not to interpret the experience of others but rather to trust the process and the enormous individual variations that are possible.

The group of co-journeyers must also avoid making the error that guide equals leader. The guide is understood by everyone as one who assists and enables. This is an ancient role, that of *hierophant* of the mysteries. In this tradition the guide is the midwife of souls, the evocateur of growth and transformation. In becoming guide, then, one knows oneself to be part of a continuity stretching across millennia, and in guiding these modern initiations of Odysseus, the guide takes on a role of the greatest challenge and responsibility. When we act as guide, we therefore invest the role with our High Self.

The guide needs to have the capacity to be both part of the experience and an observer of the journey of the other travelers. He or she must be able to judge sensitively the amount of time needed for the journey (only approximate times are suggested in the text), and to use the experiences flexibly. The experiences described are not cast in stone and will doubtless gain much from the suggestions and additions of the group and the guide.

Before each meeting of the group, the guide will have read the process material aloud several times to himself or herself, sensing the nature of the journey and allowing his or her voice and timing to reflect that experience. The voice must not be intrusive, but it must remain clear, audible, and expressive of the particular experience. Wherever music is called for, the guide must rehearse with the music in order to integrate voice, sound, and timing of the process, always knowing, however, that the timing may well shift depending on the needs and experiences of the group.

The guide may also want to have one or more "soul catchers" present. These are members of the group selected because of their ability to be sensitive to the needs of others.

Thus, even while going through the experiences themselves, part of their consciousness will remain available to help others should this be required. However, soul catchers must remember that part of helping others often lies in knowing when to leave people alone, and not intrude unnecessarily on their experience. The soul catcher may also enjoy guiding the guide through the experience once the group journey has ended.

Treading Gently

In working with this material, it is most important that members of the group refrain from acting as therapists or theologians. Professional therapists and theologians may find this very difficult, but it is imperative that they practice their profession only during regular working hours. Comments I have heard, despite repeated pleas to refrain from making them, have included, "You really are blocked!" and "I can see some enormous anger stored up there," and even "You clearly are spiritually immature." Such remarks are inappropriate here even if they seem accurate and you intend them to be helpful. Acceptance of people for who and what they are in the present moment is critical to the practice of sacred psychology. Each person is perfectly capable of interpreting his or her own experience and can invite the comments of others if desired.

One of the great advantages of sacred psychology is that it invites the participant to move into high witness, to tap into forgotten wisdom, and to practice nonobtrusive spiritual intimacy with others. One is always in a place to see the other as God-in-hiding, and to be so seen oneself. Many of the processes given in this book allow for the practice of deep empathy maintained in a variety of ways—the gentle holding of the hand of your partner while she or he is describing experience or reflections; eye to eye contact whenever appropriate; and, above all, careful and compassionate listening that knows when to speak out of one's deepest wisdom and when to maintain silence, communicating understanding and respect by eye or gesture alone. The sharing of powerful experience and reflection that accompanies the processes of this book—especially when done by a group—requires that people enter into a state of mutual trust. Thus after the sharing I have found it to be a good and satisfying thing to express words of appreciation to each other for the sharing and the trust given. One might say, for example, "I am honored that you shared so deeply of your experience with me."

Please, please, keep in mind that there is no such thing as doing any exercise wrong. This is a journey of the soul, and each person will have his or her unique way of approaching it. In fact, whenever possible—CHEAT! Do the exercise differently, or add other ideas or images or actions with which to enhance the process. And whatever else you do, throw self-criticism away—it is not in the Odyssean mode.

AFTER each adventure is over, you may want to take some time for private reflection and for recording your experience. For those who will be voyaging solo—as well as for individual participants in a group—the understanding of sacred psychology and of the journey of Odysseus will deepen as you add to your journal. Be sure to record your experiences in drawings, musings, quotes, dreams, questions, and whatever else asks to be written down. This kind of expression will engage you in the most fascinating kind of conversation there is—an exchange with the inhabitants, the crew, of your own inner dimensions.

Reflections on the experience may be shared with one or two others or, if the group is small enough for each person to have a say, with the group as a whole. While some may feel reluctant to relate in this way, I have found that the process of verbal sharing generally enhances and deepens everyone's experience. *Guides,* in the matter of sharing and reflection you will need to strike a happy medium between encouraging the maximum expression and participation in all the processes and being careful not to overstep anyone's boundaries.

OF TIME AND THE MYSTERIES

The entire journey of *The Odyssey,* with the fourteen chapters presented here, can be performed over different time periods. It can even take place over a very long weekend, although some may feel this is too compact and intense. However, many have discovered this condensed sequence to be extremely powerful because of the immediate continuity it provides for all the stages in the Homeric myth. I have found it best to incorporate the discussion and experiences of this book in a four- or five-day period. But in actuality, any convenient time frame will work; in fact, groups could meet once a week for a number of months and focus each meeting on a particular chapter and its exercises.

A list of suggested musical compositions, as well as notes detailing books and articles mentioned in the text, will be found at the end of this book. This information is designed to enhance your understanding and experience of the journey of Odysseus.

A tape series drawn from actual seminars on this material and utilizing much of the content of this book is described at the end of the book. Individuals and groups may wish to have these tapes and occasionally use the process parts for their own sessions. These tapes can also serve as a model to the guide for tone of voice, pacing, and rhythm. They are available from the address listed at the end of the Musical Selections appendix.

While this book stands alone as an introduction to mythic journeys of transformation, I strongly advise that it be used in conjunction with my book *The Search for the Beloved: Journeys in Sacred Psychology.* This work contains substantive discussions of the background, both ancient and modern, of sacred psychology, and outlines the psycho-spiritual assumptions and mythic structure from which its practices flow. The book also offers basic exercises designed to attune the mind and body to the work of sacred psychology as well as presenting several other experientially based journeys of transformation.

CHAPTER 1

The Odyssey as Transformational Myth and Mystery

TELL me, Muse, of the man of many ways, who was driven far journeys, after he had sacked Troy's sacred citadel. Many were they whose cities he saw, whose minds he learned of, many the pains he suffered in his spirit on the wide sea, struggling for his own life and the homecoming of his companions. Even so, he could not save his companions, hard though he strove to; they were devoured by their own wild recklessness, fools who devoured the oxen of Helios, the Sun God, and he took away the day of their homecoming. From some point here, goddess, daughter of Zeus, speak, and begin our story.[1]

LET us begin our experience of the power of myth by looking through the lens of one of the most famous and beguiling examples of a dramatic journey of transformation. This journey, with its mysteries and initiations, gave its hero, Odysseus, the fullest possible experience of adventure and despair, lostness and foundness, mute tragedy and thrilling triumph. Of even more importance, it demanded that he engage in initiations, which drove him past the realistic world of his much-vaunted mastery into wonderlands peopled by paradox where he was tested and honed into deeper life and higher knowing.

The story also contains a remarkable element: It tells us what can happen in a life that includes a deep and committed friendship with an archetypal power, that is, a power that emanates from a reality deeper than our own and that can guide and sustain us. In this case, that power is the goddess Athena.

The first line of *The Odyssey* sets the theme: "Tell me, Muse, of the man of many ways . . ." The word in Greek for "of many ways" is the descriptive *polytropous.* Other translations refer to a man of many devices, many capacities, even many turnings in his character as well as in his journey. Odysseus is indeed a man of many ways. He is the exemplar of the many-potentialed being, the man who has seen everything, can do everything, and, at least with his intellect, can understand everything. We study Odysseus for his utter potential.

His journey and its many levels of reality call forth these potentials in ways that have embodied the principal models, or paradigms, of challenge, response, and growth in the Western imagination. Across space and time his influence has been immense. Odysseus holds us in thrall, whether we be ancient Greek schoolboys or modern inquirers into the possible human. Entrepreneurs of every ilk name their ventures after him. From travel agencies to motion picture companies, "Odyssey" is blazoned across signboard and stationery to imply the adventurous nature of the business. "This is the cutting edge," these companies seem to say. "We are the state of the art, and to deal with us is to be caught up in excitement and innovation." Unfortunately, these companies often discover to their sorrow that the real meaning of the name Odysseus in ancient Greek is "trouble." What's in a name? Usually more than one bargained for.

In his wanderings, Odysseus finds a full spectrum of archetypal patterns. There is the heavy-handed savagery and tunnel vision of the cave-dwelling Cyclops, and its opposite in the complex sensibilities of the highly civilized Phaeacians. He meets kind hosts such as Aeolus, god of the winds, who feed him and help him, but he also encounters the ruthless giant Laestrygonians, who feed on him and try every way to destroy him. Odysseus and his crew are tempted to dwell in mindless bliss with the Lotus-Eaters, and are lured to oblivion by the Sirens. They meet with mindful, quick-witted advice from the messenger god Hermes, but also wild ruinous wrath from the sea god Poseidon. Odysseus encounters eroticism in its dangerous and devolutionary character in Circe, the nymph who reverses evolution by changing men into wolves and pigs. But there is also eros in all its subtle delicacy and fresh awakening in the young Nausicaa, Odysseus' rescuer on the Isle of the Phaeacians. And he gains an understanding of the past on his visit to the ancestors in the Underworld as well as knowledge of the future from the shade of the blind prophet Tiresias.

Odysseus' voyage, with all its physical dangers and thrills, may also be perceived as a progressive journey into the far more chilling cartography of inner space. As our hero plunges deeper and deeper into this realm, he finds himself with fewer and fewer resources and friends, until at last he washes ashore on Calypso's Isle with nothing remaining of his former selfhood. Here he stays for a full seven years as the beloved consort of this minor goddess whose name has the same root as the word "eclipse." This, as Cedric Whitman describes it, is "the nadir, the quiet center of the magic world" from which grows the intensity of his longing to return home to Ithaca, which in turn prompts the gods to reconsider his fate and allow him to begin his magical trip back. The breaking out of this womb of the ocean, "where the navel of the sea lies," begins with a violent confrontation with the Poseidon-maddened sea. This, in turn, leads Odysseus from the deep world of archetypal folk to the mid-world of the Phaeacians, a people of the in-between who dwell, Homer tells us, at the boundary between humankind and the gods. And it is only these beings of an ideal and balanced society who embody the sacred conjunction of divine and human and thus have the power to bring Odysseus back home to Ithaca.[2]

AT another level, *The Odyssey* can be read as a paean to resourcefulness. In essence, it is a story of survival by means of the ability to change, adapt, transform, and skillfully orchestrate all circumstances. This is a critical theme for our work of self-unfolding, as it shows how resourceful people can be when they consciously begin to create their reality. Odysseus creates his world by risk, choice, tenacity, and action. Like us, he often fails. But in failing he discovers even deeper resources that reflect his truer self.

One of his most persistent difficulties is in failing to see the consequences of his choices. His actions are marked by flamboyance and little or no forethought. Consider that his ten-year odyssey begins with a careless decision to attack the innocent Ciconians instead of immediately setting sail for home after his triumph at Troy. This piratical episode, although such actions were condoned in the Heroic age, still smacked of *hubris,* of god-challenging pride, and thus invited inevitable retribution. This is a quintessential example of the ways our heedless choices pull us into adventures and diversions far off the beaten track. Ironically, these seemingly random choices, which may even be experienced as blunders, provide the real stuff of our lives—the context and the content for growth into consciousness.

In his excellent essay on "*The Odyssey* and Change," Homeric scholar Cedric Whitman shows that, in the realms of the Lotus-Eaters, the Cyclops, and the Laestrygonians, it is Odysseus' chronic curiosity, not need, that demands the exploration of these lands, for neither he nor the crew are pressed by any urgent necessity. The same is true in the case of Circe—as his anguished companions point out to him. But their caution never prevails. If there is risk and adventure looming before him, Odysseus plunges into it, dragging his fear-filled companions along, often to their doom.

Odysseus may be driven to these places by the wrath of

gods—as all of us are at one time or another driven to outrageous experiences and places by circumstance—but it is he, and we, who choose to explore them. And yet, after his intimacy with Circe—symbolic perhaps of what happens when we enter into intimacy with our own deeps—the usual kind of choice disappears, and we, like Odysseus are committed to a world of wonder and soul-charging circumstances.

Essentially, Odysseus is left with no choice until he has lived with Calypso for seven full years. For the ancient Greeks, seven years symbolized a major phase in life as well as in myth, and in music, as in the seven notes of the musical octave. This octave of time is given him so that he may integrate all his learnings. After that, we see a clear contrast between the wily, arrogant master of disguises who consorts with Circe and the half-dead, salt-encrusted wreck of a man who washes up on the Phaeacian beach to be saved by a young girl. After the gestation years with Calypso, Odysseus appears before Nausicaa with only an olive branch to cover his nakedness, all disguises gone. It is she who gives him the possibility of rebirth.[3] Now he is ready to begin a new life and also a new series of disguises, which are at once more humble, more real, and thereby more effective—for example, assuming the role of the beggar in his own suitor-ridden home. This is possible now because he has become a much larger being and is in conscious touch with more dimensions of inner as well as outer reality.

THIS great change in Odysseus has been nurtured by his friend and partner in the archetypal world, the goddess Athena, who also provides the impetus for his return home by pleading his case before her father, Zeus, and the other gods. It is the power and nature of this crazy friendship that gives us new understanding about how humans and "gods," or spiritual potencies, mutually evolve each other—how, in the words of Nikos Kazantzakis, we become the "saviors of God."

What are these gods to the Greeks? They are not simply men and women writ large. Nor are they merely personalized and then deified qualities of love, war, fertility, authority, and death. Rather, they are felt presences who underlie and inform our existence. They are at once real and yet possessed of a reality that is more fluid than our own. They live closer to the storehouse of creation and therefore have greater access to the patterns and possibilities that reside there. Their abode on Mount Olympus is not only high, it is deep as well, and from its depths spring the potencies that charge the world of time.

The gods are not God; rather, they are aspects or emanations from the One spiritual reality. They serve as bridges between the One God and our own humanity, rivers to the Source, whose greater "humanness" serves to engage and illumine our own. The stories and myths that accrue around them show that they are never static but are themselves involved in growth and learning. They are numinous borderline persons who require interaction with human beings in order to extend themselves, while we need their promptings and knowledge to give us our impetus for living and learning. Both gods and humans, then, are always available for transition into wiser and deeper versions of themselves.

The Athena of *The Odyssey,* patroness of heroes and innovators, of those who live life to its fullest and live life at the edge, is herself at a transition point. She is evolving from the archaic and militant Mycenean deity of citadels, reflected in the raging war goddess of *The Iliad,* into the goddess of wisdom, of culture, and of civilization. This evolution of an archetype is an important informing motif of *The Odyssey* and is, I believe, the reason the entire poem is under the dominion of Athena. At a depth level it tells us as much about the growth of a god as about the growth of a hero. It is as much about the evolution of spiritual powers as it is about the growth of human consciousness. Studied from this perspective, *The Odyssey* becomes a sacred text and a drama of the highest mysteries. To help us understand how critical this point is, let us put *The Odyssey* into its historical perspective, and then, going farther back in time, track the cultural sources of the Goddess.

THE HISTORY OF *THE ODYSSEY*

The Odyssey was probably assembled in its present form in the eighth century B.C. by "Homer" from many oral traditions and bardic "lays" with their convention of stock epithets and repeated formulas such as "rosy-fingered dawn," "wine-dark sea," and "much-enduring Odysseus." Who "Homer" actually was has been the subject of much scholarly debate for centuries. Whether he was one person or many, whether he was the author of both *The Iliad* and *The Odyssey* as well as other epics, or whether "Homer" was the name given to a collective of poets and bards reaching across centuries is still very much of an open issue.[4] Robert Graves and Samuel Butler even think that in the case of *The Odyssey,* "he" was a "she," a Sicilian priestess of Athena who gathered the oral material and re-formed it into her own epic masterpiece. There is also the well-known tradition that Homer was blind, and one can only wonder whether this purported blindness reflects the fact that no one will ever really be able to "see" Homer's true face and identity. My own belief is that, although traditional formulas and oral poetry transmitted and shared by generations of bards are included throughout the Homeric epics, the overall design of the poems with its rich detail and dazzling intricacy shows evidence of a single creative intelligence that could not have been the result of a committee of authors' work over centuries. Thus the likelihood of "Homer" having been a single eighth-century poet of enormous craft and genius. Whether he himself was literate, since a written alphabet was available although not widely employed at that time, or dictated portions of his epic to a scribe is also a question that occupies scholars. Perhaps the most balanced view is to be found in the work of classicist Eric Havelock, who suggests that Homer's eighth-century rendering was an intermingling of oral recitation and partial alphabetic transcription.[5] It is generally believed that a final written form of the Homeric poems was available in the sixth century B.C. With regard to the possibility of an original written text by Homer, I tend to agree with George Steiner, who writes, "I venture to guess that Homer was the first great poet in Western literature because he was the first to have understood the infinite resources of the written word. In the zest of the Homeric narrative, in its superb architecture, flashes the delight of a mind which has discovered that it need not deliver its creation into the fragile trust of memory. . . . It is entirely possible that the original 'Homer manuscript' was something unique and that it was kept in the jealous possession of a bardic guild (the Homeridae). The newly established Panhellenic festivals of the eighth century created an audience for the 'sons of Homer.' These singers may well have preserved the *Iliad* and *Odyssey* in a small number of canonic texts until their wider publications in sixth-century Athens (what scholars call the Pisistratean Recension)."[6]

This was a time of transition that marked the end of a dark age and the beginning of a new high civilization. The epic itself is concerned with events that occurred some four hundred to five hundred years earlier, in the twelfth and thirteenth centuries B.C.

The date of the Trojan War is generally put at around twelve hundred years before the Christian era. This was the peak of the Heroic Age, the era of the "bronze-clad Achaeans" of Greece, who were descendents of the Indo-Aryan invaders. The label "Indo-Aryan" is generic for the waves of invaders that conquered many peoples during this period. Among them were the Aryans of India, the Hittites and Mittani of the Fertile Crescent, the Luwians of Anatolia, Kurgans in eastern Europe, and the Achaeans and later the Dorians in Greece and Crete.

These waves of invaders became secure in their power following the collapse of the ancient and remarkable "peaceable kingdom" of the high Minoan civilization of Crete around the fifteenth century B.C. We know of this collapse not only from the ruined urban centers of Crete, such as the palace city of Knossos (circa 1450 B.C.), but also from other evidence indicating that sea raiders were wreaking havoc and destruction throughout the Mediterranean and Aegean world, even threatening the once-invincible strongholds of Egypt.

To this were added earthquakes, tidal waves that drowned coastal towns, and volcanic eruptions of unprecedented force and destruction such as the one that demolished the island of Thera. These natural disasters were accompanied by social cataclysms and mass migrations of peoples all around the eastern Mediterranean.

A Division in Consciousness

It has even been suggested that so mammoth were these upheavals that the resulting trauma to humanity caused divisions in consciousness and a major neurological shift in the brain from right to left hemispheric dominance. To understand the implications of this monumental change in human perception we first need a brief review of recent brain research on the functions of the two hemispheres. This research suggests that many of the polar but complementary ways of human thought processes are the result of the specialized functions in the right and left hemispheres of our brain. Although cach of thesc functions is mutually shared, they tend to be more localized in one hemisphere or the other. Thus, while the right hemisphere is the site of spatial, visual, intuitive, subjective, and analogical thinking, the left hemisphere specializes in temporal, verbal, analytical, objective, and linear ways of perceiving the world. Operating in tandem through the connective bridge of the corpus callosum, the bicameral brain integrates its functions so resourcefully that time and space, words and images, the cataloging of data and the wild freedom of the unbridled imagination can work together.

In *The Origins of Consciousness in the Breakdown of the Bicameral Mind,* a curious and ingenious study of this phenomenon, Julian Jaynes offers the hypothesis that in the time before this traumatic series of events, consciousness operated very differently from its workings today. Both people and societies lived under the authority of the bicameral, or two-chambered, brain. Thus, all mandates, orders, volitions, and other aspects of the cultural superego issued from certain areas of the right hemisphere and were transferred to certain areas of the left hemisphere, where they were heard as auditory hallucinations telling people what to do.[7]

These hallucinations of the bicameral brain were received as admonitions of the gods. According to Jaynes, this made for a very different kind of culture and consciousness, for "there were no private ambitions, no private grudges, no private frustrations, no private anything, since bicameral man had no internal 'space' in which to be private, and no analog 'I' to be private with. All initiative was in the voices of the gods."[8]

Jaynes' hypothesis is questionable insofar as we have no neurological evidence that the relationship between the two hemispheres of the brain changed suddenly thirty-five hundred years ago. But his brilliant if eccentric work certainly gives further credence to evidence that profound changes occurred in the consciousness, behavior, and manner in which people reflected upon themselves and their relationship (or lack of relationship) to spiritual realities. Whereas before, people had ready access to archetypal visions and voices (a phenomenon whose physiological function or receptor is generally localized in the right hemisphere of the brain), the traumas of this cataclysmic time silenced the "voices" of the gods. Such a loss of guidance and succor made for widespread anxiety, as shown in these painful lines from the Babylonian *Theodicy*, written about the time of the Trojan War, a poignant foreshadowing of the Hebrew Psalms:

> May the gods who have
> thrown me off give help,
> May the goddess who has
> abandoned me show mercy.

We see this tragic phenomenon in Odysseus himself, for he, whose very name means "trouble," is one of those seaborne invaders and destroyers, a late contributor to the time of troubles and a major representative of the breakdown of consciousness. Small wonder then that the goddess Athena, who had been for him "ever near," seems to abandon him for the next ten years.

The Great Goddess and Partnership Societies

What was consciousness like before this radical shift brought about by geological and human disaster? Jaynes says that the bicameral mind of this earlier era created "noble automatons who knew not what they did." Recent research, however, suggests to me that this earlier consciousness was far more complex than Jaynes allows, reflecting not a dominance of one hemisphere over the other, but rather a congruence of both hemispheres. Such an integration may have provided a deep sense of partnership between men and women as well as human and spiritual powers.

As the remarkable, if highly controversial, work of Marija Gimbutas and others has shown, the culture of old Europe, from about 7000 to 3500 B.C., was essentially a neolithic agrarian economy centering around the rites and worship of the Great Goddess.[9] The findings of archaeologists James Mellaart in Çatal Huyuk in Turkey and of Gimbutas in southeastern Europe reveal civilizations of extremely complex and sophisticated arts, crafts, technology, and social organization. Further, as such advocates of these findings as Riane Eisler suggest, the evidence seems to indicate that these were basically non-patriarchal partnership societies, with descent and inheritance passed through the mother, and with women playing key roles in all aspects of life and work.[10]

What was it like to live in these cultures governed by the goddess archetype? In all likelihood the emphasis was on being rather than doing, on deepening rather than producing and achieving. Process was more important than product, for the Great Goddess was preeminently a deity of process, of the natural rhythms of life and their unfolding in the cycles that govern nature. Thus, she was worshiped for her many aspects—as Earth Mother; guarantor of fertility; guardian of childbirth; protector and sustainer of growth in children, crops, and animals; as healer, helper, and source of inspiration and creativity; and as the Lady of the Beasts, lady of arts and poetry, ruler of death.

Most important of all, her ways were ones of peace. Thus, in the period under consideration, the art is non-heroic; indeed, there are no representations of heroes, conquests, or captives—that came later, much later. Instead, the art abounds with scenes and symbols from nature, with Sun and water, serpents, birds and butterflies, and everywhere, shrines, votive offerings, images, and figurines of the Goddess. The artistic emphasis is never on the straight line but on the meander and the spiral, implying the many turnings of the dance of life. All in all, one gains the impression of a gentle, high culture, nurturing, playful, and pacific.[11]

This culture was exported to Crete, where it flourished in populous well-organized cities, multistoried palaces, networks of fine roads, productive farms, an almost modern system of drainage and irrigation works, a rich economy with high living standards, and the lively and joyous artistic style so characteristic of Cretan life and sensibility. Again, certain scholars suggest that this was a culture of male-female equality and partnership, and again too, the spiritual authority and guiding principles were those of the Great Goddess.[12] Here the Goddess was seen in her triple manifestation, with her shape-shifting finding its correspondence in the seasons and the phases of the Moon. Thus, she appears as maiden (spring and the new Moon), fertile mother (summer and fall and the waxing and full Moon), and wise old one (winter and the waning Moon).

The Goddess in her threefold form is found the world over in myth, theology, legend, and literature. In ancient Greece she appears in many goddess triads, perhaps the best known being her disclosure in the Eleusinian Mysteries as mother (Demeter), daughter (Persephone), and the wise one of magic (Hecate). In Arthurian legend she appears as the maidenly Lady of the Lake who gives Arthur his sword, as his wife Guinevere, and as his magical half sister Morgan le Fay.

In both the earlier and later civilizations of Greece, an aspect of the Triple Goddess in her role as patroness of arts, crafts, and sciences was personified by Athena. In her study of pre-Hellenic goddesses, Charlene Spretnak offers a beautiful meditation on the myth of Athena, which describes perfectly this earlier role of the Goddess.

> In the Minoan days of Crete an unprecedented flowering of learning and the arts was cultivated by Athena. Dynamic architecture rose to four stories, pillared and finely detailed, yet always infused with the serenity of the Goddess. Patiently Her mortals charted the heavens, devised a calendar, kept written archives. In the palaces they painted striking frescoes of Her Priestesses and sculpted Her owl and ever-renewing serpent in the shrine rooms. Goddess figures and their rituals were deftly engraved on seals and amulets. Graceful scenes were cast in relief for gold vessels and jewelry. Athena nurtured all the arts, but Her favorites were weaving and pottery.
>
> Long before there were palaces, the Goddess had appeared to a group of women gathering plants in a field. She broke open the stems of blue-flowered flax and showed them how the threadlike fibers could be spun and then woven. The woof and warp danced in Her fingers until a length of cloth was born before them. She told them which plants and roots would color the cloth, and then She led the mortals from the field to a pit of clay. There they watched Athena form a long serpent and coil it, much like the serpents coiled around Her arms. She formed a vessel and smoothed the sides, then deftly applied a paste made from another clay and water. When it was baked in a hollow in the earth, a spiral pattern emerged clearly. The image of circles that repeat and repeat yet move forward was kept by the women for centuries.
>
> As the mortals moved forward, Athena guided the impulse of the arts. She knew they would never flourish in an air of strife, so She protected households from divisive forces and guarded towns against aggression. So invincible was the aura of Her protection that the Minoans lived in unfortified coastal towns. Their shipping trade prospered and they enjoyed a peace that spanned a thousand years. To Athena each family held the olive bough sacred, each wor-

shipped Her in their home. Then quite suddenly the flowering of the Minoans was slashed. Northern barbarians, more fierce than the Aegean Goddess had ever known, invaded the island and carried Athena away to Attica. There they made her a soldier.[13]

These gentle civilizations perished at the hands of the marauding bands of invaders, the latest in the long line of Indo-Aryan warrior nomads. These conquerors not only imposed their own rigid rules but shattered the finely wrought symbiosis among humans, nature, culture, and spiritual realities. Their consciousness divided, their loyalties uncertain, the invaders felt both drawn to and terrified by the gentle complexity of the high civilizations in which they found themselves. They were both fascinated and frightened by the pervasiveness of its eroticisms. Thus, they muscled and armored themselves against the enticement of its sensualities. They feared, dreaded, and violated the places and persons who bore witness to the ongoing communication between the seen and unseen orders, which they themselves had long since lost.

We see a late version of this in *The Iliad* when the holy communicant and prophetess, Cassandra, is ravaged on the altar of Athena. Thus, to maintain his separateness, the patriarchal hero invader, in Greece, in India, and in the Fertile Crescent, dreads the caress. When he comes close, it is to subdue by duel or rape.

The Goddess and the Hero

Not that these invaders did not adopt many of the ways and skills of the more ancient cultures. The Achaeans, for example, assimilated much of the Minoan culture. But they did so in such a way as to tear out the feminine threads in the cultural tapestry, leaving a ragged social fabric, missing many pieces.[14] The suppression of the rich and complex feminine characteristics of the goddess Athena is typical of this rending of culture and consciousness. Being too powerful a spiritual force to remove, she is instead preempted by the Achaean patriarchy to become Daddy's girl, the spirit of Zeus, born shrieking a harrowing cry that frightens even the gods as she emerges fully armored from the top of his head.

One wonders what lay in this cry. Was it perhaps the cry of outrage of one forced to live a lie, to inhabit a projection? This is hard enough for humans; one can only imagine how devastating it must be for divinity. Caught in the dreams of the long dark night of the heroic ages of Mycenean power and might, she is constrained to be a warrior goddess and protector of the citadels of power.

But one can never contain an archetype for long, certainly not one of such antiquity and complexity. Even when she is raging through *The Iliad,* her deeper nature is there *in potentia.* And in *The Odyssey* she is clearly in transition. All her acts attest to this shift, which explains all her changes, her disguises, her transformings. Her transition is not only to grow beyond the heroic image thrust upon her and to acquire again some of the fuller dimensions she had in earlier times, but also to become something more—a goddess who transcends both the Minoan and Mycenean visions of her, a goddess of transformation, who partners the evolutionary journey of both individuals and culture. For Athena, it is as if what had been seeded in Minoan culture emerges again after many centuries of being kept in the dark of the heroic brain. With *The Odyssey* she emerges as a transpersonal and transformational goddess, one who is no longer merely the patron of imperial adventure but is now the guiding spirit who helps refine and deepen the culture of the homeplace.

I believe that this "homeplace" is much more than its literal meaning. Rather, it is a symbol of the mystery of congruence and confluence of the brain-mind and its possibilities. I also believe that it is the cultural memory and yearning for this once and future confluence that drives Odysseus—with the hidden guidance of Athena—into experiences and initiations that serve to reeducate his mind and soul to this very congruence and the possibility of partnership. It is only after such reeducation that he is able to go home and become a conscious partner with both his wife and his goddess.

Odysseus yearns for home just as home yearns for Odysseus. He lives equipped for the macro-world—the world of heroic adventures. And yet, he yearns incessantly for the micro-world. Home is not only where the heart is—home is the pivotal purpose of *The Odyssey*. In the beginning, home is a wasteland, ruined by feasting and riotous suitors. In the end, home is cleansed and restored. Odysseus' major task is to put his home—his local culture and civilization—to rights. But, before he can do so, he must embark on a great voyage of self-discovery through all the other realms of being. The Odysseus who leaves Troy is not equipped to return home. He must be debriefed from his warrior attitudes, and from his repression of the feminine and all that suggests. Thus, Odysseus, whose name so fittingly means "trouble," is Achaean man writ large: brilliant and resourceful, but also greedy, arrogant, and piratical. A much-needed humbling and consequent deepening at the hands of the last representatives of the old Triple Goddess culture (Circe, Calypso, Nausicaa) is required to end his dark age and to create a new order of being upon the Earth.

The Trojan War stands as the Western model for war's reality. It is also the model for the thought forms of Western humanity about the feminine. We recall that the judgment of Paris was seen as the metaphoric cause of the war. The story begins when Eris, the goddess of strife, discovers she has not been invited to the wedding of the mortal Peleus and the sea goddess Thetis, and, true to her name, she hurls strife into the occasion. She tosses a golden apple marked "for the fairest" into the wedding feast on Mount Olympus.

Three great aspects of the Triple Goddess appearing as Athena, Aphrodite, and Hera claim the apple, and Zeus is called in to judge among them. He refuses, perhaps because he knows that all three aspects of the Triple Goddess are complementary to each other, that no one of them can outrank the others. He decides instead to test humanity and asks that the choice be made by a man—in this case Paris, the most beautiful of men, son of Priam, the king of Troy. Hermes brings the three goddesses before Paris for the contest. At first, the young man refuses, saying that it is not the province of human beings to arbitrate among the gods. He would prefer to divide the apple in three parts, giving each goddess a part. Hermes insists that Paris choose among them, and each of the goddesses does her best to persuade him in her favor.

From this episode we learn what happens when the Triple Goddess is forced to be seen as separated from the essential unity of her parts. Those parts are demoralized and diminished into bribery and competition, and the feminine loses some of its ancient power and dignity. Thus does the culture of the blade rend the fabric of the Triple Goddess culture of the chalice.

The story then becomes a tale to instruct and edify a would-be hero in the ways and means to choose his Shakti—his feminine energy-giving power. Paris does not choose Hera, who would give him wealth and power, nor does he pick Athena, who would give him victory in battles as well as great wisdom. Instead, he chooses Aphrodite, who flirts with him outrageously as she displays her splendid charms, promising him dominion over the most beautiful woman in the world, Helen of Sparta, who is already married to Menelaus. It is his abduction of Helen to Troy that gives the Achaean Greeks an excuse to attack Troy, at that time a wealthy and alluring trading colony of the immensely rich and powerful Hittites.

With the Goddess divided and diminished, woman is now seen as something to be kidnapped, conquered, and won. Indeed, *The Iliad* opens with the conflict of the principal Greek leaders and warriors Agamemnon and Achilles over a captive Trojan woman, Briseis, and the need to possess her. Achilles grows petulant and then wrathful. And it is the consequences of this wrath of Achilles that compose the terrible but epic incidents of which Homer sings in *The Iliad*.

In a similar vein, Odysseus begins his adventures by sailing north to Ismarus to plunder the town and possess the women. As this is no way for a man to return to his wife, Zeus blows him around for ten days until he reaches the land of the Lotus-Eaters—dreamland. From this time until he reaches the shores of Ithaca—ten years later and fast asleep—he never encounters another human being, only monsters, faerie people, and nymphs. His is now a visionary journey of initiations into self-discovery.

The nymphs are his guides in these initiations, leading him into inner mysteries that demand an appreciation and honoring of feminine wisdom. The nymphs also serve as surrogates for the three great goddesses whom Paris judged: Circe, the temptress, is the counterpart of Aphrodite. Calypso, a middle-aged nymph with whom Odysseus spends seven full years (in Greek terms, the symbol of a lifetime), is the stand-in for Hera, the wife of Zeus and the representative of wifely and family matters. Nausicaa, the young and clever girl who saves Odysseus and becomes his friend and champion, is the counterpart of Athena, the chief ally of Odysseus. In his involvement with these nymphs, Odysseus receives his first initiation: that of honoring and learning from the female powers that had been so abused by Paris and the conquering Greeks.

In a sense, Odysseus' journey into Mystery is about the restoration of the unity of the Triple Goddess through the awesome experiences and initiations of Odysseus. *The Odyssey* reweaves what *The Iliad* had torn asunder—the fullness of the Great Goddess in all her qualities and manifestations. These feminine qualities must be recognized and assimilated in order to enjoy a proper dynamic relationship in which male and female energies meet as partners—that is, equal, but not the same, for the polarity must be there for relationship and creativity to advance.

There are other initiations as well. And in all of them Odysseus finds himself tested by a reality that is larger and more mysterious than any he has ever known in his life. The wily and cunning hero, unfailing conqueror of the ways of the external world, is conquered and deepened by the great powers of the internal world. Those very powers that are the domain of the Triple Goddess—powers of insight and imagination, of psychological growth and spiritual awakening.

This is also the case with us and our present attempts to re-create the landscapes and innerscapes of our culture and ourselves. We can only begin to green the current wasteland by personally engaging in more levels of reality, by investigating the range and depths of the ecology of inner and outer space, and by bringing back rich traveler's tales of our discoveries. I hope that this book provides a vessel to launch such an adventure.

Seeing Anew with Ancient Eyes

The Odyssey, with its message of the necessity for a balance between inner and outer experience and of masculine and feminine expression (and, from our perspective, a congruence in the utilization of all parts of the brain), influenced the creation of a high civilization that reached its apogee in Hellenic Athens. This great city, named for its patroness, Athena, became for a time the place where inward reflection and outward action achieved perhaps the most fruitful resonance that the Western world has ever known.

How different indeed was the psychological world of these Greeks from our own. We in the present day persist in looking for cause and effect and remain monotheistic (having one god or supreme principle), monophrenic (having one personality), and monocular (having one way of seeing) in our epistemology. We tend to think that everything can be known in a straightforward, linear fashion. All we need do is accumulate enough facts and look at them rationally and the truth—of which there is only one—will reveal itself.

At its worst, our Judeo-Christian bias can make us suspicious of other modes of thought and of other styles of reverence. There is only one God, and the many things of this world are but passing phantasms, of no great validity compared to the all-encompassing province of the One. Fundamentalisms flourish under this view; regarding those who think differently as poor misguided fools at best, and dangerous and demonic at worst. Our more traditional science, derived from this cultural base, is not much better. Its practitioners have set themselves up as the ultimate elitist corps—the judge as well as the jury in determining the nature and function of all realities through the holy writ of the scientific method.

But the Homerically inspired Greek mind, which found its finest flowering in the Athens of Pericles, was polycentric, (having many centers), polytheistic (having many gods), polyphrenic (having many selves), and polyocular (having many ways of seeing), conceiving of many different causes—all of which provided a rich weave of explanation. They viewed reality as a field of unity in diversity with the One, deriving its Oneness only from the interconnecting patterns of the many.

The Greek concept of reality, and especially of the nature of the psyche, is very close in some ways to the exciting things happening in recent scientific understandings of the nature of physical reality, which is coming to understand the universe as a unified existence, a web of interdependent fields and relationships. Anthropologist Gregory Bateson has offered a theory of the unity of mind and nature, showing how the conscious mind is a subsystem of a larger system of Mind. Everything—rocks, trees, starfish on the beach, you and I—are all interrelated in the great ecology of Mind, or Pattern that Connects, which some people call God.[15]

The English botanist and theorist Rupert Sheldrake has presented impressive evidence pointing to the possibility that the habits or laws of nature are not static but can change their form and functions through new discoveries and the adaptation of new habits. Through what he calls "morphogenetic fields," invisible organized fields weaving across time and space (and within which we are all connected), act as blueprints for new structures. Seeding the morphogenetic field adds new forms and behaviors to the species "memory," and all organisms can then draw upon it. This means that, once a substance or an individual or even a society learns a new behavior, the causative, morphogenetic field of that entity is changed, and the next substance, individual, or society learns the new behavior much more easily and quickly. According to Sheldrake, the more an event is duplicated, the more powerful its morphogenetic field becomes.[16] Thus, people in the twentieth century learn to operate machinery and ride a bicycle much more quickly than people did in the previous century. Similarly, our children learn how to work with computers faster than their parents.

Then there are physicist Ilya Prigogine's Nobel Prize–winning studies of nonequilibrium dynamics, which recognizes how a higher order emerges from the fluctuations and energy dispersals created through the arrival of new information into a system. Prigogine has shown that as more information or more stimulation enters a system, whether it be a molecular system or the systems of cities, cultures, or even of the psyche, the system is driven to make more and more interconnections, becoming gradually more complex, until it suddenly shifts into a coherent new form. This describes one way in which evolution occurs and higher order arises out of seeming chaos.[17] These views taken together with other new approaches to the nature of reality, such as *chaos theory* and the *holographic* view of the brain/mind system, grant perspectives in which ancient myths and modern physics are found to be remarkably correlative. The term "chaos" derives from the Greek word *chaino*, which refers to the deeps, the great mysterious, the potent void. In many mythic and spiritual traditions this void is not empty but is pregnant with patterns in which all potentialities abide. As scripture shows how the Great Pattern Maker stirs up the void to create the world and all living things out of the inexhaustible treasure house of chaos, so chaos theory concerns itself with the dynamics of the universal laws of pattern formation. This it does through the study of chaotic irregularities found in nature and society—disorder in the sea, the weather, the heart, the brain; the irregular fluctuations in wildlife populations or in the even wilder stock market. By modeling these fluctuations and aperiodic recurrences it discovers innate order and emergent form inherent in even the most chaotic of systems.[18]

The holographic view of the brain/mind system starts with the analogy of the hologram in which every part of the picture is contained in every other part, enfolding the form and structure of the object photographed within each region of the photograph itself. Neurophysiologist Karl Pribram has used this analogy to show how countless holographic images could be stored in brain cell synapses so that memory, images, sound, and action are embedded as wholes in distributed patterns throughout the brain. Using the fluid mathematics of Fourier transforms, he describes the intricacies of nerve impulses traveling between cells through a network of fine fibers on the cells. He speculated with great specificity on how, when the impulses cross the cell, the fibers move in slow waves that are then encoded throughout the rest of the brain in a manner that is analogous to the hologram. Like the hologram then, memory storage is ubiquitous throughout the brain, each neuron a marvel of hologrammatic efficiency able to store billions of bits of information in a tiny space.[19] Nobel physicist David Bohm takes this analogy even further when he suggests on the basis of quantum theory that there are two orders of reality. One is the primary order, which is implicate, enfolded, harboring our reality in much the same way as the DNA in the nucleus of a cell harbors potential life and directs the nature of its unfolding. This is an order of pure Beingness, pure frequency, consonant with the realm of Plato's Forms or Whitehead's Primordial Nature of God. Buddhist and Hindu philosophies have similar metaphysical systems and psychologies to account for this primary order of pure potentiality.

In this primary order there are no things and there are no movements as we understand them. It is a realm that transcends specification, a hyperdimensional reality that knows neither here nor there, neither space nor time.

Bohm refers to this primary order as the frequency domain. I prefer to think of it as the primary place from which the forms of reality are engendered, pervading all our processes and, potentially, totally available at any part of our reality. To me, it is the source of archetypes and those patterns of possibility that are waiting at the threshold of existence to enter the world of space and time.

Bohm speaks also of a secondary order which is seen as a second-generation reality and as such is explicate, unfolded, manifest in space and time, *the decoded hologrammatic image of reality. All apparent movement and substance, the world of space and time, then, are of the secondary order.*[20]

What Bohm is suggesting, then, is that we live in a holographic universe in which the world of space and time is but the unfolded or explicate order deriving from the underlying hologram of the implicate, enfolded order. Taken together with Pribram's premise this suggests that our brain/mind systems are holograms looking at the great Hologram of the universe. Or, as Meister Eckhart once put it, "The eye by which I see God, is the same eye by which God sees me."[21]

One thing we can say about these views of the new science is that they allow us to enter upon a universe strangely resonant with the ancient Greek notions of the interconnectedness between things. Indeed, *things in themselves* are coming to seem not as dead or inert, but actually filled with their own kind of dynamism, depth, and even inner life. Soul is being returned to the world in ways that recall the Greek manner of seeing mind and nature as immanent in psyche and soul.

For the ancient Greeks, *psyche* was not a thing but a *process,* a dynamic continuum and relationship among humans, gods, and nature. The Greek notion of psyche was one of radiating but personalized fields that cross-fertilized all structures of reality, making archetypes available to men, and making intimate the universal patterns found in nature and story alike. As Charles Hampden-Turner observes about the Greeks in his splendid book *Maps of the Mind:*

> They walked with Truth [Apollo] and Beauty [Aphrodite] at their sides. They raced with daemons of excellence, the spirits of past athletes running beside them, urging them on. They travelled with Hermes, danced and drank with Dionysius, and sailed the seas under the guardianship of Poseidon. They fought for the rights of married women, children and the home with the tenacity of Hera and harvested the crops with Demeter beside them . . . The concept of psyche gave the Greeks their infinite love and delight in nature and an extraordinary courage in exploring it. Into every nook

> and cranny of the world the spirits of gods or heroes had already ventured. Men crossed the seas in the path of Odysseus, entered labyrinths of mind or nature wherein Theseus had already slain the Minotaur. . . .[22]

By perceiving psyche as a resonance phenomenon, a radiant field of living energies that include gods and cosmic principles, the building blocks of mind, myth, and nature, the human being has the capacity within his or her mind and body to become an instrument through which the world can be re-created and the soul of humankind can touch the creative Source of all becoming.

The Greeks knew they had done this: Witness Pericles' reflections on the soul of Athens delivered in his famous funeral oration in 430 B.C. "Mighty indeed are the marks and monuments we have left. . . . Future ages will wonder at us, as the present age wonders at us now."

Athena: The Friend in Court

Which brings us back to Athena, the goddess and namesake of all this wonder, and the initiator of the action in *The Odyssey*. The most benevolent member of the Greek pantheon, she also has the widest scope for her archetypal activities—wisdom and justice, weaving and other crafts, childbirth and the nurturing of cities, grace and valor. These are the forms and functions Athena again reclaims and represents by the time of the writing of *The Odyssey*. This wide range of human-centered activities touching all arenas and conditions makes her a divine model for the possibilities of human wholeness.

When we meet Athena in the opening episode of *The Odyssey*, she is displaying the compassion that comes of such wholeness as she argues the case for Odysseus before her father, Zeus, and the Olympian gods. She speaks of his cleverness and of the sacrifices he made to the gods on the plains of Troy, of his present trouble and sorrow, imprisoned in the middle of the sea, the kept man of Calypso. She reminds them that it has been almost twenty years since Odysseus has seen his home. The first ten were spent in Troy. Then weeks were spent wandering from one harrowing adventure to another, and he lived a year with Circe. Then, finally, he landed on Calypso's island, the great stuck place of his life. It is perhaps some small comfort to us to note that the actual famed adventures took only a few weeks—apart from the year spent with Circe, the rest of the time he was stuck in the middle of nowhere. Thus, like most of us, he bides his time waiting, longing, hoping for something to happen so that he can get on with his life.

Zeus reminds Athena that this fate had befallen him because he incurred the hatred of Zeus' brother, the sea god Poseidon, for putting out the single eye of Poseidon's son Polyphemus, the Cyclops. Poseidon, the god of the sea, of the unknown, the mysterious, the unfathomable, is clearly the one god to have it in for Odysseus. Cunning and brilliant in the known ways of the world, Odysseus is in some sense the first modern man, but like modern man he has ignored his own deeper nature. Necessarily then, his learning must come out of the deeps, which he has mishandled. For from these deeps, as we have seen, come the stimulus and occasion for most of his adventures in a larger experience of reality.

But Grace is a function even higher than the remedial power of the deeps. Odysseus' education has gone far enough, and so Athena argues that, after all he has patiently endured, it is time for the gods to help him return home. Zeus agrees but asks how this may be brought about without arousing Poseidon's anger. Athena jumps into action, suggesting that Hermes, the messenger of the gods, and guide for the soul's journey, be immediately dispatched to Calypso's island to demand that she free Odysseus from her tender net. Athena herself with the consent of the other gods will now don her winged golden sandals and fly to Ithaca. There, in disguise as an old family friend, she will put heart into his son Telemachus and have him "speak his mind to all the would-be bridegrooms courting his mother, the wastrels who have been butchering his sheep and his cattle in heaps."

Twenty-eight hundred years after it was written, this episode, which I call "the friend in court," still serves as a telling model of how our own inner wisdom can help us move out of our stuck places and illumine our transitions. Often, some quickening agent of the Life Force, some stimulus from the archetypal world, is needed to help us get on with it. This can perhaps be interpreted as the entelechy, the seed pattern within us, the most potent and most personal of evolutionary principles, which constantly seeks to remind us that we are that grand intersection between cosmology and biology, and that the universe seeks to grow through our becoming.

EXERCISE: The Friend in Court

HERE begins the first of the exercises, or processes, that follow each chapter of *The Hero and the Goddess.* In this particular process we are going to attempt to tap into a symbolic or archetypal expression of the entelechy principle operating in our lives. Entelechy is all about the possibilities encoded in each of us. For example, it is the entelechy of an acorn to be an oak tree, of a baby to be a grown-up, of a popcorn kernel to be a fully popped entity, and of you and me to be God only knows what. It is possible to call upon the entelechy principle within us in such a way that it becomes personal, friendly, and even helpful. This entelechy principle can be expressed symbolically as a god or a guide. We feel its presence as the inspiration or motivation that helps us get life moving again after times of stress or stagnation. There are many ways to engage the symbolic forms of the entelechy principle. One way can be found in traditional Bhakti yoga, the "way of devotion." Here, one practices constant awareness and passionate lovingness to the deity or guiding principle in order to embody its identity. In these primarily

Eastern sacred psychologies, this loving resonance often leads to a sense of deep union with the deity or archetype, and consequently to an expansion of one's own consciousness and perspective. This form of deity yoga is one of the main practices of the current Dalai Lama.

Another way to touch into the entelechy is through shamanic means. Shamans are those healers and visionaries who learn to align themselves with natural forces both within and without in order to use these energies for healing, for renewal, and for bringing into the profane world the transformational powers of sacred time and space. Shamans are able to orchestrate themselves on the continuum of states of consciousness to serve as bridges between ordinary reality and the powers, the archetypes, of the transpersonal realms. Using prayer, chant, song, dance, drumming, meditation, and other means, shamans are able to alter their consciousness and dissociate from their local selves in order to identify or even merge with the archetype, and thus acquire some of its powers or abilities. The art and disciplines needed to enter into so special a relationship are enormous, which explains the reverence in which shamans have been held for millennia.

This exercise offers a more secular process for engaging the entelechy—the larger sense of the purpose and meaning of our lives—by calling upon an archetypal "Friend in Court." We will do this by enacting a courtroom drama in which this friend is called upon to speak about us from a larger, or Olympian, perspective. Whether we do this alone or within a group setting, we will each assume the role that Athena plays in *The Odyssey* when she speaks before the court of the gods on Mount Olympus for the sake of Odysseus, her favorite in the human world.

Just as she became his Friend in Court, so you will discover within yourself a guiding archetype, an entelechy self, who will serve a similar function on your behalf. In doing this, you will gain something of the perspective of that archetype and be able to observe with both compassion and detachment the mortal that you are.

You will find the force within that guides and protects you, that serves as your ally and champion. From the place where this force resides, you will view your life. This will enable you to see yourself in a new way and allow you to release negative or derailing habit patterns and choose consciously those steps that lead to a life of growth, courage, and creative action.

MATERIALS NEEDED: A small bell for the guide to ring to indicate time. A drum to be beaten during the chanting of the line from Friedrich Hölderlin's poem "Patmos" (see page 66).

MUSIC: Music may be used, if the guide recommends it, during the time when the "gods" are speaking for their humans. Slow, powerful chanting music, or music with a steady drumbeat has been found to be particularly effective (see Musical Selections, Area II, page 415). This must be played very softly, so the participants will be able to hear each other.

INSTRUCTIONS FOR WORKING ALONE: First, read these instructions and the script for the guide several times, until you become thoroughly familiar with the process. It may take a little preparation time for you to assemble or create what you need, so make sure you allow yourself enough time to experience your process fully. Be sure to make two signs of the opening and closing chants of the Hölderlin poem you will be reciting and post them in your sacred space.

Begin by choosing your music to chant and dance to. Then choose the portions of the script that you wish to record on tape for you to play back and follow during the process. Remember to leave pauses of sufficient time to allow you to do the work. Having to remember to keep turning the tape player on and off can be very distracting and break into your deep level of connectedness with your Friend in Court. As you record your voice reading the script, feel the majesty and eloquence of Homer's words filling your thoughts and rolling off your tongue. You will be your own guide on this journey, so call upon your Higher Self to be present in you, to infuse this tape with all that is best and wisest within you.

Be sure to create a sense of sacredness in the space in which you will be doing the process. Begin by making it neat and orderly. Some people clear and sweeten the ambience of the space by burning sage, or sweet grass or some other herbal incense, and wafting the cleansing smoke into all the corners of the room, or the area you will be using. Other people use the sound of bells or a drum or chanting. You, yourself, may wish to have a special bath and dress in ceremonial clothing of some sort.

When all is in readiness, reenter your space with a deep sense of the sacredness of your purpose. Remember to bring your journal and pen. Begin to play the music you have chosen. You may wish to stand in the center of your sacred space for a moment and offer a prayer or invocation to the "gods" who will accompany you on all your journeys throughout this book. You may also wish to offer a special invitation for the guidance, blessings, and help of your Special Friend, the tutelary deity whose presence is of greatest importance to you, as Athena's was to Odysseus. At the end of the processes always remember to thank this deity for his or her help—even today the gods enjoy "offerings" and tend to respond to them favorably.

As you are invoking your Special Friend, reach out—physically, spiritually, psychically—to its dimension of beingness. Feel your Special Friend join you in this sacred space you have created for the two of you to dance together through space-time. Feel the loving presence, the blessings and joyful laughter that are part of the beingness of your Special Friend.

Now, start the tape of the script for the guide that you have made for this journey. Begin by chanting the lines from Hölderlin's poem "Patmos," and let them slowly carry you into a meditative movement in which you feel the forces of the archetypal realm rising within you.

After a time with this meditation, come to stillness. Then, seeded with this deep knowing, begin to speak aloud about your client, "your human," yourself. Sense the presence of other witnesses from the archetypal realm as you do this. When you have finished, come again to stillness and allow time to hear what the unseen others may wish to add. After some consideration, make a final summary statement. Then, stand up and walk counterclockwise reciting the words given at the close of this process (see page 69).

To deepen and enhance your experience, record what has happened in your journal.

You may also want to do this exercise with one other person, perhaps a person with whom you are having some temporary difficulties, to allow both of you to shift perspective and bring a higher wisdom to bear on the situation. Or you can do this alone as a gestalt process by playing first one role and then the other, dialoguing back and forth as yourself and as the other person.

Another way of doing this is to dialogue with this person in your journal. Put your name on the upper left-hand margin of the page and ask the other person in this dialogue to speak about you as well as about himself or herself during the process of the Friend in Court. Then put the other person's initials in the left-hand margin, and simply write down whatever pops into your head. Don't edit it, or even reread it at this time, just let the words flow through you onto the page. Just continue asking more questions and writing down whatever enters your mind until everything that needs to be said has been said. Also be sure to record your impressions of this entire process in your journal when you are finished.

SCRIPT FOR THE GUIDE: We will begin in a traditional way, by chanting together. As you chant, allow your consciousness to shift into rhythm and resonance, and into the power and yearning of the words we speak and call out with each other. The lines from Hölderlin's poem "Patmos" will set the conditions for the entrance of the archetypal Friend in Court.

> Near is, but difficult to grasp, the God.
> But where there is danger, the saving powers also rise.

[**Note to guide:** You may want to have written these words in large letters on a poster board or slate so that people can learn them quickly as they chant.]

As you repeat this chant many times, move throughout the room, letting your voice and gestures express the meaning and power of the poem. Reach for the god, feel the forces of danger, and sense the rising of the saving powers. [The guide leads the chant, keeping time with a drumbeat, and allowing several minutes for it to continue.]

Keep chanting, but now begin to allow the god or principle of the deepest wisdom in you to be expressed through dance or movement. This symbolic entelechy principle, this "god," should be personal and unique to you and need not belong to any roster of known gods or symbolic forces. Dance the god and let the god dance you. [The guide should allow this to continue until the chanting and dancing peak and you sense the saving powers are indeed ready to rise.]

Now, gather in groups of no fewer than three and no more than six. This is the Court of the Gods. Each person will incarnate an archetypal Friend in Court, speaking for the needs and needed changes of his or her own local life, and referring to one's local self in the third person.

It is important while playing the role of the godly Friend in Court that you truly enact this archetype with appropriate change of voice, gesture, language, and energy. You will bear yourself with the presence and power of one who belongs to and is completely comfortable in the archetypal realm.

In this role you speak for the life of your human self from an Olympian perspective, allowing yourself as god or goddess to observe the causal weave of circumstance that informs the life, the strengths and weaknesses, the lacks and the possibilities of your human. Observe where this person is coming from and where he or she could be going. Above all, state what is needed in this life to get on with it. In Odyssean terms, what would enable your human to get off the island where he or she is stuck and go home to your "Ithaca." Should your human not feel stuck at this moment, then, as god or goddess, deal with the state of transition that your human may be experiencing; offer the help he or she may need to complete this transition.

The perspective of the gods is always helpful and empowering. Should your local human feel any negativity about your life, you must be careful not to let your god partake of it. Here is an example of *what not to do.* In this instance a man named Larry has assumed his god self. The god is now speaking:

God: "Consider my human, Larry. What a miserable wreck he is. Why did I choose such a loser for my human? He has no friends—who could put up with him? He has no prospects—and why should he, the lazy bum! And what's more, even I can't stand him."

* * *

It would be far better for the Friend in Court to see his client from the perspective of the rich gifts inherent in every human being, the gifts that can be discerned from the larger perspective of the "god." Here then is another version of the Friend in Court speaking for the same human:

God: "Consider my human, Larry. A remarkable person with many rare gifts. Among them is the gift for understanding the tragic side of life. This has given him a caring and compassionate nature which he shows in so many ways, both large and small. Although he worked behind the scenes, he was there putting in many hours so that the peace marches could happen. It is he who volunteers for community service, he who lends a helping hand. He has sought meaning through many paths, has glimpsed many ways of discovering and refining one's true self. His relatives would perhaps call him a dilettante, but I ask you to remember that the root word for dilettante means 'one who takes delight in.'

"Larry is a seeker. His army experience was traumatic for one so sensitive. Nevertheless, he learned that he was a survivor and has persevered in spite of all obstacles. His courage is immense. Yet he is very shy and it is difficult for him to make friends, but once he has made one, he is loyal and helpful to an extraordinary degree. He is one of those few who has the gift for transformational friendship.

"His path at present is unclear. He needs to deepen in order to find the source of who and what he is. He needs a challenge that will encourage and develop all of his talents and give him a sense of his uniqueness and usefulness in the world. There is an important role in this present world for a man like Larry. Tell me, gods, how do you see his life being set on a more productive path? How can we help Larry reach his 'Ithaca'?"

The actual telling by the "god" of the life journey of his or her human will of course be much longer, and may involve the setting forth of a certain number and pattern of experiences and life situations of that human. The other "gods" listen with attention and compassion, and after the god who is speaking for the human client presents the "case," they then offer helpful, thoughtful, and high-minded suggestions. They speak only out from the High Self—they do not try to do "therapy." After one god has finished speaking for his or her human [Guide: allow ten to fifteen minutes], the next god assumes the role of the Friend in Court for his or her human.

[The guide should indicate the end of the allotted time for each god's statement by ringing a bell. After all the gods have finished speaking for their humans, the guide will give the following directions.]

In the light of further reflection and the briefs presented by the other gods, each god is now allowed several minutes to give an overview and a summation of the life and needs of his or her human charge. Remember the example of Athena, who was able to give active suggestions for what was needed and to volunteer for service herself.

[The guide will keep time and allot two minutes or so for each god's summation. When the summation by all the gods has been completed, the guide will say:]

Rise now and let the group of gods form a circle with left hands joined in the center. Walk slowly counterclockwise chanting these words:

> Near is, and available to hold, this Human.
> For where there is openness,
> We saving powers are here and known.

[The guide lets this continue for several minutes.

If you are working alone, also walk counterclockwise around a center point with your left hand extended into the center. As you chant the words for several minutes, try to sense the "presence" of the gods who have come to join you in the circle.

At the conclusion of this process, the guide may advise each member of the court to give thanks and honor to the other members for their support. The court can close with a dance of the gods with appropriate celebrational music, and then resume their individual human selves. When this concludes, the participants should be encouraged to record their experiences in their journals.]

CHAPTER 2

The Beginning of the Hero's Journey

As you set out for Ithaka
hope your road is a long one,
full of adventure, full of discovery.
Laistrygonians, Cyclops,
angry Poseidon—don't be afraid of them:
you'll never find things like that on your way
as long as you keep your thoughts raised high,
as long as a rare excitement
stirs your spirit and your body.
Laistrygonians, Cyclops,
wild Poseidon—you won't encounter them
unless you bring them along inside your soul,
unless your soul sets them up in front of you.

Hope your road is a long one.
May there be many summer mornings when,
with what pleasure, what joy,
you enter harbors you're seeing for the first time;
may you stop at Phoenician trading stations

to buy fine things,
mother of pearl and coral, amber and ebony,
sensual perfume of every kind—
as many sensual perfumes as you can;
and may you visit many Egyptian cities
to learn and go on learning from their scholars.

Keep Ithaka always in your mind.
Arriving there is what you're destined for.
But don't hurry the journey at all.
Better if it lasts for years,
so you're old by the time you reach the island,
wealthy with all you've gained on the way,
not expecting Ithaka to make you rich.
Ithaka gave you the marvelous journey.
Without her you wouldn't have set out.
She has nothing left to give you now.

And if you find her poor, Ithaka won't have fooled you.
Wise as you will have become, so full of experience,
you'll have understood by then what these Ithakas mean.[1]

WHEN you sail into the harbor of Ithaca today, you pass a small island with a sign on it. The sign reads:

EVERY TRAVELER IS A CITIZEN OF ITHACA

You know then that you are truly home. Until this moment you may not have known the goal of all your travels, but you know now. Ithaca, the homeplace of the Western mythic imagination, has given you that most splendid journey, the road to self-knowledge. You walk her streets, climb her hills, sit over retsina and shish kebab in her cafés, watch her olives being pressed, her goats being milked, her young girls dancing the ancient round dances, and you know that it was all worthwhile.

All those wanderings, meanderings, being blown off course, meeting monsters of recalcitrance and angels of opportunity, feeling surprised by joy, shocked by unspeakable circumstances, and always, always, finding yourself caught for a long time on the island of frustration that you realize only at the last moment was also a place of integration, of gestation. And, finally, your inner ally, your partner in the depth realms, takes your part and calls you home, home to Ithaca. And when you sit on the bench by the harbor and watch all those other travelers come in—on yachts and dories and ferryboats—you feel a contentment so sweet, a fulfillment so rare: now you understand what Ithaca means.

In his great poem "Ithaka," the modern Greek poet Constantine Cavafy gives us the metaphor of our quest for the Odysseus in ourselves. We wish for his sake that it could have been spoken in some transhistorical dream to the original Odysseus when first he set out from Troy. But then would he have seen his journey differently? Would he have learned as much as he did? Perhaps it was his capacity to experience his odyssey fully that qualifies Odysseus as guide on the journey to the deepest reaches of the soul.

How many people seem untouched by even the most extraordinary experiences because their goal was held so tightly that they simply "weathered" the experience of attaining it? What was Nixon's term? " 'They' toughed it out." But they apparently grew not a smidgen on the voyage to that goal, and thus they never discovered what the road to Ithaca really means.

The emphasis in Cavafy's poem—as in Homer's epic—is on process. The process is more important than the goal. Perhaps this is the reason we have so many feminine initiators in this story of a man who begins as a goal-minded adventurer and ends as the deepened master of process. The nature of the feminine is to revere and understand process, the process of gestation and birth, the process of the body's cycles, the process of child-raising and development, the process of unfolding in the agricultural season, the inner knowing of right times and wrong times. That intimate, attentive sense of process is part of what Odysseus learns from the great demigoddesses, nymphs, wise women, and weavers he encounters during his ten-year soul's journey home to Ithaca.

The rising feminine sensibility of our own time provides, above all else, a conduit for the restoration of process in today's realities, which are as complex and uncertain as those Odysseus met. He found devourers and diminishers, and so do we. Ours chew up the natural world, spew out nuclear wastes, set us awash in a sea of drugs, and seduce the innocent through the siren call of media hype. Suddenly there are Laestrygonians and Cyclops in the middle of Iowa. Suddenly, too, opportunities come our way that were never there for our grandparents. Opportunities for partnering the planet, for becoming responsible for biological governance, for regrowing our minds and bodies to be adequate vehicles for the Earth's new story. We are on the road to Ithaca, whether we know it or not. We are about to embark on the Hero's Journey.

THE HERO'S JOURNEY

Heroes always emerge in a time of dying—of self, of social sanctions, of society's forms, of standard-brand religions, governments, economics, psychologies, and relationships. In answering the call of the eternal, they discover the courage to perform the first great task of the hero or heroine—to undergo all the gestations, growth, and trauma required for a new birth. This occurs so that they can then serve as midwife in the larger society for the continuum of births necessary to redeem both the time and the society in which they live and bring them to a higher level of functioning.

Thus, the second great task of the hero or heroine—as *The Odyssey* and many other myths show us—is to return to the world. Plato tells us that, after receiving illumination in the vast world of eternal realities, philosophers must go back into the cave of ordinary society.[2] In just such a fashion, Jesus comes back from the desert. The Buddha returns from his ascetic meditations. And Odysseus returns, at last, from his voyage into the depth world. All are deeply changed; some are transformed. And they immediately begin teaching the lessons they have learned of *palingenesia*, of life renewed and deepened.

The dearth of heroes in our time—or worse, the media's

treatment of them as banal—has created a dangerous trend. For we have lost the high and holy service of those who could bring us and our world the much-needed new births, the next steps in the creation of a global society. Perhaps, we might argue, it is right for the heroic tradition to be in abeyance for now. Perhaps it is necessary for that image to die to its old forms so that it can be remythologized, reborn in the light of the Earth's spirit calling us to a new humanity. Perhaps this new form of heroism is one that will take into account the rise of women to full partnership with men, the impossibility of war, the complexity of current social forms, the rapidity of communication, and the need for a global sensibility.

LET us look at the classical Hero's Journey as it is summarized in a diagram from Joseph Campbell's *The Hero with a Thousand Faces.*[3]

Drawing upon several hundred examples of this journey, Campbell offers us this synopsis of the Hero's Journey as it is experienced in the cycle of myths throughout the world:

> The mythological hero, setting forth from his common day hut or castle, is lured, carried away, or else voluntarily proceeds to the threshold of adventure. There he encounters a shadow presence that guards the passage. The hero may defeat or conciliate this power and go alive into the kingdom of the dark [brother-battle, dragon-battle; offering, charm] or be slain by the opponent and descend in death [dismemberment, crucifixion]. Beyond the threshold, then, the hero journeys through a world of unfamiliar yet strangely intimate forces, some of which severely threaten him [test], some of which give magical aid [helpers]. When he arrives at the nadir of the mythological realm, he undergoes a supreme ordeal and gains his reward. The triumph may be represented as the hero's sexual union with the Goddess—mother of the world [sacred marriage], his recognition by the father-creator [father atonement], his own divinization [apotheosis], or again—if the powers have remained unfriendly to him—his theft of the boon he came to gain [bride-theft, fire-theft]; intrinsically it is an expansion of

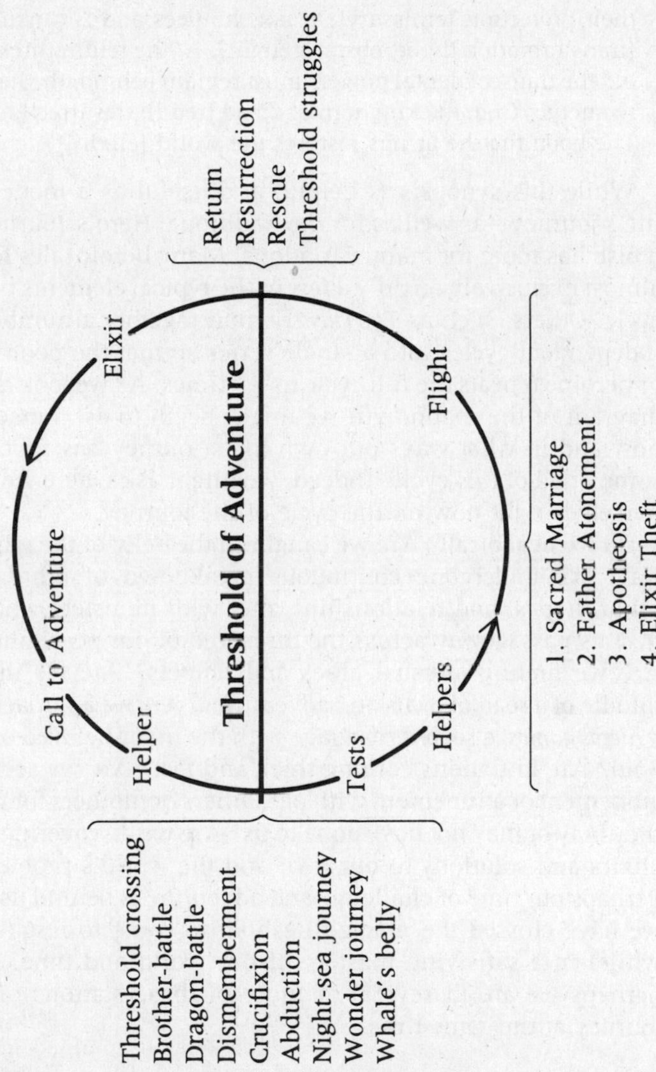
Threshold of Adventure
Call to Adventure
Helper
Threshold crossing
Brother-battle
Dragon-battle
Dismemberment
Crucifixion
Abduction
Night-sea journey
Wonder journey
Whale's belly
Tests
Helpers
1. Sacred Marriage
2. Father Atonement
3. Apotheosis
4. Elixir Theft
Flight
Return
Resurrection
Rescue
Threshold struggles
Elixir

> consciousness and therewith of being [illumination, transfiguration, freedom]. The final work is that of the return. If the powers have blessed the hero, he now sets forth under their protection [emissary]; if not, he flees and is pursued [transformation flight, obstacle flight]. At the return threshold the transcendental powers must remain behind; the hero reemerges from the kingdom of dread [return, resurrection]. The boon that he brings restores the world [elixir].[4]

While this synopsis is helpful and useful as a model for life's journey—as well as for the traditional Hero's Journey—it also has room for many variations. Many heroic tales focus almost exclusively on only a few of the typical elements of the cycle. Others, such as *The Odyssey,* pull together a number of independent cycles into a single series so that the poor hero or heroine repeats the full cycle many times. As we look at the diagram of the monomyth we might begin to ask ourselves how and in what ways our own life's journey has followed some or all of this cycle. Indeed, we might ask where we find ourselves right now on the cycle of the journey.

Do we hear a call? Are we caught in the belly of the whale? Have we undergone continuous breakdown of our body, mind, hopes, and relationships, met with monsters who refuse us passageway across the threshold of our possibilities? Are we finding unusual allies and helpers? Are we in the middle of a road of trials and adventures? Are we approaching a *hieros gamos,* a sacred marriage with the inner Beloved of the Soul? Are initiations coming thick and fast? Are we seeking atonement or attunement with our fathers or mothers for what they may or may not have done to us? Are we discovering rare elixirs and solutions to our own and the world's problems? Perhaps our time of challenge and adventure is behind us and we have crossed the magic threshold to come to rest (for a while) in a satisfying mastery of our world and time. And perhaps we are in several or more of these stations of the journey at the same time.

THE SACRED PSYCHOLOGY OF THE HERO'S JOURNEY

These mythic transformational journeys are best understood through the premises of sacred psychology. In nearly all traditions, sacred psychology assumes that the deepest yearning in every human soul is to return to its spiritual source, there to experience communion and even union with the Beloved. This relationship is then expressed in the deepened and renewed forms of our daily lives. Thus, the methods of sacred psychology involve processes that enhance the connection between our local, time-bound selves and the ultimate reality. These processes have the effect of regeneration and of *palingenesia*, the deepening of life, so that one comes gradually to enjoy a more complete and accurate self-image, with a stronger, more flexible body, an amplified mind, a compassionate heart, an active soul, and a new life focus on high service.

The themes from sacred psychology that relate to the renewal of the soul are many, and most have mythic components:

- There is the Sacred Wound, which reframes life's cruelties and betrayals, both physical and psychological, in such a fashion that we come to see them as gateways to deeper understanding, greater vulnerability, and empathy.
- There is the Mythic Journey of Transformation—the story of the soul's journey—upon which we embark again and again with ever-deepening consciousness and high purpose.
- In the Discovery of the Larger Story, we become willing to see our individual lives as part of a Great Life, and everyone and everything we meet upon the way as essential participants in the unfolding myth of life on Earth.
- We may encounter a series of Initiations into Our Own Depths. Through these experiences we discover that initiations come to us in many forms, in many ways. And almost

all of these will contain elements—some, perhaps, unpleasant and painful—that invite and incite the depth structures of the psyche to rise so that we may move to a new stage.

- Another theme of the mythic journey is Partnership with Spiritual Allies for the regreening of the world. This requires actively pursuing our relationship with archetypes through meditation, visualization, journaling, drawing, dancing, and other forms of work on our inner selves, but now in the company of others. Such community activities generate the energy, excitement, and information needed to assist in the task of creating a new world.
- And finally, at the journey's end, we experience Union with the Beloved of the Soul—our personal archetypal representative of God, of All Being. Through sacred psychology, we become citizens in a universe larger than our grandest aspirations and more complex than all our dreams.

ODYSSEUS' JOURNEY OF TRANSFORMATION

For Odysseus, the road to Ithaca follows much of the pattern of the traditional Hero's Journey. As we experience *The Odyssey,* we will redream the image of the Hero's Journey to discover how it can become a potent and viable metaphor to help us with the continuing transformation of ourselves and our society. We will add maturity to the heroic image and discover the tasks and gifts of that maturity. The mighty talismans, the secret helpers of the traditional journey, become the findings of physics, neurophysiology, and research into consciousness and human capacities. To these are added the primordial archetypal forces that give us their initiations from the cornucopia of cosmic gifting. These are the emblems and the guides of our strengthening.

As we encounter demi-goddesses and faerie folk and magical circumstances, we will discover their personal meanings for us in the symbiosis we develop with the great patterns of creation that nature gives us. We will learn and relearn how these archetypal persona are continuous with ourselves, and we will find new ways of being in partnership with them. Rather than simplifying, we will complexify. We will join ancient and modern forms into eccentric but viable unions, merging the deepest and most archaic powers within us with innovative scientific forms. We will become Athena and Hermes, shape-shifters, for whom all things are possible. We will become Telemachus and Penelope. We will become the Lotus-Eaters, the Cyclops, Circe, Calypso, the Phaeacians. But above all, we will become Odysseus, the man of many ways, who, on the road to Ithaca, discovers who he really is.

Before we begin with the journey of Odysseus, let us examine the classical Hero's Journey as it contains the adventures of Odysseus (see diagram on page 80).

With *The Odyssey,* however, there is an additional pattern present. We can see that while the surface or "horizontal" pattern follows closely upon the stages of the Hero's Journey, there is another, deeper journey, a "vertical" pattern that reenacts the stages of the ancient Greek Mystery cults and their initiations by the feminine divine powers.

The rites of the Mysteries provided powerful initiatory journeys of anguish, grief, loss, redemption, knowledge, and ecstatic union with the god or goddess. During the journey one "died" in some sense to one's old self and was reborn to a higher self or even to identity with goddess or god. One also received special knowledge and training as part of one's initiation into deeper life and its meaning.

Often, the journey followed the story of the suffering of gods and goddesses, with the training coming from the representatives of the goddess—as in the cult of the Triple Goddess in the Eleusinian Mysteries—in her aspect as Persephone, Demeter, and Hecate. This most renowned of all the Mysteries assured a powerful experience as the participant witnessed the tale of Demeter losing her child Persephone to Hades, the god of death and the underworld. Persephone becomes queen of the underworld while her mother, suffering immense grief, searches everywhere for her, and as goddess of agriculture causes the crops to die and the world to become a wasteland.

The Story of Odysseus as the Hero's Journey

The Call to Adventure as Blunder
THE SACK OF ISMARUS
Dismemberment—seventy two men of Odysseus' crew killed.

Supernatural Agents
POSEIDON AND ZEUS
who blow the ships of Odysseus for nine days across the ocean to approach the *threshold between the worlds* in LOTUS LAND.

They sail from there to the land of the *Threshold Guardian*—the Cyclops, a *monster* who continues the *Dismemberment* by eating six of the men.

THRESHOLD OF ADVENTURE

THRESHOLD BETWEEN THE WORLDS

The Belly of the Whale
THE CAVE OF THE CYCLOPS
where Odysseus disclaims his name and uses his wits to get past the Cyclops.

From there he sails to the Island of the winds where he finds a *Supernatural Ally* in AEOLUS, who gives him a bag in which are kept the contrary winds. The men release the winds, which inaugurates a *Road of Trials* and an *Initiatory Journey*. Further *Dismemberment* is had at the hands of the LAESTRYGONIANS. CIRCE changes the men INTO PIGS. Odysseus is saved by a new *Ally*—HERMES. Circe gives him further *Initiations* by sending him on a *Night Sea Journey* to the UNDERWORLD, to the SIRENS, past SCYLLA and CHARYBDIS, and to the ISLAND OF HELIOS. In the last *Adventure*, *Death* occurs for all except Odysseus.

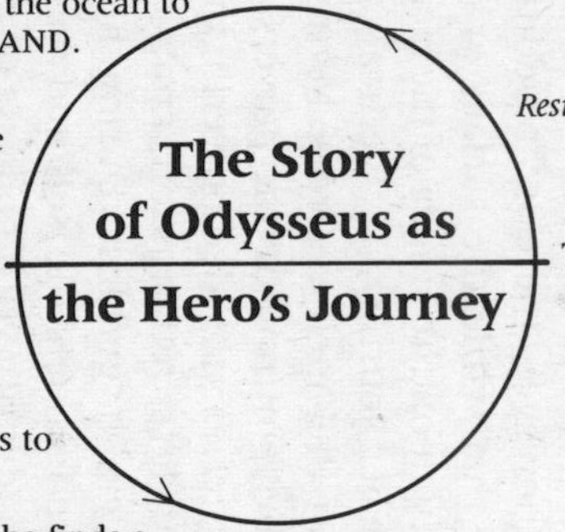

Hieros Gamos—Sacred Marriage with the Goddess with CIRCE (one year). CALYPSO (seven years). These unions anticipate the final *Hieros Gamos* with Penelope (the remaining years of Odysseus' life). *Father Atonement* with Zeus comes through his Ally, the goddess Athena. *Apotheosis* and *Elixir* of immortality offered by CALYPSO, which he refuses.

Magic Fight Back with the help of NAUSICAA, ARETE, ALCINOUS, and the PHAEACIANS, as well as ATHENA.

Supernatural Ally
The meeting of ATHENA and ODYSSEUS. *Rescue and Return* of ODYSSEUS—the beggar in Ithaca.

Resurrection of ODYSSEUS before the Swineherd, TELEMACHUS, the nurse, and PENELOPE.

Threshold Struggle
Contest of the bow and Killing of the suitors.

The Restoration of the Kingdom
Odysseus, now wiser and fully initiated at the hands of the feminine powers, is now worthy of ruling with PENELOPE. He is master of two worlds.

But then, aided by Hecate, a goddess of wise magic and of crossroads, Demeter is able to find and recover her child for part of the year, during which time there is a renewal of life on Earth.

What else happened during the initiation into the Mysteries? We know very little, but from what can be recovered from early Christian commentaries, we gather that the initiate underwent a physical and symbolic night descent into the underworld, where the initiatory experience occurred. A fragment of a work by the Greek poet Pindar says of the initiates upon their return: "Happy are they who having beheld these things, descends beneath the Earth. They know life's end but also a new beginning from the gods."[5]

That "Homer" was familiar with the Eleusinian Mysteries we know from the Homeric Hymn to Demeter, with its special Eleusinian section. That "Homer" either consciously or unconsciously crafted a journey through the Mysteries into *The Odyssey* is, I feel, a valid and illuminating way of approaching this great epic of consciousness. As Joseph Campbell tells us, whereas the Hero's Journey speaks to the more masculine voyage of consciousness, the Mysteries address the subtle but equally harrowing journey of deepening in the realm of those powers and knowledges which, during Odysseus' time in Troy, "had been waiting unattended, undeveloped, even unknown, in that 'other mind' which is woman. . . ."[6]

However it happened, it is the conjunction of these two ancient and sacred patterns that makes *The Odyssey* a book for once and future times. Odysseus' soul journey serves as a force field illuminating whatever and whoever comes into its presence, regardless of culture, era, or circumstance.

THE FIRST ADVENTURE: THE SACKING OF ISMARUS

The adventures of Odysseus are told to his kind hosts, the Phaeacians, at the banquet they hold for him after he collapses on their shores and is rescued by Nausicaa (Books Nine to Twelve). After revealing his identity, for until then he had been incognito, Odysseus begins his tale by relating what happened to him after leaving Troy. Following much of the pattern of the traditional Hero's Journey, his voyage began, as many do, with the "call to adventure." In his case the call was disguised as a blunder.

Many of us think of the call to adventure as a cosmic tap on the shoulder, a divine "Yoo-hoo!" But how many of us can claim to have received such a greeting? Therefore we feel that we have never heard such a call. It is, however, my belief that any action—especially a big "mistake," a blunder—may turn out to be a call to the deeper life. Often, our big mistakes lead us into experiences we never thought to have.

And this is how it happened with Odysseus. This cunning hero of Troy, at the peak of his success and powers in the ways of the heroic world, should, by all that is right and decent, have gone directly home, a mere two-week sail, and tended to the affairs of Ithaca for the rest of his days. But this is where his chronically activist nature, which is fine for the battlefield but a disaster for normal life, gets in the way.

Odysseus leaves Troy with his twelve ships, each containing twelve men—144 men in all. This emphasis on twelve, which we will find throughout the Odyssey, tells us that something of major import is going on. For twelve is the great cosmic number. It is the number of the signs of the zodiac, the number of hours that traditionally divide day from night, and multiples of twelve appear frequently in mythology. The hero who bears the code of twelve is the hero of the Sun, and, like the Sun at high noon, is at the peak of his powers. Odysseus, a solar hero, skilled and triumphant in the ways of the world, shines brightly in the day of ordinary reality. And the number twelve is a testament to his complete mastery over the daylight world.

But the Sun must set, and the solar hero must descend to a world beneath the horizon, for a "night journey" into realities over which he has no mastery. There he will be subject to the Moon Mysteries of the feminine powers. Only then can he rise again, many years later, humbled and humane, with the experience of the full cycle of reality—solar and lunar, masculine and feminine.

But, at the outset of *The Odyssey,* with all the machismo of solar destructive power, our hero launches a private raid on Ismarus, a Thracian town. Essentially he says to his men, "let's go north a little, just a couple of days out of the way, and see what extra booty we can find." So he and his twelve ships go to Ismarus. As he later tells the Phaeacians: "And there I destroyed the city and killed the men. We spared the women and plenty of cattle and goods, which we divided to give each man a fair share."

In other words, ravaging and rapine. Odysseus realizes they should get out of there fast, but his men insist on holding a big eating and drinking party on the beach. While they're at it, the Ciconians, the people from the surrounding area, rally and kill six men from each ship, seventy-two men in all. As the remaining men flee on their ships, their brutal deed is followed by inevitable punishment in the form of a tempest sent by Zeus, which rips the sails of their ships to shreds. Blown out of control for nine days, they are carried beyond the bounds of the known world, probably to some place in North Africa.

The blunder has a very large role to play in virtually all journeys of transformation, heroic or otherwise. It often marks the transition from one way of life to another. One of its subtleties is that it may not seem significant when it begins. In fact, it can even be socially permissible, hardly a blunder at all. Pirate raids, for example, were normal occurrences in the Heroic age. So what made the gods so angry? Was it that Odysseus' chronic greed and curiosity, coming on top of a ten-year pattern of rampant warring at Troy, had led him to overstep the bounds of appropriate action? Was he overwhelmed by his crewmen?

Or perhaps the blunder was inevitable. For Odysseus' very identity as well as his name is tied up in trouble. The patterns of warring may have become so deeply planted in his character and behavior—as well as in all those who had spent ten years at war—that he no longer knew any other way of existence. That the trauma of war can leave profound and seemingly unyielding tracings on mind and body we have seen in the tragedy of so many Vietnam veterans who seem lost to the society to which they returned.

Let us begin to delve into our own lives for blunders we too may have made. Let us seek out those patterns of behavior that have been so deeply planted in our existence, through culture, conditioning, family, and profession, that we have become their unwitting victims.

For those of us who have been launched on a journey of transformation, this pattern of behavior may mean a fall into a disordered and disordering reality that plunges us into the Mystery of the night journey of our own souls. Often, it is only after major mistakes, caused by our troubling Odyssean traits of conditioning, that we can be moved beyond complacency and so enter into the pathos of soulmaking. These "signs," "mistakes," "blunders," can become the evolutionary stimuli to the growth of one's humanity.

Perhaps this is where Charles Darwin is wrong when he says that it is the ability to adapt that signals the mark of an evolving being. Perhaps, for the human species at least, it is the *inability* to adapt, the impetus to make interesting errors, to pull one "bummer" after the other, that finally pushes us to the point of such excruciating pain and frustration that we are forced to start to make new choices, and to find the will and the courage to carry them through. When we look at our friends in the animal world, we see clearly that in many ways dogs and cats learn much more quickly than we do and do not continue to commit the same blunders.

We, like Odysseus, sail off to Ismarus again and again, persisting in automatic behavior. The inevitable results help us accumulate a store of disasters that will eventually create the stimulus for change. Chances are, as we think over our lives, we discover that great movement has come out of great mistakes. Such mistakes are almost always freely chosen events—unlike the conditions that attend wounding. When we are wounded, it is often from the outside. When we blunder, it is often a conscious, freely choosen act. We must ask ourselves, Why did I marry that man or that woman? Why did I choose that particular career? Why did I go to that school, that church, that institution? Why did I do it? Why did I make that choice? Was it for reasons of pride, ego, or the expectations of family or society? However we came to choose to continue in the old ways and not harken to the potential for change around us, it is the way of the reciprocal universe that the deeper order of things sees us and, choosing us as candidates for initiation, blows us off our culturally conditioned normal course to the very edges of our known world.

As we enter the great themes of the Hero's Journey as it was taken by Odysseus and his family, remember that *The Odyssey* has always served to illumine the understanding of the problems and potentials of any culture wherever and whenever it has been read or recited. Across space and time, it speaks dynamically as well as poignantly to the complex necessities of the present human condition.

The Call as Blunder

The Call-Blunder as a Personal Historical Happening

IN the story of Odysseus, the call-as-blunder comes in two forms. The first form is the blunder he makes when he refuses to go directly home after the Trojan War ends, and instead sails north to lead a pirate raid on Ismarus. This big mistake initiates his adventures and sufferings. The second form is the persistent blunder that comes of his own chronic curiosity and refusal to let well enough alone. This character-trait-as-blunder leads him into constant difficulties, adventures, and ultimately, deepenings. It also keeps him away from home for almost ten more years.

We will now explore both of these forms of call-as-blunder as they may have occurred in our own lives. Let us begin with the call as the big mistake. I will use an example from my own life story as an example.

When I was about twenty and had just graduated from Barnard College, I took a long trip through Greece. Shortly after arriving in Athens, I found myself sitting in the little temple of Athena on the Acropolis holding three telegrams in my hand. I had been the recipient of a number of Off-Broadway awards for acting and directing and was experiencing the unusual pleasure of being "in demand."

One of the telegrams was from a major Hollywood studio offering me a seven-year contract. Having grown up in a show business family I knew about those "contracts" and wasn't interested. The second telegram was from a Broadway producer inviting me to play the title role in *Jane Eyre* opposite an actor more famous for his swashbuckling roles than his talent. Besides, he was three inches shorter than I.

The third telegram, however, was my equivalent of a Trojan triumph. It was an invitation from the great New York director and producer Joseph Papp to play the lead in *Twelfth Night* at the annual Shakespeare festival in Central Park. Everything in me was thrilled by this prospect. I could feel the adrenaline rising to catapult me down the Acropolis and onto the next plane home.

"Yes! Yes! Yes!" all my years of training for the theater shouted.

"No," a still, quiet voice whispered.

"What do you mean, no?" I retorted.

"No," it replied. "If you say yes to this it will mean a life in theater and films."

"That's right," I exclaimed with enthusiasm. "Let's go!"

"No," it countered. "Your life can have a different meaning, a different direction. You can be part of a larger story."

"Larger than being in the theater?" The notion seemed shocking, almost amoral.

"Yes."

And that was that.

WHAT DO YOU MEAN, NO? my father the comedy writer and my mother the former actress wired back in outrage.

And then there was the Greek chorus of telegrams from my

friends. "You're Crazy! You're Asking for Trouble. You're Going Against Destiny. God'll Getcha for This."

For a while it appeared they were right and I (or the still, quiet voice) was most definitely wrong. Over the next month it seemed I was part of some harrowing Homeric saga, with the forces of nature conspiring either to punish me or test my mettle. Like Odysseus, I had my problems with Poseidon. At his temple at Cape Sounion, in a spirit of romance and in imitation of Lord Byron, I decided to dive into the wine-dark sea. Unfortunately, a six-foot Portuguese man-of-war jellyfish was waiting to snare my hands and arms as I dove through it. Many hours later, itching furiously, I sailed to a small Greek island little known to most travelers, where the boat stopped only once in a while and there was no communication with the outside world. My hands bubbled and swelled into alien appendages and the itching was torturous. Had it not been for the *deus ex machina* of a fine physician's landing quite by accident (ha!) on this little nowhere place, and tending to my hands with the latest in cortisone treatments, which he "just happened" to have with him, I would have lost my hands, if not my life, for gangrene was on the verge of setting in.

A month later, having blithely eaten and drunk everything offered me, I came down with typhoid fever in a remote village in Crete. And so it went for a year or more—an endless series of Odyssean life-threatening situations, crushing losses, and inexplicable events, all calculated to wake me up or cut me loose.

Finally, I decided to go to graduate school, where because of the unusual nature of my studies of myth and symbol, I was invited to participate in innovative research into the phenomenology of the deep psyche. This led to my meeting with the man I married and our setting up a foundation to do research in human capacities. This in turn led to my books, and teaching, and seminar work all over the world, and my working with many different cultures in helping to create programs to enhance human as well as social development.

Looking back, I do feel that my life has, in all likelihood, been part of a much larger story than it would have been had I not committed the blunder of saying no.

If I were to diagram this it would look something like the following:

JUST SAY NO
YES?
NO.
FILM
JANE EYRE
12th NIGHT
Now, for a tasty morsel!
JAN
Year of Catastrophe
LIFE FORCE
POSSIBLE HUMAN
MIND GAMES
SEARCH FOR THE BELOVED
LISTENING TO THE BODY
Consciousness Raising
M. MEAD
Ph.D.
DEEP PSYCHE
Psychophysical Exercises
GRAD SCHOOL

The Call-Blunder as a Chronic Character Defect

The second kind of call to adventure masquerading as a blunder occurs through constant recurrence of a chronic character trait. We persist in behaving in a particular way, even though the consequences are known to us. These can be either for good or ill, or both, but generally they lead us further into the adventure of the soul, tripping up our expectations, fooling our reflexes. As we have seen, Odysseus' most persistently trouble-making character trait was his insatiable curiosity. And on those occasions when this curiosity did not lead to trouble, it led him into experiences for which he had no training.

My own chronic blunder, which continually serves to call me into all kinds of soul-stretching experiences, is ironically my excessive willingness to say yes. I've drawn you a diagram (see page 90) to show how my pattern tends to play itself out.

I've begun with a circle with my image in the center saying yes. Then radiating out are the images of the requests to which I'm saying yes.

—"Come work with an order of nuns halfway around the world for a month with no salary."

"Yes."

—"Could you please take this big dog in, even though you already have three other dogs?"

"Yes."

—"Would you please write a preface for my book? And for mine? And for mine? And for mine?"

"Yes. Yes. Yes. Yes."

—"Would you please come and give a workshop in Africa, followed by training executives in Hong King, followed immediately by working with villagers in South America?"

"Yes."

* * *

WORK, YES
SALARY, NO
TEMPUS FUGIT!
WOOF!
Adopt Me!
GLUM
IDEAS
THOUGHTS
INSIGHTS
OH NO! . . . . . NOT ANOTHER ONE!
YES
"Would you please write a preface for my book?"
And mine, too?
And me?
Me Too?
So, when is Jean coming?
INTERNATIONAL MAIL
Please come to Africa!
And to Hong Kong.
And to Brazil!
MAIL
MAIL
MAIL
PLEASE FIND...
PLEASE COME...
PLEASE GIVE..

—"We've just flown in and we've got to see you now and have you guide us in this project for the next few days. I know you're trying to finish a book but this is important and . . ."

"Okay, come on over."

—And then there are all the letters that come in, often hundreds a month: "Could you find me a . . . ? Can I have a scholarship to your . . . ? Would you please give me a bibliography on the mind and . . . ? Could you write me a recommendation for . . . ?"

"Yes. Yes. Sure. Of course."

Now I go back to the pictures and I draw in the consequences of saying yes, for good or ill. I sketch my lungs, which rebel from too many trips around the world by giving me pneumonia. But you also see me getting new ideas and insights about the planet and its cultures from all that traveling. These insights allow me to be called upon to advise and work with many intercultural and governmental agencies worldwide in the field of individual and societal development.

There is a symbol for all the new information I'm getting by having to read all those extra books for which I've promised to write prefaces. And then there is the line that leads from the nuns to other religious communities where I'm called to help in spiritual-formation programs. This in turn keeps my spiritual life active and causes me to be blessed by meeting people who are radiant in spirit.

There are other negatives, of course, as we see that I do not have enough time for myself or for my own writings. Also, necessarily, there are those I disappoint, for I run out of time and am unable to fulfill my promises to them. Or, I do manage to keep my promise but have to do a hurried and harried job that I'm not satisfied with. But there are many positives as well. Taken together they show a life that says yes to too many calls, but which is enriched by this process and, it is hoped, is able to be helpful to the people and context of the calls that I've answered.

When I finally look at both these diagrams together, I see that they portray a life that has deepened because of calls taken and blunders made. They tell a story and reveal a journey and, to some extent, the meaning of a life that was not immediately apparent.

They open up perspectives that give me a deeper appreciation of the dynamics of my life—blunders, flaws, and all. And, who knows, they may perhaps render me a little more judicious in the future when I hear the call.

Now let us each enter into this process and discover our own mappings of *The Odyssey* of our lives.

TIME: One and a half to two hours.

MATERIALS NEEDED: Large sheets of drawing paper for each participant. A variety of drawing materials—crayons, colored pencils, pens, Magic Markers, and so on. There should be enough to be shared by all participants.

MUSIC: Quiet, non-intrusive music from Area I may be played if desired. However, music is not essential to this exercise.

INSTRUCTIONS FOR THE SOLO VOYAGER: This process can be done alone by making a tape of the script for the guide and by carefully following the instructions for the group. Be sure to leave pauses of the right length, giving the correct time cues in the script. However, in this case, you may want to turn off the tape for the longer portions of the exercise. Also see the note on page 94 for the solo voyager.

SCRIPT FOR THE GUIDE: I would like you to get your drawing materials together for this exercise and find a partner to sit near.

[After this is done the guide continues.]

Now I'm going to ask you to remember a critical choice you made that you—or your friends or family—considered a blunder. Some blunder you made in the past that led you to all kinds of unexpected learnings and adventures. The blunder need not have been dramatic at the time; in fact it could have been a very ordinary, even predictable action. But it resulted in a series of circumstances that, in one way or another, served to carry you on a journey into other levels of yourself.

Just as Jean Houston drew her own blunder, I'm asking you now to also draw your blunder and its consequences. You might begin by sketching the blunder in either a graphic or a symbolic form at one corner of the page.

Then indicate the path it took you on, drawing the consequences as events or people or feelings like the map of an Odyssean voyage. Next to each event you may wish to write a few words indicating the meaning of the drawing. But always try to sketch in a picture or symbol to indicate each of the consequences of the call-as-blunder as you see it.

You have twenty minutes to do this exercise. If you should finish earlier, go back to the drawing and reflect further. See if you remember other consequences, and if you do, sketch them in. [Twenty minutes.]

[After the time is up the guide will say:]

Put that drawing to one side and take another sheet of paper. Now, would you please draw a large circle on the sheet of paper, filling up most of the space. [One minute.]

Looking at the blank center of the circle, begin to reflect upon the nature of the chronic trait that you believe causes you to blunder in your life. For Jean Houston it was the tendency to say yes to any call or request that came along. What form does it take for you? Is it a tendency to fall in love, to keep on taking courses, to follow your heart rather than your head? Is it a set way of thinking about things, a certain kind of curiosity, or a private addiction? Could it be a tendency to make choices to please other people, or to shoot off your mouth, or to act out of impulse? Is it acquisitiveness that drives you, or a greediness for new experiences, or a need to see people as all good or all bad?

Whatever it is, it is unique to you, and you know what it is because of its constant recurrence in your life. Find the major form it takes and draw yourself in the middle of the page in a way that indicates the nature of your chronic blunder. [Three minutes.]

Now, as in Jean Houston's diagram, please begin to draw the consequences of this chronic blunder in your life. Do it in such a way, if you can, that the mapping of these consequences indicates something of the unfolding of your life, the journeys of the body, mind, and soul that have been yours, the adventures for good or ill that have come your way. Some of these will be single consequences, but many will be interlinked with others—a looping network of effects rather than just a single path. Draw these now please. [Fifteen to twenty-five minutes.]

[The guide should check with the participants after fifteen minutes to see if they are finished, or if not, to determine how much more time they may need. After the time is up, the guide will say:]

I ask you now to turn to your partner, and as you look at the two diagrams you have drawn, tell the story of your call to a larger life as it has emerged in the pattern of blunders in your life. Your story should reflect both the big blunder of the first diagram as well as something of the chronic blunders of the second diagram.

Tell your story using noble, Homeric language, if you can. Yes, you want your mouth to become full of blood—rich in metaphors and images. This vibrant language is what you will use to couch the story of aspects of your life as it seems to emerge from these two diagrams.

Tell your story as Odysseus told his story to the Phaeacians on that long evening thousands of years ago. You might want to include the activity of the gods—their help, or interference—if it seems that you see it there.

Let one partner speak for ten minutes, and then the other. I will keep the time and tell you when the first ten minutes are up. Then the second partner will speak and I will again let you know when the second ten minutes are over. [Twenty minutes.]

FOR THE SOLO VOYAGER: You may want to speak your story into a tape recorder as the Odysseus of your own life. When you are done, meditate quietly for a few moments. Then get up from where you are and seat yourself somewhere else in your sacred space, for you are going to play the part of the Phaeacian audience.

Now, replay the tape. And, as your Odyssean voice begins to speak, listen to your own rich tale as if for the first time. Hear with astonishment and wonder the heights and depths to which you have traveled, the perils you have encountered, the allies you have made, the deep losses and amazing success you have experienced, and the great wisdom these travels through life have brought you.

When the tale is done, you might want to dialogue—aloud, or in your journal—with both the voyager and the listener within you; or allow them to dialogue with each other. Have you questions to ask or insights to offer? Then, follow the guide's instructions for writing down your epic tale.

[At the end of the twenty minutes, the guide will say:]

Wherever you are, stop and listen, please. I ask you now to write out your story, but do so with verve and rich language, as if you were a Homeric bard writing your own story. Try to avoid saying, "And this happened. And then this happened, followed by this happening." Rather, write it in a pungent, bardic, Homeric form. For example, here, in a few sentences, is how Homer told the entire story of Odysseus:

> Sing in me, Muse, and through me tell the story
> of that man skilled in all ways of contending,
> the wanderer, harried for years on end,
> after he plundered the stronghold
> on the proud height of Troy.
>
> He saw the townlands
> and learned the minds of many distant men,
> and weathered many bitter nights and days
> in his deep heart at sea, while he fought only
> to save his life, to bring his shipmates home.
> But not by will nor valor could he save them,
> for their own recklessness destroyed them all—
> children and fools, they killed and feasted on
> the cattle of Lord Helios, the Sun,
> and he who moves all day through heaven
> took from their eyes the dawn of their return.
> Of these adventures, Muse, daughter of Zeus,
> tell us in our time, lift the great song again.[7]

You will have only ten minutes or so of clock time to do this, but that will be equal to all the time you need to write your story Homerically.

You might even want to begin as Homer did: "Sing, O Muse, of that man . . . of that woman . . ." And then tell your story. And don't worry that you've never written like this before. Practically no one ever has, But this is your opportunity to do so. And now begin. [Ten to fifteen minutes.]

All right. Those of you who are not finished just keep on going. And as you continue writing, as background, I'm going to ask those of you bards who have finished and who would like to share what you have written to read it in full, passionate, Homeric voice so that both mortals and gods can hear you.

[The guide continues to invite these readings until it seems that all who want to share have done so. The guide also elicits comments from the voyagers on what they have learned from this experience. Here are some typical examples of the variety of writings that have come out of this exercise from seminar participants.

I sing the song of myself as I have lived my life,
Yielding which carried me on the flow of myself through
    places mundane and magic, places of peace and
    pain.
Gathering, then holding, and on again, with a knowing
    which came only after its reason had drowned.
Yielding and flowing, until it seemed that all I had named
    and believed were swept away in my great wise
    unknowing to the full emptiness I fear and love.
Deeper than I was or am or will be.

And here see that the energy source of life, the sun,
has traveled 'round to direct the bud in its allotted time,
from seedling, blind in its bed, accepting nurture with no
    object to tending on,
to spreading roots, and now grounded, as the shoots to
    leaves have turned.
Blowing in the wind, accepting change and dancing
    movement, not against the force,

and in so doing, to see the sun, energy and joy, life
strength, begin to return in kind, embracing plant,
and growth and strength enable reaching up and out with
full blossom beauty.
And accept what has to be, for that too is important, to
let go and drop petals and one day prepare the
flower for the fall.

*

Child of grief, so darkly come, seeks in eyes a hope of love
and joy.
Finding none, he dreams a world of dark beauty to fill his
mind.
Every new moment holds the promise of discovery of his
goddess dream.
All other worlds recede.
Blind to warm love, holding fast to fantasy, gods come to
crush this dream and wisdom leaks through.
Heart full of hope the genius power brings, as fantasy
made real fades to become light.

*

Sing, O Muse, of Jocelyn,
Daughter of Celts and the wild Lays of England,
Bearer of ancient wisdom and blood of royalty,
who, though laid low in childhood by disease, rose out of
the safety and stifling of parental dictums to an
awareness of her divinity and power.
Through her battles against both male and female
domination and social conformity she gained
credance for her right to opinion and decision.
Her beauty and open heart, her magical healing powers
and her connection to both the Earth as mother
and to the Light as mentor, light, guide, and
spiritual lover.
Her tale is of risk over safety, joy over sorrow, surrender
over control, and laughter over rigidity.
Her story is of celebration of everything.

*

Sing, O Muse, of that man who traveled all the world by
    sea, by earth, by air, to seek what he might find at
    home.
Sing of his days of spreading books like seeds to young
    minds sent to him through wars, repressions,
    tragedies around the globe.
Tell of his travels in deep inner worlds, through levels of
    the mind by swinging pendulum or cards of arcana
    with symbols bright.
Tell him where he will find the sacred space where all trails
    join in one.
His Ithaca. His Ithaca.

*

So you see what happens when you start with the blunder, the call. You see the play of the consequences of your chosen actions. By telling it Homerically as Odysseus told the Phaeacians his story, and then writing it down, you make your life epic. The patterns of your life reveal themselves poetically, in ways they are rarely seen.

This is not therapy, rather, it is the root form of therapy. It is *therapeia*, the Greek word that means "support" and "caring." But it also carries a secondary meaning—"doing the work of the god"—or, in our terms, doing the work of the whole. Here the first part of the Hero's Journey, the call-as-blunder, provides a form of *therapeia* through which you begin to see the richer weavings of your life.]

CHAPTER 3

The Lotus-Eaters

AFTER the debacle with the Ciconians, Zeus sent a tempest that ravaged the ships of Odysseus. Then, after a brief respite on shore, he set sail with his remaining men only to meet with foul winds that blew them about mercilessly for nine days.

In recounting this adventure to the Phaeacians, Odysseus tells them that on the tenth day of being blown off course they "set foot on the Land of the Lotus-Eaters, who eat a flowery food." Those of his men who ate of the "honey-sweet fruit" fell into bliss, lost all interest in returning home, and wanted to stay there munching, devouring, slurping up lotus for the rest of their lives.

Does lotus present a Lethe-like metaphor of forgetfulness (Lethe being the mythological river that the newly dead cross in order to forget their lives) or does the tale actually tell of a food that turns the mind to inward and mythic realities? Or does it perhaps tell of the wages of greed, in our time the toxic values of a society devoted to consumerism and rampant materialism? Whatever it was, Odysseus had to drag his men weeping and wailing to the ships, tie them up, and stow them under the rowing benches in order to rescue them from this seductive and bliss-ridden place they thought was paradise.

It is interesting that this passage, only one paragraph long, has gripped the imagination of so many people for nearly three thousand years, with much of the sentiment being on the side of the lotus-eaters. They have been compared in recent times to hippies, pot smokers, and eaters of visionary vegetables. And perhaps there is some truth in the perspective of viewing the lotus-eaters as psychedelic dropouts who prefer bliss to the "real world."

However, in the context of the story, this episode is also about removing oneself from everyday existential life and entering the inner, visionary realms. It is the passing from the world of waking consciousness to the world of dream; from the world of rational expression to one of metaphorical speech; and finally from the bound, structured world of the local self to the more fluid and surprising levels of the mythic and archetypal domain, where the self moves from concern with the personal-particular to that of the personal-universal.

In the traditional Hero's Journey, this represents one's ambivalence toward entering a state of consciousness that can cross the great threshold of reality into the realm of amplified power. The extreme reluctance of Odysseus' crewmen to leave this land tells us that something of real import and worth is going on. The crewmen stand for the non-ego parts of the self, the non-ego parts of the hero, and represent the value of what Odysseus, as the dominant will or ego, is resisting with all his might. He dreads the crossing of the threshold into a world for which he is unprepared and which he can never master. If we look at the story literally, the crewmen were right to want to stay in Lotus Land. If they had remained, they would have survived the journey.

But the important point for us is that life must evolve in both realms. We must learn to dwell in both the inner reality of the Lotus-Eaters and the active world of Odysseus.

Eating the Lotus/ The Dance of Will

TIME: Thirty minutes.

MATERIALS NEEDED: A delicate-sounding bell, and "lotus."

You will need to provide some extraordinarily delicious food, of which merely a taste will suffice to evoke gastronomic raptures. Here is my suggested recipe, but feel free to offer your own most delicious dish. We have found that sweet dishes—dessert-type foods—work best. **Note:** Please have a variety of food prepared in case some participants are allergic (perish the thought!) to chocolate. Delicious ripe fruits seem to make excellent alternative lotus.

MUSIC: Play a selection from Area II, such as Deuter's "Ecstasy" for the journey in Lotus Land. Play rousing Greek dance music such as "Zorba's Dance" by Manos Hadjidakis (Area III), for the "Dance of the Will."

INSTRUCTIONS FOR THE SOLO VOYAGER: Make a tape of the script for the guide, leaving appropriate pauses, and prepare some of your own favorite "lotus" to eat.

SCRIPT FOR THE GUIDE: I have prepared some very special lotus for you. Technically speaking, it is not a mind-altering substance, but it can have a delicious effect on both your body and mind.

To begin, I want you to get as comfortable as you can, lie down or sit up, whatever you prefer, just be very comfortable. Close your eyes and begin to breathe. . . . You are being filled with the winds blowing you to Lotus Land. [Deep breaths are modeled.] AHH-AHH.

Jean Houston's Sacred Recipe for Lotus (Minted Chocolate Mousse)

8 large eggs (room temperature)
1 12-ounce package bittersweet chocolate morsels
1 teaspoon instant coffee granules
1/2 teaspoon cinnamon
10 tablespoons boiling water
2 teaspoons mint extract (or to taste)
1 teaspoon vanilla extract
3 tablespoons brandy or favorite liqueur
1 cup heavy cream
1 angel food cake, freshly made (optional)
small cups and spoons

Separate the egg yolks and whites. Put the chocolate morsels into a blender along with the coffee granules and the cinnamon. Add the 10 tablespoons of boiling water and blend for about 30 seconds or until the chocolate is melted. Add the egg yolks, the mint extract, the vanilla extract, and the brandy or liqueur and blend for 1 minute. Next, add the egg whites and blend for 2 minutes. Place the mixture in a large bowl and chill in the refrigerator for the next 4 hours, or until set.

When ready to serve, whip the heavy cream, adding a little sugar if desired. Spread the whipped cream over the mousse and serve as described below, being sure that each participant gets a little cream with their "lotus."

For even more ecstatic pleasure, increase the chocolate mousse recipe by half and mound the mousse on the top and sides of an angel food cake, and then cover both cake and mousse with whipped cream. Serve each participant a large piece of cake, mousse, and whipped cream.

AHH-AHH. AHH-AHH. . . . The winds carry you to the magical land of the lotus-eaters. . . . There, as you relax on the shore, the lotus will be brought to you. Listen for the sound of the magic bell as I lead you deeper into Lotus Land. The lotus will come in a little cup, with a spoon in it.

Now it is being given out. And for those of you who cannot eat lotus that has either sugar or chocolate in it, we have alternative lotus. Raise your hands if you would prefer the alternative lotus.

[The little cups of "lotus" are given out.]

Without opening your eyes, smell the delicious scent of it. Now, begin to eat the lotus. Let it dissolve slowly in your mouth. Savor every tiny bit. . . .

Let the taste of lotus begin to quicken your inner imagery. Let it carry you gradually into a realm of myth and fantasy. . . . Follow the lotus inward as you swallow it, for it is very powerful as well as very, very wonderful. . . . Let the lotus take you inward and deeper, and deeper and inward. . . .

Extremely relaxed now . . . so relaxed . . . just melting with the lotus, letting it carry you deep, deep, passing into a place of extreme relaxation where you cross a threshold into realities that are flowing colors . . . yellow, green, bronze, blue, purple . . . flowing colors, all kinds of colors . . . and these colors gradually take on form . . . beautiful forms . . . shapes and images from tales of wonder. . . . And you watch, and you relax into them. . . . Just let all those beautiful, delightful, fantasy images stimulated by the lotus flow through you or flow past you. . . . What you are tasting becomes imagery . . . exquisite, beautiful forms . . . and tastes . . . and scents . . . and sounds . . . and feelings.

Just think of pure lusciousness flowing over you. Ripe peaches and apricots. Delicate smells of wildflowers. Gentle flowing waters and cascading falls, carrying you to another realm. A realm of faerie bells of gold and silver . . .

[Tiny, delicate bells are gently sounded here and continue sounding.]

It seems as if the sound of these bells is carrying you across another inner threshold into the world of Faerie—into a realm of myth and magic and fantasy. The images here may not yet be specific, but they are images that are gently bringing you across the threshold from this world to the world of dreams, the fertile, exquisite world of imagination.

Inward and deeper. Being carried inward, inward, deeper, deeper. . . .

If there is anyone who would like some more lotus, please raise your hand.

[More of the lotus is given out.]

Just follow the taste of the lotus as it carries you inward and deeper. . . . Just follow the images through the tastes, which will bring you gently . . . and so beautifully . . . and deliciously . . . and exquisitely . . . to your own inner fantasy world.

Going deeper, following your own images. I will give you five minutes of clock time, equal subjectively to all the time you need, to experience this realm of dream, of myth, of imagination. Letting the images and the feelings just come as pleasurably and naturally as they came to the lotus-eaters. . . . [Five minutes.]

How long has this been going on? Tell me from Lotus Land. How long? Forever? Keep dreaming, and as you dream in Lotus Land, let us hear what other lotus-eaters are dreaming. If you are a lotus-eater who has entered into a particularly lotus fantasy place, raise your hand and I will come and touch you on the forehead. Though you remain in Lotus Land with your eyes closed, you will be able to tell the other dreamers what you are experiencing there.

[If participants raise their hands, the guide should call on several people to tell their experiences. If you are voyaging alone, stop the tape and—remaining in the energy and ambience of Lotus Land—write briefly of your visions in your journal.

After several minutes of this dreamy telling of experiences in Lotus Land, the guide will speak sharply:]

Odysseus says: "Enough! Enough! Come back! Come back! Come back!" And we begin to pull you up. Come back! Come back! Come back to the ship. Come back as we perform the Dance of Will. Come back and pull each other up. Pull each other up. Pull each other up. Pull each other. Pull each other up. Yes! Pull each other up. Pull each other up. Play Odysseus for each other.

By the gods, you can be a lotus-eater, but you've got to be Odysseus too, or nothing will happen. Where's your willpower? Where's your courage to be? Where's your need to get on with it?

Pull each other up. Pull each other up. Yes. Pull each other up. Drag each other into the boat. The boat is that way. I know you don't want to go. But the boat is that way. You've got to get back to that boat. You have to go. Come back. Come back into the place of the boat. Come back to the place of the will.

Yes! You're going to do a Dance of Will because you've got to get back into will, some kind of will, not just dreamland. Come back. Please come back. You can't remain a bliss ninny. Dreamland is fun, but you'll just turn into a vegetable there. Please. I know, you'd love to spend your life as a happy vegetable, but you have to get back to that boat! Kicking and screaming, yes, but back into the boat with you. Oh, yes. Oh, yes. Back into the boat. Back into the boat. Back into the boat. To the boat. To the boat. Back into the boat. Back into the boat. The boat. The boat. Get into the boat. The boat. Get there. Come on. Back into the boat. Oh, yes. Oh, yes. Oh, yes. Back into the boat.

Our voyage has barely begun. Please. Back into the boat. Back into the boat. Back into the boat.

Okay, group. Wake up! Wake up! We have to go on. So make a big circle, and stand strongly on your two feet on the deck. Now remember Ithaca. Remember your home. We're going to dance a Dance of Freedom, a Dance of Will, a dance of charging up the spirit to get on with it when you'd rather delay, procrastinate, vegetate, fall into fantasy. It's time to wake up now! It's time to dance the dance of Odysseus.

[Rousing Greek dance music, such as "Zorba's Dance," is played here and all the participants dance vigorously while the guide continues to remind them to wake up. At the end of the music the guide can lead the participants in a Greek chant, *"Ego Odysseus"* (pronounced Eh-go), meaning, "I am Odysseus." This will naturally become another rousing round dance.

If you are voyaging alone, experience being both Odysseus and his lotus-eating companions. Shout "Wake up!" as Odysseus. Then, as the crewmen, pull and resist, pull and resist. Be Odysseus forcing his men into the ship. Be a crewman dragging your feet and painfully hauling yourself aboard. Once safely in the ship, play rousing music, and chanting *"Ego Odysseus,"* dance passionately around your sacred space.]

CHAPTER 4

The Cave of the Cycylops

"... a monstrous thing and fashioned marvelously. Nor was he like to any man that lives by bread, but like a wooded peak of the towering hills."[1]

HAVING entered the realm of mythic space and magnified power in Lotus Land, Odysseus and his men now embark upon the Road of Trials. In the Hero's Journey, this is a time of incredible tests and adventures. Joseph Campbell reminds us that this is where "the hero moves in a dream landscape of curiously fluid, ambiguous forms, where he must survive a succession of trials."[2] Storytellers and bards, epic poets and novelists have always described this state most vividly, and filled it with rollicking and miraculous adventures.

This ruse of the storyteller serves to mask the dread that we all feel before a region of mind and being that is both unknown and unbounded. It occurs whenever the comforts of given space and time are dissolved—in deserts, in the wilderness, on the uncharted seas, or in the labyrinth of our own unconscious life. There, demons and monsters and primal forces are felt to be lurking, each and every one of them waiting to get us! Odysseus clearly remembers this dread as he tries to justify to the Phaeacians his reasons for entering the land of the Cyclops, the place of his most harrowing adventure.

His first justification is anthropological. He wanted to "go and find out about these people, and learn what they are, whether they are savage and violent, and without justice, or hospitable to strangers and with minds that are godly."[3] He discovers the country to be a gentle and fertile island, abounding in sheep and wild goats, where everything grows without sowing or plowing—wheat, barley, vines. The Cyclopeans have no government or laws, but live in hollow caves, each a law unto himself. Nor do they build or sail ships.

The second reason Odysseus gives for his exploration is entrepreneurial. He is no sooner off the boat than his pioneering eye assesses this goodly land and his acquisitiveness awakens. Almost immediately he begins to imagine what a "civilized" group of people could do with such a land.

His third reason is rampant and fearless curiosity. This leads him to choose twelve men, the best in his company, for this adventure. Together they enter a vast cave. The occupant is away, but there are lambs and kids, each penned by age and kind, and there are many cheeses stored and pails of whey. Odysseus' companions urge seizing these and leaving, but he refuses. He is curious to see the occupant, and he cites the tradition of that time, which requires the host to offer a guest gift to any visitor. We see then that greed is his fourth reason.

These four reasons tell us that Odysseus is caught between the archaic heroic age and a more culturally advanced society. His acquisitiveness and impatient curiosity are tempered, though barely, by his anthropological and entrepreneurial interests. They impel him and his men toward the initial stages on the Road of Trials. First they must pass the Threshold Guardian on the way to falling into the Belly of the Whale.

The Threshold Guardian, often a monster, often of an alien

turn of mind, guards the entranceway to the deeper world. We must prove ourselves worthy and able to make the passage to another realm by fooling the guardian's expectations, by outwitting its monstrous presumption. A worthy adversary, the guardian is often a creature of fixed habits and immovable attitudes. At worst it swallows us, and turns us into a replica of itself. At best it calls forth our pluck and cunning. In our waking world, the guardian may show up as the supervisor, church, parental attitudes, place in society, or even entrenched habits. We are challenged to find ways to get around these dragonlike guardians, lest we become just another assistant dragon, keeping others from their quests and possibilities.

The Belly of the Whale describes the stage in which the hero is swallowed by the unknown—be it a whale, a wolf, a sarcophagus, a cave. There, in one way or another, he or she experiences a deathlike state, or dissolves, or disclaims identity, and subsequently must exhibit extraordinary powers or talents in order to return or to get past the Threshold Guardian. The tales of Hiawatha and Heracles, Osiris and Red Riding Hood belong to this genre, and the world is made richer by their triumph.

We know the Belly of the Whale in many guises. It can take the form of a depression or even of a strong need to get away from it all. It can be a period of intense interiority when we seem numb and unresponsive to others, but where we are nevertheless aware of stirrings and changes.

For Odysseus and his men, the Belly of the Whale is this cave he is determined to explore. It belongs to the Cyclops (meaning "round-eye")—in this case, the one-eyed giant Polyphemus, a son of the sea-god Poseidon, and a most daunting Threshold Guardian. While Odysseus and his men are inside the cave, Polyphemus returns, carrying a great load of wood and making so much noise that Odysseus and his men flee fearfully to the darker recesses of the cave. Polyphemus then sets about his homey evening chores, lifting a huge stone to fill the doorway, a stone so heavy "no twenty-two of the best four-wheeled wagons could have taken that weight off the ground."[4] He then begins milking his ewes and goats, and places under each her lamb or kid.

Only as he rekindles his fire does he spy the cowering men, instantly recognizing them for what they are—seafaring ravagers. But to Odysseus, the ravaging of Troy was glorious; as he tells the Cyclops: "We are the conquerors of Troy!" He then goes so far as to ask Polyphemus for a present, invoking Zeus, the god of hospitality. But the Cyclops cares nothing for Zeus or the Olympic pantheon; he glories in the strength of his primitive condition. "Zeus Almighty be damned and his blessed gods with him," he roars. "We Cyclopeans care nothing for them. We are stronger than they are."[5] And to prove his point he grabs, kills, and eats with great relish two of Odysseus' men for dinner, washing down his horrible meal of human flesh with a huge draft of goat's milk.

When dawn comes, he has two more of the men for breakfast. And then he drives his animals out to pasture, replacing the stone to make sure that the men stay trapped inside the cave. Odysseus, imploring Athena for help, devises a plot. He and his companions prepare a long stake of green olive wood. He sharpens its end, chars it in the hot fire, and hides it beneath the animal dung. He then conspires to get Polyphemus drunk that night on wine.

Now, the wine of ancient Greece did not taste anything like the wine we know today. It was thick like syrup, and was often heavily flavored with honey, thyme, aloes, and juniper berries. Most people today would find it awful. Even then they had to water it down to avoid toxic intoxication. However, Odysseus offers Polyphemus the thick, unwatered wine that he had been given by Maron, a priest of the Ciconians, as a reward for saving his life and his family. Odysseus suggests to the giant, "Maybe you'd like a little wine with your dinner?"—another meal of human flesh, two more of the men.

Polyphemus laps up the wine, drinking abundantly of it. In a state of benign inebriation, he asks Odysseus to tell him his name so that he may present him with that famous guest gift. Odysseus replies that his name is Noman (*Outis* in Greek, a variation of his own name). The drunken monster then jokes,

"Noman shall be last eaten of his company and all the others shall be eaten before him. That shall be your stranger's gift."

And at this point, Polyphemus lies down, his thick neck drooping sideways, and falls asleep. Homer tells us in his inimitable descriptive fashion that "wine dribbled out of his gullet with lumps of human flesh, as he belched in his drunken slumbers." As Odysseus tells the tale:

> . . . Then I drove the pole deep under the ashes to grow hot, and spoke to hearten my men that no one might fail me through fear.
>
> As soon as the wood was on the point of catching fire, and glowed white-hot, green as it was, I drew it quickly out of the fire while my men stood round me: God breathed great courage into us then. The men took hold of the stake, and thrust the sharp point into his eye; and I leaned hard on it from above and turned it round and round. As a man bores a ship's timber with an auger, while others at the lower part keep turning it with a strap which they hold at each end, and round and round it runs: so we held the fire-sharpened pole and turned it, and the blood bubbled about its hot point. The fumes singed eyelids and eyelashes all about as the eyeball burnt and the roots crackled in the fire. As a smith plunges an axe or an adze in cold water, for that makes the strength of steel, and it hisses loud when he tempers it, so his eye sizzled about the pole of olive-wood.
>
> He gave a horrible bellow till the rocks rang again, and we shrank away in fear. Then he dragged out the post from his eye dabbled and dripping with blood, and threw it away from him, wringing his hands in wild agony, and roared aloud to the Cyclopians who lived in the caves round about among the windy hills. They heard his cries, and came thronging from all directions, and stood about the cave, asking what his trouble was.[6]

There then ensues the famous play on words between *Outis* (Noman) and *me tis* (some one). *Me tis* itself is a pun on the chief characteristic of Odysseus, his *metis,* which can variously be translated as his wit, skill, wisdom, and intelligence, and which has brought this successful punning to the following conclusion:

> "What on earth is the matter with you, Polyphemos?" they called out. "Why do you shout like this through the night and wake us all? Is some one [*me tis*] driving away your flocks against your will? Is any one [*me tis*] trying to kill you by craft or main force?"
>
> Out of the cave came the voice of mighty Polyphemos: "O my friends, Noman [*Outis*] is killing me by craft and not by main force!"
>
> They answered him in plain words:
>
> "Well, if no one [*outis*] is using violence [*biazetai*], and you are alone, there's no help for a bit of sickness when heaven sends it; so you had better say your prayers to Lord Poseidon, your father!"[7]

The interesting play on words that I have indicated in Greek, *metis biazetai* tells the truth of the story. The intelligence *(metis)* of Odysseus has triumphed over the violence *(bie)* of the Cyclops.

> With these words away they went, and my heart laughed within me, to think how a mere nobody [*outis*] had taken them all in with my machinations [*metis*].[8]

Now it remained for Odysseus to use all his wits and cunning to figure out how to get out of the blocked cave. But the Cyclops himself solved this problem. Groaning in agony, groping with his hands, Polyphemus lifted the stone from the door and then sat there with his hands outspread, ready to catch anyone who tried to go out with the animals. Odysseus consulted with his own intelligence to good advantage, saying, "All kinds of schemes and machinations I wove in my wits [*metis*]," and settled on the plan of lashing together three large fleecy rams of the flock. Six of these triads of large rams he lashed together, so that a man could cling underneath the middle ram while the side rams gave protection from the groping hands of the Cyclops. For himself, he chose a great ram, the finest of the whole flock, and snuggled beneath his belly of thick fleece.

Came the rosy-fingered dawn, and nineteen rams, along with the rest of the flock, poured out of the cave, bearing the seven remaining men. In a poignant and pathetic moment, the Cyclops asks the last ram, the fine huge one that carries Odysseus, why he leaves last, who always was first out of the cave to the soft grass and rivers, and is the first into the cave at evening. Does he miss his master's eye that the cursed Noman blinded?

Several critical symbolic events occur in the story of the Cyclops, some version of which appears in many of the mythologies of Europe. In this case, though, it is not your usual monster story, but rather, as Joseph Campbell notes, a primal initiation tale. Consider that the penetration of the eye—"Bull's-eye"—is analogous to the symbolic piercing of the Sun door into the other world. The symbolic name Noman is the statement of divestiture from the claims of the local self that the initiate must make before being allowed to enter the passage to the yonder world: "Because he did not assert his secular character, his personal name and fame, Odysseus passes the cosmic threshold guardian to enter a sphere of transpersonal forces over which the ego has no control."[9]

There is also Odysseus' identification with the ram, which is often understood to be a solar animal, as with the Egyptian solar ram-headed god, Amun. This sets Odysseus in the mythic constellation of the solar hero whose initiation consists in going down into darkness for a long period of time, only to rise again greater than he was before. With Odysseus the initiation is a double one, for he not only succesfully passes the Threshold Guardian, he is also swallowed up in the darkness of the blocked cave (the Belly of the Whale). There he must harness all his skill and resources to save himself and his men.

The fact that these resources are constantly identified with *metis,* and Metis is the name of the Titaness mother of Athena, is an important clue. Metis, the first wife of Zeus, and the principle of wisdom, was swallowed by Zeus in order to defeat a prophecy proclaiming that a son born of Metis would be greater than Zeus. Nevertheless, Athena has incorporated this deeper mother wisdom in spite of her aberrant birth from the head of Zeus. Odysseus' use of his hidden *metis* mirrors the hidden intelligence and skill of his goddess ally. This strong emphasis on *metis* makes it clear to us that somehow Athena is present.

To sum up, here we have a monster, son of the god of the deeps, standing literally in the cave that is a threshold to the deeps. The person who invades the cave moves past the threshold by divesting himself of the power and force of his name and reputation. This means Odysseus is now about to enter the great journey. The episode in Lotus Land was but the beginning of his descent. As Noman he crosses the threshold in the cave of the demi-god with the one eye and finds himself in mythic space and time.

But Odysseus' all too human pride rises once again as soon as he feels himself safe. He cannot resist, like an artist signing a canvas, telling the Cyclops exactly who he is. Once on the boat, he taunts and mocks the furious Cyclops, and the boat narrowly misses being broken up by the huge rocks that Polyphemus hurls at him. His crewmen plead with Odysseus to be quiet, but he continues his tirade, boasting to the Cyclops, "I say, Cyclops! If ever anyone asks you who put out your ugly eye, tell him your blinder was Odysseus, the conqueror of Troy, the son of Laertes, whose address is in Ithaca."[10] That's a pretty thorough statement of self-identity. He gave everything but the zip code.

Polyphemus then recognizes the fulfillment of an old prophecy—that he would lose his sight at the hands of Odysseus. But he'd always expected a tall, handsome fellow, not a whippersnapper like Odysseus! (Throughout *The Iliad* and *The Odyssey* we are constantly reminded that Odysseus is not very tall. In fact, he's quite short, with little bandy legs, a huge barrel chest, and a great head of red hair. That is why the goddess Athena is always trying to make him taller and more beautiful than before.)

The Cyclops then prays to his father, Poseidon, that Odysseus, the conqueror of Troy, son of Laertes, whose address is in Ithaca, may never reach his home. But should he get there, may he come late and in misery, having lost all his companions, in another man's ship, and find tribulation at home. All of which comes to pass.

To modern consciousness, the story of the Cyclops bears a poignancy rarely felt by commentators of the classical period, who universally perceived Polyphemus to be a ruthless and disgusting barbarian. The perception of the pathos of Polyphemus is a modern sensibility, not unlike the pang we feel for Shakespeare's Caliban in *The Tempest*. The perpetration of too much oppression of Third World peoples, of too many exploitative ventures by colonial powers, have left scars upon our collective conscience.

In the blinding of Polyphemus, we feel the obliteration of our own innocence. For indeed, the Cyclopeans lived in a state of primal innocence. They knew nothing of government nor agriculture, yet things grew for them without effort. Theirs was a kind of primitive golden age, a barbaric Paradise. But in such a Paradise one sees with only one eye—without perspective. Nor is there a Cyclopean Serpent around to seduce them into eating of the tree of greater knowledge and perspective. (Unless it can be argued that Odysseus plays this initiatory role.)

Perhaps primal innocence must be wounded in order to move on to the next stage. And the stage after that. And the stage after that. Until perhaps this series of woundings brings us to the highly civilized but compassionate stage of the extraordinarily evolved Phaeacians. There is more to this than meets both eyes. As we note in the diagram of the Odyssean Hero's Journey on page 80, the protectors of opposite sides of the magic threshold are the Cyclops and the Phaeacians. One provides the means by which Odysseus is sent into the mythic world of trials and challenges; the other releases him from that world and enables him to return home.

In many other ways they are also polar opposites. The Phaeacians are practitioners of highly civilized manners and mores. Their many arts and virtues, as well as their advanced technology, stand in extreme contrast to the primitive and barbaric Cyclopeans. But these polarities become more intriguing when we discover that the Phaeacians are relatives and were once neighbors of the Cyclopeans. Poseidon is not only father to Polyphemus, he is also grandfather to Alcinous, king of the Phaeacians. Generations before, the noisy violence of the Cyclopeans forced the Phaeacians to emigrate. Yet, although they now live apart, they still share many similarities, albeit reflected differently in the state of their development. Neither group knows war or trading, and both are isolated from the doings of the world that Odysseus and his men inhabit. And they both are blessed with the favor of the gods.

The Phaeacians are known as the ones who are "near to the gods," among whom the divine personages come and go without disguise. Indeed, the gods have imparted to them the products of a divine technology: gardens of remarkable fertility, magic ships that move swiftly under their own guidance to any destination.

The Cyclopeans on the other hand, in spite of their impiety and scorn for the gods, also receive the divine gifts we have seen. Zeus makes their lands grow all kinds of grains and vegetables without any work on their part, and Poseidon immediately responds to the request of his son Polyphemus to punish Odysseus.[11]

This kind of complex interrelationship between superhuman and subhuman realities will be reflected throughout the adventures of Odysseus as he moves alternately between one and the other. Elements of both are combined in this voyage of initiation to deepen his character. As Jenny Strauss Clay has noted in her excellent study, *The Wrath of Athena:*

> Thus both the brutish Cyclops and the goddess Calypso live in caves. The cannibalism and immense stature of the Cyclops are shared by the Laestrygonians, who, on the other hand, have a city, king, *agora,* and are capable of communal effort—be it only to destroy intruders. On the floating island of Aeolus, Odysseus receives the same hospitable treatment

> he later gets from the Phaeacians. There, too, he tells his story to his host and receives a *pompe,* a means of return, in the bag of winds. . . . These and other combinations which Odysseus encounters suggest that the sub- and superhuman may have more in common than one originally suspects.[12]

Odysseus will discover his finer identity somewhere between the two realities. His regeneration will come from both, and both will give him the necessary trial and triumph to enable him to attain a fuller humanity with which to return home to Ithaca. Thus his is ultimately a richer experience than that of the denizens of the sub- or superhuman worlds. For they know not suffering or toil as does Odysseus, nor are they able to journey through multiple realities as he can. He intrigues the gods with his *metis,* his endurance, his vulnerability, and he gains their respect and partnership. He does not bore the gods, while the Cyclopeans and the Phaeacians possibly do. Their enterprise is static, while his is transformational.

Self-Divestiture—Becoming Noman and Putting Out the Eye of the Cyclops

WE are about to perform an exercise in divesting ourselves of our usual sense of self, particularly as it relates to our identification with our name. We are about to become Noman or Nowoman. But as this is our own metaplay, our own Mystery journey, we can change and expand upon the actions of Odysseus. Using a process of rhythmic repetition, we will initially state our identity very fully, and then proceed to confuse it, and then to lose it. Finally, we will join in a dance of unity and become Everyone.

Next we will create a double line with however many participants in the group we have. Thus six participants will form two lines of three; eight participants will form two lines of four, etc. Our partner will be the person opposite us in the other line. Holding our partner's hands, we will imagine that we hold a long pole with a charred, sharpened point like the one Odysseus and his men prepared. Using that pole we will forcibly put out our most negative or monstrous quality, especially the one that flattens our perspective on life and creates tunnel vision by refusing to let us see anything else. This is our Cyclopean eye and will be represented by a large drawing we will each make.

TIME: Forty-five to sixty minutes.

MATERIALS NEEDED: Large sheets of paper and drawing materials. A drum. A container or large decorated wastebasket.

MUSIC: Rousing music for dancing a dance of freedom and liberation.

INSTRUCTIONS FOR THE SOLO VOYAGER: This exercise in self-divestiture requires that you make a tape so that you can follow the processes with an imagined partner. As you read the script for the guide into your tape recorder make sure that you include the special places in which added suggestions are given for working alone. After you have done this, but before you begin the exercise, imagine that there is sitting opposite you a good friend (either one who exists in real life or in your imagination). This person would be sympathetic and available to you in participating in such an exercise. Reach over and shake their imagined hand, greeting them by name—their own name if they actually exist or a name you give them if they exist only in your imagination. Try to have a sense of breathing in rhythm with them so as to set up a greater sense of rapport. Do this for several minutes. Now turn on the tape recorder and begin the exercise.

SCRIPT FOR THE GUIDE: What is it that keeps you Cyclopean? What is it that keeps you in a state of limited vision and automatic behavior? What would be some examples of your Cyclopean behavior? Here are some answers that others have given.

> Always looking at the negative.
> A sense of impending disaster.
> Chronic melancholia for no reason.
> Gluttony.
> "I'm so tired."
>
> Laziness.
> Self-doubts.
> Self-destructive tendencies.
> Self-toxicities.
> Approval seeking all the time.
> Envy.

What would be some examples of your Cyclopean behavior? [The group gives examples.] Now I ask you to take a big sheet of paper and draw an outline of the front of your face. This face should take up most of the paper. Now draw a single huge eye on this face to represent your Cyclopean side.

[As the participants draw the eye, the guide can say such things as:]

As you draw your Cyclopean eye, don't try to deal with many bad habits at once. Rather, single out the big one, your worst pattern, the one you would really like to poke out. As you draw this huge eye, think what it is that you would happily let sizzle and boil away under a red-hot stake, as did the eye of the Cyclops. This episode contains such pungent, primal imagery; we can smell and touch and feel as well as see the bubbling of the burning eye.

Let us use that kind of imagery to get rid of our negative junk. Because the more vitally you engage the images of putting it out, the less amorphous it becomes. It is no longer just a vague feeling—"I'm so negative," or "I'm so lazy." If you think of it as something that singes and crackles, hisses and sizzles, then you have greater clarity and power over it.

You see, the Greeks had a very powerful, primal psychology. Many Mediterranean people do. They believe in rooting out, literally, various destructive patterns—whereas we say, "Oh, let's understand it fully. Let's talk about it. Let's analyze it and get to the bottom of it, and then maybe it will go away." Unfortunately, what happens is that we become so interested in it, we set up housekeeping there. We open a land development agency on the inner acreage of our own complaint. The old Mediterranean psychology is something else again.

Let me pass on this note from Jean Houston: "As a child I discovered this psychology when complaining to my Sicilian grandmother, 'Oh, I feel so bad. I have such a pain!' And she'd ask, 'Where isa da paina?' And I'd answer, 'Oh, I don't know. I just feel terrible.' And then she'd reply ferociously, *'Eh, Gina, killa da paina!'* I mean, this is not something you would think that a sweet little old grandmother would say. And then she would top it off by proclaiming proudly, 'Why be weaka *whena you canna be stronga!*' "

Mediterraneans believe in taking on strength to put out weakness. It may not have the subtlety of a hundred-dollar-an-hour psychiatric consultation, but what it lacks in sophistication it more than makes up for in vigor. In this case, we take on strength to put out the tunnel vision of our own hurtful habits.

We begin with the self-divestiture at the entrance to the other world. This process helps us discover how to pass the Threshold Guardian, for it is by releasing our fixation on our local identity that the healing powers are able to rise.

SCRIPT FOR THE SOLO VOYAGER: Sit down and imagine the other person sitting opposite you. This will be your imaginal partner. Sense this imaginal partner sitting there as vividly as you can. . . . Raise your right hand, and as you do have the feeling that your partner is mirroring your action. Do the same with your left hand and his or her right hand. Next, make a variety of movements and feel your "partner" mirroring these movements back to you. . . .

After doing this for several minutes begin to breathe very deeply through the center of your body. . . . Breathe very deeply so you get a sense of your breath being pulled up through the middle of your being as you inhale, and then down as you exhale. Get a good sense of this movement. . . . Continuing this process, imagine your "partner" sitting opposite you breathing in the same way. Breathe together now, aware of the breathing in both bodies. Be aware first of one, then the other, shifting your awareness back and forth until the two bodies are breathing together. Continue doing this for several minutes. . . .

Now, play the tape of you reading the script for the guide—or follow the instructions given next. Imagine that you hear your partner speaking his or her name as well as repeating the words given.

SCRIPT FOR THE GUIDE: Find a partner and sit opposite each other. Now, I want you to repeat your own name out loud and rather fast. Out loud and fairly fast. Just repeat your full name. Over and over again and simultaneously to each other. Really put your full sense of identity into it. Don't go on automatic. Put your full identity into it. Feel and express the pride in your name as Odysseus felt his. "I *Am* Mary Smith. I *Am* Mary Smith. I *Am* Mary Smith." [The guide repeats his or her own name.]

Just keep repeating your own name over and over again. . . .

Now, keep on repeating your own name—but louder. [Two minutes.]

Now repeat your partner's name as if it were your own. So if I'm sitting across from Sally Jones, I'll say: "I am Sally Jones. I am Sally Jones. I am Sally Jones." Back and forth. Over and over again. Both of you repeating the other's name at the same time.

And keep staring at each other as you do this, very intently, so it seems that you are assuming the other's identity as well as the name. Really get into being this other person. [Two minutes.]

Now quickly repeat, "My name is Nobody. My name is Nobody. My name is Nobody. My name is Nobody. My name is Nobody. My name is Nobody. My name is Nobody. My name is Nobody. My name is Nobody." [As with the other repetitions, the guide continues to repeat this along with the group.] [Two minutes.]

Now repeat to each other, "I am No One. I am No One. I am No One. I am No One. I am No One. I am No One. I am No One. I am No One. I am No One. I am No One. I am No One." [Two minutes.]

Now stop and reflect, without speaking, to each other on the state of your identity—or lack of it. [Thirty seconds.]

And taking your partner's hands, begin rocking back and forth, looking each other in the eyes, and saying, "I Am. I Am Not. I Am. I Am Not. I Am. I Am Not. I Am. I Am Not. I Am. I Am Not." [The guide continues to repeat this along with the group, with different shadings of emphasis, over the given time period. The pace becomes more and more accelerated.] [Two minutes.]

Now rocking and repeating, "I Am. I Am You. I Am. I Am You. I Am. I Am You. I Am. I Am You." Rocking back and forth. "I Am. I Am You. I Am. I Am You. I Am. I Am You." [The guide continues to repeat this with the group.] [Two minutes.]

Now rocking and repeating, "I Am Me. I Am You. I Am Me. I Am You. I Am Me. I Am You. I Am Me. I Am You." [The guide continues to repeat this with the group, gradually accelerating the pace.] "Me. You. Me. You. Me. You." [Two minutes.]

"We Are. We Are One. We Are. We Are One. We Are. We Are One. We Are. We Are One. We Are. We Are One." [The guide continues to repeat this with the group. Gradually, the chant turns into a song accompanied by drumbeats.] [Two minutes.]

"We Are Everyone. We Are Everyone. We Are Everyone. We Are Everyone. We Are Everyone." Get up with your partner and dance. "We Are Everyone. We Are Everyone. We Are Everyone." [The guide continues to repeat this with the group, turning it into a song accompanied by drumbeats. The chant and the dance of partners continue for some time at the discretion of the guide. The dance may begin to take a variety of forms, generally starting as a circle dance and becoming a weaving line of dancers.]

[If you are a *Solo Voyager,* again strongly imagine your partner's presence. Continue chanting with the tape, imagining that you can hear your partner's voice chanting too. Then stand up and begin to dance with your imaginal partner. You are not dancing alone, you are partnered in this triumphant dance.]

One. One. One. One. One. One. One. One. One. One. One. One. One. One. One. [This is chanted by the guide to drumbeats for an extended period.]

The One and the Many. And the Many and the One. The One and the Many. And the Many and the One. The One and the Many. And the Many and the One. The One and the Many. And the Many and the One. [The guide continues to chant and dance this with the group until the process reaches its climax.]

All right. Now take your drawing of your Cyclopean eye, line up with your partners in a double line that is no larger than four partners, that is, eight people. [The guide allows the necessary time for this to happen.] Putting your drawings down, let all partners join hands in the line and vividly imagine that together you are holding a smoking stake with a red-hot, charred point at the end. Feel the heaviness of the stake. Know how effective it will be for putting out the eye of tunnel vision. Practice together shoving that stake into the Cyclopean eye. All together now. One. Two. Three. Shove! Practice turning the stake in the eye so that it sizzles and boils.

[*Solo Voyagers,* enlist the aid of your imaginal partner in putting out the Cyclopean eye of your drawing. Feel your energy enhanced by this presence as you both shove the red-hot stake in the Cyclops' eye.]

[When the guide sees that the group has had sufficient practice, he or she will say:]

Let the first person in the line take the drawing of his or her own Cyclopean eye and hold it up in front of the line. Name what it represents so that it can be poked out. Make sure that you voluntarily agree to this symbolic act.

Speak out the name of the quality you want to get rid of, the one represented by the eye of the Cyclops—sloth, melancholy, negativity, laziness, envy—whatever it is. The rest of you who are holding the stake, repeat the name of that quality as together you shove and bore it out of the person's drawing. Really bore through the eye of the paper with your joined hands. Keep repeating the quality of tunnel vision, the particular eye of the Cyclops, as you do this together. If the quality is envy, you would all shove with the imagined stake at the eye of the drawing held in front of you, repeating, "Envy. Envy. Envy."

[The guide will then direct the process so that after each "Cyclops" has been through this process, he or she will go back in the line as a stake bearer and the next Cyclops will stand in front of the line with his or her drawing and state what each Cyclopean quality is. After they have lost their "eye," they will step back into the line and the process will continue until all members of the line have had a chance to be both stake bearer and Cyclops.

Often it will happen that the particular Cyclops will be representing a quality that others in the line can respond to as being one of their own negative traits. Then the event may take on an even stronger and more passionate quality. The guide may have to remind the participants to be mindful not to hurt each other. Only the symbolic drawing is to be hurt.

When everyone is finished, some rousing music and an accompanying dance of freedom can be performed by all. One very effective dance can be created without music but with a drumbeat with the guide drumming rhythmically and singing, "We are Everybody," and inviting the group to join in. If it is a large group, then generally the individual "Cyclopean" groups may want to dance together.

The *Solo Voyager* may want to play a small drum and/or a tape of drumming and dance rhythmically—with the imaginal partner—chanting "We are Everybody" for quite some time. Lose yourself in the chant, in the dance, in the drumming.

This dancing and singing continues, with many variations on words and rhythm, until the guide determines the natural ending place. Then the guide will say:]

We need to go a further step than Odysseus was able to do. Let us now gather the many pieces of paper that represent our destroyed negative qualities, and place them in this container where they may be treated with the respect they deserve, the respect due the worthy adversary. Let us also replace the energy of the now-empty Cyclopean eye socket with a quality or qualities that we wish to take on. Such qualities might be compassion, discipline, affirmation, awareness, or joy.

As you bring your torn papers to the container and place them in, speak out loud the name of the quality you wish to have fill the empty place in yourself. Have the sense that you and Odysseus are granting new vision, new hope, new possibility to Polyphemus as you do this. After this is over, a member of the group may want to take responsibility for seeing that these papers are burned ceremonially so that the energy of these negative qualities may be dissipated and transmuted. Or the group may wish to do this together.

[After each member of the group has placed his or her torn paper in the container and proclaimed the new quality, the entire group can join in a song or dance of celebration.

After a break, the group will get back together and perform the next exercise in this series—The Great Homeric Brain Exercise.]

The Great Homeric Brain Exercise

THIS process helps sharpen our intelligence so that we, like Odysseus, can get out of the caves when we need to.

We know that Odysseus is full of machinations and wiles, the result of his *metis,* his high intelligence, and the almost constant use of his mind and sharpening of his wits. He is always endlessly inventive, able to devise brilliant solutions to the many problems he faces.

Following the example of Odysseus, we are about to sharpen our own brains. We will use a right brain/left brain exercise with images from *The Odyssey.* The style but not the content of this exercise derives from one that Robert Masters and I developed to increase the brain's capacity to consider multiple possibilities and to enhance the fluidity of creative and conceptual thought and expression.[13] In this process, we will "speak directly" to the brain, exercising its capacities, and actively recruiting it as an ally for the purpose of higher mental and emotional functioning.

Although I work with the metaphor of right and left sides of the brain in this exercise (you may wish to review pages 45 to 47 and to read pages 162 to 166), I cannot claim that it actually exercises the function of two distinctly separated hemispheres of the cerebral cortex. Instead, this exercise seems to integrate many functions of the brain, bringing together words and images, senses and emotions, the abstraction of numerical symbols and the unity of the mind field.

NOTE: This exercise will be effective only if one knows the complete story of *The Odyssey,* since many of its images are drawn from later portions of the book. If any reader and participant has not read *The Odyssey,* then it is advised that he or she read the remaining chapters in this book in order to have a good sense of the story and its imagery. This exercise can be repeated again and again as one progresses through the processes of later chapters. Repetition will only serve to enhance mental functioning as well as provide a deep familiarity and appreciation of the journey of Odysseus.

TIME: Sixty minutes.

MATERIALS NEEDED: None.

MUSIC: None.

INSTRUCTIONS FOR THE SOLO VOYAGER: If you do this process alone, you will need to put it on tape, remembering to leave pauses long enough for the images to develop and be reflected upon.

SCRIPT FOR THE GUIDE: Close your eyes and direct your attention to your breathing. Allow the rhythm of your breath to become regular. As you do this, allow your consciousness to rest in your left eye. Keeping your eyes closed, look down with your left eye. Now up. Look to the left. To the right. Up. Down. Right. Left. Up, down, right, left. Up, down, right, left. Allow the left eye to circle clockwise. And counterclockwise. Clockwise. And counterclockwise. . . .

Now, shift your attention to your right eye. Keeping your eyes closed, look up and then down with your right eye. Repeat this several times. Now move your right eye from right to left a number of times. Allow your right eye to circle to the right and then to the left, clockwise and counterclockwise. Notice whether it is easier with the right eye or with the left.

Relax your eyes. Release the muscles around the sockets, and feel your eyes getting soft. Rest for a minute. . . .

Keeping your eyes closed, direct your attention and your breathing to the right side of the brain . . . and now to the left. Shift back and forth easily a few times, breathing and focusing on each hemisphere of the brain as you do so. . . .

And now, again placing your attention on the left eye, go on a journey through your left brain by moving your left eye. Have a sense of circling with the left eye all over the left brain. . . . Continue traveling throughout your left brain with that left eye, but now have a sense of experiencing a wondrous Mediterranean Sea voyage as you travel along the various passageways and sea lane turnings of the ancient world encoded in your left brain. Breathe deeply into the left brain as you do this. . . .

And now place your attention on your right eye. Again, take a journey through your right brain by moving your right eye. Have a sense of circling with that right eye all over the right brain. . . . Now, continue traveling through the right brain with the right eye, and once again have a sense of experiencing that wondrous Mediterranean Sea voyage as you travel along the various passageways and sea lane turnings of the ancient world encoded in your right brain. Breathe deeply into the right brain as you do this. . . .

Now, with both eyes, circle throughout your whole brain. Activate the ancient world of the old brain. Actually, have a sense of your eyes going way back there toward the back of the skull and circling in the older parts of the brain—in the area that is sometimes referred to as the reptilian brain. Circling and circling and circling. Breathing very deeply as you travel in this most ancient part of the brain which oversees so many of your survival functions and basic life energies. It is the brain of attention and arousal helping you to maintain stability in an ever-changing world. Continuing to circle and travel in this ancient brain, a brain that loves habits, rituals of sameness, things staying on an even keel.

Then focus with your eyes around the middle of your head, on the midbrain, what is referred to as the old mammalian brain which contains the limbic system, the hypothalamus, the parts of your brain that affect heart rate, blood pressure, respiration, digestion, hormonal activity, pleasure and pain. It is a very emotional part of the brain. So circle now with your eyes in this midbrain, circling and wandering through this part of the brain that controls your mood, your emotions, your sense of reality, how and in what manner you love or hate or feel indifferent about people or things. . . .

Have a sense now as you move your eyes through your brain that you are making the journey of Odysseus, with all its different twistings and wanderings and turnings back on itself. . . .

And now, using both eyes, breathing and circling throughout the whole of your brain, charge your brain with energy, with adventure and excitement. Charge your brain as both eyes circle throughout the whole brain. . . .

You are making tremendous circling passes in your brain with your eyes. Meandering, journeying through the great passageways of your brain. And as you do this—charging your brain with adventure, with excitement—you will begin to activate your latent Odyssean brain.

Breathe deeply. I should be able to hear you breathing now as you follow the adventures of Odysseus from place to place. Starting at Troy, its citadel still burning on the hill, travel north to the land of the Ciconians. See the sacking of Ismarus somewhere in your brain. Then, be blown across to another part of the brain where you land in North Africa at the land of the Lotus-Eaters. And then off again across the Mediterranean to the island of the Cyclops, and from there to the isle of Aeolus, Lord of the Winds. Now you're traveling past the island of the giant Laestrygonians. Keep going. Let your eyes take you across your brain to Circe's island. And from there to the Land of the Dead. Here, your eyes circle down and around, around and down, down and around, around and down. Then come up and around, around and up.

Moving now past the Sirens, past Scylla and Charybdis, to the Isle of the Sun. Past the Isle of the Sun, you find yourself traveling in mad, chaotic circles, lost, circling wildly with your eyes, being flung around around and around as Odysseus is shipwrecked after his companions have eaten the forbidden cattle of the Sun. . . .

But now, circling more calmly, circling horizontally at the level of your eyes as widely as possible inside your head. Circling inward horizontally, making smaller and smaller circles with your eyes until you get down to a space inside your brain that is so small there is no room for circling. You want to fix on that space—try to hold it. Fixing on this place at the center of your brain we will call the Isle of Calypso, this place where you will try to stay focused for a while. If you lose this central place, make more large circles with your eyes. Circles . . . circles . . . letting the circles become smaller and smaller until you get back to this small space, staying fixed on Calypso's Isle for as long as you can. . . . [One minute.]

Now, focus again on both hemispheres of the brain. Focus on both hemispheres until you see or imagine on the left brain a digital clock blinking the numbers one through twelve. A digital clock blinking the numbers one through twelve. . . .

On the right hemisphere, see or imagine the twelve ships of Odysseus setting off from Troy. . . .

Now, on your forehead, over your left brain, tap a slow, even beat with your finger. . . .

On the right brain, see, hear, or imagine as vividly as you can the men on Odysseus' ship rowing to the beat of a drum. . . .

Now on the left brain, spell Odysseus. . . .

On the right brain, see Odysseus. . . .

On the left brain, spell Telemachus. . . .

On the right brain, see Telemachus. . . .

On the left brain, spell Penelope backward. . . .

On the right brain, see Penelope from her back as she sits at her weaving.

On the left brain, see the name of Tiresias with its letters in a circle. Trace the letters in a circle with the eye of your left brain. . . .

On the right brain, plunge downward through the Earth, feeling the falling, circling movement, until you reach the underworld and see the shade, the ghost, of Tiresias. . . .

On the left brain, pick and pack the lotus berries for shipment to a friend of yours, making sure that you stencil the address on each box and get the same number of berries in each box. . . .

On the right brain, eat the lotus and see what happens to you. . . .

On the left brain, write on parchment a series of reasons and arguments to the Cyclops as to why he should not eat you. . . .

On the right brain, be a part of the line of Odysseus' men who poke out the eye of the Cyclops. Feel the rough wood in your hands. Smell the burning flesh. . . .

On the left brain, scrape and tan the hide of an ox that will hold the winds. . . .

On the right brain, get inside the bag of winds and listen to the stories and voices of the winds. . . .

On the left brain, be Circe's animal keeper. Organize the various meals of mash, acorns, and barley for the animals. . . .

On the right brain, feel yourself to be one of Odysseus' men, an archaic heroic seafarer. Now—turn into a pig! And now become a human again, but younger and more beautiful than before, knowing the lessons that one learns from being a pig. . . .

On the left brain, consider several arguments for and against life after death. . . .

On the right brain, visit heroes, heroines, or other great ones that you know about in the land of the dead and speak with them. . . .

Now, like Tiresias, be a woman in your left brain, and at the same time, be a man in your right brain. . . .

Now at the center of the brain, in the corpus callosum, the ridge where the two hemispheres come together, bring these two energies together and be both at the same time. . . .

On the left brain, see how many turns of rope it takes to bind Odysseus to the mast while you pass the island of the Sirens. . . .

On the right brain, listen to the songs of the Sirens. We're told they're songs about knowledge. Let your head be flooded with this music of knowing. . . .

On the left brain, navigate your way between Scylla and Charybdis. . . .

On the right brain, be the great monster Scylla taking a bath in the whirlpool of Charybdis. . . .

On the left brain, be Odysseus figuring out how many days

you have been on Calypso's Isle. Remember it's been seven full years. . . .

On the right brain, sit by the seashore of Calypso's Isle, feeling an enormous nostalgia and longing for home, wherever home is for you. . . .

Now, in the center of your forehead see the Sun rise on a day on Calypso's Isle. Follow the Sun with your eyes as it goes through the sky of your skull up to the top of your head and then sets in the back of your head. Then, still following with your eyes, continue circling downward somewhere within your face, and rising again in your forehead. All these days spent on Calypso's Isle. Follow the Sun rising on Calypso's Isle, going up to the top of the Heavens, which is the top of your skull, setting toward the back of your head. Follow it as if your eyes were turned around in your head—looking inward. Continue circling down into the darkness, and coming up again to your forehead. Follow this inner Sun, rising and setting on Calypso's Isle, with your eyes for many days. . . .

And now, on your left brain, you have been shipwrecked. All you have are a few floating pieces of wood and some thongs of hide. In the rolling waves, you are trying to weave and tie these scraps of wood together with the thongs to make a raft. . . .

On the right brain, swim for your life toward the shore of the Phaeacians. . . .

On the left brain, meet the lovely young girl Nausicaa on the shore. . . .

On the right brain, feel yourself changing, changing from someone humbled, reduced to nothingness, changing, being lifted up, being made more beautiful, more glorious, than before. Feel that miraculous change within you. . . .

Now on the left brain, try to enumerate to the Phaeacians your main adventures since you left Troy. . . .

On the right brain, join the boys in their dance with the balls. . . .

Now, try to stay very focused, as we reverse the images that we've just given to the right and left. They will be for the most part the same images reversed, but this time done more quickly. . . .

On the right brain, see a digital clock blinking the numbers from one through twelve, but see it blinking in Roman numerals. . . .

On the left hemisphere, see or imagine the twelve ships of Odysseus setting off from Troy. . . .

On the right brain, tap a regular beat on the right forehead. . . .

On the left hemisphere, see, hear, or imagine as vividly as you can the men on Odysseus' ships rowing to the beat of a drum. . . .

On the right brain, spell Odysseus. . . .

On the left brain, see Odysseus. . . .

On the right brain, spell Telemachus. . . .

On the left brain, see Telemachus. . . .

On the right brain, spell Penelope backward. . . .

On the left brain, see Penelope from the back. . . .

On the right brain, see the name of Tiresias with its letters in a circle. Trace the letters in the circle with the eye of the right brain. . . .

On the left brain, plunge downward through the Earth, feeling the falling, circling movement, until you reach the underworld and see the shade, the ghost, of Tiresias. . . .

On the right brain, pick and pack the lotus berries for shipment to a friend, stenciling the address on each box and getting the same number of lotus berries in each box. . . .

On the left brain, eat the lotus berries and see what happens to you. . . .

On the right brain, figure out and write on a parchment a series of reasons and arguments to the Cyclops as to why he should not eat you. . . .

On the left brain, be a part of the line of Odysseus' men who poke out the eye of the Cyclops. Feel the rough wood beneath your hands. Smell the burning flesh. . . .

On the right brain, scrape and tan the hide of an ox that will hold the winds. . . .

On the left brain, get inside the bag of wind and listen to the stories and voices of the winds. . . .

On the right brain, be Circe's animal keeper and organize the various meals of mash, acorns, and barley for the animals. . . .

On the left brain, feel yourself to be one of Odysseus' men, an archaic heroic seafarer. Now turn into a pig. Now turn into a man younger and more beautiful than before, having the knowledge of what it is to be a pig. . . .

On the right brain, consider several arguments for and against life after death. . . .

On the left brain, visit heroes and heroines as well as other great beings that you know about in the land of the dead and speak with them. . . .

On the right brain, see how many turns of rope it takes to bind Odysseus to the mast while you pass the island of the Sirens. . . .

On the left brain, listen to the song of the Sirens, the song of knowledge. Let your head be flooded with this music of knowledge. . . .

On the right brain, navigate your way between Scylla and Charybdis. . . .

On your left brain, be the great monster Scylla taking a bath in the whirlpool of Charybdis. . . .

On the right brain, be Odysseus figuring out how many days you have been on Calypso's Isle. Remember it's been seven full years. . . .

On the left brain, sit by the seashore of Calypso's Isle, feeling an enormous nostalgia for home.

Now in the center of your forehead see the Sun rise on a day on Calypso's Isle. Follow the Sun with your eyes as it goes through the sky of your skull up to the top of your head and then sets in the back of your head. Then, still following with your eyes, continue circling downward somewhere within your head, and rising again in your forehead. All these days spent on Calypso's Isle. Follow the Sun rising on Calypso's Isle, going up to the top of the Heavens, which is the top of your skull, setting toward the back of your head. Follow it as if your eyes were turned around in your head, looking inward. Continue to circle down into the darkness and your face, and come up again to your forehead. Follow this Sun rising and setting on Calypso's Isle with your eyes for many days. . . .

Now, on the right brain, you have been shipwrecked and all you have are a few floating pieces of wood and some thongs of hide. In the rolling waves you are trying to weave and tie these scraps of wood together with the thongs to make a raft. . . .

On the left brain, swim for your life toward the shore of the Phaeacians. . . .

On the right brain, meet the lovely young girl Nausicaa on the shore. . . .

On the left brain, feel yourself changing from someone humbled, reduced to nothingness, changing, being lifted up, being made more beautiful, more glorious, than before. Feel that miraculous change within you. . . .

On the right brain, try to enumerate to the Phaeacians your main adventures since you left Troy. . . .

On the left brain, join the boys in the dance with the balls. . . .

Now we will resume the story in Ithaca.

On the left brain, be Odysseus in Ithaca looking and feeling glorious after he's been transformed by Athena. . . .

On the right brain, be Odysseus disguised as a beggar and feeling poorly. . . .

Now be glorious on the right brain and beggarly on the left. . . .

On the right brain, you are weaving, as Penelope is weaving, a mantle by day. . . .

On your left brain, you are unraveling the weaving. . . .

Now weave the mantle on your left brain, and at the same time, unravel it on the right. . . .

Now weave the mantle on your right brain, and at the same time, unravel it on the left. . . .

On the left brain, shoot arrows across to the right brain, where there are twelve axes in a row. Shoot arrows from the left brain to the right brain through all the holes in the ax heads, feeling in the left brain the aiming and the shooting, and in the right brain feeling the arrows going through one ax hole after another. . . .

On the left brain, destroy the suitors. . . .

On the right brain, make peace. . . .

Now make peace on the left brain as well. . . .

In the center of the brain, meet Penelope and experience your time of mutual recognition. . . .

Now feel the figure of the goddess Athena touching your left brain with light, sending golden energies to the left brain. Feel as if your left brain is being charged with the energies of goddedness. . . .

Now do the same thing with Athena touching your right brain with these godded energies of golden light. She is charging your right brain. Breathe deeply into your brain as you receive this. Breathe very deeply. See the figure of Athena wearing her goatskin mantle with the head of the Gorgon in the center. Beneath it she wears the long, elegant, ancient Greek dress. Her head is helmeted and she carries a spear in one hand, a shield in the other. She radiates golden energies of light to your entire brain. . . .

Now, taking a favorite god or goddess by the hand, a Greek one this time, explore the labyrinthian windings of your left hemisphere, having a sense of sacrality moving in the left hemisphere, the sacrality of your left brain with its ways of data processing, of taking in knowledge, of understanding the logic and process of things. Wander with this god or goddess through the left hemisphere, having a sense of this left hemisphere being filled with potency, with capacity, with sacrality. Keep breathing into your brain while you do this. . . .

See or sense approaching you a favorite god or goddess. Take this deity by the hand and begin to explore the labyrinthine windings of your right hemisphere, the place of intuition, of seeing patterns as a whole, of space, of visualization, of creativity. As you explore these windings in the right hemisphere, have a sense of evoking the capacities, the potential, the power, of the right brain; bring sacrality to this hemisphere as you go hand in hand with the god. . . .

Sense behind you a great pantheon, an assembly of the gods behind you, sitting on top of the corpus callosum, the ridge that joins the two hemispheres. With the pantheon of all the gods—all the psycho-spiritual forces and powers gathered together—let all of you together meditate as one being upon the whole brain. Breathe deeply into the whole brain—the left brain, the right brain, the old brain, the new forebrain. Sense its infinite connections, its tremendous capacities. It is a universe in itself. Sense the glory of it. . . .

And as you meditate on it, strengthening connections where they need to be strengthened, begin to speak directly to your whole brain. Speak to the brain about improving its function and the deepening partnership you will share with it. Meditate on this, making friends with your own brain, making friends with the pantheon of spiritual powers now sacralizing the brain. Keep breathing very deeply. . . .

Breathing deeply into this whole brain, suggest to it that you wish its functionings to get better and better; that new connections between the right and the left hemispheres will be made; that new connections as well between the older and newer parts of the brain will be made. And if you wish, suggest also that all kinds of latent potentials become activated. Think of your brain as a great friend. Suggest that more cells will become available to you as you and your conscious self begin to work in partnership with this friend who has been with you through many adventures, many Odyssean trials and voyages, a true partner in the journey of life. . . .

And if you wish, place your hands about half an inch above your head and caress the field around your brain. Sense it as a triumphant old voyager who is ready to come home to you as you are ready to come home to it. Together, you are in the Ithaca of a new creation, ready to work in partnership and in deep friendship to create a whole new world, to create the circumstances for which a deeper life, a deeper soul, a deeper purpose, a deeper commitment, can come into time. . . .

In the next couple of minutes, just caress this brain, feeling the connections between you, the conscious self, and the brain, as these connections deepen and the friendship deepens from this day forth. . . .

See if your brain wants to tell you a story or perhaps to give you something. Just listen to it. The story may come in words or images or feelings, or just a sense of a pattern of connections. It may actually be a story. But listen now. Receive from your brain what it wants to give you—word, image, insight, impulse, perhaps even story. [Two minutes.]

And now, if you have some intention for the further adventures, the further voyages of your life, know that from this time forward you can enlist your great friend, your brain, in partnership. Together, in partnership, so much can be done, so many potentials can be released. The *metis* that is in your mind and soul can be released. If you have some intention for your life, some desire to get out of a cave in which you may be stuck, or even some particular path to Ithaca, give your brain that intention now, so that together the two of you can work for a much richer, fuller, deepening life, one in which you are truly in partnership with the godded self. [Two minutes.]

When you are ready, you can open your eyes and look around the room. What do you observe? Have your perceptions changed in any way? What is your mood? What is your sense of reality? Do you feel as if your possibilities have changed? Notice these things.

Then, in your own time and at your own pace, come back. Knowing that from this time forth you and your brain, the godded brain with its pantheon of possibilities, are now in relationship, in partnership. For you have gone so far together in the Odyssean voyage of your life.

You might want to take some time now to write in your journal, under the heading "Cave of the Cyclops," what it means to have been No One and Everyone; to have gouged out the tunnel vision of a limited sense of self, and to have spoken directly to your new friend the brain and activated the quickening of your *metis.* You can do any or all of these things. You can even speak about what your mind, your *metis,* now knows and what you are truly capable of, with the intelligence that has been sharpened and deepened.

Then, when you are ready, look around the room and sense and feel and know what it is to have the brain activated on many more levels.

[**NOTE:** This exercise can be repeated again and again as one progresses through the processes of later chapters. Repetition will only serve to enhance mental functioning as well as provide a richer sense of the journey of Odysseus.]

CHAPTER 5

The Island of Aeolus

AT this point in the Hero's Journey, the protagonist is clearly in need of supernatural allies and a good rest, and that is just what he gets. Odysseus and his men sail to the floating island of Aeolus, another son of Poseidon—the one to whom the gods have given the responsibility of the care and control of all of the twelve winds. Aeolus lives in a palace of bronze with his wife and his twelve children—six sons and six daughters—who are married to each other.

Odysseus makes nothing of these incestuous relationships, nor are they seen as the brother-sister royal marriages of Pharaonic Egypt. Rather, they serve as symbols of utter self-sufficiency, a reality so complete that it needs nothing further to enhance itself. The two halves of the cycle of completeness (the brothers and sisters) are in union with each other and presided over by the god of winds, of high spirits, of *pneuma* and of *spiritus*. Twelve is also the number of the signs of the zodiac, another symbol of completion. In the Homeric Bronze Age, bronze is the strongest material known; thus a bronze palace is the symbol of both strength and, again, self-sufficiency.

In this state of equilibrium, strength, and breezy high spirits, they spend a great deal of time feasting, for the table is laden with innumerable delicacies, and the palace is always filled with the steam of cooking. Odysseus, whose often-stated idea of a fine time is a good and plentiful dinner with interesting companions, enjoys himself immensely in his month-long sojourn there. He fascinates his hosts and keeps them enthralled with his tales of Troy.

Aeolus grows very fond of Odysseus, and when at last his guest is ready to leave, gives him the skin of a nine-year-old ox that he has made into a bag. In it, he has bottled up all the blustering and dangerous winds. The bag is then tied with a silver wire, with only the west wind left to blow freely that it might carry Odysseus' ships quickly to Ithaca. Aeolus makes Odysseus understand that on no account must the wind bag containing the contrary winds be opened. On no account allow your wind bag to be opened! Good advice for all of us.

After nine days of swift and uneventful sailing, with Odysseus awake and holding on to the sail the entire time to make sure of a quicker passage home, all grow exultant as they approach the shores of Ithaca and see the people of their native land tending fires on the shore. Odysseus is so relieved to be home that he lowers his guard, and falls into an exhausted sleep. He says the equivalent of "All right, boys, you bring her in. It's only about another hour to go. Isn't that marvelous? I'm worn out from always handling the sails. I'll take a short nap so as to look nice for Penelope."

Did you ever do that when your goal was in sight? In one way or another you fell asleep or dropped your vigilance. And what happened? Out to sea!

With their captain (their consciousness) asleep, Odysseus' men let their greed and curiosity run away with them. They say, "What do you suppose is in the bag? Come on. He's always shared everything with us. How come he's not sharing that? I'll bet you he was given a really big present. Time for our presents!" This kind of expectation and sharing was apparently quite common among ancient Greek seafarers. Indeed, the men's actual words show that there is a kind of proto-democracy if not anarchy at work here:

> See now, this man is loved by everybody and favored
> by all, whenever he visits anyone's land and city,
> and is bringing home with him handsome treasures taken from the plunder
> of Troy, while we, who have gone through everything he has
> on the same venture, come home with our hands empty. Now too
> Aiolos in favor of friendship has given him all these
> goods. Let us quickly look inside and see what is in there,
> and how much silver and gold this bag contains inside it.[1]

And in their greed they open the bag of winds, only to let loose a tremendous gale. All the contrary winds in the bag leap out and the ship is blown back to Aeolus. In his distress, Odysseus considers diving overboard for a quick suicide, but decides to endure his outrageous misfortune and, grieving, lies down and hides his face.

Once on land, Odysseus goes again to the great bronze palace of Aeolus, whom he finds busy at his usual feasting with his wife and children. He shocks the family by explaining what has happened and asks again for their help. This time Aeolus refuses, reasoning that if such contrary misfortune is still plaguing them after so much magical and supernatural help, it must be that some god has cursed them for a very good reason.

Joseph Campbell comments that the adventure with the winds is a symbolic expression of inflation followed by deflation.[2] Odysseus and company had come so close to their goal they thought that the adventure was over. But, in fact, it had many more years to go. Sound familiar? When we come so close to what we want that we can see the fires on its shore and think it is so near that we can just drift in—that is exactly the moment when we may be in for a rude awakening. For life as teacher has many more lessons in store. It is particularly dangerous when the voyage has been made easy by the grace of the gentle west wind and the confinement of contrary forces and we mistakenly believe that our own power has brought us here. This inflated view is invariably followed by deflation, leaving us stranded mid-ocean with our sails torn away in the wild gales of harsh reality.

In psychological terms we would say that, when the essential being of our Odysseus self sleeps, the less mature selves of our inner crew will undermine the purposes and intentions of that essential self. Most mythological thinking, and the mythic psychology of the ancient Greeks in particular, assumes that we are all polyphrenic by nature—that is, we have multiple selves within us, some of whom are mature, while others are not. Each of these selves carries a different quality, a different strength as well as shadow.

Each of us contains as part of our polyphrenic crew a wide and willing group of players: child, parent, worker, dreamer, lover, trickster, ecstatic, melancholic, follower, leader, wise elder, holy fool, and the myriad gods. All these and others populate our personal myth as well as make up the inhabitants of our inner life. This is why myth speaks so deeply to us, for it presents in powerful and dramatic scenarios our own stories writ large, and with many of the same characters. Thus, James Hillman's potent plea for a renewal of mythological or archetypal psychology: ". . . the soul's inherent multiplicity demands a theological fantasy of equal differentiation."[3]

Primal and myth-making cultures have always known this and have provided rich theological as well as mythological fantasies and psychologies to account for this multiplicity of selves. They give these various personalities different "names, locations, energies, functions, and voices, angel and animal forms, and even theoretical formulations describing different kinds of soul."[4]

The modern Western focus on a dominant egoic self not only inhibits the development of our many other selves, it also contributes to the splitting and fragmenting of the personality, and generally plays havoc with the psyche. These other selves, seeking the recognition and fulfillment that the ego self refuses them, go off on their own—aliens in the landscape of the self, strangers in a strange land. Eventually, they can even become saboteurs, fracturing the psychic landscape with the power of their unintegrated needs. Then we feel split, fragmented, at war within ourselves. This is especially true when the governing ego is itself immature and jealous of its prerogatives.

This state of chronic internal rebellion can be circumvented by the conscious intervention of an entelechy self, that is, the deepest level of our personality, the storehouse of the larger picture, the codings and potentials for what we can be. The entelechy self has the capacity to train and mature all the other selves. In the mature personality, the entelechy self gradually replaces the dominance of the ego self, while also encouraging the development of the other cast of characters contained within the total self. This is why I often say that if schizophrenia is the disease of the Western psychological condition, then perhaps polyphrenia (the orchestration of our many selves) is our potential health.

The old Mediterranean psychology affirms this, honoring the existence of many different selves within us—so many, in fact, that they could be considered a kind of crew. If, like Odysseus and his men, your crew is not engaged by consciousness (the captain), if you do not put *metis* into each part of yourself, then some aspect of your whole self is going to keep sabotaging all your best efforts. If you have a splendid mind, but neglect the body, chances are the body will take its revenge in gradual breakdown and chronic complaints that will only serve to distract the mind. If you have a well-developed mind and body, but neglect the emotions, you are almost certain to acquire psychological problems that will derail you in many wounding ways.

The heroic requirements of Odysseus' life cause him to neglect the development of his crew with disastrous results. He is the kind of person who always wants to be the baby at the christening, the bride at the wedding, the corpse at the funeral. After all, it was his insistence on manning the sail by himself for nearly ten days that brought him to the state of exhausted sleep within sight of his journey's end. Through his inability to trust and develop his crew, Odysseus quite literally inherits the wind and loses his home for another ten long years.

This whole episode could also be interpreted in sociological terms. One might say that it shows how the individual journey is always thrown off course by the collective will. Think about how many of your own intentions and personal quests have been beset by long detours because of the response of the collective. Whether it was the collective of habit, of cultural expectation, of professional limitations, of family, of friends, of "what others will think," the collective mind-set has often diminished your possibilities and undermined your goals. Joseph Campbell comments: "Odysseus had not yet released himself from identification with his group, group ideals, group judgment, etc.; but self-divestiture means group-divestiture as well."[5]

Only at our peril can we underestimate the difficulty of the task that faces all of us in the great journey. Divesting ourselves of old habits and old ways often requires our separation from the tried-and-true community as well. As we begin to move into new ways of being, we often discover that we simply cannot continue on the journey clothed in the habits and mind-set of our "crowd." There is nothing for it but to walk away from that crowd and its easy but enervating identity.

Divesting ourselves of a group identity—especially one that we've long been part of—often forces us to lose for a time the pacts and contacts that give meaning and sureness to life. And what is often harder to take, those we have left behind do not understand. They think we're weird, or remote, or no longer "responsible." They are especially estranged by our high spirits: "You actually seem to think you know where you're going!" As with Odysseus' men, they feel that we are keeping something valuable from them. They feel abandoned, betrayed, unloved, misunderstood.

If we let guilt overwhelm us, we might succumb to the pressure and fall back into the welcoming arms of the collective embrace. The prodigal returns. Hurray! It was all a bad dream anyway. Business as usual—only more so. But from here on out, entropy sets in and the self dies a little more each day.

Suppose, however, we do not immediately return. Suppose that, instead, we honor the divestiture that has occurred. Suppose we allow for the loneliness and grief and that period of intense self-reflection that often accompanies the process of spiritual gestation and psychological growth. Then, should we choose to return to the group in some way, we will return with ways and means that are more conscious, with many more of our resident selves awake. Now, there is much less possibility of our "falling asleep" from the lull of the crowd, or settling into automatic behavior from the demands for sameness.

However, in staying awake and staying conscious, we carry within us the difficult assignment of evoking awakeness in the other sleepwalkers. This, as many have found, can place us in the position of being always servant and never lord. In subtle and sensitive ways we empower consciousness whenever we can; we "walk our talk."

Thus, in most every great mythic or scriptural rendering of this theme of divestiture, the god-human journeys away from the requirements of society; he or she goes off into the desert, up a mountain, or into the forest, often having lost all friends, possessions, and social esteem. So divested have they become that they are capable of being filled; so humbled that they are ready for initiation into the larger reality.

In *The Odyssey*, divestiture becomes explicit and horrifyingly concrete when, after leaving Aeolus for the second time, the men row day and night for six days, with no friendly winds to help them. On the seventh day they land on the shores of the Laestrygonians, a grim place whose harbor entrance is narrow and bounded on both sides by precipitous cliffs. Odysseus sends out three men to reconnoiter.

Their adventure begins with unholy innocence; they ask a young girl who is drawing water from a running spring about the king and people of this place. She points them to the high-roofed home of her parents. There they meet first the mother, a gigantic being whom they "hated on sight." She sends for her husband, who is attending a town meeting. When he appears, also gigantic, he grabs one of the men and prepares to eat him. The young girl's parents have turned out to be giants with insatiable appetites for just such people as Odysseus and his men.

The remaining two evade capture and run back to the ships to warn their companions. Rowing valiantly out of the harbor in an attempt to escape the now fully aroused citizens of Laestrygon, they find themselves bombarded by stones and boulders hurled by thousands of giants who smash their ships and spear the swimming men like fish. Only Odysseus' ship makes it back out to sea. In fear of their lives his men "put their backs to it." All the rest are lost.

After the debacle of the winds and the refusal of any further friendly help from Aeolus, Odysseus must now know himself to be an enemy of the gods. No wonder he covers his head. But he chooses life and its teaching rather than suicide. And life, taking seriously his willingness to learn, begins its deeper teachings.

It is fascinating to me that this first adventure at the hands of the feminine powers is the exact opposite of the last—the encounter with the Phaeacian princess Nausicaa. In both there is a meeting with a young girl at a source of running water. And in both there is an immediate referral to the queen, the girl's mother. This first experience ends in devouring destruction—man's greatest fear before the female powers. But because Odysseus perseveres, and through his further adventures becomes initiated into the wisdom of the feminine, his final meeting before returning home is one of enhancement, enrichment, play, and love.

But for now, the divestiture is almost complete. They are ready for the first great initiation into larger realities at the hands of the feminine. And, indeed, they will soon meet their guide, Circe of the braided tresses.

The Winds of Aeolus

TIME: One hour.

MATERIALS NEEDED: Everyone should have his or her journal out and available. Balloons and long pieces of string for each participant.

MUSIC: A recording of the sounds of wind played in the background can be very effective here. The guide can raise and lower the volume of the recording wherever appropriate to the script.

INSTRUCTIONS FOR THE SOLO VOYAGER: First, read through the rest of the instructions. Then make a tape of the script for the guide, allowing sufficient time for each part of the process. It is very important to a deep understanding of the story to enact all the events as fully as possible. So visualize yourself in your ship surrounded by the other members of your inner crew, and whenever needed, use your journal to dialogue with them.

In the sequence that requires you to blow up balloons, blow up a different balloon for every member of your inner crew, speaking aloud the specific kinds of inflation to which each is subject. Later, call out aloud what the world owes you. As the exercise progresses, keep visualizing your other crew members and enact the raising of your sails, the letting loose of the winds, the endless rowing, the escape from the Laestrygonians, more rowing, losing parts of yourself, calling out the names of the parts you're losing, more rowing, until you collapse, exhausted, on Circe's Island. When you have finished the process, be sure to treat yourself to a celebratory feast.

SCRIPT FOR THE GUIDE: We will now explore this episode of the winds of inflation and the storm of deflation. To begin with, let's all get reacquainted with the members of our inner crew and their demands. Please take your journals out and quickly list a number of members of your crew. For example, a typical list might include: the Great Mother, the Whining Scold, Mr. Know-It-All, the Wise Old Woman, the Envious One, the Artist, and others.

After you have listed these members of your crew, next to each of them give some example of the kind of inflationary statement they might make about themselves. Also list the kind of thing they could say about what the world owes them. For example, next to Mr. Know-It-All, one might write, "I am an expert on so many things. It's everybody's loss that they don't listen to me. I should have my own show on television in which I give my ideas for solving the world's problems." Begin now to quickly make these lists of your crew and their remarks. [Ten minutes.]

Share the balloons and the string, at least several per person. Form small groups of no fewer than four people and no more than eight. These are your boats.

Sit down in your boats please, in a circle facing each other, and listen carefully. We are going to explore in a whimsical fashion the control that our secondary selves exert over us. We will experience quite literally the nature of inflation followed by deflation. Each one of you is now to speak your inflation. Do this consciously, as you are blowing up the balloon. With each breath make a statement of self-inflation. Each breath and statement can come from a different member of your crew. Or, you can think of the statements as coming from the collective gathering of your crew.

It could go something like this. "I'm a very good teacher." Blow into the balloon. "I work harder than anyone I know." Blow into the balloon. "I know more about dog psychology than anybody." Blow into the balloon. "I'm kind to nearly everybody." Blow into the balloon. "I tell great jokes." Blow into the balloon. "My chocolate mousse is spectacular." Blow into the balloon. And so forth. Try not to burst the balloon by overinflating it. Speak some aspect of your inflation before each breath. When the balloon is stretched about as far as it can go without popping, then tie it up, letting a long piece of string hang down from the knot. If you need more balloons to speak the varieties of inflation of your various selves, then by all means use them.

Begin now, with the members of each boat sitting in a close circle facing each other. Now speak your inflation as you blow up your balloons. You and your companions can choose to do this one at a time or all of you simultaneously. Also feel free to tell the truth about things you're really proud of—the qualities and characteristics that have carried you a long way toward your goal.

[The guide allows enough time for this to happen, generally five to ten minutes, depending on the size of the group.]

Now, I want you to take the string and tie all your balloons together to make one great bag of wind. As you do this, keep speaking your inflation, as did Odysseus' crew. Now we add another element. Let all of the different crews bring your bags of wind together and tie them like a great sail. While you're doing this, speak about what the world owes you—just like Odysseus' crew's saying, "Hey, we deserve an equal share of that treasure."

Speak it out now. Speak out about what the world owes you. Tie your balloons together so that you have one big sail, one big wind bag. Put your sails up as you brag. Keep it up. Speak what the world owes you as we voyage together with our wind-bag sails. Remember that the west wind is blowing strongly. Rattle the sails as you continue to travel in the Good Ship *Inflation.* Sail on, carried by your wind bag, speaking all the time about what the world owes you.

What does the world owe you? Speak it out. Give examples of what you've often said or thought about what the world owes you. I'll walk around and listen and call out what some of you are saying as you all speak out.

The following are examples of some of the things people say that the world owes them during this exercise:

- A lot of money.
- Applause, an audience.
- Fun, good times.
- Recognition.
- Smartness.
- Adulation.
- Deification.
- Joy, rapture, emotion.
- Eternal approval.

What does the world owe you? Keep your wind bag up there. What does the world owe you?

- Loving, supportive relationships.
- Winning the lottery.
- Wealthy children.
- Parties.

What does the world owe you?

- Clean water.
- A safe neighborhood.
- My own sailboat.

What does the world owe you? Speak it out.

- Being able to eat chocolate without getting zits.
- Millions and millions of dollars.
- Love, love, and more love.

What does the world owe you? What does the world owe you? Keep those bags of wind up.

[After this has gone on for three to five minutes, the guide will say:]

Now you just know that all those good things are probably inside those balloons. They are in those wind bags just waiting for you to get them. Here we are nearly at Ithaca, nearly home, and we can just coast in. The boss has gone to sleep, so we can finally get what it is we know we deserve from the world. All those things others have and refuse to share with us. Let's get at those bags! Let's tear them open and find out what's in there. [As people "open up" their wind bags the room is filled with the sound of the popping of many balloons.]

Oh, oh. Big mistake. No more wind. Now we have to row. Right? Well, there's nothing to do but get in formation like a rowing team and begin to row. We've got no sails. We've got no wind. So we have to row. Row. Row. Row. Just keep rowing. Row. Row. Row. Row. Row. [The guide continues to keep the rhythm of the rowing throughout, by saying "Row. Row. Row."]

And as you row you get released from all kinds of things. Ego. The pride of your lesser selves. Instead, there is only humiliation.

And deflation. And endless rowing. Row. Row. Row. Row. Just keep it up. Keep it up. Keep rowing together as I talk to you.

We finally make it back to the Island of the Winds, but our host, who was so kind before, slams shut his great bronze doors and tells us to leave immediately. More humiliation! We are now to be treated as enemies of the gods!

So we row some more. Row. Row. Row. After many exhausting days we come to a narrow harbor on a forbidding shore. We find ourselves in the land of the Laestrygonians, and the humiliation and deflation continue. In fact, it is worse than we could ever have imagined. At first, the place seems friendly; a young girl sends us to meet her mother. But her mother is not friendly—in fact, both the girl's parents and all the people of this dreadful place are voracious giants who see us as tasty morsels in their food chain! We run back to the ship, pursued by the Laestrygonians, who chase after us and spear us like fish, and we lose many parts of ourselves.

Then it's time to row some more. To row for our lives! Row. Row. Row. Rowing away from the killer cannibal Laestrygonians as fast as we can. Row. Row. Row. Row.

Keep rowing. But pay attention. Be aware of what it is you're losing of the crew, of yourself. Row together, in sync with each other, or you won't get anywhere. Row together. Row. Row. Know what it is you're losing. Feel the parts of your crew drop off. Feel the parts of yourself drop off. Feel the dropping off.

Keep going. Keep going. Row. Row. Row. Row. Feel the parts of yourself falling away. Feel the ego self losing parts of itself to the Laestrygonians. Keep on losing parts of yourself—losing, losing. Deflation. Deflation. Losing. Keep going. Losing more. Getting tired, but keeping going. Going. Going. Going. Row. Row. Row. Row.

Keep going. Losing. Calling out the parts of yourself that are dropping off. What's falling off? Call out what you're dropping. What you're losing, what's being captured, or even killed and devoured. Speak out what's being lost in yourself. Speak it out. Speak it out.

Keep going. Keep rowing. Keep speaking it out. Keep going. Keep going. Keep going. What is falling off? Keep speaking it out. Keep going. Keep going. Row. Row. Together. Row. Row. Speak what's falling away. Utter deflation. What's falling away? Speak it out now:

- Pride.
- Vanity.
- Adulation falling away.

What else? What are you losing? Keep going. Keep going. What's falling away? What else is falling away?

- Weight.
- Self-destruction.
- Disorder.
- Pride.
- Physical beauty.
- Fear.

Let it fall away. Keep rowing. Ego is certainly going. Ego is going. Row away the ego. Keep going. Row away the ego. Row away the inflation. Row away the pride. Row away the junk. Keep going. Together, row. Row. Call it out. Fear. What else is falling away? Pride. What else? Contradiction. What else? Arrogance. What else? "Get-rich-quick schemes." Falling away. All falling away. Keep going. Row. Row. Row. Row.

Faster now. [The rowing is paced faster and faster.] Row. Row. Row. Pride. Ego. Self-hatred. Row faster. Row. Row. Row. Row. Row. Row. Row. Row. Row. Row. Row. Row. Row. Row. Row. Row. Row. Row. Row. Row. Row. Faster. Faster. Faster. Until . . .

. . . You collapse finally on Circe's Island. Circe's Island. Now just rest for two days there, mourning that which you have lost, that which you have left behind. All those lost, immature shipmates. All those parts of yourself that didn't work anymore. Just feel them release, release, release.

Having let go, find yourself now on Circe's Island, a land of meadows, and beautiful lakes, and flowers, and deer browsing in the fields. A place perhaps of magic and of new possibilities. Feel yourself ready to take on the strangeness and the beauty of the next adventure. Circe's Island, a gentle island, a place of transformation, of initiation, of a year-long training in a deeper reality.

On shore allow that which has fallen away to return to the soil.

Feel the freedom of the release. Gradually, the sweet waters and the Sun and the gentle rains restore your weary spirit as you rest for two days on Circe's Island. Much leaner in mind and spirit than you were before, prepared now to take on the great initiation. Rest now without speaking on Circe's Island. [Two minutes.]

Gradually begin to feel the need for more life in you, for more action. As Odysseus now, go hunting. Shoot a stag and bring it to the shore where your companions are. Offer it as a feast to get your spirits and your body up for the next initiation, the next adventure.

[This is a good time and place in the journey for the group to share food or have dinner together.]

CHAPTER 6

The Island of Circe

SO, humbled, ravaged, and reduced in numbers, utterly deflated—at least for the time being—Odysseus and his men are divested of the accoutrements of their heroic past. Removed entirely from the proud domain of the warrior society in which he had once dwelled so cocksurely, Odysseus is now ready for a series of major initiations by the feminine principle. This comes to him through the graces of Circe.

Circe belongs to the ancient and powerful tradition of the "Initiator as Temptress"—she who lures men to experience the Mysteries of regression in the service of transformation. In this she resembles, indeed, perhaps descends from, such Middle Eastern courtesan-divinities as Ishtar, who can be alternately cruel and beneficent. She also bears clear descent from the goddess-queens of Old Europe, who were venerated as the sources of the magical and creative life of the community, and who took as consort a man of unusual abilities. He would, for a time, share her Mysteries and a portion of her prestige, only to eventually suffer seasonal death and rebirth.

J. G. Frazer's extensive studies of this practice give us a glimpse into the reasons behind the rite:

> People feared that if they allowed the man-god to die of sickness or old age, his divine spirit might share the weakness of its bodily tabernacle, or perhaps perish altogether, thereby entailing the most serious dangers on the whole body of his worshippers who looked to him as their stay and support. Whereas, by putting him to death while he was yet in full vigour of body and mind, they hoped to catch his sacred spirit uncorrupted by decay and to transfer it in that state to his successor. Hence it has been customary in some countries, first, to require that kings should be of unblemished body and unimpaired mind, and second, to kill them as soon as they begin to break up through age and infirmity. A more stringent application of these principles led in other places to a practice of allowing the divine king or human god to live and reign only for a fixed period, after which he was inexorably put to death. The time of grace granted to limited monarchs of this sort has varied from several years to one year or even less.[1]

The rich ritual strata that weaves in and out of *The Odyssey* suggests that Odysseus himself may have descended from these dying and rising consorts of the goddess-queens. J. A. K. Thompson proposes that parts of the Odysseus myth show evidence of inheriting themes from the earlier Mother Goddess culture, that Odysseus is an *Eniautos-Daimon*, which translates as "year spirit." Thus, the sacred king or year king is "thought to die and come to life again, or to be obscured for a season only to reappear in renewed splendour."[2] The story of Odysseus, especially in the Circe episode with its year-long cycle, shows a definite correlation with this pattern.

The fact that, as a very young man, Odysseus was seriously wounded by a boar and bears the marks of the boar's tusk upon his thigh, testifies further to this correspondence. Throughout the Mediterranean region and to the east, the boar is often seen as the killer of the consort of the goddess—as, for example, in the case of Aphrodite's lover, Adonis, or of Tammuz, the consort of Ishtar. The boar is considered to be a most sacred animal, a precious sacrifice to the gods, and an essential element in many ancient dramas of initiation. Further, as I will discuss later, Odysseus, the solar hero, desired by several goddesses—Circe, Calypso, and the divinely inspired Nausicaa, as well as by his goddesslike wife—has 360 boars at home as a major part of his substance. The significance of 360 boars is further testimony to Odysseus' metaphysical identity as a solar hero. The number 360 refers to the days of the year in the ancient calendar. These days were thought to be the property of the sun. This property translates for Odysseus into 360 porkers. With Circe (see page 166), he is about to have to do with the mystery of the pig in a very big way.

Yet, Odysseus can always be counted on to deviate from the archaic and mythical tradition, for he reproduces it only in part—refusing its requirements for annihilation in order to die into divinity. He asserts his living humanity at every turn. What makes *The Odyssey* so fascinating is the way in which the ancient ritual pattern demanding that "the king must die" is woven together with the newly emerging consciousness represented by Odysseus, which asserts that "the king must live," and that he must learn everything he can from the goddess-queen. The death journeys that he undergoes must be ritual rites of passage and learning in the depth worlds, not literal dyings. Thus, the new king-consort dies to the ingrained habits and immaturities of his little local self and rises to the refinements of a deeper matured self.

However, in order to learn from the goddess, one must first pass the test of her magic threshold. Those who come to her in a state of heroic inflexibility and immaturity are transformed into wolves, lions, and pigs. In other words, all who come to her in the pride of their earned position in the world are forced to revert to earlier stages of their development in order to be humbled and then remade into finer beings.

This is a familiar theme to us all. Whenever we are so trapped in the awareness of our own excellence that we feel we've really "made it," the initiator of the next stage comes along to mock us or betray us into seeking yet another, deeper, broader level of understanding and growth.

The whole genre of Native American shamans—such as those we meet in the Carlos Castaneda books about Don Juan—teaches us that the initiator can be one who laughs at and taunts us while putting us through our paces. We also remember painfully the teacher who humbled us, the friend who jeered, the relative who found us ridiculous. Thus, our initiator is often a humiliator, one who turns us to *humus*, making certain we are earthy and grounded before we learn to soar.

But great initiators—like great teachers—receive as well as give initiations and learnings. So it is with Circe of the braided tresses. After her time with Odysseus, she no longer needs to use humiliation as an initiatory device. Now, by her very being, she is able to evoke a higher stage of awareness in her victim-initiates. The goddess herself is evolving. This theme of developing mythic powers (discussed in Chapter One) is as vital to us now as it was to the generation reflected in the Homeric epic. We and they have repressed or forgotten the knowledge of the part of the self that holds and honors goddess nature.

Twelve hundred years before Christ, the patriarchal view held by the warrior-chieftains was that women were there to seduce or to mother. The meeting with the feminine principle as equal, as partner, as evocateur, largely belonged to the past. Nevertheless, the cultural memory of matrilineal and matrifocal energies, as well as the sacred danger and extraordinary power of woman, continued to haunt these chieftains. This is preeminently apparent in *The Odyssey* in that, apart from the Cyclops, the principal monsters and all the initiators are female. Odysseus himself, married to the brilliant and resourceful Penelope, as well as being on the path of initiation by the feminine powers, discerns a possibility not seen by such heroes as Jason, Hercules, Achilles, and Agamemnon; one that includes a partnering of the inner and outer feminine, as well as schooling in the depths by goddess knowledge. Let us hear from Homer how this comes about.

After the men lay grieving for several days on the beach, Odysseus rallies them by killing an antlered stag and preparing a feast. Then he sends a party off to reconnoiter, for he has seen smoke rising in the woodland beyond. The men soon discover the halls of Circe:

> They found in a dell the house of Circe, well built with shaped stones, and set in a clearing. All round it were wolves and lions of the mountains, really men whom she had bewitched by giving them poisonous drugs. They did not attack the men, but ramped up, fawning on them and wagging their long tails, just like a lot of dogs playing about their master when he comes out after dinner, because they know he has always something nice for them in his pocket. So these wolves and lions with their sharp claws played about and pawed my men, who were frightened out of their wits by the terrible creatures. They stopt at the outer doors of the courtyard, and heard the beautiful goddess within singing in a lovely voice as she worked at the web on her loom, a large web of incorruptible stuff, a glorious thing of delicate gossamer fabric, such as goddesses make.[3]

So, singing and weaving, the goddess with the bright braided tresses lures them in. Throughout *The Odyssey* the earthly feminine powers—Circe, Calypso, Penelope—are seen weaving threads and wearing braided hair. They hold the powers that weave things together; they braid realities into gossamer webs that make it possible to recover something of what had been lost after the warrior-nomad invasions.

Once Odysseus' men are inside her domain, Circe mixes a potion of fine wine, barley, cheese, and honey into which she also stirs magical drugs. After they have drunk it down she touches them with her wand and they all become grunting, bristled pigs—"but the minds within them stayed as they had been before." She then herds them into sties and gives them acorns and beechnuts and cornel beans to eat. But one of the men, who suspected a trap, waited outside for a long time, and then managed to escape back to Odysseus. Filled with sorrow and terror at the disappearance of his companions, he tells Odysseus what he fears. Odysseus immediately slings his bronze sword and bow across his shoulders and goes raging toward Circe's palace.

However, the vengeful Odysseus is intercepted by the god Hermes, disguised as a beautiful young man, who clasps his hand and warns him of the powers of Circe. He then advises Odysseus to confront Circe not as witch and temptress, but rather as a great teacher of the Mysteries.

Now, Hermes, whom we met on page 61, who is both the messenger of the gods and the guide to the underworld, is also the one who brings opportunity. He is the god of *kairos*, the potent time when transformation can happen. In early Greek usage, *kairos* also referred to that moment in weaving when the two sets of warp threads are opened and the weft thread, carried by the shuttlecock, can be passed through—the moment when the new fabric (lives, fate, cloth) is actually being created.

It is significant that the gods who play the most important role in helping Odysseus are Athena and Hermes, acting as a kind of brother and sister pair. In earlier stories, Hermes appears as something of a knave, a trickster, while Athena, particularly in *The Iliad*, is seen as a fierce promoter of war and heroic action. However, at this point, in the eighth century B.C., the two gods are at their own moment of *kairos* in the Homeric telling of *The Odyssey*. They are themselves transforming into more evolved spiritual and psychological forces. Hermes begins to assume his role as a soul guide, or psychopomp, to the Mysteries and to the depths. Here, he is identified in part with Thoth, the Egyptian god of magic and mystery, while Athena is becoming the great goddess of creativity, of civilization, and of the weave of transformation. As the two gods are being deepened at this moment, the goddess prompts her brother to actions that serve not only to grow human beings, but to grow themselves as well.

This is a key part of the Mystery being played out here—the Mystery of the deepening of archetypal powers. The Hermes who meets Odysseus on the way to the palace of Circe is no longer Hermes the thief and trickster but a god who himself is developing beyond his archaic persona and is hoping to encourage his cousin Circe to develop as well. His method of accomplishing this is to persuade Odysseus not to approach her as a hero bent on rescuing his endangered men, but rather as a possible initiate into her sacred knowledge. This is a very powerful moment in the history of consciousness because it means that the depth world has resolved to extend itself.

As the god of *kairos* and of opportunity, Hermes brings the windfall, the unexpected but fortuitous happening at the right moment. In Odysseus' case, Hermes reaches down and pulls out of the ground a certain herb called *moly,* which has a milky white flower and black roots. Scholars have argued for centuries about the botanical identification of this plant and have offered speculations that range from visionary vegetables to garlic. Whatever its true designation, it is a plant with a strong root system and leaves that reach up to Heaven—a "great-rooted blossomer," in Yeats' poetic phrase. Hermes tells Odysseus that this particular plant of virtue, *moly,* will turn Circe's drugged brew into something innocuous.

In our age of extraordinary toxicity, when pollutants of body and mind are on a rampage, we yearn for some version of that *moly* to render the poison of our lives innocuous. How wonderful it would be to find ourselves suddenly free of toxic behavior and ready for *kairos.* Ready for opportunity, for Hermes, and for a true meeting with Circe.

Along with the plant to detoxify Circe's brew, Hermes also gives Odysseus very specific instructions. He says, "As soon as Circe gives you a tap with her long rod, draw your sword at once." What is a sword in the symbolic realm? It is often a metaphor for discrimination. At the right moment of opportunity you must move with decisiveness and discrimination. Hermes then details the decisive act that Odysseus must take:

> . . . rush upon her as if you meant to kill her. She will be terrified, and will invite you to lie with her. Do not refuse, for you want her to free your companions and to entertain you; but tell her to swear the most solemn oath of the blessed

gods that she will never attempt any other evil against you, or else when you are stript she may unman you. . . .[4]

So Hermes prepares Odysseus in the same way a guide to the Sacred Mysteries might have done: At the right moment act with decisiveness and join with the goddess if she invites you. By approaching Circe this way, Odysseus will surprise her into knowledge of her own vulnerability. This will remind her of what it is to be human, while awakening her capacity to evoke human refinement through the path of love rather than regression.

Here we have a man who is willing to meet the goddess in full union and not be lured into regression. How often have we dissipated some of the high moments in our lives by being unwilling to meet them fully? Instead of allowing ourselves to fulfill an opportunity of high promise and evolution, we fall into regression or depression, or a state of feeling less than human. This makes us incapable of utilizing those peak moments as vessels to carry us into new life, so we create a stockpile of unused "highs" and let them molder like old cars.

I believe this great passage in *The Odyssey* is about learning how to listen for instructions when the gods send their messengers, about how to recognize those fragile and all-too-fleeting moments when the possibility of High Mystery opens to us. Then, when *kairos* calls, we can move swiftly, wisely, and in full mindfulness of that critical junction between evolution and devolution.

This meeting between Odysseus and Circe—between she who carries the wand of transformation and he who carries the sword of discrimination and full human development—is also about how, as we engage the "gods," the psychospiritual principles, with all our human power, we call them forth in their full mystery and potential. A key teaching of most Mystery schools and schools of spiritual training involves the knowledge that we grow the god as well as the god growing us.

Odysseus does as he is told. In Homer's words:

> . . . I found myself at the doors of the lovely goddess' palace. Here I halted and gave a shout. Circe heard my call, came out at once, and opening the polished doors invited me in. Filled with misgivings, I followed her indoors and was asked to sit down on a beautiful chair with silver decorations and a stool for my feet, while she prepared some pottage in a golden bowl for me to drink and for her own evil purposes threw in some poison. When I had taken the bowl from her and drained it, but without suffering any magic effects, she touched me with her wand and sharply ordered me to be off to the pigsties and lie down with my friends. Whereupon I snatched my sword from my hip and rushed on Circe as though I meant to kill her. But with a shriek she slipped below my blade, fell at my knees and burst into tears.
>
> "Who on earth are you?" she asked. "What parents begot, what city bred such a man? I am amazed to see you take my poison and suffer no magic change. For never before have I known a man who could resist that drug once he had taken it and swallowed it down. You must have a heart in your breast that is proof against all enchantment. I am sure you are Odysseus, the man whom nothing defeats, the man whom the Giant-slayer with the golden wand [that is, Hermes] always told me to expect here on his way back from Troy in his good black ship. But I beg you now to put up your sword and come with me to my bed, so that in love and sleep we may learn to trust one another."[5]

When she has sworn not to unman him, he accepts her amorous invitation. It would appear that what is being played out here is an Odyssean variation of a most ancient fertility rite of initiation.

The same symbols that one finds in the quest for the Grail—the chalice and the sword—are also in evidence here. So too is the issue of the never-healing, emasculating wound of the Fisher King, that both creates and reflects the wasteland all around. In the Grail legend, the kingdom of the Fisher King—who can only lie on his side and fish, so terrible is his endless agony—is in ruin and chaos. The ground is spent and sere, the crops no longer grow, nor do the waters flow, and a darkness has descended on the hearts of the people. And yet the castle of the Fisher King contains the sacred emblems of the Holy Grail as well as the sword and lance of Christ's passion.

Only the preordained knight of the Grail—Percival in some legends, Galahad in others—can save the kingdom by coming at the right time and asking the correct question: "Who serves the Grail?" After the question has been asked, the king arises from his bed of pain, now completely healed, and the wasteland becomes a rich and fertile land once again. Eventually, the Grail knight becomes the new king of the Grail Castle. Only the one who has enough passion for the possibilities inherent in life to ask the great question can save the kingdom.

This Grail story has remarkable parallels to the tale of Odysseus, for at the time when we first meet him on Calypso's Isle, his kingdom in Ithaca is in chaos, and his substance is being wasted by the riotous suitors who have been feasting every day at his palace. The chief residents of Odysseus' kingdom, his wife, Penelope, and his now twenty-year-old son Telemachus, live in a state of chronic despair, as do the servants still loyal to his memory. In this case the king has been missing for twenty years rather than being incurably ill. But, like the Fisher King, Odysseus' wound of absence is caused by a heedless act, a major blunder. (We are never quite sure what the blunder of the Fisher King was—all we are told is that it was the cause of his condition.)

Odysseus, however, assumes the roles of both Fisher King and knight of the Grail. Like the king, he is forced to fish in his own unconscious self (fishing always being the symbol of accessing the symbolic worlds). But just as the Grail knight has to wander through many years of initiatory adventures in order to ready himself for a return to the Grail Castle, so Odysseus wanders for twenty years. And it is only upon his return to the wasted kingdom of Ithaca at just the crucial time that the disguised Odysseus can ask the right questions of wife, suitors, and servants that will lead to the restoration of his kingdom.

In her renowned study of the Grail legends, *From Ritual to Romance,* Jessie Weston explored the symbols of lance, grail, and sword as they were to be found in their most ancient antecedents:

> Lance and Cup (or Vase) were in truth connected together in a symbolic relation long ages before the institution of Christianity. . . . They are sex symbols of immemorial antiquity and world-wide diffusion, the Lance, or Spear, representing the Male, the Cup, or Vase, the Female reproductive energy.
>
> Found in Juxtaposition, the Spear upright in the Vase . . . their signification is admitted by all familiar with "Life" symbolism, and they are absolutely in place as forming part of a ritual dealing with the processes of life and reproductive vitality.[6]

In the hands of Homer, while these symbols of Holy Grail and sacred sword keep their sexual context, they are deviated into instruments of violence, rather than being ritual icons of love. However, they end by serving their original purpose when Odysseus and Circe perform the ancient and ever-new ceremony of sexual union, and Circe recognizes him as an initiate. At his request she brings in the men, who look like a lot of nine-year hogs, anoints each one with a drug, and then "the bristles all dropt off which the pernicious drug had grown upon their skin. They became men once more, younger than they were before, and handsomer and taller than before."[7] In other words, they had evolved, a situation that quite possibly was reflected in the ancient rite wherein some kind of ritual of restoration was performed.[8]

THE TRIUNE NATURE OF THE EVOLUTIONARY BRAIN

From this episode we can learn to recapture our capacity for recapitulating earlier stages of our evolution and to anticipate the next levels of our unfolding. In a single lifetime we seem able to traverse a million years of development forward and backward. We look in the mirror and wonder, "Who is that dinosaur?" At other times we feel allied with a nature so noble that it appears more suitable for a utopian society ten thousand years into the future than the world of today. This may be because, as Paul MacLean, former chief of the Laboratory of Brain Evolution and Behavior at the National Institutes of Mental Health, has convincingly proposed that our brain has evolved over time into what he calls "the triune brain."[9] In the diagram below we note the placement and evolutionary development of the three brains.

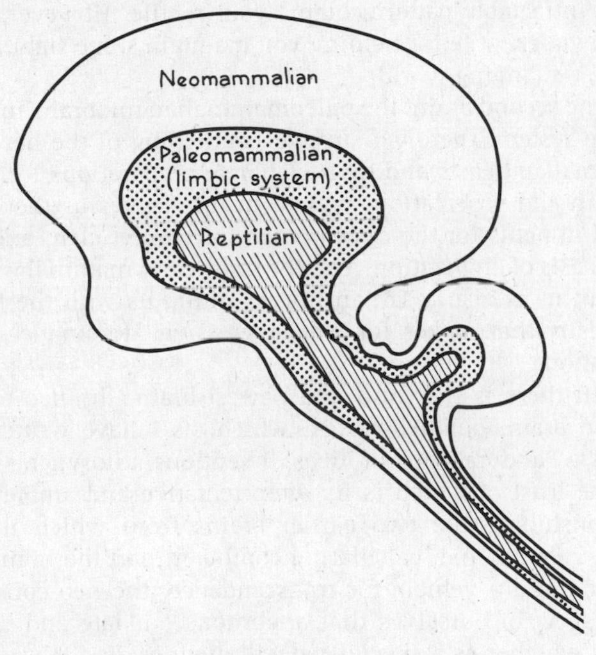

The glory of the human brain/mind system is that we each contain a part, albeit tiny, of those protoplasmic globules floating in an early ocean. In the recesses of the older parts of our brain we contain the fish, the reptile, and the amphibian, who still to some extent govern our survival attitudes as well as those patterns that call for the maintenance of habit and stability.

This first and earliest of the brains is known as the reptilian brain, and we feel its effects every day. We find, for instance, that the routine and ritually driven behavior of reptiles and amphibians translates in our human expression into obsessive-compulsive acts and a tiresome devotion to a large variety of habit patterns. When you find yourself stuck in the rut of an intractable pattern, blame your reptile. However, also thank your reptile for helping you maintain some stability in an ever-changing world.

In the second brain, the paleomammalian midbrain and the limbic system, there yet survives something of the herds of mammalian beasts and their elaborate preparations for partnership and procreation, which, in turn, gives us the emotional impetus for the development of family, clan, and the early basis of civilization. Yet, the same early mammal within each of us is also a Trojan horse, gifting us with the brain chemistry that makes for war, aggression, dominance, and alienation.

Then there is the third and newest brain, the neo-mammalian brain, our neo-cortex, which, as I have written, is itself "a Pandora's box of ideas, inventions, idiosyncrasies—not the least of which is its often tentative and ambiguous relationship to the two earlier brains from which it has sprung. Part a cold, calculating computer, part the home for paradox and a vehicle for transcendence, the neo-cortex is that aspect of ourselves that apportions our fate and determines whether as a species we will grow or die."[10]

We are given the future in the prefrontal cortex, the most recent growth spurt of the neo-cortex, which in its crucial link with the older emotional palette of the limbic system enables us to look inward, gain insight into the feelings of others, have compassion, reflect upon where we have been, and orchestrate all of these to become all that we might be. Thus, we might be said to contain, in our neurological makeup, some hundreds of millions of years of past memories and who knows how many aeons of knowing into the future.

In our lifetime, not only do we play many parts, we also seem to recapitulate earlier (and possibly later) species as well. Why, we wonder, after years of pursuing personal development, do we suddenly regress to fanged-lipped screechings and monkey mayhem upon middling provocation? And then, in the midst of real tragedy we rise to an angelic state of equanimity and beneficence. This phenomenon is far more interesting than mere neurosis. It belongs to the fact that we are a loaded transevolutionary species. Therefore, whenever someone says, "Are you ever crazy!" you can respond with, "No, I'm just a loaded transevolutionary species." That will take the wind out of their sails—to use a Homeric metaphor.

Nevertheless, because of our comprehensive makeup, we remain the most vulnerable of beings. The early mammal in us continues to slip on ancient banana peels and suddenly we're back a million years. "Grrrrr!" we growl—and wonder where that came from. This transevolutionary anarchy is further complicated by the hauntings of earlier stages of our cultural evolution, making it a very ambiguous and difficult thing to be human right now. As long as we were protected in tribe, in clan, or in a very limited, bounded culture, with explicit laws regarding transgressions and taboos, Thou Shalts and Thou Shalt Nots, we knew what we should do and how we should act. All our teeming transevolutionary entities could be kept contained.

But now, much too suddenly, we are the first generation without taboos, without a culture that tells us in no uncertain terms how to be, and in many cases the first generation without a strong family structure to guide us in the patterns of our ancestors. We are lost in space, loose in time, caught in a force field of historical spasm.

On top of our cultural rootlessness, we have been given

access to the immensity of everything we have been and will be, plus the plenitude of a cross-cultural smorgasbord. How can we not fail? We have to. We are Circe-ed and regressed. But also, necessarily, something keeps calling us on, luring us into becoming more than we were before we slipped backward. And this call, with its demand for communion with the god, is exemplified in this portion of *The Odyssey,* with its portrayal of the opening initiation of Odysseus, the first modern man.

The Mystery of the Pig

A fascinating question to explore in the work with Circe and her transforming power is, "Pigs? Why pigs, Circe?" We of the twentieth century fall automatically into a Judeo-Christian abhorrence for these animals. We use the word as our cruelest pejorative. But pigs meant something else to the Greeks, as well as to many other peoples of the world for whom the pig continues to be sacred. In fact, a powerful clue that the confrontation and union with Circe is an initiatory drama is the emphasis given the pig. Odysseus, the king of Ithaca, the solar hero, has 360 boars at home, while the goddess who turns men into pigs and back again is preparing them for entry into the mystery of sacrality.

The sacrifice of the pig was an essential part of the most ancient rites. They were offered as representatives of death and rebirth at the Eleusinian Mysteries and at the Anthesteria, a spring festival of flowers and new wine dedicated to Dionysus. At the great healing center at Epidaurus, silver effigies of the pig were offered to Asclepius to invoke the gift of healing and renewal from the god. Throughout Malaysia, Melanesia, Hawaii, and the South Pacific, the pig is the holiest of animals—also associated there with death and resurrection. Indeed, the island of Borneo is said to be named after the "boar."

In Celtic cultures and throughout Ireland, Scotland, Wales, and Brittany, the pig was the animal associated with the Mysteries and with the sacred underground burial vaults of kings—the barrows—again, a name derived from the ancient name for the pig. The Celtic goddess Cerridwen was said to fly over the countryside in the guise of a great white sow, occasionally giving birth and dropping piglets—and wherever they landed a Mystery School was said to form. Among the Druids, the Arch Druid, Merlin, was also known as the divine pig herder—as contrasted with the holy shepherd of Christianity. The tracks of the sacred pig can be traced around the world from Ireland to the Pacific. In fact, these tracks may be even deeper that we know, for, as Joseph Campbell has shown, the myths and rites of pig sacrifice in ancient Greece show precise analogies with those of Melanesia and the Pacific.[11]

Why is the pig considered so sacred in the collective knowing of the human race? As anyone who has ever worked with them knows, pigs are highly intelligent animals. Our ancestors believed that the pig represented the Mystery of the Earth, in which it was always rooting, and with it, a knowledge of the mystery of death and thus of rebirth in the great cosmic round. Also, the pig's going into the deeps of the Earth was symbolic of the self going into the deeps of consciousness. Among ancient peoples, including the Greeks, the underworld of death and the underworld of the psyche were often seen as continuous with each other. Indeed, among the remaining primal peoples this belief often continues.

As Jane Harrison, a member of the Cambridge school of anthropologists and mythologists in the early twentieth century, has shown, in the most ancient times the pig replaced the human as a worthy sacrificial gift for the gods.[12] Only the pig was considered equal to the gift of a human life. In fact, scarring by the boar's tusk was thought to be the marking of a sacred king. When Odysseus finally returns to Ithaca, Eurycleia, his old nurse, recognizes him as the true king, even though he is disguised as a beggar, because of the scar on his thigh. The pig is also considered to be one of the most fertile of all animals, an extremely important and significant fact for developing cultures as they were learning to domesticate animals. The pig therefore was a great provider. Like the goddess, like any kind of mother, it provided abundantly.

Pig reverence finds its icons even today. Why the fascination with the Muppet character Miss Piggy? She is no mere caricature. She is a descendant of Circe. She is a witch, an evocateur, who can take on many forms. Furthermore, she is fascinating and can carry on romances with different species—one of her favorites being Kermit the Frog—and she speaks many languages. She is an evolutionary being with a decided goddess streak to her. She is always in charge, is very glamorous, never dies, and in fact stays young forever. Miss Piggy is the modern prototype of the sacred pig. And while we may think of this as a peculiarly American mythic affectation, the Russians have an equally widespread fixation on a popular being known as Mr. Pig.

Circe, then, the Lady of the Pigs, joins with Odysseus, the Lord of the Pigs, and they live together in happiness and contentment for a year. It is implied that Odysseus becomes her pupil during that year, while she receives much comfort and, we hope, intellectual challenge from him.

The Circe story is like an archaeological dig, with many strata of meanings and messages. By transforming Odysseus' men (symbolically, the immature parts of his being) into the Mystery of the pig, the lovely goddess is initiating the men into a larger sense of life. When Odysseus, their captain, is rendered more conscious and more mindful by the ministrations of Hermes, he can join in union with Circe, thus releasing her from her own isolation. This, in turn, enables her to release Odysseus' men, who are then ready to take on the younger, more beautiful, taller, and more valiant versions of themselves. Through all these acts, the gods themselves—Athena, Hermes, and especially Circe—become instruments through which the pig redeems the higher dreams of humans, while the humans activate the higher possibilities of gods.

The Initiations on Circe's Island

THE initiation will be divided into three parts:

1. An Adventure in Evolution (Prolepsis).
2. The Leap of Hermes and the Gifting of *Moly*.
3. Union with the Archetype.

TIME: Three hours.

MATERIALS NEEDED: None.

MUSIC: Environmental sea sounds (Area I) for the evolutionary sequence, followed by highly energized music appropriate for leaping and dancing (from Area III) for the second and third parts of the process. We have found *Hooked on Classics,* volume 1, to be especially engaging for this latter process.

INSTRUCTIONS FOR THE SOLO VOYAGER: This process can be done alone with judicious use of taped scripts and artfully detailed journal work and visualizations with such imaginary beings as Hermes.

SPECIAL NOTE: The first part of this process, the evolutionary sequence, is best done outside on a lawn or a beach. The entire process, however, can be done in any fairly large, open space where no one and nothing will be hurt by people crawling or leaping around. Clear everything out of the way so that there are as few interferences as possible.

This process serves as an initiation with several component parts, each of which addresses the stages of the Circean adventure. The first uses an exercise of mine for recovering and recapitulating the genius of earlier phases of brain and behavioral evolutionary development. A full explanatory version of this process will be found in my book *The Possible Human.*[13] As I discussed there, it is possible, by engaging in the movements evocative of different stages of evolutionary development from fish to human, to activate something of the modalities of those stages as they are still present in our triune brains.

This has proved to be a therapeutic procedure as well as an enhancement of growth and integration. It often results in our gaining a deeper appreciation of the evolutionary history of our species. Because the actual movements seem to activate a "recall" of what has been lost to consciousness, there is often an apparent recovery of the genius of each stage as it applies to the human being.

For example, what is the genius, or the meta-level, of the fish when translated to the human level? Participants often respond that by virtue of this exercise, they are able to move in a more open environment. They also perceive a fluidity of opportunity, or *kairos,* in the various situations in which they now operate. Exploring the meta-level of the amphibian (a creature in transition from water to land) enhances one's ability to move with amphibious ease through different contexts and to meet the challenges of many different environments, as did that most amphibious of heroes, Odysseus.

In the context of the Circe story, when we get to the mammal stage there will be a strong emphasis on the sacred pig as a key part of the evolutionary development. When we finally reach the human stage and beyond, we will find ourselves, like Odysseus' shipmates, to be recovered humans, ready to go on to the next stage of evolution with full consciousness, "younger and taller and more beautiful than before."

What this Homeric hyperbole means when applied to participants in this exercise is that many will feel themselves to be part of the emerging evolutionary process, strongly motivated to go forward as committed and concerned partners of evolution, now that they have experienced their deep connections with the past. Many have said that in prolepsis they have experienced their spiritual dimension incorporated in flesh that has become numinous, and their physical selves as being the embodiment of their spiritual evolution. Some express a sense of profound integration with the stages of evolutionary development as well as unusual feelings of freedom and structural integration.

The second part of this initiation has to do with the gift of *moly* given by Hermes to Odysseus. This will be presented as the leap into opportunity, Hermes being the god of opportunity and of the *kairos,* the loaded time of the right moment. Together, we will perform a process in which we leap to each other and give each other several gifts of *moly* represented by the best qualities and virtues we are able to present to the world.

For the third initiation, we will take up the part of the story that has to do with the meeting and union of Odysseus and Circe. However, we will take it a stage further, and discover a way to meet and deepen our relationship with the godlike archetypal being within ourselves. This also corresponds to the deepening of Circe, as well as to the enhancement of the divine possibilities within Hermes and Athena.

1. An Adventure in Evolution (Prolepsis)

SCRIPT FOR THE GUIDE: Before we begin, please remove your shoes, belt, watch, glasses, jewelry, and anything else that could prove uncomfortable to you or to others as you move through the stages of evolutionary development. [Two minutes.]

[**NOTE:** Sea sounds are played during the following sequence.]

Begin now by sitting on the floor or the ground. Allow enough space around you to move freely. As we go through each of the evolutionary stages, the more deliberately and fully you give your consciousness over to the movements and sensations, the more complex and precisely authentic these movements will become and the more benefits you will find from this process. Remember that neither fish nor reptiles are likely to say "Excuse me" to another member of their species. Speech did not evolve for a very, very long time, and we are trying to recover connections to much older parts of the brain.

We begin with the fish stage. Lie on your stomachs now with your hands at your sides, and begin to roll gently from side to side as a fish. . . . And as you move make sure that your entire body rolls, the head and torso and lower body. . . . You are gaining now a sense of the recovery of the fish consciousness, which is coded in your brain. . . .

Notice your perceptions as you roll like a fish. How do you see as a fish? How does your world look, sound, smell, taste? Your fish skin is the organ of taste, so your sense of taste is very acute and the water brings the knowledge of your surroundings through taste. Notice too how sensitive you are to the subtle changes of pressure in the water. As a fish your tactile sense is very great. Notice now your sense of direction . . . of distance . . . of gravity in this watery environment. Sense as a fish the unconscious knowledge of the seas, the consciousness of living in an endless ocean . . . rolling . . . rolling. . . . Until full fishness just moves in. . . . You are a fish. . . . You are a fish. . . .

And should you get tired, just stop and continue the movement in your imaginal, kinesthetic body until you're able to do it physically again. That is, feel the movements so vividly in your imagination and body image that it is almost as if you are doing them. . . .

Keep rolling like a fish from side to side, knowing that by doing this you are engaging the ancient fish structures of your brain. . . .

Sense the reweaving that is going on as your entire spine moves as one from side to side. Reweaving. Freeing you from false enchantments . . . becoming released in the realm of water. Continue this for five minutes, always staying focused on the movements that you are making as a fish. [Five minutes.]

Become aware now that a new freeing has occurred around your fins. That fins are extending and developing into primitive forms of forearms. And that you feel an instinctive pulling toward the light. But still you remember the knowledge that came with being a fish. . . .

For now you're becoming one who can live in several worlds, the amphibian. The one who lives in several worlds, the world of water and the world of land. . . .

And your head is raising somewhat and there is a great tail behind you. And you pull yourself along on the forearms, still very much on the belly. Pull yourself along on your forearms dragging the lower part of your body along.

If you happen to find yourself crawling over or under others, know this to be a normal part of amphibian life and continue to pull yourself along. Don't say "Excuse me," for language has not developed yet. . . .

Your legs cannot yet move independently for you are dragging a great tail behind you. Shoulders and arms help to pull you up to the Sun. The legs are the great tail that can still descend into waters.

You taste the chemistry of the air. You've just come from being fish where your mode of communication is entirely by taste. And still having that strong taste sense to taste your reality. And smelling it as well. Notice how the world looks to an amphibian.

You have been released from the fish stage, and the genius of that stage is yours. Now you're fully within the experience of the amphibian stage in this initiation of prolepsis. And the genius of this amphibian stage is now yours, for you are able to live in several worlds at once. Continue for a while now as an amphibian, allowing your mind to be open to the brain's remembrance of amphibian life and experience. [Five minutes.]

But the amphibian, too, grows and releases beyond its limitations. Although you are still crawling on your belly, you will experience greater movement and separation in your legs, which now are becoming coordinated with your arms—your arms and legs are now moving cross-laterally with each other. For you are becoming a reptile, with its intense focus on getting where it needs to go.

Still on the stomach, moving with purpose, having acquired the genius and therefore the initiation of the fish, and the initiation of the amphibian, you are now receiving the initiation of the reptile.

You are releasing the pelvis. Great cross-lateral movements with the knees are coming up. Knees coming way up. Cross-lateral movements. . . . Notice as you continue moving how your senses have changed as an amphibian. Notice the litheness of your head movements, how you sometimes stop and pump yourself up and down on your forearms. . . . How you may occasionally hiss. . . . How does your reality look now? . . . Sound? . . . Taste? . . . Smell? . . . Feel? . . . What do you desire? . . . What do you fear? . . . Where do you want to go? [Five minutes.]

Now, gradually being released from the reptile as your blood becomes warmer. But gaining the genius of the reptile—its singular perseverance. Having received now the initiation of the reptile.

We move next into the early mammal—a lemurlike creature. Discovering what it is to be able to move on all fours with your belly rising off the ground. The blood warming. Living entirely on the land. Discovering the ability to make sounds. Discovering the sensations of the early mammal. Notice how your head wants to move . . . and your shoulders. Notice how your relationship to others begins to change. Know that as you are doing this you are activating the old mammalian structures in your brain. [Five minutes.]

And now your mammalian body and mind evolve further in many other animal forms. . . . Explore these for a while . . . the cat family perhaps . . . the bears . . . the cows . . . horses . . . elephants. Explore for the next several minutes some of the other mammal forms. [Five minutes.]

And now your mind deepens as you gradually take on the beingness and the initiation of the pig. You're not just any ordinary pig. You're the sacred pig, the pig that has the knowledge of the Earth, the depths. You are gaining now the mysterious Earth-intelligence of the pig—an animal of almost Odyssean intelligence.

Not falling into old Judeo-Christian notions about the pig. Becoming the sacred animal that the ancient Celts and Greeks knew. Not satirizing, but honoring this becoming a pig.

Feel the power of being a sacred animal. [Five minutes.]

And now from being the sacred pig, you begin to be released to the higher evolutionary forms that preceded your development as a human being. The four-legged mammal in you now begins to stand upright part of the time. Begins to live part-time in the trees and sometimes on the ground.

The little monkey . . . the little monkey . . . leaping and climbing, experiencing a greater lightness in regard to gravity and a greater freedom in the flexibility of the spine and movement of the head and neck. Listen to and make the sounds of the monkey. Notice how full of curiosity you are, how playful and in such high spirits. . . . Notice the increasing use of your visual field. Know that as you do this you are activating the brain memory and structures that relate to the early monkey. [Five minutes.]

And having been initiated into the genius of the early monkey you begin to develop further and are released into the great anthropoid ape. Feel your body becoming more massive, with powerful muscles developing. . . .

Now you can stand with greater ease and maintain balance as you swing from side to side. You are beginning to make many side-to-side movements . . . and you are probably very sociable . . . with appropriate gestures and sounds. . . . Again, become aware of your change of perceptions. How does the world look and smell? Notice your relation to distance and gravity, and to the other apes. Let the memories and muscles and brain structures corresponding to this period of evolution be activated as you enact the movements and experiences of the great ape. [Five minutes.]

And having had the initiation of the great anthropoid apes, we can be released from that stage and gradually, gradually become the early human being. Losing your protective furry covering, standing on your two feet, vulnerable and immensely inventive and adaptable. Know now that this early ancestor of yours was able to master an alien and frequently cold environment, discovering language and art and music and tools. Jaws are thrust forward, and the body fully remembers the ape it has been so recently. And yet there is an ever-increasing intelligence and capacity to plan. All this is driving you as an early human to move away from the apparent immediacy of animal life into a whole new experience of being alive in the world. . . .

And as you fully experience the initiation of the early human coded within you, both male and female, let your brain be filled with the experiences of the reality that was and is encountered and the challenges that were met and overcome. [Five minutes.]

Gradually, you are evolving into a full human being. Notice how your senses become more or less refined. How do your movements change? And your questions? And your relationship to people and your environment?

Become more and more aware of the yearnings of developing and evolving human nature, wandering and moving into villages, beginning to trade and build cultures, telling stories and discovering the written word. Building civilizations, and yet still other civilizations on the ruins of even earlier civilizations. Using increasingly complex tools. . . . Your ideas becoming increasingly complex. . . .

Keep going, coming closer and closer to the present era, closer to yourself, with all the levels of awareness that you possess in this time and space. [Ten minutes.]

Now find yourself taking on the dimensions of a humanity that has within it an Odyssean nature, making it possible to meet divine beings and not be hurt by them.

[**Note to guides:** You might want to take a break and a stretch before continuing with Part 2.]

2. The Leap of Hermes and the Gifting of *Moly*

We find we now need more godly help, and so we call upon that part of Odysseus' story in which Hermes provides the opportunity to evolve the gods by causing Circe to recognize Odysseus as a worthy initiate in her Mysteries. We are going to enact the giving of the gift of *moly* by Hermes to Odysseus.

And we will play Hermes for each other in the fullness of our humanity, having had the initiation of fish, the initiation of amphibian, the initiation of reptile, the initiation of mammal, the initiation of sacred pig, the initiations of the early monkey and the great ape, the initiation of the early human.

As a full human being, feel all of the previous evolutionary stages in yourself. Can you feel them in your body? Can you feel them through your spine? How have your perceptions changed? What is your mood and sense of reality? Notice these things. . . .

[The guide can invite response from the participants here.]

Now as we play some wonderfully energetic music we are going to leap around the room in the leap of opportunity. Hermes, a god who opens to opportunity, is also a god of leaping—notice his winged sandals. There is something about the psychology and physiology of leaping that gets one into a state to appreciate the right moment of opportunity.

Remember too, that, like Odysseus, we are at the moment of *kairos* in which Hermes is leaping toward us. When the music stops, stop yourself and turn to whoever is nearest you, and give that person *moly.* Then receive the holy *moly* from that person as well. Thus, we will play both Hermes and Odysseus for each other.

INSTRUCTIONS FOR THE SOLO VOYAGER: Follow all the group instructions, especially those below. But as you are doing this, envision the presence of the god Hermes interacting with you. Recognize him by his shining, youthful beauty, his round winged bronze hat, and his winged sandals with the thongs wrapped high up his calves. Feel his loving power, his concern for your well-being, his urgent sense of *kairos.* Listen to what he says as he hands you the *moly.* Feel the freshness of the magical herb in your hands, sense its power connecting Heaven and Earth. What has Hermes told you of the qualities of this *moly*? What qualities of your own spiritual *moly* can you gift him in return? Each of you is growing and deepening the other. Hermes leaps toward you on his winged sandals and hands you the *moly* of ———. You leap toward Hermes, your step light and feathery, and you hand Hermes your *moly* of ———.

FOR THOSE WHO ARE WORKING IN GROUPS: Now how will you give and receive *moly*? In this enactment it will not be a plant pulled up from the ground or excavated from the rug. It will be instead a particular virtue or possibility or even magic. You might say, for example, when the music stops, and you find yourself near someone, "I give you the *moly* of loving-kindness." And that person might say to you something like, "I give you the *moly* of self-knowledge."

You will both stand there together, allowing yourselves to absorb these wonderful gifts. For know that the *moly* that you are giving and receiving is also the knowledge and capacity of the plant that reaches deep into the underground roots of reality and up into the world of the full blossoming of possibility.

Don't just give as *moly* some nice idea that occurs to you. Give rather what you know is truly your gift to give, just as Hermes, the god of *kairos,* of the right moment of action, gave that knowledge to Odysseus.

Now when music begins, start leaping into opportunity.

As full human beings, with the initiations of the totality of your animal past, now goodlier, more handsome, younger, and taller than before.

[**Note:** Play leaping music.]

Leaping. Leaping to the next opportunity.

[Stop the music after thirty to forty-five seconds.)

Now find someone near you and give the *moly* you have to give. Receive that person's *moly* fully in return.

Remember, you are giving a quality that you have yourself and therefore have available to give. The holy *moly.* Again, as an example, one of you might say, "I give you the *moly* of self-knowledge." The other might reply, "I give you the *moly* of a loving heart." All right now, give each other the *moly,* playing both Hermes and Odysseus to each other. [One minute.]

[Play the music again.] Leaping again now. Leaping into your opportunities. Leaping into all your possible worlds. [Thirty to forty-five seconds.]

[Stop the music.] Find the one with the *moly,* and say, "I give you the *moly* of ———." Give it and receive that person's gift of *moly* deeply. [One minute.]

[Begin the music again.] Leaping. Leaping. [Thirty to forty-five seconds.]

[Stop the music.] Find one with the *moly.* "I give you the *moly* of ———." [One minute.]

Now, when the music starts again, leap and leap and leap toward the extraordinary so that it is as if invisible gods are meeting you and giving you their *moly.* As if the archetypal worlds themselves are giving you their *moly.* This time the music will not stop. But at times you will know that you are being met by a god or archetype and then you will have to stop in the middle of the leap to receive deeply. And after receiving you will leap some more until again you find yourself receiving the *moly* from the depth world, from the world of gods and archetypes and those who have much to give you.

[Play the music again.]

And now leap again until you find yourself met and gifted with *moly,* and then leap again. And continue that for a while. [Two to four minutes, according to the observation and discretion of the guide.]

[The music shifts into a slower section.]

3. Union with the Archetype

Begin now slowly to turn in place, turning, turning. And while you turn, listening closely to these words.

With all this *moly* of virtues and possibilities that you have received from both human and depth realities, you are now prepared to meet and join with your archetype. This archetype can be considered in several ways. It might be felt as the god self who spoke for you as the Friend in Court. It may be known as the Beloved Friend within. It may be experienced as a divine presence whom you have met before in your life, or one you have yearned to meet. In what is about to happen the relationship between you and what we are calling the archetype will be deepened and matured—just as in the mythic, symbolic story told in *The Odyssey,* the meeting and union of Odysseus and Circe deepened both human and goddess.

Continue to turn now as you bring to this meeting the fullness of your human virtue with the added possibilities and qualities that you have gained from the gifts of *moly* received from each other and from the gods. . . . Not overwhelmed by the meeting, but enriching the sense of relationship to the archetype so the archetype can deepen you and can serve as a midwife of your soul.

And continuing to turn—or if you prefer, now moving into a dance—but meeting and deepening your relationship to the archetype. . . .

Ask the archetype to be careful not to overwhelm you. Together, you will move gently, gracefully into each other's presence, experiencing the joy of mutual presence and loving communion. And in so doing, deepening the archetype, helping him/her/it reach the next stage of archetypal evolution. And that is happening now. . . .

The two of you now dancing together. The rich knowledge and communion are flowing back and forth in the dance. . . .

The two of you dancing together now. You, the human being, are now deepening through the gifts of *moly* as well as the initiation of all the evolutionary stages, and thus are able to meet the archetype in communion. The archetype is deepening through your humanity as well as through your new ability to meet the archetype fully. . . .

Feel this initiation, this mutual deepening, going back and forth. The god, the goddess, the depth self, is being welcomed and grown beyond its archaic stuckness. Not losing the ancient qualities, but strengthening them so they are more available for present and future times. For in recapturing the earlier stages of evolution, you are no longer stuck in these stages. You have now found and experienced the growth and the genius of these stages in the fullness of your human life. . . . Both you and the archetype have recovered your pasts. Both of you are meeting each other as full beings in this present moment of holy time, this moment of sacred *kairos*. . . .

And so, having been initiated, know now that as it was in the beginning, is now and ever shall be, the human and the divine dance without end. . . .

[The music and the dance continue until a natural ending occurs. After some discussion and sharing of what occurred during this entire process, the guide suggests that the participants record their observations in their journals.]

CHAPTER 7

The Descent into the Underworld

ODYSSEUS and his men have been on the island of Circe "for the full circle of a year . . . and the seasons returned as the months waned, and the long days came in their course. . . ." Thus, according to the ancient ritual calendar, it is time for Odysseus, as the year king, to meet the challenge of death. Circe, out of ritual necessity, sets Odysseus the challenge of another initiation. She will give him directions to the Underworld and guidance on how to act once he is there.

Now, the Underworld of Homer as described in *The Iliad,* but most especially in *The Odyssey,* is the place where the ghostly double, the *eidolon,* of a person goes after death. Dismal and eternally dark, it is an enormous underground cavern inhabited by these ghosts of the joyless dead. It is also colorless, featureless, and without distinctions or social position. Everyone is leveled here regardless of his or her status in life. As in other religious traditions, punishment is meted out here to those who sinned in life—formidable and often ironic punishments are given to formidable sinners.

Thus, Tantalus, voracious in life, stands in water up to his chin, eternally thirsty as the water immediately evaporates when he tries to drink it. And when he seeks to eat of the fruit-bearing trees that surround him, the wind blows all the fruit away. (Dante's inspiration for his great poetic journey to the infernal region with his guide Virgil in *The Divine Comedy* clearly owes much to Homer.)

But there is deep knowledge here for the hero courageous enough to descend into this world. In the Hero's Journey, the descent into the Underworld is also a quest for special wisdom usually denied the living. Heroes—or in shamanic cultures, shamans—meet their relatives and sometimes very special entities as well who grant them this knowledge. Heroes who successfully return to the world of the living knowing these things have conquered their fear of death and thus often gain a kind of immortality. In shamanic cultures, they are now able to mediate between the living and the dead.

Odysseus is now ready for this initiation. Having met the biological ground of existence by seeing how easily men become earlier stages of development; having received the *moly* that disenchants the toxic brew so that he himself can enchant Circe; having entered into intimacy with the goddess, he will now be initiated into the realm of the ancestors. He knows the genesis and possibility of the species. But now he has to learn its history by entering into the realm of the dead to meet his predecessors. Only there can he gain the further self-knowledge required to continue with the stages of higher initiation that will ultimately allow him to go home to Penelope.

Circe tells him that he must particularly speak with the blind prophet Tiresias, for this great sage can acquaint him with the Mysteries of past and future and the riddle of birth and death. Unlike the others, who are merely shadows flitting about, Tiresias alone has been permitted to exist in full consciousness in the world of the dead.

It is interesting to note how modern esoteric traditions treat the theme of the initiations of Circe. For example, among the anthroposophists—the followers of the teachings of Rudolf Steiner—Circe is thought to be both priestess and magician, holding the remnants of Atlantean wisdom. As the daughter of Oceanus, she is descended from one of the three rulers of the mythic-symbolic kingdom of Atlantis (the others being Poseidon and Atlas). And Calypso, the other nymph that Odysseus will meet, is a daughter of Atlas. Thus, it is suggested that both these nymphs are keepers of the depth knowledge of the high civilization that was Atlantis. Further, according to Steiner, the Phaeacians are direct descendants of the people of Atlantis, still capable of using some of their technology: they have robots for servants and their ships go at immense speeds without pilots. Thus, the esoteric tradition implies that Odysseus is being initiated into the wisdom of the old high culture that had passed away—by the very inheritors of that culture.

Of course, most classical scholars believe that the story of the civilization and fall of Atlantis, as recorded in Plato, actually refers to the violent volcanic eruption that destroyed a great deal of the island of Minoan Thera (Santorini) and sent tidal waves and earthquakes throughout the Mediterranean area around 1450 B.C. (see page 45.) Atlantis buffs, however, think Thera was only the latest in a series of geological disasters, and that previous millennia had seen the fall of a much higher society that had obviously been located somewhere in the Atlantic Ocean. The remains of this land are said to be those outcroppings known as the Canary Islands. This tradition holds that the names of actual living Atlantean rulers—Atlas, Oceanus, Poseidon—were transmuted in race memory as the names for gods and Titans in the early Greek world.

I offer this information only as an aside that intrigues me. My own belief supports the notion that Circe and Calypso are indeed inheritors of an ancient culture, but one that recalls the goddess-centered culture of Old Europe, one that has much to teach the heroic spoilers of later eras, including the present one.

Whatever is true, however, there is no question that Circe is a hierophant—a priestess who directs the initiate onto the path to deeper realities. But while she can serve as a guide, she cannot herself participate in the Mysteries, and thus she cannot grant Odysseus inner knowing. But she can give him all the necessary external information he will need to find the entrance to the Underworld, the depth world. She can tell him how to sail to the limits of the known world and come to the city of the Cimmerians, shrouded in mists and cloud, and that there he must dig a trench in the Earth to offer his gifts for the dead.

Odysseus follows the instructions of his teacher, Circe, and he and his men arrive in the Underworld, where he pours out his offerings first of barley, wine, and honey, and then blood from the sacrifice of a black ewe and ram. The ghosts then press toward him, hoping to gain some brief substance and memory by partaking of the sacrifice. It was known in ancient Greece that blood is the vital part of life; thus, the shadows of the dead required it if they were going to regain even a fleeting chimera of living vitality. But Odysseus is not to permit any of them to drink until he has spoken with Tiresias.

The story of Tiresias offers us yet another initiatory theme. Blinded by Athena, according to the law of the gods, because he had inadvertently seen her bathing in a pool, he received from her some measure of recompense: gifts of prophecy and divination, a long life (some say seven generations), and the power to keep his mental faculties intact in the Underworld.

Another account tells us that Tiresias once saw two snakes copulating. He put his staff in between them, wounding them (some say he killed the female), and immediately became a woman. He remained a woman for eight years—having a wild and flagrant time of it from all accounts. Seven full years or the beginning of the eighth year symbolizes a whole lifetime, and Tiresias made the most of it. Then one day, as a woman, he/she was walking along and again saw two snakes copulating. Again Tiresias did the same thing, putting his staff between the two—this time killing the male—and was immediately turned back into a man.

Naturally, he became a marriage counselor. Everybody started asking him questions. What was it like being both sexes? Which was preferable and why? The gods themselves were fascinated. One day Zeus and Hera were having an argument about who enjoyed sexual intercourse more, a man or a woman. They decided to call upon Tiresias since he had definitely acquired the appropriate experience and knowledge. Tiresias answered their question by saying, "On a scale of one to ten, the woman has nine parts of the enjoyment, the man only one." Whereupon the infuriated Hera blinded him permanently.

Joseph Campbell tells a funny story about this divine encounter. He says that for years he couldn't quite understand why Hera would so overreact. But in one of his seminars a woman came up to him and said, "Mr. Campbell, I know why Hera blinded Tiresias in anger."

Campbell replied, "Really! Why, madam?"

And she replied, "Because she would no longer be able to say to Zeus—'I'm doing it for you, darling.' "

However it was that Tiresias came by his blindness, he gained the deep knowledge of "inner seeing" as well as the knowledge of the androgyne, the understanding that comes of being fully male and fully female. This entitled him to serve as guide to the Mysteries of life and death, past and future.

In traditions the world over, but especially in shamanic ones, the androgynous personality is thought to have access to unusual kinds of knowledge. In these cultures, be they Oceanic or Arctic, African or Latin American, it is often (but by no means always) the shaman of indeterminate sexuality who is regarded not as a pariah but as one whose ambiguity provides gifts of great value to his or her society. In many cases these shamans are encouraged, given special treatment and training in order to be able to speak to nature, to know the ways of special plants and healing herbs, to have the knowledge of past and future, to know the pathways of the world of death.

A critical religious myth may explain part of the wide appeal of the androgyne and the numinous quality that such a person manifests. It tells of the Creator who contains both sexes, and splits apart in order to imbue the inhabitants of the

Earth with the pattern of male and female. This myth, explicit in the Hindu *Upanishads,* and implicit in the biblical book of Genesis, has many variations in many cultures.

In ancient Greece, the myth of the androgyne finds its most poignant telling in Plato's *Symposium*. Here, at a drinking party celebrating love, the most comic of playwrights, Aristophanes, tells the most tragic tale. He says that human beings originally consisted of two persons in one body, with two heads and four arms and legs. These beings were shaped like a ball, and in their completeness and satisfaction, they rolled along in ecstasy, ready and able to do almost anything. However, the Titans, fearful of the enormous power available to these extraordinary double beings, forced Zeus to split them in half, thus diminishing both their powers and their happiness, and forcing them (us) to spend their lives yearning for the missing half. This little story offers a tragicomic explanation for an essential, primary experience of the human race: We are twinned but divided selves. And according to Plato we spend our lives looking for our other half.[1]

Around the concept of the androgyne, then, there is always the suspicion that this is one who is closer to the original bisexual nature of the Creator and therefore more complete in himself/herself, having greater power as well as access to the secrets of the universe.[2] With Tiresias, we have a classical Western example of this ancient, worldwide tradition.

The blind sage is able to tell Odysseus the meaning of his destiny, the reason for his wanderings, and the goal of his initiations. In doing this he provides Odysseus with a larger perspective on his own story. First, Tiresias informs him of the nature of his religious offense—angering Poseidon by blinding his son, Polyphemus, the Cyclops. Next, he indicates the flaw in Odysseus' character responsible for the offense. This is seen as an excess of passion, which Odysseus must learn to restrain in himself and his companions if he wishes to return home. This restraint, urges Tiresias, must particularly be enforced when he and his men reach the island where the cattle of the Sun are pasturing. He warns Odysseus that he will come home alone if his men eat any of these sacred cattle.

And he paints an unhappy picture of what Odysseus will find on his return to Ithaca, though he also promises him a comfortable old age and eventually a gentle death in the bosom of the sea. But Odysseus is also warned that he will not be able to remain in Ithaca forever. He will have to leave for a while, carrying an oar over his shoulder, wandering until he finds a people who are so far from the sea that they know nothing of oars. And when someone asks, "What is that big winnowing fan, that shovel?" he is to plant it on the spot. For with the oar he will be bringing the knowledge and authority of Poseidon to a place where the sea god is unknown. Only after this mission of atonement is carried out will he be allowed to return to Penelope and live out his days in Ithaca.

On a symbolic level, Tiresias can be seen as Odysseus' alter ego.[3] Both, after all, are connected by the motif of blindness. One is literally blind, and the other can be described as metaphorically blind. Odysseus falls asleep (into unseeingness) at two critical junctures on his journey home; first, when he hands over the ship to his men within sight of Ithaca and they open Aeolus' gift of the bag of winds. Odysseus' second lapse will occur later in the story, on the island of Helios, where his men do indeed eat the forbidden cattle. Then too, Odysseus' second big blunder, the first blunder being the sack of Ismarus, was the blinding of the Cyclops, Polyphemus. This act alone delayed Odysseus' homecoming by ten long years.

Now Tiresias is telling Odysseus of his *telos*—his destiny, his unfolding, his ultimate goal. On one level, *telos* refers to both future and goal—the kind of destiny that we inherit with our birth. But *telos* is also a word that is frequently used in the Mystery tradition, where it refers to perfection and initiation. The initiates at the Mysteries were called the *telestes*, the ones who were the journeyers on the road to transformation. Therefore, for those who would live a deeper life, *telos* becomes a more flexible term. One can take one's given destiny and, through the gaining of knowledge and the practice of spiritual development, re-form one's original *telos* into a higher, finer destiny.

The physically blind but spiritually sighted Tiresias guides the spiritually blind but physically sighted hero, Odysseus. Thus, this teletic journey into the Underworld, into self-knowledge, becomes, as all such journeys are, an inner journey in which Odysseus discovers for himself what he could always have known had he not been so heroically deluded through his excessive self-sufficiency and acquisitiveness.

Having been given teletic knowledge by the blind shaman of androgynous knowledge, Odysseus is now ready to meet the Mothers. These include his own mother, as well as the mothers of famous men—of Heracles and Oedipus, of Castor and Polydeukes, of Laius and Neleus—fourteen in all. Traditions in myth and legend are filled with episodes occurring in the Realm of the Mothers. This is also the everlasting sphere of womanhood that Heinrich Zimmer has described as "representative of the timeless abode of inexhaustible life, a well of death from which life pours forth in perennial rebirth. It is a mysterious locality that has been visited by numberless legendary and romantic heroes of the world, and can be recognized under many historical transformations and belongs to our universal treasure-store of archetypal symbolic images."[4]

The Realm of the Mothers is most commonly known to us through the Grail legends, which retain elements that have come down to us from the pre-Celtic matrifocal cultures and Mysteries. It is here that the knight, being wearied of his long adventure, discovers his rest in the feminine source level in which reposes the intuitive wisdom of the Life Force, which illumines what before had been uncanny and mysterious. There, all becomes clear. And yet, this realm is always described as one of static ecstasy, of great aesthetic beauty but no passion—a place of being rather than becoming—and thus it persists in perpetual melancholy. It is also known as the realm where there is no change, the realm from which no wanderer returns. However, when it is entered by an activating soul, like the Grail legend's Sir Gawain, it once again becomes a repository of spiritual treasures that facilitate psychic transformation.

In the Mystery tradition, the Realm of the Mothers represents the depth world where you receive archetypal ideas.

This demands a radical broadening of consciousness and perspective on the part of the successful hero who is sure in the ways of the world but weak in inner knowledge. Once the hero enters the Realm of the Mothers, he is often gifted with knowledge of the patterns of things, of the real biology of how the universe works. He is told by many of the Mothers, for instance, how they had been intimate with Zeus or some other god, and how their power and the power of their progeny came from those relationships. Odysseus, who himself has just emerged from a year-long intimacy with a depth goddess, can understand the necessary communion between gods and mortals.

Odysseus is overwhelmed with sadness, however, when told by the shade of his own mother, Anticleia, that she had not died a natural death in his absence. Rather, it was grief over the loss of him, yearning for his sweet and merry presence, that slowly bled dry her ability to continue living. This offers us a tragic confirmation of how Odysseus, whose name as we recall means "trouble," brings trouble to all who love him. While his loyal wife, Penelope, spends her nights in grieving for love of him, his mother actually dies for love of him.

Odysseus, who is recounting all this to the Phaeacians, interrupts his tale at this point, for it is midnight. He really wants to rest. But he is urged by his gracious hosts, Queen Arete and King Alcinous, to also relate his encounter with the World of the Fathers. He tells them that the ice-pale Persephone, whom he met with unspeakable dread, comes and leads away the shades of the Mothers. He then meets dead heroes from the most recent to the more distant past, beginning with the fallen heroes of Troy, including Agamemnon, Achilles, and Ajax.

Agamemnon recalls with horrible vividness his own death at the hands of his wife, Clytemnestra, whom he had left for ten years in charge of his kingdom of Mycenae. She and her lover had plotted and carried out his death, stabbing him in his bath immediately upon his return from Troy. Agamemnon's litany is one of unmitigated misogyny: "Let it be a warning even to you. Indulge a woman never, and never tell her all you know. Some things a man may tell, some he should cover up. Not that I see a risk for you Odysseus, of death at your wife's hands. She is too wise, too clear-eyed, sees alternatives too well."[5] Still, Agamemnon advises Odysseus not to trust even Penelope—when he finally gets to Ithaca, he should bring his ship to shore secretly, "for there is no longer any faith in women."

Ajax will not even talk to him, his silence being an eloquent expression of how he had been so humiliated by Odysseus in Troy that he committed suicide.

In seeing Odysseus alive and well, and yet able to visit Hades, the greatest of Greek warriors, Achilles, is reminded of the ultimate pain of being dead and pronounces his fundamental despair when he says the famous words: "It is better to be a slave of a stranger and to serve a poor man on a miserable farm than to be a ruler over all the dead!"[6] This is the death knell of the heroic mentality that can become neither conscious nor comfortable in depth realms. In my opinion, it is not a statement of the futility of death but rather a recognition that the heroic mind can only assert itself in the world of space and time and cannot look inward into the timeless, spaceless realm.

Then Odysseus tells of his meeting with the legendary Fathers: Minos, Orion, Tantalus, Tityos, Sisyphus, and Heracles. Again, the theme of pain is reiterated: Tantalus is caught in a hell of endless craving; Sisyphus in a task of endless striving; while Tityos, whose belly is continually being eaten by vultures, sums it up as eternal agony. Those who have active tasks, like Orion, hunting with his quarry, or Minos, passing judgments, are at least useful and content. But what Odysseus finds, over and over again, is the pain given to others by his own heroic identity and the pain and futility shared by all the heroic Fathers. There is no way to be a hero that is not etched in the acid bath of anguish and meaninglessness.[7]

This realization moves Odysseus beyond his own time into

a new society. He finds himself especially engaged by Heracles, the hero whom he most closely resembles in terms of challenges and tests, of adventures taken and endured. Heracles tells Odysseus how, as the last of his twelve labors, he was directed to bring Cerberus, the triple-headed hound of hell, up from Hades to the upperworld, and how he was able to accomplish this deed with the help of Hermes and Athena.

This is a striking point, for in fact it is only the shadow of Heracles telling this story. The soul of Heracles, his essential being, has been transmuted into a demi-god living in great happiness with the Immortals on Mount Olympus. In his lifetime, Heracles has gone into the depth world and returned. Heracles has suffered and endured to the point that he, unlike many of the other heroes, has acquired inward knowledge, and therefore he is no longer only a shadow, no longer primarily a shade, the way Achilles is. Heracles' essential spirit went to the realm of the gods and became an Immortal. His is the step beyond Archilles.

We learn at this point that Odysseus too has a Heraclean destiny, for he is also destined to become a demi-god with Hermes and Athena as his guides. Hermes is the god who evokes the will, while Athena instructs Odysseus in considered thought and mindfulness, as well as in the ability to change form and process whenever needed. Hermes guides the initiate into the Underworld and along the path of the Mysteries. Athena guides the initiate to the supra world, the world of civilization and enlightenment. Together, Athena and Hermes help to inaugurate the new Greek epoch, which, at this point of *c.* 720 B.C., is about to begin. The Greeks are on the verge of the Golden Age of consciousness and high civilization, one that can be at once both mythical and historical, both given to the knowledge of the way things work in the world (Greek arts, science, letters, statecraft) as well as to the archetypal patterns and forms behind things (Greek philosophical thought).

Odysseus, who is learning to be conscious in the depth world, and to be mindful, a master of the ways and means, the arts and the sciences, of the breadth world, is the First Man of the coming epoch. In his painful initiation in the Underworld, he comes to the self-knowledge of his own responsibility to other individuals in his world. Without this knowledge, civilization would be impossible, and the luminous culture of Hellenic times might never have happened.

From this perspective, a tremendous amount is going on, for Odysseus is to be the first representative of this high civilization. He met eleven heroes and demi-gods in Hades—and he himself will eventually become the twelfth—a mortal who will be granted immortality, the man who completes the mythic number. Again, whenever you find the number twelve—be it the twelve ships of Odysseus, the twelve labors of Heracles, or the twelve principle heroes, you have a statement of conjunction with cosmic forces.

And as Odysseus is deepened and transformed, so too is Hermes awakened out of his trickery, Athena weaned of her belligerence, and the rest of the gods activated into more evolved archetypal principles. For a civilization can only become as great as the archetypal patterns with which it endows its gods and its depth principles. A magnificent mutuality is beginning to occur between gods and humans, with each priming the other to new growth in responsibility and a true wisdom that comes of suffering. This, I believe, is the meaning of this extraordinary descent into the Underworld. It is the key to the Mystery drama of *The Odyssey.*

Journey in the Underworld

(*Becoming Tiresias/Entering the Realm of the Ancestors and the Archetypal Principles*)

TIME: Sixty minutes.

MATERIALS NEEDED: None.

MUSIC: "Eric's Theme" from *Chariots of Fire* or some other musical selection of slow grandeur and mystery. For the walk into the Realm of the Ancestors, Irene Pappas singing *Odes* works well, as does any music that has an archaic and mysterious sound or chant-like quality.

INSTRUCTIONS FOR THE SOLO VOYAGER: First, read the script for the guide for inspiration and suggestions. You may want to tape this script with appropriate musical background—leaving sufficient pauses for sensing and knowing. However, instead of working with a partner in the exercise called "Becoming Tiresias," you will call up the inner essence of your own innate maleness and femaleness. You may want to work with images of some admired person of the opposite sex and another of the same sex as yourself for inspiration in accessing your inner knowingness. Or you may want to close your eyes and image. Or you may simply want to feel, sense, the different knowings.

Now, as you experience these deep, essential changes of beingness, you will write three dialogues in your journal:

Dialogue Number One—with Your Male Self: This will express your fresh, new awareness of maleness. Feel male awareness flooding into your beingness. If you are male becoming male, try to feel what this is like for the very first time. If you are female becoming male, is there anything new and totally surprising about this form of embodiedness? What are you discovering as you enter into your masculine self, your right-side, solar knowing? How do you carry your body; how does it move; how does it feel to you; where is your center of gravity? How do you see the world; how does your mind think; what do your eyes perceive? How do you feel about yourself? What are your triumphs, your joys? What are your wounds?

When you are ready, dialogue with your male self in your journal.

Dialogue Number Two—with Your Female Self: Feel your male self powerfully first, and then feel female awareness flooding into your beingness. Be a man learning how it feels to be a woman. If you are male becoming female, is there anything new and totally surprising about this form of embodiedness? If you are a woman making this leap into otherness, try to sense what it is like being a woman for the very first time.

What are you discovering as you enter into your female self, your left-side, lunar knowing? How do you carry your body; how does it move; how does it feel to you; where is your center of gravity? Is there anything new and totally surprising about this form of embodiedness? How do you see the world; how does your mind think; what do your eyes perceive? How do you feel about yourself? What are your triumphs, your joys? What are your wounds?

When you are ready, dialogue with your female self in your journal.

Dialogue Number Three—with Your Tiresias Self: From being a woman, now shift your awareness wholly back to your male self, your right-side knowing. No longer someone else sensing being a man, but being wholly and entirely male. Be there for a few moments. Being wholly male. Write in your journal how this whole maleness feels.

From this perspective, now shift back to femaleness, your left-side knowing. No longer someone else sensing being a woman, but being wholly and entirely female. Be there for a few moments. Being wholly female. Write in your journal how this whole femaleness feels.

Shift back and forth several times. Are there are any new and interesting developments as you become more and more accustomed to being fully male and fully female? Fully male. . . . Fully female. . . . Fully male. . . . Fully female. . . . Both male and female. . . . Wholly male and female. . . . Wholly yourself. . . . Wholly your Tiresias self. . . . Wholly your Tiresias self—the one who has experienced both sides, now embodied in a richer, fuller sense of self.

When you are ready, write in your journal. Write as Tiresias—your whole self, your true self. How did it feel being male becoming female? How did it feel being female becoming male? How did it feel to be newly aware of your maleness if you are a man? How did it feel to be newly aware of your femaleness if you are a woman? Have you learned something new and fascinating and exciting about yourself from being the other? Have you learned something new and fascinating and exciting about yourself from being who you are, but with fresh perceptions?

What have you learned from your bothness, your wholeness, your Tiresias self? Speak with this whole self, this wit and wisdom of "seeing both sides now." What can you bring from this knowing into your life now to enrich it?

The second part of the exercise, "Entering the Realm of the Ancestors," can be done by taping and then following the instructions.

SCRIPT FOR THE GUIDE: Will the men in this group please gather in a circle facing outward.

Now, will the women in the group move to the circle, each woman facing a man.

[**Note:** Should there be more women than men or more men than women, the guide will suggest that a number of women stand opposite each man, or a number of men stand opposite each woman.]

When the music begins to play, each person will become like Tiresias, experiencing something of what it is like to be the opposite sex.

And I will ask each woman to look at the man opposite her and to become a man. And I will ask each man to look at the woman opposite him and become a woman. And the man who is actually a woman will be looking at the man who has become a woman.

And the man who has become a woman will look at the woman standing opposite as a man.

So you will become your opposite gender and you will see the person across from you as the opposite gender from what that person actually is.

This will be experienced as an exchange of the essence of being male or being female—the Tiresias exchange. And then at a certain point, which I will indicate, you will resume your original gender. And then I will guide you into the Realm of the Ancestors.

As the music starts, the women will look at the men. The men will look at the women. And very gradually, as the exchange of essence occurs, the man will become a woman looking at a man and the woman will become a man looking at a woman. I'll repeat. The woman will become a man looking at the man as a woman. And as a woman, the man will look at the woman as a man. Each will have the perspective of the opposite sex.

Let this exchange of gender now take place. Let the great exchange, the mystery of Tiresias, take place. The exchange is happening now.

["Eric's Theme" from *Chariots of Fire* or a similar piece is played at this point. After the piece ends the guide will say:]

And it is said that when Tiresias met Odysseus, having as he did the knowing of both genders, he was able to tell Odysseus the meaning of his destiny and the reason for his wanderings and the goal of his initiation. He told him how he had angered Poseidon when he had put out the eye of his son Polyphemus. He told him he would come home alone if he or his men ate of the cattle of the Sun, and the havoc he would find in Ithaca. But he promised Odysseus a comfortable old age and a death near home at sea.

He also told him that he would not immediately be able to stay at Ithaca, but would have to leave for a while, carrying an oar over his shoulder, wandering inland until he found a people who knew nothing about the sea. And when someone asked—"What is that big shovel?"—then he was to plant it. Because that was the knowledge of Poseidon that he would plant, the knowledge of the oar and the sea, and then he'd be allowed to live a normal life again.

So Tiresias gives Odysseus his destiny, his unfolding, his *telos,* a word you find in the Mystery tradition, referring to the perfection of the initiate who knows past and future, who knows male and female, who knows life and death.

And now the male and female partners are moving toward each other. The woman who has been the man and the man who has been the woman are moving toward each other, becoming themselves again. And now, as who you are, share with each other some of the initiatory knowledge that you have gained in this meeting and exchange.

Speak to each other, share what you have learned in the exchange. First, speak of the knowledge of having become male or having become female. Then, share if you will any other kind of insight about the nature of life and death, or past and future, that may have come to you during the exchange of Tiresias. Share this *telos* knowledge, the knowledge of the *teleste*, of the initiate. [Ten minutes.]

Now stand up and begin to part from each other, and with your eyes closed or half closed, move slowly around this room.

THE REALM OF THE ANCESTORS

With your eyes closed or half closed, now begin to walk backward. Like Odysseus, you will be entering the Realm of the Ancestors, and, perhaps, communing with them and receiving some of their knowings.

[The chanting section from Vangelis' "Odes" is very effective played here and throughout the rest of this process. Should "Odes" not be available, a good substitute would be the first half of Vangelis' "Ignacio." In any case music with mystery and power should be selected for playing here.]

So please close or half close your eyes now and begin to walk backward. First you will begin by walking into the Realm of the Mothers, some of whom will be ancestors, some not. Walking back and back and back. . . .

Occasionally you will meet with someone with whom you will speak. Perhaps it will be someone, a woman from your own ancestry, who has passed on, your grandmother or great-grandmother, or an ancestress from hundreds or even thousands of years ago.

Perhaps it will be a wise woman from the past from whom you are not descended but who desires to reach you. Whoever it is, she will tell you something that you will wish to hear, and you will just stop and stand or sit with her a few moments and commune and be together. You will sense the presence of this ancestress or friend of yours from the Realm of the Mothers. Continue to walk back now and call forth the presence of this spirit from the Realm of the Mothers. Walk backward and as you do becoming utterly available to her presence. And when you sense her you may then wish to sit and commune with her. After you have been with her, resume your walking backward in the Realm of the Mothers until you meet someone else. . . . Should you bump into another participant, just continue to move backward.

You may go back one hundred years or two hundred, five hundred, or one thousand. Or perhaps even as far back as the time of that early Goddess Culture of Old Europe or Old Africa or Old Asia.

You will be led to the right ones who will speak to you, who will be with you now. And when that happens, you will either stand or sit and be with them for a few moments until the communication of mind or heart has been given. And then you will again resume walking backward.

But now, having experienced the Mysteries of Tiresias—the exchange and the fullness of the genders, the past and future of life and death—much more can be told you than was possible yesterday or even today. [Five to ten minutes.]

Whenever you feel it's appropriate, begin walking into the Realm of the Fathers; walking backward into the realm of the knowledge of the Fathers. Back across hundreds and even thousands of years. Communing with the Father ancestors, just as Odysseus communed with the heroes.

Do this at your own pace. Continue in the Realm of the Mothers until it seems appropriate for you to enter into the Realm of the Fathers. . . .

Enter into the World of the Fathers. Some of them may be ancestors, some not. The World of the Fathers. And if you sense the presence of one, stop and stand or sit for a few moments, conferring and exchanging essence and knowing of mind or of heart. The World of the Fathers. . . . [Five to ten minutes.]

In this journey in the Underworld we are also able to encounter the depth world of pattern, the world of the archetypal principles—of Athena and Hermes and Zeus and the guides and the gods. The depth realm. The realm where all the patterns of existence are contained.

And it may be that you find yourself charged and seized by one of the great principles of existence, one of the great creative forces. Whether seen as god or archetype, or as pure essence of love, or of beauty, or knowledge, or creativity. And if you feel that sense of Presence, stop and be with that great principle or archetype or goddedness. Walk back now into the Realm of Patterns. . . . [Five minutes.]

Continue to journey in this world that contains the Realm of the Mothers, the Realm of the Fathers, the Realm of Pattern. But this time, whatever presence you sense you can now stop and meet. . . . [Five minutes.]

Having seen these things, having journeyed in these realms, one is exalted by the words of the Eleusinian Mysteries: *"Oide men bio teleutan, oiden de di-os-doton archan"*—Blessed are you who have known these things. You know the end of life and you know the God-given beginnings. *"Oide men bio teleutan oiden de di-os-doton archan."*

Begin to walk forward now, forward through hundreds or even thousands of years until you get to the present time. Travel forward now through the timeless realms and through the millennia and the centuries. Now carrying with you the essence of those whom you have encountered in the World of the Fathers, the World of the Mothers, the World of Patterns and the archetypes. . . . [Two minutes.]

When you reach the present time, stretch out your arms in a circular arc, for you are harvesting the essence of all these ancient ones, all the timeless ones. This is the Mystery of the depth realm. You have harvested its essence and are bringing it into the world. . . .

And now, reach forward to your future descendants—either to the children of your flesh or to the children of your mind or spirit, or to both. Take steps forward to them. And give what you have gained from the depth realms to them. . . .

For somewhere in the realm of space-time, in a realm that we may even call the future, there is perhaps a descendant of yours, a descendant of your body or of your mind and spirit, who is reaching back to you and making contact. And you are reaching to them. For you are in the depth realm and you are giving them of your wisdom and your knowledge. And they are receiving from you profoundly now. . . . [Two minutes.]

And, in return, they are sharing themselves, giving to you of their wisdom and knowledge. And you are receiving from them profoundly now. . . . [Two minutes.]

Having been received by your ancestors and giving to and receiving from your descendants of mind or body, come back to the threshold of this time and this place. For you have descended into the Underworld and received the initiation of Tiresias and the communications with the ancient ones. You can now begin the journey back to your True Home.

Returning. Returning through these Cimmerian plains. Returning through the land of frost, and the portals of the depths. Returning to the surface. Bring with you this knowledge. Having received this initiation.

Returning.

[The guide will then inquire into how everyone is. After a break for writing or reflection, a discussion can follow.]

CHAPTER 8

The Sirens, Scylla and Charybdis, and the Cattle of Helios

ODYSSEUS returns from the underworld to be met on the shore by Circe. She hails him and his crew as "men overbold, who have gone alive into the house of Hades, to know death twice, while all men else die once. . . ." This qualifies them to learn how to survive the most dangerous initiatory rituals they have yet to undergo—the pathway to the Island of the Sun. Circe gives precise instructions of the way and warns them of its dangers.

Many commentators have taken this section to be just one more series of horrific adventures on the Road of Trials, but I see it as very clear guidance by Circe, in her higher role as "She who shows the sacred way" to the heart of the Mysteries. I believe the Island of the Sun, where graze the sacred cattle of Helios, is a metaphor for the ultimate stage of enlightenment. Circe knows that the exquisite dangers and tortures of making one's way to this sacred island serve as a

Western version of the fierce austerities an Eastern seeker undergoes in the quest for enlightenment. However, she also recognizes in Odysseus one who is capable of receiving that final illumination—if he chooses.

Again, *The Odyssey* represents a critical stage in consciousness in which both men and gods are being grown. As previously indicated, Circe as Enchantress belongs to a much earlier tradition in which the hero-consort of the queen or goddess would be ritually killed, and then, often as not, ritually renewed. Instead of literal death, however, Odysseus, as the goddess's consort of the year, enters the world of the dead to gain conscious, living knowledge of the Mysteries of death. Upon his return, she can set him on the path of the highest revelation in the world of the here and now. For Odysseus "insists upon living as a man, not dying into divinity, with all that that insistence implies of an individual consciousness emergent from the confines of collective understanding."[1]

Such an emergent consciousness requires knowledge of the things of the Earth, and so Circe tells Odysseus how to listen for that knowledge without being destroyed by it. He must sail past the land of the Sirens, and listen to their call, which is itself the lure of knowledge. It is said by the Sirens that he "who has heard them leaves knowing more."[2] Further, they give knowledge too "of all that comes to pass on the fruitful earth."[3] This is an immense temptation, and I know of few people, myself included, who wouldn't risk everything to listen in. To modern knowledge seekers it would feel as if we had been given access to all the programs available in the ultimate universal computer.

The Sirens' role is not unlike that of the snake in the Garden of Eden. Both promise nothing less than complete understanding of the patterns that rule existence. But the knowledge in the Sirens' song is as dangerous as that in Genesis. Eating of the fruit of the Tree of Knowledge of Good and Evil means that Adam and Eve are now vulnerable to aging and death—the expulsion from Eden—just so has the thrilling song of the Sirens brought only destruction to the ancient mariners. Such knowledge is clearly more than the ordinary human mind can contain, for theirs is a burning intelligence that will singe the mind away. Indeed, the Greek word *seirios* (siren) means "burning," and their shores are laden with the shriveled skins and scorched bones of mariners who were unable to assimilate this fiery knowing.

As in the biblical book of Genesis, this is a knowing that only a god or a godlike being can withstand. Yahweh declares that "the man is become as one of us, to know good and evil" (3:22). The sense of fiery knowing reminds us also of the *Bhagavad Gita,* when the charioteer Krishna reveals himself to his spiritual pupil, Arjuna, in the blazing radiance of his full being—the god Vishnu. The words of the *Gita,* which describe the epiphany of Vishnu as "brighter than a thousand suns," were poignantly quoted in the 1940s by J. Robert Oppenheimer upon seeing the first atomic bomb test at Los Alamos.

The siren call of the knowledge of atomic energy also devastates—and in precisely the same way. Witness the shriveled bodies and scorched skins of those irradiated by the creations of other humans who had gained the fiery knowing of atomic release. One of the anguished harrowings of our century is that this immensely thrilling and seductive call to knowledge may also carry a power capable of destroying an entire world of listeners.

Happily, the word "siren" also carries less fearsome resonances. In Greek, as Aristotle tells us, it can refer to a species of wild bee. This reference opens a whole other world of symbols. In Egypt, the bee is the symbol of the Pharaoh. In a famous Hittite myth, which tells of the disappearance of the god Telepinuu, an eagle is sent to find him, but fails to do so; whereupon the bee is given the task of locating the vanished deity. In other words, if the eagle fails, bring in the bee. And this bee is told, "Take wax and cleanse him. Make him pure, make him holy, and bring him unto me." Thus, in the ancient world, the bee and its wax possessed the powers of purification.[4]

The bee is also recognized as an emblem for the priestesses of that time, especially those attending to the cults of Demeter and Persephone, Phrygian Cybele, and the goddess Artemis, for whom the bee served as her very insignia.[5] On many ancient Greek coins you may find an engraving of a bee, symbol of the purification of the city whose medium of exchange the coin represents.

So it is that Odysseus is warned by Circe to fill the ears of his men with "sweet wax of honey"—that is, with purification—so that they cannot hear the siren call and be lured to follow it. The beeswax will also ensure that the crewmen maintain their innocent ignorance of the great interconnecting patterns of things. But if Odysseus wants to receive the godlike knowledge from the "honey-sweet" voices of the Sirens, he must be lashed to the mast so that he will not be able to jump overboard and rush to join those other listeners who stayed to hear more of the sweet fire than humans can endure, and whose bodies now are strewn on the shores.

Hungry, even desperate, for knowledge, Odysseus nevertheless has no wish to be burned on the rocks. Yet, when the "honey-sweet" voices call to him with promises of "knowing more than he ever did," he indicates by many extravagant facial expressions that his wax-deaf shipmates should untie him and let him go. They, however, obey his original instructions, which had been given to him by Circe, and instead of loosening his ropes, they add a few more bindings to lash him even more securely to the mast.

In Hellenistic times (300 B.C. and later) storytellers identified the siren song as the music of the spheres, which, once heard, so enraptures the hearer that all earthly tasks are forgotten. And so it seems to have proven with Thomas Aquinas. Once in Naples, while he was serving mass, this brilliant author of the most comprehensive theological works of the Middle Ages heard the siren song of transcendent knowing. And it finished him with his work forever.

One can imagine this huge man, said to weigh well over three hundred pounds and to stand taller than anyone around, sitting there dumbly, his mouth fallen open in perpetual astonishment, staring into space. He had heard the siren of mystical knowledge. His friend urged him again and again to speak, to tell what was happening. Finally, Aquinas replied,

"Reginald, I cannot tell you. For what I have heard and seen has made all of my other work seem like straws, mere chaff to be blown away." He died several weeks later at the age of forty-nine.

There seems to be no doubt that the lure of knowledge, the yearning to hear the music of the spheres, the all-encompassing search for a sense of the patterns of things, when pursued for their own sakes, can divert or even destroy the realization and accomplishment of our true purpose.

Have you too searched for knowledge, or for certain kinds of transcendent experiences, so far and so wide that you have lost sight of, or forgotten, your original goals? Then you have known the siren's call and understood it as the most seductive, the most persuasive, perhaps even the most passionate of calls. This hunger for knowing has become so widespread that it is small wonder that the cultural historian and philosopher Oswald Spengler defined the present stage of modern consciousness as the Faustian age, the age of those for whom the search for knowledge is everything.

What forms have the search for knowledge taken for you and your friends? Some of the answers I have received to this question have been: An extra five years in graduate school. Becoming a nun and entering the convent. LSD trips. Rock music as a call to some kind of transcendence. Organized religion that professed to have all the answers. Religious cults that professed to have all the answers. New Age metaphysics. Endless psychoanalysis. Endless workshop attendance. Traveling and more traveling. And the most frequent response of all—perhaps because it is a response I share and therefore never fail to hear others mention—not being able to pass a bookstall without buying something, certain that somewhere, in some book, I will find The Truth. These are the forms of the sirens' calls.

No sooner has Odysseus successfully made it past the sirens than he and his men find themselves in the immense dangers of the passageway between the cliffs where Scylla and Charybdis reside. Scylla, a many-headed, slavering, man-eating monster, lives in a dark cave on the sheer cliff face of one side of the sea lane; while Charybdis, a powerful, spouting, ship-destroying whirlpool, lurks at the bottom of the other cliff. These are the most fearful monsters since the Cyclops, and both of them are considered female.

Circe has warned Odysseus of these perils and advised him privately that he will have an easier time of it (and lose fewer men) if the ship veers in the direction of Scylla. She has six heads, therefore a maximum devouring capacity of only six men at a time. If they row like mad—and Odysseus resists the temptation to stop and fight—most of them will get through. Charybdis, on the other hand, is an absolute threat to the entire ship and all of its crew.

These two "perils" represent the powers of attraction and repulsion in their most symbolically destructive forms, the snatching monster and the boiling maelstrom. In Hellenistic times these images were taken to mean the dangerous and narrow path between the rock of rational, logical thought and the abyss of mysticism, through which many seekers after truth skirt a very chancy passage.

These perils, however, can also represent a dangerous voyage between decisions for many successful professionals, to whom success has come ostensibly because they have worked consistently and well in one particular focused mode or manner. And yet, there also exists a fatal, and usually growing, attraction to letting that focused success be maniacally spilled, spewed out, and dispersed all over the universe. Shot, as the saying goes, "to hell and gone!"

Do you too share this sense of being pulled apart—or of wanting to be pulled apart—by opposing forces? Anything will do, so long as it allows you to stop being steady, responsible, reliable—and bored. We seem to search out an opportunity to sail past monsters who will threaten to grab bits and pieces of our lives, chew them up, and swallow them down, belching with delight. Witness the number of successful and "happy" people who risk their reputations, their families, and even their lives, by indulging in a search for "tanginess" in inappropriate places and conditions.

On the other hand, you may prove so dedicated to remaining safe and protected that all risk-taking, life-enhancing capacities are lost. Any encroachment by the wide world becomes an invasion, and in time your ability to enter the wide world shrivels and dies. In some ways, Odysseus had it lucky. He and his men wanted to get home, and there was only one way to go. They had to take that narrow passageway; the sea made it impossible for them to go back or to hide from either the danger or the decision. We may avoid making the necessary decisions for many long years, but sooner or later the time comes when we must go forward and take our chances with the monsters.

If you make it safely past Scylla (or if you lose only six men) then you may find yourself in the maw of Charybdis, who sucks the whole ship of your life down, down, down, and who, when you feel yourself split apart, spits you back up again all over the landscape. Have you ever had nightmares about the times you barely made it past—or failed to make it past—Scylla and Charybdis? Do you feel yourself presently caught in habits or patterns whose effect on your life seem as monstrous as the images conjured up by these two horrors?

Scylla and Charybdis also bring up the issue of the destructive power of the feminine. Throughout *The Odyssey* we alternate between experiences of the feminine powers that are ultimately nurturing and those that threaten ghastly destruction. The battle we endured during our brief but painful visit to the Laestrygonians is reechoed here as we navigate the awesome passage between Scylla and Charybdis. Both the destructive feminine and the nurturing feminine must give us—men *and* women—their initiations. And if we are unable or unwilling to prepare for and undergo the initiations of all aspects of the Divine Feminine so that we may understand and celebrate our full lives on this Earth, these initiations will come to us and take us, often unpleasantly, by surprise.

Part of the initiation that prepares us for the enlightenment offered by the Island of the Sun is to experience fully our dread of the destructive feminine power and to face her in her wildest, fiercest behavior. As pained and grief-stricken witness, yes, certainly—but not as fighter. This is the advice Circe gives Odysseus when she prepares him for this stage of the journey. Odysseus of course wants to stop and do battle with Scylla when she attacks:

> But the goddess only cried out at me as an obstinate fool, always spoiling for a fight and welcoming trouble. "So you are not prepared," she said, "to give in even to immortal gods? I tell you, Scylla was not born for death: the fiend will live forever. She is a thing to shun, intractable, ferocious, and impossible to fight. No; against her there is no defence, and valour lies in flight. . . . So drive your ship past with all your might, and call on Cratias, Scylla's mother, who brought her into the world to prey on men. She will prevent her from making a second sally."[6]

Thus we learn that Scylla is virtually an immutable force. Still, *she has a mother,* Cratias—a death-dealing force of resentment and revenge from the old Mother cultures. And Cratias, if called upon at the moment of greatest need, can be persuaded to lessen Scylla's hostility to the patriarchal sailors and reduce their loss. This passage—like most of *The Odyssey*—is itself a veritable whirlpool, or a bottomless chasm in which we can submerge ourselves in our search for possible meanings. But it is both possible and enriching to understand that every female figure in *The Odyssey* represents an aspect of the Great Goddess. Thus, the true Hero must meet her as one willing to undergo all of her initiations in order to prove worthy of the title "human being."

In earlier civilizations, the women and priestesses mediated the death-bringing side of the Great Mother through ritual practices. In the time of the Heroic Age, though, the patriarchal influences were still in intense conflict with the power of the Mother Goddess, and the two—or three, or a thousand—faces of the Mother had already suffered a radical split. No longer known as life-bringer, life-sweetener, life-destroyer in one being (and therefore as a true mirror of the universe), now she was seen as one or the other—Holy Virgin, or Sex Goddess, or Destroyer. Her power—and the power of women, who also suffered this split and its accompanying projections—was thus cruelly undermined, with, I believe, disastrous consequences for the world. Thus, Homer writes of Scylla and Charybdis as the kinds of females we fear either to recognize in ourselves or to face in others: all-devouring monsters or whirlpools of overwhelming power. And that is all they are allowed to be. The men are terrified by and helpless in this encounter.

Sailing past Charybdis, the men turn green with fear as the violence of the vortex reveals the very bottom of the sea. Odysseus has of course managed to forget Circe's injunction about arming himself, and he stands on the deck in his fine "harness," with a spear in each hand, hoping to see Scylla before she sees them. While the men are mesmerized by the yawning horror of the boiling, hissing cauldron that is Charybdis, the monster Scylla snakes out of her cave and plucks up six of Odysseus' finest remaining men, one in each of her mouths. Before anyone has time to react, she hauls them to her cave and gobbles them up for all to see. Their last words are "Odysseus!"

"They were screaming and reaching out their hands to me in this horrid encounter," Odysseus told the Phaeacians. "That was the most pitiful scene that these eyes have looked on in my sufferings as I explored the routes over the water."[7] Again, as with the episode with the Cyclops, the image of the dangerous cave represents the place where the aboriginal one snatches and devours human flesh while guarding a threshold, a scene that recurs in folk tales and nightmares the world over.

Having safely negotiated these feminine perils—or at least made it through with the smallest possible sense of loss—Odysseus and his men come at last to the Island of the Sun, about which both Circe and Tiresias had given a very specific warning: The men must not eat of the sacred cattle belonging to Helios. This represents Odysseus' final test along the Road of Trials—and his most important decision. The Island of the Sun, the Island of Helios, represents the Golden Door to ultimate illumination. Once one has passed through this symbolic door in the journey of transformation, one can never return.

In light of this, we can interpret the three adventures immediately preceding as preparations for a form of enlightenment such as the yogis of the East know. That may explain the harrowing tests offered on this part of the journey. At some level, Odysseus knows he is at a place of ultimate decision. He does not want to stop at this island, knowing how dire the warnings from Tiresias and Circe were. But his exhausted men beseech him to give them a rest, to stop long enough to let them regain their strength, to mourn the ones they have lost, to eat in peace some of the supplies Circe provided.

Homer gives their speaker, Eurylochus, a speech as persuasive and poignant as any in literature:

> Odysseus . . . you are one of those hard men whose spirit never flags and whose body never tires. You must be made of iron through and through to forbid your men, worn out by labour and by lack of sleep, to set foot on dry land, with the chance of cooking themselves a cheerful supper on this seagirt isle. Instead, you expect us, just as we are, to go blindly on through the night that is overtaking us and put leagues of fog and sea between the island and ourselves. What of the high winds that spring up at night and do such harm to shipping? What port could we make to save ourselves from foundering if we were hit by a sudden squall from the south or west? There's nothing like the South Wind or the wicked West for smashing up a ship. And they don't ask leave of our lords the gods! No, let us take our cue now from the evening dusk and cook our supper. We won't stray from the ship, and in the morning we can get on board once more and put out into the open sea.[8]

Although everyone applauded these remarks, Odysseus had the presentiment that some huge calamity was soon to hit them all. But there was nothing for him to do but agree, and to get them to promise to stay near the ship and not go near the sacred sheep and cattle. After disembarking, they eat of the provisions that Circe had provided and then fall to weeping over their lost comrades until "sweet sleep overtook them in their tears."

Throughout the journey, at every stage and with every loss, Odysseus and his men mourn the crewmates who have been wrecked or drowned or eaten by monsters. They call out or recite the names of those lost companions, weep for them and grieve for them. So must we as we make the journey of transformation through our lives, for the parts of ourselves that are shorn away or engulfed by our experiences need and deserve to be named, mourned, and remembered.

The option is clear: Odysseus can end his journey at the Island of the Sun, the Golden Door. At this point he has successfully fulfilled the rigorous requirements of certain spiritual initiations. In addition to his earlier tests and learnings, he has now passed the Sirens of all-encompassing knowledge and found his way past fierce polarities and feminine aspects of destruction. Now he stands at the place of the Sun, the place of illumination. His option here would have been to take the path of India and the East and accede to the final illumination.

An interesting parallel offered in this passage is the fact that the cattle here are sacred, as they are in India; they are guarded by the goddess-nymphs who are daughters of the Sun God.[9] (Now Helios, the Sun God, was not an Olympian God but a Titan, whose activity was limited to driving his fiery chariot across the sky and witnessing good and evil deeds during the course of his journey. He did not have the importance of the far more complex solar god Apollo, and gradually his cult was absorbed into that of the Olympian.) We are not told what it is that has made the cattle sacred except that the Sun God loves to look upon their beautiful faces, horns, and hides as he begins and ends his daily journey that puts the stars to flight. These animals are not born in the usual way, they do not give birth, nor are they subject to the usual forms of death.

It may be this quality of immortality and the great love that Helios feels for them that evokes for us the knowledge that this is a place where one may find transfiguration and oneness with the Sun's light. The yellow robe of the *sanyasin,* or monk, in India is representative of this Golden Door. It announces to the world that you have agreed to live your life on the other side of that door. Thereafter, you offer yourself as a *bodhisattva* in the world—the compassionate servant to all seekers—understanding that all forms of life are sacred; you live as an illumined one.

But Odysseus is no yogi, and the Golden Door of Illumination is not to be his way, his *dharma.* What do you do when you're nearly there, but there is not your path? Generally, you fall asleep. Now Odysseus is given plenty of time to consider his path, for the next day Zeus sends gales of such incredible violence that in a moment "the black sky had blotted out the world." The men beach the ship, and during an entire month of prohibitive sailing weather, accompanied by onshore gales, the supplies give out and the men become lean with hunger. They comb the island with barbed hooks looking for game, fish, birds, anything edible. When the hunger and thirst are at their worst, Odysseus goes off to pray for advice from the Olympians, but all that happens is that he falls asleep. And of course his secondary selves, in the form of the crewmen, slaughter and consume the absolutely forbidden cattle.

Their decision was legitimate and sensible from their point of view. They believed they were dying from starvation, and while no form of death is pleasant, that seemed to them to be the worst of all. They declared to themselves that if in fact they ever did get home to Ithaca, they would build a big temple to the Sun God. But if he was so stingy as to resent having his cattle used to feed desperately hungry men, and decided to wreck the ship in vengeance, one quick gulp of drowning water is better than being pinched to death from inside.

That has always seemed to me to be a perfectly reasonable argument. In fact, there are many places throughout the story where I am in complete sympathy with the crewmen. But the result is complete disaster and final divestiture. Helios learns that his beloved cattle have been slain and this so distresses him that he threatens to go down and live in the Underworld unless the men are punished. Since this would mean that the Sun would shine no more upon the fruitful Earth, Zeus affirms that the men will be punished by shipwreck. But first come ghosts and portents. As the men eat of the cattle, "the hides crawled; the meat, roast and raw, groaned on the spits; and a sound as though of lowing cattle could be heard."[10] Six days of feasting followed, with the men putting away as much meat as they could consume. Finally sated, on the seventh day they hauled up the white sail and headed for the open sea.

Once they are clear of the island, however, a great shadow covers the ocean, followed by a fierce wild wind hitting them with hurricane force. The mast cracks and falls, the forestays snap. Zeus thunders and strikes the ship with lightning and as sulfuric fumes fill the riven ship, every single man is flung overboard, tossed into the sea to die.

Odysseus alone survives, saved only by the fierce fires of his life force. Managing to lash two timbers together, he even survives a second passage between Scylla and Charybdis. As Charybdis threatens to suck him down to perdition, he flings himself onto the branch of a great fig tree. There he hangs, like a bat, over the maelstrom for hours until it coughs up the fragment of the ship's mast and keel he had strapped together. Leaping onto these timbers, he rows with his hands away from all his losses.

And that is the climax of his spiritual voyage. The next seven years in the life of this nearly dead man will be spent in reconstitution on Calypso's Isle.

Meeting the Sirens

THE Sirens' Call can come in many ways, but here we will experience a particularly delightful, and indeed salutary, version of it. As with the Sirens themselves, people have to be dragged away from this process. It involves listening to things you have always wanted to hear about yourself.

TIME: Ten minutes.

MATERIALS NEEDED: None.

MUSIC: None.

INSTRUCTIONS FOR THE SOLO VOYAGER: Stand in front of a mirror for several minutes and say absolutely smashing things about yourself to your own image. To experience the process even more fully, make a tape of yourself singing your praises—or even better, ask a friend or two to do it for you—and play the tape while standing in front of the mirror and adding your own flattering commentary nonstop for about two minutes.

SCRIPT FOR THE GUIDE: For this process, the group needs to break up into threesomes, with one person in the middle and the other two on either side. Before we start, let me explain the procedure. The person in the middle takes the role of Odysseus, who will soon listen to the most wonderful things being said to him or her. The people on either side will take the role of Sirens, but you will also be the sailors who bound Odysseus to the mast so that he could not escape. You will do that by holding the middle person by the arms.

Then you will each place your mouth close to the ear of the middle person and begin to speak to her or him. Very close to the ear so that the two voices are inescapably pouring into the ears of the listener in the middle. You will say extraordinary and flattering things, which are more or less true, about the person in the middle. You will speak simultaneously, although each person is saying something different. It is this experience of two different voices saying different things spilling into the ear that is so dizzying and Siren-like. Speak very rapidly for perhaps two minutes. As an example, one person might be saying something like this:

"You are really the most wonderful person I know. You are so handsome and strong and courageous, and you have the best ideas and the most intelligent way of looking at things. You're cute too. I'd vote for you for president any day. Whenever you walk into a room everyone becomes alive because you're there. You light up everything. I've never known anyone with so much grace and charm. . . ."

Meanwhile the person at the other ear might be saying something like:

"Fascinating! You are the most fascinating person I know, and yet so profound. With your personality and brilliance you can do anything you want—and help everybody while you're doing it. Not since George Washington has there been your equal. And kind! You are so kind. The milk of human kindness just rolls through your veins. And good too. You're like the next step in human evolution. When I grow up I want to be just like you. . . ."

[At this point the guide might want to select two other people and demonstrate this process.]

The person in the middle just takes it all in as his or her due and basks in all the glory. Since it's coming so fast and furious this person has no time to block or doubt or disparage. He or she can only accept these wonderful things being said as the gifts of knowledge concerning true conditions from the Sirens.

After several minutes have elapsed I will call time, and the second person will go into the middle and become Odysseus while the first person will take up a new role as Siren and give as good as he or she got. Then I will call time again and the third person will have a chance to be bound to the raft and listen to the Sirens call.

Now we will begin. Separate into groups of three people if you have not already done so and let one sit in the middle. Those playing the Sirens' role, sit so that your mouth is very close to the ear of your Odysseus.

On your mark. Get set. Sirens' Call! [One to two minutes.]

Stop! Now change places so that one who had been a Siren goes in the middle, and the middle person becomes a Siren.

On your mark. Get set. Sirens' Call! [One to two minutes.]

Stop! Change places again so that the remaining Siren gets to be in the middle.

On your mark. Get set. Sirens' Call! [One to two minutes.]

Stop! Now, spend a few minutes discussing among yourselves what you have experienced.

[Almost invariably people will be giddy and quite delighted at what has happened. The guide may want to have the group at large share some of their findings after the initial sharing in threesomes. It is also interesting to discuss possible applications of this exercise in everyday life.]

Walking the Line Between Scylla and Charybdis

TIME: Forty-five minutes.

MATERIALS NEEDED: A large floor area without rugs and a good deal of masking tape, or strings taped down in many and varied paths, zigzags, circles, intersections.

MUSIC: Many short selections of many different kinds and styles of music: classical, rock, ragas, pop, ragtime, and so forth.

INSTRUCTIONS FOR THE SOLO VOYAGER: This exercise can be done alone if the instructions and the variety of music are prerecorded. When you're laying masking tape on the floor, make sure that you put odd obstacles on the path. Optimally, for this exercise, it would be helpful for you to get another person to lay out the path and its obstacles for you, so that it will be a surprise.

SPECIAL NEEDS: Throughout this process, the guide will be required to act as a diversionary expert. If the size of the group warrants it, one or more other persons may also serve in this capacity, as pests on the path.

SCRIPT FOR THE GUIDE: I'd like each one of you to very quickly make a list of the things that tempt you into diversions from your life path. List all the things that lure you away from the way you wish to go. Write them very quickly without giving them any particular thought. These diversions or distractions can be good, bad, or indifferent. They can even be lures to transcendent experience. But whatever they are, they keep you from following your Path of Possibility. You have two minutes of clock time equal to all the time that you need to make this list. [Two minutes.]

All right. Now take a minute to review the list a number of times so it's very much in your mind. Review the list. [One minute.]

Now release the list and forget it for a while.

I want each of you to find a place on one of those lines laid out on the floor. You'll try to walk the path and stay on that line, neither falling to left or right or forward or backward.

In other words, you will stick to your path, able to go past the Sirens of knowledge, past the snatching heads of Scylla and the great maw of Charybdis. Naturally, as you try to stay on the line we'll try to distract you in a variety of ways.

Even though you've just finished going over your lists of all the things that distract you in your life, you're going to try not to think about these distractions. Instead, you're going to keep your mind and your feet on the task. And the task is very simple: to stay present and stay on that line.

This is a lot like the game you played as a child about not stepping on the cracks in the sidewalk lest you fall through into some dreaded world. Only this adult version is much worse and much more difficult. The cracks on the sidewalk are everything *but* the line. As soon as random distracting thoughts come in, or diversionary tactics are played on you, you pull your focus back to the line you're trying to walk.

Above all you must not suffer the diversion of running into each other, but rather step carefully around each other in order to stay on the line. To provide as rich an experience as possible during your walk between Scylla and Charybis, we will play many different kinds of music. One kind of music will come on, and then it will stop and another kind of music will come on. All right. As the music starts, begin your walk on the lines.

[As participants walk the lines, the guide and his or her assistant(s) try to distract them by talking to them, mocking them, placing large and small obstacles in the middle of their paths, throwing balls, and so forth. Many, many different kinds of music are played, and the mood maintained by the guide and the assistant(s) should be alternately raucous, teasing, alluring, and just plain obnoxious.] [Fifteen to twenty minutes.]

You have now safely navigated your way through the straits of Scylla and Charybdis. But don't stop to celebrate, for you have yet to face the trial of the cattle of the Island of the Sun. It was there, you remember, that Odysseus' men failed to heed his warnings not to eat of the cattle and violent storms spun them away. So spin now through the room. Spin through the room. Spin through the room. Lost. Shipwrecked again. Spin through the room. Faster. Spinning faster and faster. After all that precision, now spinning, spinning. A vortex of waters spinning you like mad through the room. Spinning and spinning and spinning and spinning. Storm-tossed and spinning. [Two minutes.]

And now, as the exhausted, half-drowned Odysseus, collapse on Calypso's Isle. And rest.

[After the participants have rested for a minute or two, the guide can invite discussion of what they have experienced while walking the lines. Questions can be asked as to what happened to them physically, mentally, emotionally. Some typical responses to this process have been:

- I felt one-pointed.
- Every time the distractions came in, I lost balance.
- A symbol of about half the things I wrote on my list occurred during the walking.
- When the guide tried to interfere with me, I had to refrain from telling her her soul was in danger.
- I pretended that I was on a road that was about three thousand feet above ground, and if I responded to anything it would mean that I would lose my balance. Then at one point somebody came up and tried to pass me, and then her foot went off. And that meant in my reality that she tumbled to her death, and I had to keep going and not be distracted by that.
- Somebody put a bench on my line, and I saw it, trying to not see it. And I went under it, and then when I got to the other side, I just had to sit on the line and laugh, because it was so funny.
- I found that the incredible sense of the music made it easier to stay on the line.
- The music was an enormous distraction. I found myself stopping whenever it stopped.

In response to what this process told participants about their lives, here are some of their answers:

- My life is an immensely distractive process.
- I just got it. At one point when you urged everybody to spin, my first urge was to go comfort someone, comfort anyone. So I sought out Jerry because I knew he had a sore knee. So I was going to comfort him. And I realize in my life that's my big distraction. I get off my goal because I'm going out to nurture and comfort and be a great person.
- It was important for me to let what happened on the outside flow through rather than to fight against it. When I fought against it I began to lose the balance. I just let it move right through and the balance was very simple. This is what I've learned in my forty-eight years of living.
- It was interesting to me to note what I did with the distractions. I was vehement about them. If I came to a bench, instead of going over or under it or playing with it, I just picked it up and moved it off the line. I got to take off two benches and a blanket!

And I just felt really good about that because that's what I do when I'm successful in solving problems. I move them off the line.

Here is a case of someone distracted by her own perfection:

- Jean, I'd just like to address this to everyone. I hope this doesn't come up for me daily. I had a very mixed experience, and I feel if I share it maybe it will go away a little bit.
  First of all I think I am pretty distracted in my life and I wrote down a big list. When I got out here it was the easiest thing I have ever done to stay very centered. I had my hands in my pockets, so little did I need to use any other kind of balance. I was right on.
  And what has come up is incredible self-righteousness and arrogance. I thought nobody here listened. Nobody here heard the directions. Everybody was hopping and jumping. Everybody was stopping when the music stopped.
  And what has come up for me is that I find that I am totally consumed by arrogance and self-righteousness. Not that everybody else couldn't do it, but they didn't listen, didn't do what they were supposed to. I guess it was a kind of Sirens' Call, my constant commentary on how easy it was. "Look at all these fools and louts," I would think. "Look at them falling by the way. Look at how wonderful I am. I am perfect." And this turned out to be the ultimate distraction.

To which I replied, "See? You failed perfectly!"
Someone else responded to this by asking,

- Well, I'd like to ask her if she felt she was walking the line in her mind. Because that's what struck me as interesting because of the level. I was thinking so many times I'm walking the line with my body, and not walking it with my mind. And which am I doing now and which am I doing in my life? And I can really identify with your experience. I have that problem also.

After this discussion the guide might suggest to the participants that they take careful note in the days and weeks ahead of how often and in what ways they are distracted and what they have to do to stay focused and mindful. This metaphor of walking the line between Scylla and Charybdis can stay with you as a powerful impetus to mindfulness.]

CHAPTER 9

Calypso's Isle

WITH so many things to integrate, Odysseus needs a long period of rest and reflection. He drifts alone for nine days on a single timber, all his companions dead in the wake of the storms and boiling seas sent by Zeus. By all accounts he should, like his crewmen, have come to rest in a watery tomb. Instead, he is cast into a womb on Ogygia, the Isle of Calypso in the far west, a paradise of fertile gestation.

To speak of someone as having "gone west" in both the ancient Egyptian and Mediterranean worlds meant that they had died. But in the case of Calypso's western island, the tomb is a kind of ultimate womb with its comfortable cave, soft meadows, colorful flowers, luxurious vines, woods, birds, gentle streams, and cedar-scented air. This Elysian atmosphere is governed by the beautiful if matronly goddess who sings sweetly as she works on her loom. Notice the critical theme of weaving as symbolic of an initiatory journey under the dominion of Athena.

The nymph Calypso, daughter of Atlas, is a minor divinity whose name means "concealment," from which we get our word "eclipse." Her name also implies hiding and engulfment, and a state of absolute and utter security. Her island is in the middle of the sea, a nowhere place that serves as a womb of renewal. For the next seven full years she will be Odysseus' lover and protector. He does not leave until the beginning of the eighth year—an octave of time—again, as we have seen, a metaphor for a lifetime in ancient Greece.

During this period he is restored, rewoven, under the skillful and loving hands of Calypso, and, we presume, helped by the goddess to assimilate the lessons learned from his adventures and initiations. Here, too, he is prepared for his meeting with Penelope, for Calypso is the Hera surrogate, the one who prepares him to resume the responsibilities of wife and family and kingdom.

It is interesting to note that most of the commentators on this passage, both ancient and modern (virtually all of whom are men), view this episode with considerable anxiety. Many see it as an engulfment by the "instinctual female principle physically vital, but intellectually and spiritually lifeless."[1] Parallels are found between Calypso's Isle of Ogygia and the balmy if boring Isles of the Blessed Dead—the fields of Elysium. Typical of this response is that of a German scholar who writes: "The ideally sketched and tranquil landscape, which invites Hermes to tarry, depicts then nothing other than the meadow of an Elysium, the gardens of a western, otherworldly Island of Death."[2] The author of these words takes the traditional translation of Calypso's name, the "concealer," and reinterprets it as "she who buries."

It is presumed by these writers that, for the hero adventurer, the apparent "effortlessness of existence" would always be a kind of living death. For only in action can he find his identity; only by struggle can he maintain his reality. On Calypso's Isle, Odysseus is not being threatened. There is no battle to fight, no ship to sail. So this adventuresome hero must live without adventure for seven full years. Thus this long cohabitation with Calypso is seen by many to be his most severe trial.

Indeed it is a trial, but in the perspective of a Mystery

drama, it is a trial that accompanies death and rebirth. There is a much deeper story going on here than meets the traditional scholarly eye.

Earlier, I referred to the ancient practice of sacrificing the consort of the goddess-queen after a year's reign as the Year-Daemon. We saw that with Circe, Odysseus both reenacted as well as transcended the ancient theme of "the king must die." At some point in historical time, the literal sacrifice did cease, and instead a ritual drama of remembrance was instituted to celebrate the cycle of the rising and dying Year-Daemon. Indeed, classical Greek tragedy is thought to have had its roots in these early ritual dramas. As Gilbert Murray tells us, "the life of the Year-Daemon, as it seems to be reflected in Tragedy, is generally a story of Pride and Punishment. Each Year arrives, waxes great, commits the sin of *Hubris* [overbearing pride], and then is slain. The death is deserved; but the slaying is a sin: hence comes the next Year as Avenger, or as the Wronged One re-arisen."[3]

Odysseus, however, both continues and violates the phases of the dying god cycle. On the one hand he has, to all practical and ritual purposes, died to his old self. His ship and all his remaining companions and crew—all the many aspects of himself—have died at the hands of Zeus because of their crime of eating the cattle of a solar deity. But Odysseus continues to live, restored in the island womb of the divine Concealer. And, within the Great Cycle of seven full years, he will stand as avenger in his own home, during, as it happens, the festival celebrating the solar god Apollo.

We see, therefore, that with Odysseus, the traditional ritual measure has been extended and deepened. The killer of the hero is no longer the queen-goddess-consort. Instead of putting him to death, she hides him from the wrath of Poseidon and Zeus and nurtures him into renewed life. This reconstruction of the primitive scenario is of the order of the Mysteries—the Eleusinian Mysteries as well as those of Isis and Osiris.

However, while the Egyptian god Osiris dies to this world, killed by the wrathful god Seth, it is only through the hiding of his body and preparation of his mummy by his wife, Isis, that he is able to be resurrected as Lord of the Afterlife. But Odysseus, as hero-initiate, dies only to his lesser selves and is reborn to a higher self. His lesser selves, represented by his crew—all 144 of them (12 × 12)—undergoes complete extinction, the best of them dying last, so that Odysseus may pursue his initiatory journey of transformation.

Whether Homer borrowed from the developing Mystery tradition of his time or intuited this transformative possibility is hard to say. As the practice of the Mysteries marks a psychological advance over the primitive rites that declare the year-king must die, so the story of Odysseus and his experience of the deepening Mysteries of initiation under the guidance of the divine feminine is an evolutionary step in the drama of human becoming. Perhaps a shadowy god-king who has fulfilled the ancient ritual cycle and been put to death stands behind the mortal Odysseus. Nevertheless, even he will rise again on the celebrational solar day of his revenge against the suitors and the reunion with his beloved Penelope.[4]

So, battered, naked, stripped of all his symbolic heroic veneer, the brilliant "man of many ways" lands on Calypso's womblike island, dead to his former self. Helpless and with nothing to "do," he is virtually a newborn infant to be raised under the tender ministrations of the kindly goddess. She provides him with a regular daily life in which he has no need for the cunning and wily qualities that saw him through the Trojan victory and his subsequent adventures. Instead, he must learn to use the qualities of sensory enjoyment and emotional relationship. He has to become Calypsian. And so for years he enjoys a life of loving intimacy with the goddess, which doubtless has its salutary effects. Although we are not told anything else about his life with Calypso, the implication is that Odysseus is reasonably content with his lot until the seventh year; that is, not until the great cycle of seven ritual years is complete and the dangers at home require his immediate return does he begin to long for Ithaca. Certainly there is nothing to indicate that Odysseus suffered the degree of anguish over his lot that his commentators do.

This episode is critical for a new understanding of our own stuck places. As I mentioned earlier in this book, the famous adventures actually took only a few months. With the exception of the year-long stay with Circe, Odysseus spends most of his time with Calypso. The same kind of time frame is probably true of most of us. The exciting incidents of our lives were few and brief; then came the long, long stay in the place where routine was the order of the day. Looked at in the light of Calypso's Isle, we see this is a much more important place than we tend to give it credit for. Indeed, apart from this incident, there are few other examples in the literature of myth and symbol that indicate how vital the long resting place is to the soul's developmental journey. But it carries no excitement or charge for us, and in retaliation we name our boats, bars, and beaches "Calypso" to indicate those loose and mindless places where one can go to relax and vegetate.

True, many of us do begin to label our places of routine and relative calm as stuck places after a while. Yet, often it is these very places that give us our stability and restoration. Sometimes, however, these places are so hidden, even from us, that we feel our lives are being wasted, and we long to get back to where the action is. Yet the "action" may very well be going on—in the internal realms—with our state of external routine providing the stable conditions necessary for the reflection and reweaving of our own possible human.

This inner work is the hardest of all and, like Odysseus' reweaving, may go unnoticed and externally unrewarded. But where these conditions are met—a life of some regularity, good and trusted friends, few big surprises—one can take time to deepen one's own potential and consciousness. This is the place and time when you are best able to tend to your soul growing, where you meet hidden aspects of yourself and resolve to nurture them into valuable new attributes.

But there is yet an even more subtle hiddenness within the context of this hiddenness. In this state consciousness is lowered in order to be rewoven in the depths. It is an ultimate concealment for which traditional psychological understanding is almost entirely deficient. It feels like an utter engulfment in which one has a hard time relating to anything because the self is so deeply buried in something else. It is not the dark night of the soul. Rather, it is the necessary hibernation period presaging a fundamental renewal or restructuring of personality. Saints and mystics write about this long dry spell, and how then, almost inevitably, when the time is right, the longing begins again, and life rises to assert itself, renewed and greatly strengthened.

Perhaps what this episode speaks to is the need for Calypso Centers, halfway houses for journeyers, adventurers, wanderers, and people who are in a period of either transition or transformation. There they may feel bored, but there they can be literally rewoven, restored, grounded, loved, and made ready for the next stage of their journey. Needless to say, this would not be a community run by therapists, or at least not by run-of-the-mill therapists. Can you imagine a therapist on Calypso's Isle saying, "Odysseus, let's get it out. What was your real relationship to Circe? Don't give me any of this mystical claptrap. You had a pig fixation, and deep down you know it! Right? Right." And that would be that.

By the seventh year, Odysseus is ready for the next stage. He moves into an active state of longing. He weeps for Ithaca, for Penelope, for the sight of the smoke rising from his own hearth. His tears are as briny as the sea, and he breaks the heart of the gods with his weeping and his fixed and inconsolable looking out over the sea toward home.

And home weeps for him. There, things are as bad as they can be. Unless the resurrected savior returns, his son will be killed, his property stolen away, his wife married to another. Perhaps at some level he knows these things, for he sits scanning the bare horizon of the sea longing, longing for home. Longing for Penelope, and Penelope is on the other shore, perhaps three hundred miles away, longing for Odysseus. And on Olympus, Athena says before the court of the gods, "Enough. He is ready. The time is now."

> O Majesty, O Father of us all,
> if it now please the blissful gods

> that wise Odysseus reach his home again,
> let the Wayfinder, Hermes, cross the sea
> to the island of Ogygia; let him tell
> our fixed intent to the nymph with pretty braids,
> and let the steadfast man depart for home.[5]

Hermes speeds his winged way to the island, pausing in admiration of the paradise he finds there. After taking some refreshment of ambrosia, the food of the gods, he gives Calypso her orders from the higher Olympian powers to release Odysseus.

She responds with anger over what she describes as Olympian resentment and spite over goddesses who find human lovers. But she is willing, though grudgingly, to let him go. And Calypso does so with that generosity of spirit that informs her kindly nature. She goes down to the seaside where Odysseus sits in his usual place of weeping and longing, and says to him:

> Poor man, no longer mourn here beside me nor let your lifetime fade away, since now I will send you on, with a good will. So come, cut long timbers with a bronze axe and join them to make a wide raft, and fashion decks that will be on the upper side, to carry you over the misty face of water. Then I will stow aboard her bread and water and ruddy wine, strength-giving foods that will keep the hunger from you, and put clothing on you, and send a following stern wind after, so that all without harm you can come back to your own country, if only the gods consent.[6]

She makes one last attempt to persuade Odysseus to stay with her. She lovingly cooks him a delectable meal (still, we gather, his favorite form of entertainment) and then warns him of the many hardships he will still have to endure before returning to Ithaca. He would be wise, she says, to stay with her and accept the gift of immortality. She reminds him that Penelope is no match for her in beauty. Odysseus' response, tactful and resourceful as it is, marks the turning point in his life:

> Goddess and queen, do not be angry with me. I myself know that all you say is true and that circumspect Penelope can

> never match the impression you make for beauty and stature. She is mortal after all, and you are immortal and ageless. But even so, what I want and all my days I pine for is to go back to my house and see my day of homecoming. And if some god batters me far out on the wine-blue water, I will endure it, keeping a stubborn spirit inside me. . . .
>
> So he spoke, and the sun went down and the darkness came over. These two, withdrawn in the inner recess of the hollowed cavern, enjoyed themselves in love and stayed all night by each other.[7]

Odysseus refuses the "euphoria of eternity" and the lure of timelessness, lest he lose his identity and his own mortal fulfillment in his homeward journey to Ithaca and Penelope. Had he chosen eternity, all his adventures, initiations, and deepenings would have been in vain. He would have ended up, like so many other fabled consorts of goddesses, as an undying effigy of his mortal self, finished with time, space, and destiny. The tale would have ended at the turning point, no human point would have been made, and *The Odyssey* would have been idiocy.

His refusal to leave the world of time affirms the importance of time and timing in the story. Hermes comes at the right moment to release Odysseus, just as he showed up right on time on the path to Circe's Palace to give Odysseus explicit instructions as to how to save himself and his men from Circe's time-regressive magic. The *kairos* is opened when the hero is ready. The leap of opportunity can only be successfully taken at the right moment.

Many Western people grow up thinking that every moment is the right moment, that opportunity knocks and knocks and knocks. "Seize the day," the saying goes, and the rush is on. Perhaps that explains our serious pathology of timing, one result of which is the disease of cancer. Certain cells multiply at the wrong time and a malignancy forms out of time-warped matter. Our economics, politics, and even cosmetics constantly conspire to fool time. But time, as Odysseus so wisely discerned, cannot stop for humans. All its phases must be endured for any joy to be known, any knowledge to be gained, any healing to be had. So in this superb parable of timing, the pure adventures take a short while, the initiations take longer, and then a very long time is required to gestate and deepen, before the time is ripe to re-create the world anew.

The wise and prescient Calypso knows this, and even though she greatly desires him to share her timeless life, her loving nature deeply understands his mortal needs. She releases him and even helps him find the materials to build his raft. Perhaps she too, after so long an intimacy with Odysseus, as restorer, mother, lover, companion in paradise, has also deepened and grown. In helping him get on with it, who is to say that she has not herself been released from the womb of ocean. Certainly all those bars, beaches, boats, and other balmy places bearing her name may be a fair barometer for her Odysseus-inspired outreach in the wide world of other times and further places.

Gestation and Rebirth on Calypso's Isle

WE will now experience a number of processes that can enable us to remythologize the great stuck places of our lives as gestation islands, places and times where we were allowed to integrate our life's learnings, rewoven, and finally birthed into new possibilities for our lives. These processes, which represent the seven full years of Odysseus' stay on Calypso's Island, should ideally be performed over the course of an all-night event. Therefore, earlier in the evening, after the participants have shared supper, they would begin with Part One, the initial exercise of reflecting with a partner on the stuck places of one's life. This would be followed by Part Two, the experience of the enhancement of the body and mind through music.

Then, in Part Three the participants will sleep through the night in a room large enough to hold them all with their bedrolls close together. This will be an experience of gestation as one sleeps. While in the "womb state," the guide and his or her assistant(s) will read from *The Odyssey*, especially books five through nine—the adventures of Odysseus. During this reading, the sound of ocean waves rhythmically rolling up a beach should play in the background.

Toward morning, the guide will initiate Part Four, the Blessed Birth, and bring the participants to full awakening and "rebirth." Part Five will complete the process by emulating Odysseus' yearning for Penelope by the shore, as together we clarify the nature of our yearning for the beloved and prepare ourselves for this meeting.

TIME: Eight to fourteen hours.

MATERIALS NEEDED: Everyone must be supplied with a comfortable bedroll, which will allow him or her to sleep together on the floor. An optional suggestion is that they wear comfortable loose white clothes both for the evening processes and to sleep in, following the ancient Greek belief that the color white attracts dreams. Foods for supper and breakfast should be brought to be shared.

MUSIC: A wide variety of music, which will be described for each section.

INSTRUCTIONS FOR THE SOLO VOYAGER: These processes can be adapted by using a notebook to record the answers to the questions of Part One. Parts Two, Three, and Four can be put on tape, although you will have to interrupt the flow of the process in the morning by turning your tape player back on. As for the reading of *The Odyssey* through the night, while it is not essential, you might want to record a ninety-minute tape of your favorite parts of Odysseus' journey so far and put it on an auto-reverse tape player to play all night as background. Or, you might choose some particular favorite cassette of poetry or music or sea sounds and play that all night on an auto-reverse tape player. Part Five is readily done alone.

Part One: Remembering Stuckness

SCRIPT FOR THE GUIDE: We will now each find and sit with a partner. Together we will ask each other a series of questions that will help us remember our places and times of being stuck. When, where, and how in our lives did we feel, as Odysseus did, that we were caught on Calypso's Isle and could not get on with our lives. The times and places need not have been negative. In fact, they could have been very nurturing and supportive, as was Calypso's Isle for Odysseus. However, this may be small comfort for how we felt when we were on them. We may even have a certain amount of resentment about them that keeps us from enjoying the full benefit that they provided.

We will now attempt to deepen our understanding of what may have been going on at a deeper level during that time of seeming sameness and stuckness. You and your partner decide who will be the first questioner and who the first answerer. The questioner will ask the series of questions as I give them to you, and the answerer will answer them.

[When the partners have chosen, the guide will say:]

The first question for the questioner is: "Tell me, from one particular time in your life, how, when, and where you got stuck for a longer period than you would have liked?" Please ask the question and let the answerer respond. [Five minutes.]

The next question is: "Who or what nurtured or supported you during this period, and what long-term effect did it have on you?" [Five minutes.]

The next question to ask is: "How, in retrospect, were you deepened or in some way enhanced as a result of this long period of being in the stuck place?" [Five minutes.]

The next question is: "What was really going on within you during this period that up to this moment you may not have been conscious of?" [Five minutes.]

Now the questioners will ask their partners: "Please tell the same story that you have just told, but recast it in the form of a story or a myth, referring to yourself only in the third person." You might say, for instance: "Once upon a time, there was a magical princess, filled with a mighty and adventurous spirit, who got shipwrecked on the Isle of Babies. There she cared for many long years for nothing but babies and wondered what her life might have been like had she chosen to continue with her adventures instead." The myth should carry the story beyond the point of stuckness, even if the answerers have not actually gotten beyond that point themselves. Begin. [Ten to fifteen minutes.]

[When the time is up, the guide will have the questioner and the answerer reverse roles and repeat the above instructions. When both have completed this process, the guide will have the group share some of their understandings of the place and meaning of Calypso's Isle in their lives. Many will find that these places were much needed and necessary stopping points where they integrated previous life lessons learned. Further discussion could address what kinds of understandings members of the group might bring to any future sojourns on Calypso's Isle so they can benefit from these places, seeing them as opportunities for deepening rather than harbors of stagnation. After a break for dinner, and perhaps time for some singing, dancing, games, jokes and/or storytelling, the guide will begin the next process.]

Part Two: Reweaving the Body and Mind with Music

SCRIPT FOR THE GUIDE: We are about to perform a series of exercises that celebrate the healing influences of Calypso on Odysseus. We gather that after shipwreck, mourning, and despair, he grew strong and vibrant under her tender ministrations. In some sense his body was "rewoven" by her sensuous care and the nurturing environment she provided. In this process we will use music to effect just such a reweaving of our own bodies and nervous systems. The music will reach us through synesthesia, or cross-sensing. This will stimulate new growth in our perceptual abilities as well as greater capacity for enjoyment of music and other related pleasures.

To start, I would like you to find a place to lie down.

[If there is still sunlight outside and a pleasant place to sit or lie down and absorb the Sun, the guide will include the following process. However, this process can also be done on an imaginal level indoors. The guide will say:]

I want you to go outside [or imagine you are outside in a beautiful sunny spot] for about twenty minutes. There, I would like you to sit or lie down on the ground and receive the Sun. Allow yourself to feel the Sun streaming through your body. Pay special attention to the feeling of the Sun's rays streaming through your heart and throat. Have a sense of real communion with the solar light. Try not to speak to each other during this process. Stay focused on the light and its flowing into your body.

At the end of that period I will call you back with a bell. You will come back very quietly and lie down in the place you have chosen, still maintaining awareness of the Sun in your heart. Then we will begin the process of listening with light and enhancing the body and mind with music. [Ten minutes.]

[The process then continues after the participants return from being out in the sun and lie down in the room. Even if the previous stage of going outside was omitted, or the Sun exercise was imaginal, the directions that follow are the same. The guide now says:]

I ask you now to feel that you are able to hold an image of light in your heart.

From Japanese experiments measuring the output around the energy centers, or *chakra* system, of the body, we know that when one woman concentrated upon and opened her heart *chakra*—the energetic center of love and compassion—the measuring device showed a continuous stream of high-frequency energy. In addition, the photoelectric cell placed near her heart increasingly registered the presence of more and more light.

Now we are going to turn up the light in our own hearts—the light that is in the cosmos, that is in you. Focus your attention on the area of your heart, allowing it to become a radiant Sun. Let that Sun stream out a light that is love, that is joy, that is the abundance of being, to every organ and artery and cell of your physical being. Let that inner Sun radiate in concert with the rhythms of your body, let it pulse with your breath, until there is no part of you that is not suffused with light.

Tune the light of your heart to even greater brilliance, so that it streams clear and triumphant into any remaining dark mental and emotional crannies. Every cell and system and organ sings with light. Every brain wave, every heartbeat, every thought stream is filled with the deep and powerful oneness of this light of love. Light that will soon become music as well. Let this light of love continue to stream through you.

I'm going to begin to play some music for you. A very beautiful and sensuous song such as Calypso might have sung for Odysseus. But know that it is possible for you to hear music very differently from the way you normally hear it. You are now able to hear music over the entire surface of your body. Not just hearing with your ears. Over the entire surface of your body, where there are countless end organs that can be stimulated by the music. Your entire body can hear. Your entire body, illumined by the light of love, will hear the music. And your body is also able to experience this music as touch and sensation, music touching you everywhere.

[Here the guide plays a beautiful and soulful song like the ones found on albums by Nana Mouskouri.]

Now, as the music plays, you are going to make use of this capacity of your skin and of your touch centers to hear the music with your whole body, to be touched by the music, all of your being evoked and touched by the music. It can be an extremely pleasurable sensation. The music, swirling around you, passing in and out of your light-filled body, your sensitivity increasing with every note.

You become more and more sensitive, more and more responsive to the music. Now you are experiencing the music rapturously, exquisitely, with all of your body. Your flesh, your skin, all of you is totally involved in this awareness of the music.

And now, as a very, very different kind of music begins to play, all of your senses will participate. As well as hearing the music and being touched by the music, you will see the music. You will taste the music. You will smell the music. You will experience total and intense sensory involvement.

[Here the guide plays music from Area II like Vangelis' "Chariots of Fire."]

Keep the heart illumined. Keep the heart shining brighter and brighter. The light and music are moving in you. All of your senses are responding individually. And now all your senses will make an integrated, orchestrated response, each sense reinforcing every other sense, all of your senses coming together to create one powerful climactic whole as the Sun continues to stream brightly from your heart through your entire body.

And now the music will shift again. And again, all of your senses will participate in the music. You will see the music, taste it, eat it, smell it, hear it, be touched by the music.

[Here the guide plays music from Area II such as Smetana's "The Moldau."]

But this time the music is invested with light. The light from your heart is filling the music. Music bursting with light. Within you, the light-laden atomic structure of your physical beingness is dancing to the music, as well as seeing, touching, hearing, smelling, tasting the music. A very intense experience of music as light. The light-filled music seizes all your senses, moves through you, fills you with light. The music becomes light. And you hear the sounds of light.

As the music shifts again, you will continue to feel with all your senses, but this time you will also experience the music emotionally.

[Here the guide plays *West Meets East* ("Improvisations"), (Album 3, side 1).]

A rich variety of emotions can sweep through you—happy or sad, nostalgic or ebullient. It will seem as if the whole story of the human race is playing through you. You will see the music, taste the music, smell the music, hear the music, be touched by the music—a total intense sensory adventure.

But you will also feel a deep involvement, a sweeping emotion containing all the passions of human history. The entire history of the human race is playing through you. Playing through your bones like flutes and violins. Playing your muscles like a cello. Playing the drum of your heart. The music of all humanity playing through you now. You are the instrument being played by the Universal Human.

And now you will just be music from many times and places. You will just be music. Music as light. Music as the Sun. Music that will play you. Music from the twelfth century, from the eighteenth century, from East, from West, from North, from South. Music from all centuries, from all times, from all space. It will be as if the entire history of the human race will play through you now.

[Music from many different cultures and times should be carefully selected and put together for a cycle of about five to ten minutes of music. The person who is running the tape player should be careful to gently fade out one piece before another begins. At the end of this cycle there might be played a well-known inspirational song such as "Amazing Grace" or the "Ode to Joy" of the last movement of Beethoven's Ninth Symphony. As this plays, the guide will say:]

Join in now and sing, sing either this song or your own song. Sing with all parts of you. Feel yourself as music now. All parts of you are music, music that is light that is love that is music. Let the music that is you shine forth in the song.

[Once the singing has reached its appropriate energy level, and the concert feels ready to end, the guide and helpers will create a pattern on the floor with the bedrolls and sleeping apparatus so that the participants can readily find their own spot. The pattern can be in lines, or arranged radially like the spokes of a wheel. However it is laid out, it must allow for pathways so that participants who get up in the night don't trip over the other sleepers. The guide says something like this:]

Now that the music has entered our bodies and we are fully part of the music and the light, it is time to enter the deep darkness of Calypso's Cave, so that we may sleep through the hours of the night while the goddess completes her reweaving work on our bodies and psyches. When we awaken in the morning we will be ready to set out for home, for Ithaca again. Let us now quickly and quietly prepare for bed. Make sure that you have your journals and pens by your side so that you can easily write down your dreams whenever you awaken. When all are in bed, Calypso will speak to you.

[Participants prepare for bed.]

Part Three: The Gestation Through the Night

MUSIC: An environmental tape of ocean waves begins to play as the participants take care of any prebed needs and find their way to their sleeping places. The ocean waves play all through the night.

SCRIPT FOR THE GUIDE: [As the participants settle in, the guide speaks for Calypso—if the guide is a man, please ask a woman to speak for the goddess.]

Beloved adventurers, heroes and heroines, the time has come for you to rest deeply and sleep sweetly here in my cave. While you sleep you will hear the waves break on my shores; feel yourself lulled and rocked by this primal sound. You will hear the story of *The Odyssey* read to you all during the night. It will be very soft, perhaps out of your hearing range, but the story, which is now your story, will enter your psyche once again. In your deep, sweet, comfortable sleep, you will relive the adventures of your own great life voyage. This time, you will experience them on a spiritual level as my loom, working like the music, gently opens your awareness, separates any strands of pain that may have blocked or damaged you, surrounds them with healing power and color, and reweaves all of your being into new patterns of understanding. As I work with my loom on your life and your being, you will feel how totally I honor and love you for the gifts you have brought to my island here in the center of the ocean.

All through the night, I, Calypso, will weave and reweave your body, your life, your heart, your psyche. And all through the night you will feel the great love that Calypso feels for her Odysseus. As you hear the sounds of the ocean and the voices reading the text of your life adventures, and feel my loom weaving its enchantment all through your inmost self, you will be strengthened and prepared to take the next stage of your journey.

In the morning you will awaken with new awareness of the next part of your life. And you will be ready to bid farewell to me and to my cave of healing and wholing. But for now, my dear adventurers, sleep, sleep, gestate. Allow yourselves to be rewoven. Sleep. Sleep. Sleep. . . .

[The volunteer readers should read only as long as comfortable and without strain for the voice, no more than an hour. Devise a system of reading order so that those who are waiting to read may sleep as long as possible and be awakened only a few moments before their reading time. After one's reading time, it may feel right for the reader to spend a few moments in silent vigil for the sleeping Odysseans, and in meditation upon the reweaving that needs to be accomplished in his or her own life.]

Part Four: Awakening

SCRIPT FOR THE GUIDE: [Early in the morning, as the group begins to stir and wake up, the guide and several assistants should move among them, touching and massaging their heads, feet, and hands very gently and murmuring to each Odysseus something like:]

It is time to wake up now, my Odysseus. It is time now to awaken and begin to plan your journey away from this island. Your family and home are calling you. You must wake up now. Hold on to any dreams you had in the night. Record them in your journal, and listen for the information they have to give you about the next stages of your life. It is time to wake up now. Remember your dreams. Remember your dreams. Record your dreams. But it is time to wake up now. Penelope and Telemachus are yearning for you. It is time to continue your journey home.

[During the shared breakfast, participants should also share their dreams. Discuss them together in the light of being rewoven and prepared for the deeper life. Pay particular attention to any theme of yearning that may have emerged, as it may relate to "going home," to becoming who one really is, to discovering one's deeper potentials for fulfilling one's life purpose.]

INSTRUCTIONS FOR THE SOLO VOYAGER: Record your dreams and impressions in your journal. Dialogue with your inner guide—with Calypso or with Hermes or your own Great Friend—about the larger, deeper elements of your journey. Simply write down your name in the left-hand margin and address a question to your inner guide. Then write your guide's name in the left-hand margin, and open your mind and heart and spirit to this great dimension of loving knowingness.

Remember that you can "hear" with your whole body now. Feel your guide near you, speaking to you. Whatever thoughts now enter your mind, write them down. Ask more questions if you need to. And again, write down any thoughts or flashes of insight, any words or images that come into your mind. When the dialogue ends, go back and give it a title. The act of finding an appropriate title that sums up the gist of the dialogue will offer you a powerful clue to where you are in your own journey, and the issues of greatest concern to you.

Part Five: Yearning for the Beloved

After breakfast, the dreamwork may continue if you have discovered any common themes, or if there is more to be done on the sense of reweaving. Once the guide senses that the night process has safely gone as far as it need go, participants should be encouraged to sit quietly with paper, drawing materials, and pens in order to begin the next stage.

MUSIC: Any soft, evocative sounds, perhaps the same played for the first section of the music process performed in the night, to call up memories of the Calypso nurturers in our lives. (Georgia Kelly's composition for the harp, "Seapeace," would be an excellent choice here. Then a haunting, yearning piece, such as Alan Hovhannes' "Mysterious Mountain," to symbolize the aching for home and home's aching for us. For the closing, a farewell song, which the participants may create on the spot, followed by a happy song of embarkation, perhaps even literally: Enya singing, "Sail away, sail away, sail away," or "Orinoco Flow" from her album *Watermark*.

SCRIPT FOR THE GUIDE: We are now going to do something Odysseus never had the chance to do—as far as we know. We are going to write a poem or a letter or draw a picture expressing gratitude to one of the Calypsos of our lives. Sitting quietly, comfortably, and easily now, let your mind roam back over the conversation you had last night about your stuck places. Was there a Calypso at work helping you to gestate and reweave your life—and did you have the opportunity to say thank you appropriately? You may never send this thank-you—in fact, the recipients may be people whose names you never knew, or they may have died. But somewhere, somehow, this expression of gratitude will enter a new kind of World Bank, a morphogenetic field of good feelings, where it will be available to be used when an expression of grace is deeply needed.

As the music plays, remember now any Calypso who gave you a moment—or seven years—of safe harbor. Let the feelings of your appreciation rise through your body, until your hand yearns to write or draw. Then let the hand pour out an expression of your feelings. Listen to the music and let the music carry you back until you feel yourself once again in that safe harbor and in the presence of the nurturing one. [Allow ten minutes or so.]

Now, knowing that the process of expressing your gratitude to Calypso may continue, let it be complete for this time. Shift your attention now to that which is calling you. Put your pencils and paper aside for a moment. Let yourself drop into the being of Odysseus as he sits on the shore of Calypso's Island, having received the necessary gestation and reweaving. He has been in the presence of the archetypal powers for long enough; it is time to go home to the human world and fulfill his work there.

[The music shifts to a more plaintive, haunting melody.]

What parts of your life work have yet to be accomplished? What is it that you know you must do in order to feel fulfilled, that you have achieved what you came to do? Who is calling out to you to say that they want your partnering? Who or what stands in your life in the place where Penelope and Telemachus stand for Odysseus? What do you really, really, passionately want?

Feel yourself sitting on the rocky shore looking out over the wine-dark sea toward home, toward your Ithaca. What is it? What does it look like? See or sense your Ithaca as that something you most richly desire. Unless we bring in the power of the emotions and allow that emotional power to feed our thoughts and our imaginings, we will not be able to make our way home. So let your emotions loose; feel what Odysseus felt as he yearned for home, weeping the great salt tears of longing for his beloved wife and, yes, his beloved job as King of Ithaca. [Allow a few moments for the music to evoke this longing.]

Speak out loud, so that at least your own ears can hear what you are deeply yearning for. Describe your Ithaca in words or images loaded with meaning for you. As you do so, feel now from across the water that Ithaca, that Penelope, yearning so wildly for you. Whatever it is—a project, a person, a life work, even a need for knowing—feel your yearning for it. Feel the ways it is calling out, longing for, searching for, yearning for you. [Allow five minutes.]

Once again take up your paper and drawing materials and begin to write about or draw your yearning, your Beloved, your Ithaca. Draw also or write about the mutual energy that is forming over the distance between you as your Beloved, your Ithaca, yearns for you.

Here is a poem by Judith Morley that will give you a model for expressing your yearning. It's called, appropriately:

YEARNING

I am a tear
longing for a cheek
to roll upon . . .

I am . . . a hungering
to have again
the dream
in which I heard
the melody
that holds the stars together
and apart.

I am . . . an ache
to feel the rending
in the center
of that silent mushroom cloud
that cracks me open,
sucks the marrow from my bones,
with pain so shrieking
through the raw interstices
of wounded flesh
that I finally know again
the agony
the passion
and the ecstasy of how it all began . . .

I am . . . a thirst
to be the waters
falling back to earth,
every cell a drop of rain,
every drop of rain

a tear
longing for a cheek
to roll upon.

[Allow twenty minutes for the writing of the sense of yearning. Keep the music going throughout the writing time. When the time has elapsed and people seem to be finished or at least well embarked, ask for volunteers to share some of their work.]

SCRIPT FOR THE GUIDE: We have said thank you to Calypso. We have felt and expressed our great longing for the Beloved. We have experienced the great longing the Beloved feels for us. It is time now to say farewell to this island in the middle of the ocean; to say farewell to our nurturing, loving weaver. We need to make our way home to the place where the Beloved waits. No matter how frail our craft, how weak the boat we fashion, no matter how wildly Poseidon throws us around, we must try to make our way home.

This is what Odysseus does. But one thing is lacking. He has endured and experienced fully his adventures, he has undergone many initiations, he has loved and been loved by immortals, and he has been granted time to integrate his learnings. But he has not yet had the opportunity to tell his story to a group of wise and interested listeners. Through the cruel offices of his old enemy Poseidon—with whom he has not yet made peace—Odysseus will soon be washed ashore on the island of the Phaeacians, and there he will find the audience for his story.

But now it is time to say good-bye to Calypso and sail away toward Ithaca and the Beloved.

[Music of good-bye should be played and a celebrational dance performed that represents a joyful embarkation for home and the hoped-for reunion with the Beloved.]

CHAPTER 10

The Isle of the Phaeacians

ODYSSEUS leaves Calypso's Isle knowing that he's setting out to sea at high risk and with inadequate equipment, a state true of many of us when we leave our places of safety and surety. In such times we are challenged to our utmost and seem to have few external resources to rely upon. So Odysseus navigates his raft by the constellations, sails filled by Calypso's gift of a following wind.

For seventeen days he happily sets a steady and uneventful course, but on the eighteenth day, within sight of the land of the Phaeacians, Poseidon spots him, and all hell and fury breaks out. Night springs from heaven, and the storm winds clash together as Odysseus and his raft are assaulted again and again.

He would surely have perished had not a sea goddess, Ino, taken pity on him and lent him her veil to tie around him, making him unsinkable. Ino herself had once been a mortal, the daughter of King Cadmus. She had leaped into the sea with her infant son, Melicertes, to save him from his frenzied father. Once there, Zeus took pity on her and turned her into a sea divinity known as "the white goddess." Finding Odysseus cast into the sea by the fury of Father Poseidon, she was naturally sympathetic and Odysseus was saved.

After swimming for two days and two nights in wintry seas, he finally comes near the jagged rocks of the Phaeacian shore, but turns away knowing that the heavy surf would smash him to pieces. Desperately weary, he nevertheless continues to swim, looking to the shore, hoping to see a beach. Suddenly, he spies the mouth of a river. With the little strength he has left, he prays to the river spirit to be his protector. The spirit agrees, the current slows, and he is able to cast his briny, swollen body on the land. There he collapses underneath some olive bushes into exhausted sleep. He is too tired even to consider where he is or what may happen next.

In point of fact, he has landed on the shores of the ideal community and he is about to meet the ideal girl, the princess Nausicaa, one of the loveliest figures in literature. Charming, witty, and wonderfully knowing, she also represents the best that humanity has to offer, and serves as Odysseus' first guide as he is welcomed back to the human world. In the trinity of goddesses, Nausicaa is a surrogate for Athena. And Athena herself has prepared her for this meeting with Odysseus by sending her a romantic dream. When she wakes up in the morning she is filled with joyful premonitions about finding a husband. This so energizes her that she feels a sudden zeal to do something useful—she decides to do the palace laundry.

Wheedling a wagon and mules from her father, Nausicaa sets off with her handmaidens to a river by the shore. There they merrily wash the clothes and set them out to dry. This gives the girls time to bathe and anoint themselves, enjoy a picnic, dance, and play ball. The ball naturally does what balls do at the beach; it rolls away into the water.

Their cries of laughter and dismay awaken Odysseus. At first, he wonders whether he has fallen among monsters or gods—or is there a remote chance that he could finally be among real people, people he can talk to and understand.

Breaking off a branch of an olive tree to hide his nakedness, he emerges from his hiding place. But his battered, salt-encrusted hulk scares the daylights out of the girls, who scatter down the beach.

This is a first for Odysseus. In ten years, this is the first time he was not the frightened but the frightener. He must be among humans! Only one of the girls stands her ground, Nausicaa, for Athena has put courage into her heart. Athena has also possibly put honey into Odysseus' speech, for his words to the young girl create a masterly confection no adolescent could resist:

> I am at your knees, O Queen. But are you mortal or goddess? If indeed you are one of the gods who hold wide heaven, then I must find in you the nearest likeness to Artemis the daughter of great Zeus, for beauty, figure, and stature. But if you are one among those mortals who live in this country, three times blessed are your father and the lady your mother, and three times blessed your brothers too, and I know their spirits are warmed forever with happiness at the thought of you, seeing such a slip of beauty taking her place in the chorus of dancers; but blessed at the heart, even beyond these others, is that one who, after loading you down with gifts, leads you as his bride home. I have never with these eyes seen anything like you, neither man nor woman. Wonder takes me as I look on you.[1]

Imagine being fifteen years old and greeted in such a fashion! Here is the Odysseus beloved of Athena—tactful, gallant, a weaver of words, able to persuade anyone of anything, a man who in spite of all his losses is never at a loss. He even gently implies a possible love relationship, saying, "May the gods give you everything that your heart longs for, may they grant you a husband and a house and sweet agreement in all things, for nothing is better than this."[2]

When he asks her for a rag to cover his nakedness so that she may show him the town, she agrees with alacrity, adding that he is clearly a fine and intelligent fellow. Obviously, Nausicaa is wondering if this man is the dream-promised husband. She takes charge of the situation, calling the other girls back, and providing him with food and clothes after he has bathed.

After Odysseus scrubs himself down, Athena makes him beautiful, topping his head with hyacinthine locks and stretching him taller than before. When she sees his transformation, Nausicaa remarks to her handmaidens that this formerly unpromising-looking stranger now looks exactly like a god. She wistfully adds, "If only the man to be called my husband could be like this one, a man living here, if only this one were pleased to stay here."[3]

The transformation of Odysseus from a foul-looking, battered adventurer into a radiant, handsome presence signals the beginning of the reunion of Athena and Odysseus after more than nine years. Since leaving Troy, the goddess, although always protecting him, could not appear in person, because of the wrath of the gods he has called down upon himself. Also, as the human extension of Athena in the world of space and time, he had compromised both her nature and his through his various blunders. Now, after all his trials and learnings, he is chastened, deepened, and finally worthy of the goddess, and will represent her nature in this world. From this moment on, she will be constantly about, in one form or another, using her godly skills to assure his well-being.

Nausicaa is coquettish as Odysseus accompanies her back to the city, warning him that they will need to enter the city separately lest some lowlife stir up scandal by saying, "Who is this handsome and distinguished stranger with Nausicaa? He'll be her husband no doubt, I suppose. . . . Perhaps a god descended in answer to her prayer and he will make her his forever. Better for her if she finds her husband from some place else, since she scorns all the local fellows. . . ."[4]

This flirtation, worthy of Scarlett O'Hara, cannot be taken too seriously, and Odysseus maintains a balance of the fatherly and the courtly in his attitude to the young girl. As one commentator has put it: "With the immortal Circe and Calypso, Odysseus had no age, but with Nausicaa he is a mature man. Much of the humor in their encounter stems from this discrepancy of ages, which attracts them to each other and yet helps to keep them apart."[5]

Nausicaa brings Odysseus to the grove of Athena, where he prays that he will be well received by the Phaeacians. After leaving Nausicaa, he encounters the goddess herself, disguised as a young girl who shows him about. Without his knowing it, she covers him with a magical mist that hides him from all inquiring eyes. As he walks through the land, Odysseus meets what he has missed for decades—the ordered beauty of a high civilization. Everything seems balanced and harmonious—the elegant ships, the beautiful harbor, the fine meeting places, the long lofty walls of the city, intricately fitted into the surrounding rocky hills. He enters the city through elaborately symmetrical but flourishing orchards and vineyards surrounded by orderly rows of a great variety of vegetables. Two springs flow here; one irrigates the orchard, while the other runs to the palace to supply water inside. It is the finest collaboration between man and nature that Odysseus has ever seen.

At the center of this artful landscape stands a testimony to purely human genius, the palace of Alcinous. It is a shining wonder with its bronze-plated walls, its circling frieze of lapis lazuli, its silver pillars and golden doors. Gold and silver dogs guard either side of the threshold, and inside, golden boys stand on pedestals holding flaming torches. Fifty women are busy within grinding grain and weaving lush fabrics.

Superb artisans, craftsmen, inventors, sailors, and agronomists, the Phaeacians stand in diametric opposition to their distant relatives the Cyclopeans, whose only skill appears to have been cheesemaking. As Norman Austin says in *Archery at the Dark of the Moon*, his superb study of *The Odyssey*: "The polychromatic, polymorphous scene in Alcinous' palace reveals an organically functioning community, the first *polis* Odysseus has seen since leaving Troy, just as the monopolistic industry in Polyphemus' cave reveals the monocular character of its inhabitant."[6]

In the Homeric scheme of things, what is this place? The Phaeacians themselves suggest that they exist halfway between humans and gods. Is their society meant to be a model of civilization to come, or a remembrance of a civilization that once was? I suspect that they are both, but that the strongest influence comes from the past, and that Homer has created the land of the Phaeacians from a folk memory of Aegean matrifocal civilization before the coming of the patriarchal invaders.

The latest research tells us of these matrifocal cultures; the Phaeacians seem a remarkable approximation. This is evidenced by the outlying pastures; the exotically decorated and beautifully laid-out palace; the sophisticated gardens with their rich variety of produce; the women weaving complex textiles in the palace; the palace as a center for art, music, poetry, dance, singing, and games; the men meeting in the harbor among the fishing and trading vessels; and their great skill as navigators.[7]

Additionally, their lives are regulated by much ceremony and many courtesies, as befits a high, aesthetic culture. As in the earlier Minoan and Cretan societies, the men's domain is the harbor and the sea, while the women attend to most of the town life and the affairs of the household. In meeting the Phaeacians, are we also meeting memories of Knossos and other Cretan and Minoan civilizations?

Further, like earlier Aegean city-states, it appears to be a partnership society, with men and women sharing the dominion and the decisions. This is particularly evident in Nausicaa's warning to Odysseus when he enters the city not to bother with the king, but to go directly to the one who makes the real decisions about who stays and who goes—her mother, Queen Arete. She is a formidable lady, a favorite of Athena, and the arbiter in all disputes. But she maintains her reserve when Odysseus enters, bows, and throws his arms around her knees in supplication, entreating her help in a passionate and heart-rending speech. She responds by granting him formal protection, but does not stand on ceremony when she recognizes that he is wearing clothes she herself has made. "What man are you, and whence? And who was it gave you this clothing? Did you not say that you came here ranging over the water?'' What the queen is really asking here is: ''What is your relationship with my daughter?''

Odysseus does not respond directly. Rather, he offers a brilliant and poignant description of his stay with Calypso and what befell him after leaving her island, ending with a true account of his meeting with Arete's daughter, but he does not yet reveal his true identity. With this speech Odysseus creates the enormous impression he intended. Old Alcinous is so bowled over, he immediately offers him Nausicaa in marriage and many properties beside. But the king also understands and delicately suggests that the stranger may have another home that he will really want to return to right away. Alcinous agrees to consult with his people about arranging for his conveyance. As the poet tells us, ''long-suffering great Odysseus was happy.''

The next morning Alcinous and Odysseus go to the assembly place, but not before Athena. Disguised as Alcinous' own herald, she has spoken privately to each citizen, saying, ''Come with me, leaders of the Phaiakians and men of counsel, to the place of assembly, there to find out about the stranger who is new-come to the house of wise Alcinous, after wandering on the great sea, and in shape he is like the immortals.''[8]

Needless to say the assembly place fills rapidly to see this marvelous stranger, and marvel he is, Athena having just drifted a magical grace about his head and shoulders and, as usual, making him taller than before. (Poor Odysseus seems to grow and shrink regularly according to Athena's aesthetic whims.)

At the assembly, the gracious and generous Phaeacians grant him his wish and make ready a large black boat requiring fifty-two strong rowers to carry him home.[9] After making a sacrifice in honor of this event, and after the feasting, all grow silent in order to hear the great bard Demodocus sing. His choice of material that day happens to be the famed quarrel between those hero-warriors Odysseus and Achilles! Hearing the sweet bard sing his song, Odysseus, still incognito, cannot control his weeping, and tries to cover his head in his mantle.

Only the perceptive Alcinous notices his guest's sorrow and suggests a change of program: "Show the stranger how well we do in athletic contests!" The young men try to lure Odysseus to try his mettle in the sports, but he begs off, claiming his mind is more on cares than on games. One young man, perhaps jealous of the older man's reception by the royal family, taunts him rudely, claiming that he declines only because he has no gift for sports, being built more on the lines of a merchant, one who cares only for profits.

Odysseus responds to this rudeness both spiritually and physically. On the spiritual level he speaks of two different kinds of grace: One man may be a match for the gods in body, but his words may lack grace; another may be less noted for beauty, "but the god puts comeliness on his words, and they who look toward him are filled with joy at the sight, and he speaks to them without faltering in winning modesty, and shines among those who are gathered, and people look on him as on a god when he walks in the city."[10]

To make his answer physically, Odysseus stands up, picks up the discus, and casually hurls it farther than any of the Phaeacians had ever dreamed possible. He adds to their astonishment by claiming that he has similar skills with the bow and arrow as well as the spear. Kind Alcinous diplomatically saves the Phaeacian honor by suggesting they show the stranger their expertise at the dance. His speech is a model statement of the life and entertainments of a non-militaristic society: "For we are not perfect in our boxing, nor yet as wrestlers, but we do run lightly on our feet, and are excellent seamen, and always the feast is dear to us, and the lyre and dances and changes of clothing and our hot baths and beds."[11]

And as the glorious young dancers execute their marvelous steps, "Odysseus gazed on the twinkling of their feet, his heart full of wonder." To accompany the dancers, Demodocus sings a bawdy tale of the way Aphrodite and Ares were caught *in flagrante delicto* in a bed especially engineered by her husband, the club-footed Olympian blacksmith Hephaestus, to spring a tight net around them so that they could not escape. When the cuckolded Hephaestus calls for the gods to come and witness the adulterous pair in his trap, only the male gods come and roar with Olympian laughter at their predicament. The goddesses stay away out of a feeling of embarrassment for Aphrodite and their sex. The song tells of the humiliation to which even the gods are subject when the bounds of propriety are transgressed.[12]

For all the burlesque humor of the song, it presages the far grimmer episode that will occur in Ithaca within a few days.[13] For then it will be Odysseus who sets the trap and bloodily revenges himself upon the suitors in Ithaca, who, in their desire for his wife, have also been wasting his property and destroying the inheritance of his son, Telemachus.

The song is followed by a brilliant demonstration by the young men of the intricate Phaeacian dance with a ball. Then come the guest gifts. Each of the twelve Phaeacian lords sends to his home for a rich gift for Odysseus. He will return far wealthier than ever he was before he lost his loot to Poseidon. So gifted, Odysseus bathes and prepares himself for the major banquet in his honor. On the way to the feast, he meets Nausicaa for the last time. Both look their best, and their parting, though inevitable, is poignant.

> Then Nausicaa, with the gods' loveliness on her, stood beside the pillar that supported the roof with its joinery, and gazed upon Odysseus with all her eyes and admired him, and spoke to him aloud and addressed him in winged words, saying: "Good-bye, stranger, and think of me sometimes when you are back at home, how I was the first you owed your life to." Then resourceful Odysseus spoke in turn and answered her: "Nausicaa, daughter of great-hearted Alcinous, even so may Zeus, high-thundering husband of Hera, grant me to reach my house and see my day of homecoming. So even when I am there I will pray to you, as to a

> goddess, all the days of my life. For, maiden, my life was your gift."[14]

That is all. Nausicaa has advanced the cause of Odysseus as far as she can, and now her part is over. Many readers have expressed sorrow at this parting, feeling it to be "like a musical phrase left incomplete." And yet nothing else could really happen. The classical style requires the parts to be subordinate to the whole, that the episodes be secondary to the higher purpose. There can be no romance, even though we sentimental readers might desire it. As scholar W. B. Stanford noted: "From the point of view of ethics, Penelope would have good reason to view any liaison between her husband and Nausicaa very differently from the Circe and Calypso incidents. There was no supernatural sanction on Nausicaa's side."[15]

Still, one wonders what happened to the luminous girl, and some authors, like Samuel Butler and Robert Graves, suggest that what happened is that she turned around and wrote *The Odyssey*! Drawing upon Butler's hypothesis, Robert Graves wrote a delightful novel with this premise, *Homer's Daughter*, a tale of Nausicaa herself, a princess and priestess of Athena in Sicily. Their hypothesis draws upon the fact that the whole of *The Odyssey* is predominantly pro-woman, unlike *The Iliad* or other Greek epics of the time. Also, it contains extraordinary knowledge concerning women's crafts, especially weaving, while seamen have cited some real mistakes about ships and the running of ships unlikely to have been made by a male writer.[16] True or not, it is a delicious hypothesis and worthy of the character and temperament of Nausicaa.

At the banquet, Odysseus asks the singer Demodocus to tell the story of his greatest exploit, the episode of the Wooden Horse. (Remember, the Phaeacians still do not know who he is.) Always the dramatist, and with a theatrical sense of timing, Homer wishes this to be the prologue of Odysseus' revelation of himself as the author of the famous stratagem.

> Sing us
> the wooden horse, which Epeios made with Athene
> helping

the stratagem great Odysseus filled once with men and
brought it
to the upper city, and it was these men who sacked Ilion.
If you can tell me the course of all these things as they
happened,
I will speak of you before all mankind, and tell them
how freely the goddess gave you her magical gift of
singing.
. . . He sang then how the sons of the Achaians left their
hollow
hiding place and streamed from the horse and sacked the
city,
and he sang how one and another fought through the
steep citadel,
and how in particular Odysseus went, with godlike
Menelaos, like
Ares, to find the house of Deiphobos,
and there, he said, he endured the grimmest fighting that
ever
he had, but won it there too, with great-hearted Athene
aiding.[17]

Listening to the song, Odysseus dissolves into paroxysms of weeping. After ten years of initiations and learnings he is no longer the same cool Odysseus, the sacker of cities. His former pride in his heroic accomplishments has now turned into pity for the victims of his conquest. The Homeric description is as powerful as it is revealing:

As a woman weeps, lying over the body of her dear husband, who fell fighting for her city and people as he tried to beat off the pitiless day from city and children; she sees him dying and gasping for breath, and winding her body about him she cries high and shrill, while the men behind her, hitting her with their spear butts on the back and shoulders, force her up and lead her away into slavery, to have hard work and sorrow, and her cheeks are wracked with pitiful weeping. Such were the pitiful tears Odysseus shed from under his brows. . . .[18]

Having learned so much from women, this identification of Odysseus with the plight of women in wartime indicates the great change that has come upon him. The sensitivity we saw him use with Nausicaa and the family of Alcinous is now extended further into a universal compassion. His hitherto suppressed sympathies, the hard mask of his warrior stance, has dissolved with the tears that overwhelm him. The full brutality of heroic action stands revealed in all its starkness. The Trojan War is now seen for the unspeakably cruel and barbaric exercise that it was, and Odysseus, the chief architect of the Greek victory, condemns himself and the ways of war.

After such an outburst, the subtle Alcinous alone "remarked him and recognized him." But instead of revealing the name of his guest, he chooses the more tactful strategy of inviting Demodocus to lay down his instrument, for "from the moment when the divine singer began his song our guest has not ceased from bitter weeping. Surely, some great sorrow surrounds him."[19] He asks Odysseus to take the place of Demodocus and tell his tale, who he is and where he comes from, where he has been, what and whom he has seen, and what his connection is to the subject of Demodocus' song.

To the rapt audience, Odysseus tells his name and then his tale, a song that exceeds in beauty and incident and profundity any the Phaeacians have ever heard. And what is so wonderful and mysterious about it is that it is no travelogue, but a full recounting of the stages of the Hero's Journey, and a story of initiations and rapprochement with the depth world, the world of women, and the Mysteries of the inner journey.

He interrupts his tale but once, at midnight after he has told of his meeting with the great queens in the Underworld. It is then that the living queen, Arete, gives him her admiration and confidence and says to the Phaeacians, "What do you think now of this man before you for beauty and stature, and for the mind well balanced within him."[20] He has won over Arete and is now literally home free, for as Athena in the form of Nausicaa had warned him, he must win over Arete's mind, the mind of the great human woman, if he is to finally achieve his return home. His journey through the reality and minds of goddesses—that is, with the depth feminine—has prepared him for reconciliation with woman in her human form.

Finally, the tale is finished and Odysseus has brought his story up to the present: "So he spoke, and all of them stayed stricken to silence, held in thrall by the story all through the shadowy chambers."

And Alcinous understands why this man of many ways and many mysteries can never become his son-in-law. He calls for further gifts to be given his esteemed guest, clothing and gold and cauldrons and tripods, lavishly worked metals, the masterworks of the Mycenean world. At dawn, the Phaeacians bring many treasures down to the ship. And while Odysseus falls into a deep but sweet sleep, the fifty-two rowers bring the ship swiftly to Ithaca.

His sleep is described as one like death. It is the sleep of a man who, in both the journey of the hero and the journey of the Mysteries, is finally fully initiated. This being so, he has in some sense died to the old Odysseus, and can be reborn back into the world of space and time, a fully realized man. And so when he awakens from this blessed but deathlike sleep, it will not be to disaster as it had been on previous occasions. He will awaken having crossed the magic threshold between the worlds, home at last in Ithaca.

Caring Like the Phaeacians

NAUSICAA'S care for the homeless, shipwrecked Odysseus is an inspiration to us all. She sees beyond his naked desperation to the person within, and offers that person food, clothing, and hospitality. Equally important are the roles her mother and father play in their generous hospitality to the unknown stranger, which includes giving him the opportunity to tell his story fully before a sympathetic and understanding audience. Then, loading him with gifts, they provide for his journey home.

This story of ancient hospitality and empowerment provides a model for action in our treatment of those people who have suffered today's equivalent of massive shipwreck—the homeless, most of whom are women and children; the runaways; the refugees who come to this land having no friends or knowledge of our language and ways; the crack babies and people with AIDS; those who have been disempowered by losing their jobs or by other shifts in the economy; the older ones left lonely or caught in uncaring agencies; and so on.

Like the generous and caring Phaeacians, the individuals or groups who are working through this book can covenant to seek out some stranger or strangers among the contemporary shipwrecked ones in their vicinity and instead of giving charity at a distance or help from a sense of superiority, truly provide deep recognition as well as practical assistance. Above all, listen deeply to their stories, and in council, as the Phaeacians did, be willing to agree to provide some tangible "boat" that will allow them to make the next part of the journey to where they need to be. This ongoing project would be the individual's or group's commitment to that noble way of life "between humankind and the gods" that the Phaeacians embodied.

TELLING THE STORY

The central books of *The Odyssey* are actually part of a wonderful and elaborate literary device, perhaps even a ruse, that Homer sets up so that Odysseus will be invited by the Phaeacians to tell the story of all his adventures. This gives him the opportunity to simultaneously remember them, recite them, and reflect on them deeply. He describes all the stages of the Hero's Journey he has survived: the call, his blunders, the crossing of many thresholds, the endurance of many trials along the road of that name and so forth. But he also offers his account of the initiations into the Mysteries that he has undergone, and of his rapprochement with the depth world, with his meeting of the ancestors, and the guidance and nurturance he has received from the feminine powers. His story is of coming into fullness through the Way of the Mysteries as well as through the more traditional Hero's Journey.

We will now engage a process I call "The Epiphany of the Moment."[21] We will employ it as a process to reveal the depths and dimensions of our own stories through a rapid reflection on the main episodes of *The Odyssey*.

We prepare for this session by doing the following assignment: Throughout the preceding day, several times an hour, we will stop whatever automatic, ordinary thing we're doing and become luminous to the moment. In other words, we will experience the moment as one in which all of creation is at hand and we know ourselves to be a part of it. Every seemingly trivial act or happening is filled with "epiphany," filled with the sacred, and abounding with meaning, relevance, and multiple associations. As we experience the grandeur in the ordinary, we will quickly make a note of it and then describe fully the revelational qualities it contains.

This epiphany can occur when we are brushing our teeth, locking the door, running for a bus, standing on line at the supermarket, or even considering some event that may have occurred in the past, say when we were five. Here, for example, are several "epiphany of the moment" poems that Judith Morley wrote while doing this process. (In fact, she has written and brilliantly performed several books of poems using this method.)

CATCHING THE BUS

The bus on wheels and I flying afoot
arrive at the corner
sim-ul-tan-e-ous-ly
Ah!
Synchronicity comes to the real world
What a good day this is going to be

I have caught the bus
I have not caught the flu
and I remembered
to pull out the plug
of the electric coffee pot
before I left the house.

STANDING ON LINE AT THE SUPERMARKET

Lifting the parcel
Off the supermarket treadmill
I hear myself saying:

I HATE all this
waiting in line
for a loaf of bread

Well, then!

Would I have Loved
my work
were it

felling the trees
clearing the brush
piling the rocks
plowing the earth
watching the moon
bedding the seed
praying the rain
battling the bugs

standing with gun cocked for marauder
racing raccoon to the first tender ears
picking the yield in the wild August sun

husking it
drying it
scraping it
pounding it
and baking it—for my bread

Would I have Loved
my work
then?

WHEN I WAS FIVE

When I was five
Margie Gahn said
I was *not g r a c e f u l enough*
to be in her dancing class
but I could WATCH.
I thought I was pretty good.

When I was nine
Miss Laughinghouse said
I was *not t u n e f u l enough*
to be in her singing class
but I must LISTEN.
I thought I was pretty good.

When I was forty-seven
Merle Levine said
I was *not e v o l v e d enough*
to be in her consciousness-raising group
but I might AUDIT.
I thought I was pretty good.

If they had said
come dance with us—
come sing with us—
come grow with us—
Oooooooooohhhhhhhhh
What a difference!

TIME: One hour.

MATERIALS NEEDED: Paper and pencils.

MUSIC: No music required.

INSTRUCTIONS FOR THE SOLO VOYAGER: This exercise is easily done alone by making a tape of the script and by following the instructions. Be sure to leave the appropriate time on the tape for doing the work.

SCRIPT FOR THE GUIDE: We are now ready to begin a process by which we rev ourselves up by making z-z-zing sounds for some seconds, after which I will suddenly drop in an image drawn from *The Odyssey.* You will experience this image as a charge to come up with rich verbal or poetic associations that relate to your own life and thought. Each Homeric episode will serve to harvest the essence of your life. You will immediately write these knowings and associations down. You will have no more than two minutes to rapidly write down each poem or epiphany of the moment based on *The Odyssey.* Than we will begin z-z-zing again, after which another Odyssean image will be given you to write about. As you make the zzz-zzz sound, allow your whole body to vibrate slightly with this sound. Feel the sound going down your spine and then down your arms and legs to your hands and feet. Let your whole body hum with the zzz-zzz-zzz.

Get ready now. Have your pencil and paper ready? All right, begin. Zzz-zzz-zzz. Zzz-zzz-zzz.

[The guide continues to do the sound with the group for about a minute. Then the guide says:]

SACKING ISMARUS! [Two minutes.]

All right. Here we go again with the sound. Zzz-zzz-zzz-zzz-zzz-zzz. [One minute.]

THE LOTUS-EATERS! Relate it to your own life. Quickly. An epiphany of the moment. [Two minutes.]

[The guide continues to give the directions using the same timing throughout.]

Zzz-zzz-zzz-zzz-zzz-zzz. THE CYCLOPS! . . .

Zzz-zzz-zzz-zzz-zzz-zzz. THE WINDS OF AEOLUS! . . .

Zzz-zzz-zzz-zzz-zzz-zzz. MEETING WITH CIRCE! . . .

Zzz-zzz-zzz-zzz-zzz-zzz. THE DESCENT TO THE UNDERWORLD AND THE MEETING WITH TIRESIAS, THE ANDROGYNE! . . .

Zzz-zzz-zzz-zzz-zzz-zzz. THE WAY PAST THE SIRENS! . . .

Zzz-zzz-zzz-zzz-zzz-zzz. SCYLLA AND CHARYBDIS! . . .

Zzz-zzz-zzz-zzz-zzz-zzz. CALYPSO'S ISLE FOR SEVEN YEARS! . . .

Zzz-zzz-zzz-zzz-zzz-zzz. I AM ODYSSEUS! . . .

Now would you please turn to one other person, and just as Odysseus recited his adventures to the Phaeacians, would you and your partner please read to each other what you have written for each adventure. Begin. [Five minutes].

INSTRUCTIONS FOR THE SOLO VOYAGER: Read your notes into a tape recorder with great passion and power. Then play the tape back, listening to the voice and the stories as if for the very first time. Find an epiphany in your own imagination!

Examples from seminars of Odyssey Epiphany Poem Cycles:

THE SACKING OF ISMARUS

Why do I want to pillage,
tear and rip apart,
each time a tiny word,
pierces me and hurts my heart.

When, oh when will
the world be named
innocent and free
of hurting me.

* * *

Ismarus sacked by me?
Me, who would never harm a fly?
But wait!
What cities on the shores
of others' hopes and plaintive dreams
Have I ravaged by my all too ready wit
and caustic common sense?

THE LOTUS-EATERS

The Lotus-Eaters call
to lull me, soothe me,
swallow me
within the tender melting

boughs of those so
gracious trees.

The power of their call!
Sleep and dream.
Dream that you lived and
did not care
whether you lived
or dreamed.

* * *

Am I the taster or the tasted?
Am I the eater or the eaten?
Lotus dreams waft me into mindless bliss
Bliss that opens my margins so wide
I no longer know nor care where I leave off
And You begin.
Let me Be. I Am not going anywhere.

THE CYCLOPS

Single seer!
Wheel-eyed one!
When your eye turns,
Can you see the world
upside down?

What a vision!
No wonder heroes cannot stand you.

Warning: We put out eyes which
do not see the way we do!

* * *

Under the ram again, clinging to fleece,
I once more escape your hungry hands.
Yahhh Cyclops! If anyone asks who put out your only eye
Tell them it was Christopher Columbus
And I came to steal your cheese and sacrifice your sheep
To my one true church.

THE WINDS OF AEOLUS

The winds of Aeolus
toss me

like a piece
of cork
across the hurly-burly
river-seas of life.

Am I a Frisbee in the playful
hand of some amusing god
who wants to see how far
surprising out I fling?

Yearning to feel myself
a boomerang
flung aptly out,
feeling the moment of
Whang!
Turn!
right back to laugh
into the eyes of my
aboriginal and oh-so-playful god.

* * *

Winds winding down as I slide to middle age.
Is this the still center of the hurricane
Are there yet stormier times in store
Or am I finally at rest, soft breezes cooling
The fires of my life.
Hey Spiritus! Come out, come out, wherever You are.

CIRCE

Why, silly man, did you come along
and make the lady change us back
again to human beings.

What is this human stuff anyway?
Nothing but snort and snout and snuff,
rooting around in life trying to
find the truffles.

When we were pigs we knew.

* * *

Circe, have Mercy.
I too have turned men into pigs.

But for me, they stayed that way.
Send me please an Odysseus to reverse the formula.
I too will have them younger and taller
And more beautiful than before.

TIRESIAS

Tiresias in the Underworld
Delves blind to warn us what may come
Of living.

What does he see there?
How discern the trace of light
That guides my life
Along the shadowed cavern roads
Where death is king?

I can't see, I cry. It's so dark I can't see!

Open your eyes, let blindness enter.
See nothing and know all.
When darkness rules, only the blind
Can see.

* * *

Tiresias a blind prophet of old
Was bisexual, bi-temporal and bold
He knew future and past
How your horoscope's cast
But was sadly the ultimate scold.

THE SIRENS

Wild bees,
Burn me! Pour your burning
In my honeyed ears.
Does honey burn?
Oh, yes!
Sweet fire,
Ignite!
Burn all,
Even my bones,

And let my spirit wander
On this shore forever.
My bones dry out,
Still I sing with you,
I know! I know!

* * *

Can it be? Someone is finally calling me?
I'd better go to the ear doctor and have the wax removed.
Ah, that's better. Now I can hear you.
What! You are telling me WHAT?
Oh my god.
Ohhhhhhhhh.

I AM ODYSSEUS

I am Odysseus.
I am trouble.
But I am kindness too.
A force of nature moves in me
Shaking the foundations
Bringing peace to the violent
And unleashing the tame.

* * *

I Am Odysseus,
  On surface of the seas I seek out unknown shores,
    forever widening the margins of myself.
  I try to encompass everything.
  Or, do I learn as I go deep in caves
    to become the surface of the midnight sea,
    nothing, yet reflecting everything?

NOTES AND SUGGESTIONS FOR FURTHER DISCUSSION AND ASSIGNMENTS: Part of your practice can be to pay attention to all your actions, but especially little ones. These might include cleaning the sink, or tying your shoe, or noticing some local drama with a neighbor. Stop and write an epiphany of that moment. Do at least two or three each day. Create a little journal within your Odyssey journal called "The Epiphany of the Moment." Pour the gift of rich language and cosmic associations into the things of every day. That's how we create epic consciousness—the ability to see each thing as luminous with possibilities and associations.

Notice what happens as you work with these epiphanies. By relating any part of your story or any moment of your life to *The Odyssey,* or any myth, you will find your story illumined, for a myth is a force field. And by giving yourself insufficient time, a minute or two at the most, you don't have time to block. Working in poetic forms allows the fullness of our experience to come through because we transcend the usual limitations of our grammatical experience.

If you continue creating epiphanies for a while, you will discover that your ordinary experiences really are extraordinary. Gradually, you will begin to see with new eyes and speak with rich metaphorical speech. Your mouth will be "filled with blood." This is a way to become bardic and Homeric—by raising common events to new dimensions.

One useful side effect is that you will learn to say even horrible things about yourself magnificently. If you're going to be toxic, be toxic with majesty! Instead of being "poor old me," take "poor old me" to the level of Shakespearean or Homeric cadence and join the mythic and mundane realities.

A sizable part of the brain is devoted to the linguistic structure, and to take care of it adequately we need to give it delectably juicy stuff to chew on. One way to provide it with inspiration, instruction, and exercise is to practice "The Epiphany of the Moment," and then relate these seemingly ordinary moments of our lives to the events and moments of great stories and myths.

CHAPTER 11

The Initiation of Telemachus

WHILE Odysseus sleeps, let us look at what has been happening to his son in preparation for his return. The story of Telemachus occupies almost a third of *The Odyssey*—the first four books and part of the fifteenth. Together, they are referred to as the *Telemacheia*. Indeed, some scholars feel that the story of the education of Telemachus, whose name means "Far Fighter," is so developed and complete in itself that it may once have been a separate song cycle that got pieced into *The Odyssey*.[1]

My own sense is that it was always an integral part of the larger poem, not only because its poetic unity in rhythm and theme are mirrored in the larger poem, but also because the balance of the story requires that two complete initiatory cycles be presented. For *The Odyssey* is above all a book of initiations, the first being the initiation of Odysseus into proper relationship with female powers and into the fullness of second or higher maturity.

But there is another equally important initiation, the rite of passage of Odysseus' son, Telemachus, out of boyhood into manhood. In this case the initiation is embodied within the metaphor of education. Telemachus must be educated to become the true heir of Odysseus, capable of assuming heroic stature in Ithaca. As Norman Austin says:

> The son, in order to become spiritually like the father, traces out a reduced, and to some degree symbolic, journey in imitation of his father. Telemachus duplicates in important ways the kinds of experience Odysseus undergoes. He too must brave the sea to visit unknown peoples; he too will see cities and come to know mind. There will be a powerful king and queen to receive him, as there will be for Odysseus. Like the father, the son will arrive incognito at a magnificent palace, his identity will be recognized, and he will prevail through his charm and find there what he needs for his return.[2]

In the almost magical resonance between their two journeys, each assures the success of the other. But before we explore Telemachus' remarkable rite of passage, let us look at some of the dynamics inherent in this ritual structure, one that we find is as relevant today as it was in the twelfth century B.C.

Rites of passage—that is, rites in which one is prepared and then initiated into the next stage of one's life journey—have been performed for many thousands of years and may be part of the inner coding for human development. The rite is crucial in that it allows one to "die" to an earlier stage of development and awaken to a higher one. In the rite of passage from childhood or adolescence to maturity, one dies to one's childhood and its associations and is reborn to adulthood and its responsibilities and privileges. In the course of these rites, then, one undergoes the passage into becoming a new being—from novice into full initiate. Modern life provides but a thin crust over the memory of millennia of these initiatory experiences. But, go beneath the surface crust of consciousness, and the forms and functions of these rituals are still there, often in explicit and concrete detail. Over the past thirty years, thousands of my research subjects and hundreds of thousands of my seminar participants have confirmed this time and again.

My own first encounter with this phenomenon was notable not only because of the archaic cast of the experience, but also in the way it typified the stages of the adolescent rite of passage. In the early 1960s, I was asked by government researchers to join in a scientific study of the effects of LSD on human personality. Although I was very young at the time, it was thought that as a student of the philosophy of religion and comparative mythology and symbolism, I would be able to help in identifying some of the symbolic experiences that research subjects were having. My husband, Robert Masters, and I have recorded this research in a number of books, and the following case history is a somewhat expanded version of one that occurs in our *The Varieties of Psychedelic Experience.*[3]

My subject was a diffident young man in his early twenties, not unlike Telemachus in some ways. He seemed to have little ambition and spent a good deal of time daydreaming. His father had died when he was young, and his mother had never really "found herself." He felt inadequate to the challenges around him, and although highly intelligent and well educated, did work that was far below his capacity. His reason for becoming a research subject was that he felt he needed some kind of radical "push" to get him motivated.

Several hours into his LSD session I began drumming on the table and suggesting that he envision an African rite of initiation—possibly a puberty rite. Almost immediately the young man began to describe a journey through the night to a place where a ritual was going on involving many young boys who appeared to be moving around a fire on hands and knees while being struck by much older men—graybeards and grandfathers. I asked him if he minded the beating, and he answered, "No, it is quite necessary if I am to be reborn." He then described himself as being wrapped up in some kind of animal skins. I asked him if he knew what kind of skins they were, and was told: "Sheep . . . goat . . . I remain three days and am then reborn." (I found this especially noteworthy, for it echoed other initiation rituals in which the symbolism of birth is almost always found alongside that of death.)

He then spoke of gaining some special knowledge while he was wrapped up, some deep teaching. Many stories of "how things came to be" were recounted to him, presumably by the old men. After receiving these teachings, he discovered himself to be a baby floating in fluid (presumably in amniotic fluid) and moving down the birth canal, pushed along by the contraction of muscles. He then burst into uproarious laughter, for he had not emerged onto the hospital table as expected, but rather into his own Bar Mitzvah (the Jewish rite of passage for adolescent boys).

I asked him for an explanation of the entire sequence. He answered with unusual certainty that people are born incomplete and require a second birth of a spiritual character in order to pass beyond their prolonged fetal condition. One becomes completed by engaging in some significant event or rite of passage in which one is obliged to divest oneself of the embryonic or prehuman nature and enter into the state in which one becomes fully human and fully mature.[4]

My research with LSD lasted only a few years. Subsequently I went on to take depth probings of the human psyche without drugs—using hypnosis, trance, meditation, active imagination, sensory deprivation, and other ways of altering the spectrum of consciousness in order to reach the deeper levels of subconscious knowing. This research showed me that initiatory experiences were always available to consciousness. The experience of my research subjects suggested exactly what much historical and anthropological evidence has demonstrated—that the Mystery of initiation, whether culturally staged or induced through a variety of methods, can deliver young people from shallow adolescent understanding and render their lives more fully dimensional.[5] Chastened by the vision and the teaching of aspects of reality, which include the sacred or extended reality, they must be similarly extended and take upon themselves the obligations and capacities of the adult state. They must die to their shallow natures and rise to their heightened ones.

This is a fact of existence we still seem to recognize on a

subconscious level, even while "officially" regarding these as tenets belonging to archaic societies. The deep truth is that the process by which we attain heightened awareness, maturation, and a greater sense of reality finds expression in the journey away from one's outmoded existence and into new learnings, dyings, and ultimately rebirth. As experienced in altered states of consciousness or staged ritual events or enactments (such as the ones in this book), the initiation can have a profound and frequently transformative effect upon the participant.

At the end of the session above, the young man declared himself "reborn." Later, he stated that his experience had first brought deliverance and then meaning into his life, linking his personal destiny to that of mankind and liberating him from narrow and selfish purposes.

Let us now observe how this initiation process occurs for the son of Odysseus. In good ritual fashion we first meet Telemachus in a state of utter inadequacy and living in outmoded conditions. In Book One, Odysseus is sitting by the shore longing for home, while across the sea in Ithaca, Telemachus has ceased longing for anything. He sits passively in the background, amiably weak, and with none of the yearning we have come to expect of adolescence. He whines and complains but does nothing to oppose the men who are ruining his estate. He seems incapable of making any decisions or taking any action.

Clearly, he is deeply wounded—his wounding taking the form of disempowerment, for no one has given him the attention and acknowledgment usually shown a young prince. Instead, he is mocked and mortified, and his powerlessness is constantly thrown up in his face by the suitors. Unpatterned and unparented, his father absent since he was a baby, and his mother in a constant state of grief, he has become a limp, dispirited antithesis of his father.

In this condition Telemachus would be useless as a confederate for Odysseus when the time comes to destroy the suitors and restore order to the kingdom. Thus, when Athena pleads before Zeus and the other gods for the release of Odysseus because his education has gone far enough, she also announces that she herself will attend to the needed education and training of Telemachus so that he may be made a fit companion for his phenomenal father.[6]

His education begins when Athena arrives in Ithaca in the form of an old family friend, Mentes, and views the wasteland the suitors have created with their riotous occupation of the palace. In the classical ritual scenario, this corresponds to the initial preparation of the adolescents by the elders sponsoring them. Mentes-Athena finds that while the twenty-year-old Telemachus possesses a fine natural character, he is so depressed and frustrated that he is unable to do anything to prevent the wasting of his inheritance. He sits daydreaming about his father returning out of the blue and putting the wastrels to rout. However, he is actually the only decent person in sight, and he accords Mentes-Athena the finest hospitality, welcoming him/her as an honored guest. Telemachus tends to his guest's every need, giving him the finest place and choicest chair, washing and feeding him, and offering him the tastiest morsels as he inquires about Mentes' family.

Athena on her part maintains her human role until the very end and proceeds to educate Telemachus in what will become known as the Socratic mode, by question and answer. Through the course of their conversation there are no superhuman epiphanies, shape-shiftings, mysterious lights, or thunderclaps, only a steady, lucid exchange of information and opinion. Following the dictates of courtly society, she answers all his questions first, and only then inquires into his situation. Is he really Odysseus' son? He certainly looks like him. With the wise Penelope as his mother, his future will surely be a glorious one. But why is all this riotous banqueting going on? Are not these rude feasters making free with his house in a most improper way?

With only a few questions, Athena has reminded him of his potent heritage and the contrast between it and the present conditions in the house. It is a brilliant psychological maneuver to draw him out and begin his true education. As Norman Austin has so aptly put it, the parody of the wedding feast and the parody of song that greets Mentes-Athena "reminds Telemachos, the host, of the embarrassing truth that the guests are not guests but pirates, and the hosts their prisoners. Guests who have become pirates, hosts who have become unwilling prisoners, a presumptive widow, a presumptive son—that is Ithaka when the poem opens."[7]

Telemachus tells his visitor of the wasteland created by the suitors, how they are eating him out of house and home, and that they probably intend to kill him. He tells too about how his mother hates the idea of remarrying with one of them even though she refuses to drive them away. As for his father, Odysseus has ceased to exist for Telemachus, having left a legacy of only sorrow and tears. Indeed, he is even uncertain about his paternity, though his mother affirms that Odysseus is his father.

To this melancholic litany Mentes-Athena responds with wide sympathy. Yes, indeed, it would be just the thing if Odysseus could show up right away and lead the suitors to a bitter wedding with death. But in case that doesn't happen, would it be possible for Telemachus to start to grow up and stop acting like an infant? Instead of dreaming heroic fantasies, consider how they may be put into action. Someone his own age, Orestes, has just done such a thing:

> You are no longer a child; you must put childish thoughts away. Have you not heard what a name Prince Orestes made for himself in the world when he killed the traitor Aegisthus for murdering his noble father? You, my friend—and what a tall and splendid fellow you have grown!—must be as brave as Orestes. Then future generations will sing your praises.[8]

The goddess then gives advice, which she expressly describes as *education*, and this begins his progress into maturity. She counsels him to make a formal protest about what is happening before an assembly of the honored men of the island, and then take a ship and twenty men and go in quest of his father. First, he should voyage to Sandy Pylos to ask old King Nestor for news of his father, and then on to Sparta, where he will inquire the same of Menelaus. Telemachus is immensely heartened by this "education," and feels that Mentes has spoken to him as a father to a son. He urges his guest to stay a little longer. "No," says Mentes-Athena, who then changes into a bird and flies up the chimney!

Telemachus is left bemused, but filled with courage and confidence. He knows that a god has come to inspire him and get him moving on the path to manhood and to redemption of the social order. As readers, we can only wonder how it would feel to entertain an old family friend, hear extraordinary and useful advice, and then watch this person transform into a bird and disappear up the chimney. I suspect one would feel up to any challenge. And that is just how Telemachus feels: seized with a new power, like a human springtide.

In typical adolescent fashion, he immediately asserts his newfound belief in himself before his mother. She makes her first appearance in the story by coming downstairs to ask Phemius, the bard, to stop singing sad songs of the tragic return of the warriors from Troy. He knows so many other tales and ballads, she complains, why can't he sing one that doesn't remind her of her own sorrow. "Sing something happy," she asks.

Telemachus, however, publicly reprimands her by saying, "Mother, the bard has to sing what the bard has a mind to." (We hear echoes of Homer's own sentiments in this.) Besides, Troy marked the end for many another man; Odysseus is not the only one who failed to return. He then orders her upstairs to tend to her weaving—he would be master in the house.

Penelope returns to her rooms in a state of wonder: Her depressed adolescent boy is asserting himself for the first time in his life! Telemachus then turns to the suitors and tells them to stop brawling, to stop eating up his provisions, and to stop destroying his estate. Further, he orders them to appear at a full public assembly the next morning where he can give public notice that they must quit his palace. "I will be master in my own house!" he announces for a second time, to the astonished suitors.

Here we have the classical tale of new growth being

prompted out of the rich fertilizing manure of the decaying social order. (There is plenty of real manure lying around, Homer tells us in no uncertain terms.) Telemachus has been stimulated to assert his new maturity in the face of the decadent maturity of the suitors who squander, befoul, and ravage their borrowed nest. This episode presages the later genre of Tales of the Wasteland. Indeed, the Percival story is of a similar order, with the Grail Castle corresponding to Ithaca. In *The Odyssey,* however, the Grail is not a sacred object, but a missing sacred person. Telemachus will go in search of this person, perhaps not so much to find him as to become worthy of his heritage.

After being tenderly prepared for bed by another elder, his nurse Eurycleia, the boy-about-to-become-a-man plans his strategy and journey. The next morning, however, the council meeting in Book Two is a fiasco and all strategy fails. Telemachus is not yet a match for the suitors, and his boyish appeal to their nonexistent sense of justice carries little weight, especially when he ends his speech by bursting into tears. All he really gains from the assembly is pity, and the leader of the suitors, Antinous, whose name means "anti-mind," blames their prolonged banqueting on Penelope. She has been deceiving them by her ruse of weaving and unweaving the shroud of her father-in-law, Laertes. She had told the suitors that she could not marry until the shroud was finished, and so to gain time had, over the past three years, unwoven at night what she had woven by day.

However, even though Telemachus has proven himself ineffective and unready, he has raised the essential motif of the justice of Odysseus compared to the injustice of the suitors. And, in fact, he prefigures with his words the educational discoveries he will make on his upcoming journey. Howard Clarke makes this point aptly in his study of Telemachus by pointing out the crucial lines in Book Two where this occurs:

> He describes Odysseus' kingship as fatherly in its gentleness (line 47), and he will see gentle and exemplary fathers in Nestor and Menelaus; the food wasted by the Suitors in

their revels in Ithaca (lines 55–56) will be consumed in order and harmony in the feasts in Pylos and Sparta; the wine that intoxicates the Suitors in Ithaca (line 57) will become a tranquillizer in Sparta; and the weakness he protests here (lines 60–61) will be overcome by confidence and resolve before he sees Ithaca again.[9]

Both poetic symmetry and ritual necessity require Telemachus to leave Ithaca immediately and receive further education at the hand of noble humans. As he tells Antinous, the most baneful of the suitors, "I am old enough to learn from others what has happened and to feel my own strength at last."[10] Athena is there to lend her godly power to assure this happening, turning up this time as another old family friend, Mentor, whose name means "teacher." As Mentor she helps Telemachus fit and man his boat—even taking on Telemachus' own form to gather and instruct the crew. She then advises him on his journey, and travels with him as far as Pylos.

What happens next in this journey of education follows both the classical form of a boy's initiation into manhood and stages of the traditional Mystery religions, particularly the Eleusinian Mystery.[11] The first part is consonant with the initiatory night journey or night theft of the boy away from his home. In examples found the world over, an older man takes, or even sometimes steals, a boy away from his home and mother at night in order to begin his initiation into adulthood. In Telemachus' journey we have a variant tradition known as the night-sea journey; nevertheless, he leaves under the cover of darkness and without Penelope's knowledge.

However, Telemachus has Athena-Mentor accompanying and advising him. In directing his initiation, she resembles the older men of any number of archaic rituals of initiation into adulthood. But where they are often dressed as gods, spirits, and other mythic beings (witness, for example, the kachina dancers of the Hopi, who wear masks and carry sacred objects of gods and spirits), Athena, the goddess, is "dressed" as a human, and in this form provides instruction.

Athena also plays the part here of the *mystagogos,* who in the Mystery tradition serves as guide and initiator to a deeper life.

The traditional initiation next demands that the young initiates travel to some sacred ground. (In the Eleusinian Mysteries, after suitable sacrifice and preparation, the candidate for initiation traveled from Athens to the sacred ground of the Telesterion at Eleusis in the company of a *mystagogos.*) Rites conducted on sacred ground are believed to reactivate mythic events and mythic time, bringing back the power of the primary mythic moment so that the candidate for initiation opens up to primordial aboriginal creative time and space. Often the sacred ground is thought to be related in some way, if not identical to, the place where the great mythic event or story occurred. At Eleusis, for example, it was thought that this was the very place where Demeter had stayed in her search for her daughter Persephone. In boys' initiation rites, one is taken to the place where gods or sacred ancestors have performed some world- or culture-creating event. These events are generally told or enacted by performers who may assume the mode, dress, and even something of the essence of the gods or demi-gods involved in those events.

The sacred ground for Telemachus would have to be in the Peloponnese, around the original site of Mycenean civilization, and under the governance of Nestor and Menelaus, two of the surviving royal victors of the Trojan campaign. He must travel away from his life of limited possibilities and childhood expectations to the sacred ground of Pylos and Sparta to learn more of his father and family background, and to receive the education required to move him to manhood.

A second phase of the process of education through initiation has the boys sequestered in fearful seclusion (as with my research subject's "remembering" being wrapped for three days). This harrowing experience is a genuine risk and can sometimes result in literal death. More often, thankfully, it allows the boy to die to his inadequacy and be reborn as a man capable of taking on the challenges of the adult state. As part of this ritual, the boy is given secret tribal knowledge—myths of creation and creators, stories of the early struggles of the godlike founders of this culture with primal destructive power. These stories inaugurate the young initiate into the great tradition. He becomes storied too—the latest in the long line of heroes and preservers of his society's deepest purposes and morality.

On his dangerous night journey to and from Pylos, Telemachus accomplishes these initiatory requirements, and in fact the danger becomes critical when the suitors attempt to waylay and kill him on his return journey. And the sacred knowledge imparted to him by the older men, Nestor and Menelaus, contained the quintessential myth of his society. Even though it is recent history, the story is fast becoming mythic in its telling and its repercussions in the Greek psyche. This "new myth" is the story of the Trojan War and the *Nostoi* (tales of the Return), which educate Telemachus to the splendor and tragedy of heroic experience. Additionally, he is educated in the older cultures of Sparta and Pylos, with their high standards of noble culture and manners, something he cannot learn in his ravaged home.

Arriving at Sandy Pylos on the occasion of a great feast, Telemachus is shy at first about speaking to the legendary Nestor. His inadequate upbringing has left him with no skill in making speeches, and no training in courtly procedure. He feels little more than a bumbling bumpkin. Athena-Mentor, however, assures the young prince that the gods have been watching over him since his birth, and wherever his innate knowing fails him, the gods will supply him with the necessary wit. Telemachus does in fact do a credible job in his account of himself and his search for news of his father.

Nestor's response is a long reminiscence of Troy and the return of the victors, ending with the tale of the death of Agamemnon and of Orestes' revenge. In alluding to the action taken by Orestes, Nestor offers him the *paradeigma,* the example for imitation. As German scholar Werner Jaeger says, "the appeal to the example of famous heroes and traditional instances is an integral part of all aristocratic ethics and education."[12] In candor, Telemachus tells Nestor that he doubts whether the gods would give him the strength to bring vengeance to the suitors.

Then, in words that ring with delicious irony, Nestor says, "I only wish that bright-eyed Athene could bring herself to show on your behalf some of the loving care she devoted to your illustrious father in the course of those hard campaigns of ours at Troy. For never in my life have I seen the gods display such open affection as Pallas Athene showed in her championship of Odysseus. Ah, if only she would love and care for you like that."[13]

Telemachus finds the idea that Athena would actually care for him too stunning for his mind to contain. No, the likelihood is that he will never see his father again: "That which I hope for could never happen to me, not even if the gods willed it." This is skepticism bordering on blasphemy, especially in the light of Athena's own presence at his side. One suspects the goddess of laughing to herself as she jumps in to chide him: "Telemachus, what a thing to say! However far a man may have strayed, a friendly god could bring him safely home, and that with ease."[14]

As if to confirm this, Athena soon abandons her Mentor disguise by publicly changing into a sea eagle and flying off. Needless to say, Telemachus' stock rises appreciably. The next day a banquet is given in his honor, before which he is given a bath by Nestor's own daughter. This signals the beginning of his rebirth, as he emerges "looking like a god." Nestor then lends him horses, a chariot, and his own son Peisistratus to accompany him to Sparta. From Nestor he has learned noble codes of conduct and *paradeigma* that he can imitate. He has been publicly honored and feted by men and gods, and now he is ready to enter into the far more elaborate society of Sparta.

Telemachus and his new friend Peisistratus arrive in the midst of a double wedding of Menelaus' son and daughter, entering a gleaming palace of Olympian splendor, which befitted "the richest man in the world." But equally rich is the welcome the two young men receive and the elaborate hospitality that is extended them. By now, Telemachus has become a quick study, and he enters this urbanely elegant society with grace and composure. His only *faux pas* is to be overheard by his host as he whispers loudly to his friend comparing the wealth of these surroundings to the court of Zeus.

The gracious Menelaus puts him at his ease by contrasting his treasures with his sorrows. Too many terrible things occurred in the acquisition of these rich things—the murder of his brother Agamemnon by his treacherous wife Clytemnestra, the ruin of one previous house, the untold misery and death of so many of his friends who accompanied him to Troy to recover Helen. He is the progenitor of incredible sorrows, the worst of which are those of Odysseus. This preys upon his conscience and ruins whatever pleasure he might have enjoyed in his present rich life.

Having been enchanted with the heroic world of Nestor and with his tales of brave deeds and noble codes of honor, Telemachus is now being exposed to a phenomenon that attends more sophisticated rites of passage: disappointment or disenchantment with the "ideal" world, in this case, the world of heroes and riches acquired while fighting for a "just" cause.

Again, this phenomenon of disenchantment is found in many cultures, for it serves to further the awakening of the young person from belief in the appearance of things to pursuit of their essence reality. Among the Hopi, for instance, children grow up regarding the kachinas as the "real" gods who come to their village at intervals to perform awesome acts and marvelous dances. Wearing the heads of birds and storms and clouds, carrying the power of cosmic forces, they bear the stories of origins and contain the secret knowledge of the tribe. They are the tribal myths incarnate. Then, one day, when children reach a certain age, they are taken down into the sacred *kiva,* or meeting place, to await a kachina dance. They listen with mounting excitement as the drums play the rhythm of the dance and the kachinas begin to enter the *kiva*. But they are without their masks. And, worst of all, they are their own fathers and uncles! This is a wrenching and traumatic experience. As one Hopi woman recalled:

> I cried and cried into my sheepskin that night, feeling I had been made a fool of. How could I ever watch the Kachinas dance again? I hated my parents and thought I could never believe the old folks again, wondering if Gods had ever danced for the Hopi as they said and if people really lived after death. I hated to see the other children fooled and felt mad when they said I was a big girl now and should act like one. But I was afraid to tell the others the truth for they might whip me to death. I know now it was best and the only way to teach the children but it took me a long time to know that.[15]

In his penetrating discussion of disenchantment, Sam Gill, a scholar of Native American religious traditions, observes:

> With the unmasking of the kachinas the naiveté of the children is shattered all at once and forever. The existence of the kachinas, the nature of one's own destiny, the trust in parents and elders, and the very shape of reality itself are all, in a flash, brought into radical question. The children can either accept the world as bereft of meaning, with Hopi religion as a sham, or find some deeper sense in the ceremonies and objects which had come to mean so much to them. Necessarily then, they begin their religious life in a state of serious reflection and in quest of an understanding of the sacred profound enough to sustain their new life. There is tremendous incentive for the children to listen even more carefully to the stories of the old people and to participate in the ceremonies with a new seriousness.[16]

One discovers similar modes of disenchantment in what at first might seem dissimilar spiritual traditions. Consider, for example, the initiation ceremony of a young Zen monk. He sits the night long meditating in front of a beautiful but delicate statue of the Buddha. During the course of this meditative night journey it may even seem that the Buddha is inhabiting the statue. The next morning, the elder monks come in and snatch up the Buddha-filled statue and hurl it to the ground, where it breaks into many pieces. The young monk is told, "We are throwing the Buddha to the dogs." This traumatic act of destruction and disenchantment of the image of the Buddha serves to shock and then awaken the initiate to the higher reality of the Buddha-nature, which cannot be found in a particular object.

In the Christian tradition we have the apostles and the three Marys witnessing the death and entombment of Jesus. But then, three days later, when they roll away the stone before the entrance to his tomb, they discover it is empty. This is also an experience of shock and disenchantment—one that leads finally to the grasping of a higher knowing.

In all of these rites of disenchantment, the initiate is moved from naive belief through the crisis of disbelief to the active pursuit of the deeper meaning behind the events. What had once been a vehicle of awe now becomes a symbol pointing beyond itself to a fullness and complexity that require continued growth and constant reflection to comprehend it. At its best, such is the consequence of disenchantment.

In the Homeric version, a double purpose of disenchantment is served. On the one hand, the court of Menelaus with its profound sadness and regret represents the twilight of the once-vaunted heroic age. The air of disenchantment that pervades the court announces the fact that it is time for an end to heroes. Menelaus, chief initiator of the Trojan War, pronounces the end of an era, the dissolution of the heroic world. On the other hand, Telemachus is being asked directly and indirectly to discern a higher form of nobility within the death throes of this age, a form that does not imitate, but, rather, transforms and betters the old mold. Whether he manages this task we never really discover, but the seed has been planted. If Telemachus cannot succeed, then his descendants may. It is they who will be the inheritors of the Homeric journey through disenchantment with the old ways and a reawakening to that vision of human, artistic, and social possibility that will eventually lead to the creation of one of the noblest civilizations the world has ever known.

As Menelaus bemoans the fate of the Greeks after the fall of Troy—most especially Odysseus—tears roll down Telemachus' cheeks. Menelaus begins to suspect who the youth is, but is too discreet to say so immediately. Formal recognition is left for his wife, Helen, to give. At this point she enters, looking like Artemis, the virgin protectress of wild things. Like Artemis, Helen bears a golden distaff and is accompanied by a group of women, each one carrying precious gold and silver accessories for her weaving. On the surface then, she is as radiant as one of Menelaus' many treasures, but is she worth the cost of so much sorrow?

Helen immediately recognizes Telemachus by his likeness to his father. This recognition puts everyone in mind of Odysseus, and the tears of remembrance and regret flow freely. It is then that Helen brings out the drug nepenthe, "banisher of sorrows," and slips it into the bowl in which their wine is mixed. We are told that it "had the power of robbing grief and anger of their sting and banishing all painful memories. No one that swallowed this dissolved in wine could shed a single tear that day, even for the death of mother and father, or if they put his brother or his own son to the sword and he were there to see it done."[17]

When all had drunk their drugged wine and felt suitably detached, Helen, like the tripmaster she was, guided them into another mood to discover pleasure through storytelling. This is another important experience in the milieu of disenchantment. To remember the past fully, husband and wife must chemically distance themselves from it, for its scars run deep, and the pain is ever present. Indeed, as Helen and Menelaus recount stories about Odysseus, it becomes clear that strong tensions still exist between husband and wife. Both tell of Odysseus' inventive cunning that brought about the Greek entry into Troy.

Helen tells us that the master of disguises flogged himself until he looked like a slave and then, dressed in a filthy rag, he explored the streets of Troy. Only she, Helen, was clever enough to penetrate Odysseus' disguise. The story is told in a way that highlights her intelligence and days of glory. She tells how Odysseus had trusted her as his peer with his plans for the Greek victory and that she had rejoiced, for she had by now repented her Aphrodite-spawned infatuation with Paris (who in the meantime had been killed) and, suffering a complete change of heart, wanted her daughter and Menelaus back, "who had all one could wish for in the way of brains and good looks."

Menelaus counters with a very different version of her behavior in his telling of Odysseus' Wooden Horse stratagem. Knowing that the Greeks were crouched inside the gift horse, Helen walked three times around the horse with her new Trojan paramour Deiphobus, brilliantly mimicking the loving voices of each of the men's wives. These impersonated endearments almost made the Greeks give themselves away, but for the resistance of Odysseus, who forced the men to keep quiet. One can almost hear the hidden agenda in this conversation between the two, who are speaking to each other as much as to Telemachus. Emotions are still steaming beneath the polite and prosperous exterior. As one commentator has noted:

> Menelaus and Helen cannot discuss this past, because each has participated in it in a different, or rather opposing, manner. Menelaus knows that Helen never conclusively broke with the Trojans, never allowed her momentary twinges of shame to disturb for long the pleasant tenor of her life; and Helen knows that she enjoyed the power which she had over history to provoke such war, could not help but be attracted by the frivolous Paris, could not avoid abusing the uxorious Menelaus. Such recollections cannot be obliterated even by periodic draughts of nepenthe, even by the glittering surroundings of the Spartan palace.[18]

As for Telemachus, he has been given a front-row seat on one of the greatest soap operas of all times. Part of his education here is learning from Helen and Menelaus how to handle complex and subtle emotions in a civilized way. One can only hope that it also gives him greater appreciation of his mother's extraordinary fidelity.

The next day Menelaus tells Telemachus what and how he knows of Odysseus' whereabouts. At the end of his own seven years' wanderings in the eastern Mediterranean he found himself *in extremis* in Egypt. There his sufferings were pitied by the daughter of Proteus, the Old Man of the Sea, and she taught him how to hide himself in seal skins to fool her father as he tended his flocks of seals. Then he was told to enlist the help of three others to grab Proteus and keep on holding him while he transformed himself into a variety of creatures and things. If they proved successful in constraining him, he would tell them what they wanted to know.

Succeeding in this plan, Menelaus asks Proteus first what he should do to appease the anger of the gods so that he can go home, and second, what happened to his companions. It is then that he learns of Odysseus' captivity on Calypso's Isle and also what happened to his brother, Agamemnon. He was then urged by Proteus to hurry back to his own homeland.

This point is not lost on Telemachus. His education in Sparta complete, he now desires to return home. Menelaus offers extended hospitality, which Telemachus courteously refuses. With grace and wit he also refuses Menelaus' gift of horses, for they are unsuited for the rocky, mountainous terrain of Ithaca. Instead, he asks for a gift that he can carry. Menelaus expresses his admiration at this: "I like the way you talk, dear lad: one can see that you have the right blood in your veins."[19] Telemachus is given a royal send-off carrying his gifts of a gold-and-silver mixing bowl made by Hephaestus himself and a fine embroidered robe woven by Helen to give to his future bride.

The ensuing books of *The Odyssey* tell of Odysseus' trials and adventures. We resume the *Telemacheia* in Book Fifteen, with Athena inspiriting Telemachus with an urgent desire to return home. Again Menelaus presses him to stay and tour the countryside, and again Telemachus refuses, offering as his reason that he might lose something precious from his home. The meaning is only too clear, for it is at this time that Odysseus is making his way to Ithaca. Our boy has now become a self-possessed young man of action, schooled in the forms and the emotions of the noble life, but also properly disenchanted with it at the same time. Telemachus is ready to partner his father and help create a new order in Ithaca. He is ready too for phase three of the rite of passage.

The third phase of initiation generally has to do with some scarring—the creation of a "conspicuous mark of adult male status." Archaic and aboriginal societies have inflicted the mark through circumcision, subincision, elaborate decorative scarring, and even the removal of a joint. This phase then leads into a fourth—the revelation of certain sacred objects and/or sacred beings.

These last stages in the classical process of initiation are generally embedded in long, difficult, and dangerous journeys. Often, as in the walking of the Australian aboriginal's Songlines, or the journey of the initiates from Athens to Eleusis, the initiate retraces the paths taken by the mythical ancestral beings. And this is precisely what Telemachus does. In returning to Ithaca on his night journey, he emulates his father's perilous sea path. The part of Poseidon is taken by the suitors, who have made plans to waylay his ship and kill him. Phase four of his initiation occurs almost immediately after his escape, when he experiences the revelation of his father's living presence in his disguise as an old beggar. There is also the revelation of the presence and guardianship of Athena, who, for all practical purposes, is the totemic deity of his tribe.

There are other initiatory details as well. For example, as we will see in the final chapter of *The Odyssey,* Athena precedes Telemachus and Odysseus into the great hall of the palace on the eve of battle bearing a golden lamp that illumines the walls and pillars with an unearthly blazing light. This corresponds to the concluding rituals in the Telesterion at Eleusis, where reports tell of a sudden blaze of light that shines out upon the initiates, welcoming them into immortality. The required ritual scarring occurs when Athena controls the spears that are thrown by the suitors and allows Telemachus to be cut near the wrists. She then lifts high her "man-destroying" goatskin aegis emblazoned with its gorgon's head of writhing snakes to terrorize the suitors and send them flying. This emphasizes the fearful power of the tutelary deity or totemic guardian, which contains both glory and terror.

These are the paradoxical accoutrements of the protector. Ancient civilizations (and a few modern ones) had a tremendous sense of their spiritual guardians, but in our modernity we have denied and even lost this sense of protection. Perhaps that is why we, and our planet, are presently so vulnerable. The great protector is almost always like Athena—blazing light and writhing snakes. Or like Shiva—with calm, ascetic, benign face as the Creator, and dancing on demons as the Destroyer. Or like Manjushri/Yamantaka of the Tibetans—the sweet, graceful, utterly lovely and gentle child god on one side. And on the other—BAH!—the thousand bloody heads and lolling tongue of the destroyer of evils, demon-faced Yamantaka.

The initiate or spiritual adept can call on different aspects of the divine force by using "mantras," sacred sounds and words that, when repeated, can both call forth the spiritual presence and charge one's own mind with their power and meaning. That is because, in Hindu and Buddhist practice, the mantra incorporates the divine. Using and pronouncing the mantra correctly can orchestrate the power of the divinity. Thus one can evoke Manjushri for peaceful and serene reflection with a meditative *Om mani padme hum* ("the jewel in the lotus"). But one can also invoke the power of creative terror to put down toxicities with *Yamantaka Hum Phat!* (which means just what it sounds like). The ancient Greeks also had mantralike invocations to the gods, and these were used in ceremony and ritual, especially in the practice of the Mysteries.

I mention this because it is clear that the ancient sacred psychologies spoke to a wider range of the human experience than we are accustomed to today. Now when we try to walk the narrow precipice of logic back to the place of our terror we may not get there. This is because we are far more complex than the mere particular historical events that traumatized us. But these ancient psychologies, with their rituals, initiations, rites of passage, and profound sense of protection and protectors—both individually and communally—involved participants in a far more complex movement of the soul than our present limited, non-ritualized therapies. Perhaps that is why there is a such a strong drive to understand the nature and practice of rituals of renewal and transition through a study of remaining aboriginal societies.

With the story of Telemachus we are given a tremendous and absolutely classical rite of boys' initiation. And that is one of the reasons why fully one third of *The Odyssey* is devoted to his rite of passage: first maturity must be achieved before the depth of second maturity can be known. With the son prepared, the sacred lost one, the father, can return, and the reenchantment of the world can begin.

Creating a Night Journey

WITH the story of the stages of Telemachus' initiatory night journey as a model, the group—as well as individual readers—has the opportunity to create one or more rites of passage for adolescent friends or relatives, while serving as the "elder" allies that make the night journey possible. Also, any elders who feel their adolescent rites of passage were inadequate or nonexistent may wish to take this opportunity to plan and perform the several aspects of this night journey for themselves. They may ask friends or others in the group to serve as Athena in her various guises, as well as other tribal elders such as Helen, Menelaus, and Nestor.

Western society is generally lacking in powerful and meaningful rites of passage. This has generated endless pathology and alienation. Since *Homo* has been sapiential, ritual and rites of passage have served to provide a pattern of dynamic expression. Through them, the energy of events, or the movement from one phase of life to the next, can flow in an evolutionary process toward a larger meaning or a new stage or level of life. Rites of passage offer us ways of activating and illuminating our transitions, and provide us with the breakthroughs, the insights, the graduations that inform us of our movement from one stage to the other. But too often in our modern world, lacking as it is in dramatic and depth acknowledgment of this kind of movement, the transition is lost, and we fall from grace into the entropy of accident and chaos. With adolescents particularly, this failure by adults to set up initiatory opportunities has had horrendous effects. Though a few social rituals do exist (Confirmation, Bar Mitzvah, graduation, and the driver's license), for the most part, they fail to engage the young person in reeducation for a deeper life, with its process of dying to the old and being reborn to the new. As Anthony Stevens has noted, it appears to be:

> society at large that has abdicated responsibility for initiating the young. Traditional initiatory procedures have been allowed to atrophy with disuse because our "elders" have lost confidence in the values of which they are the custodians and no longer possess any certain knowledge as to what it may be that they are initiating the young people for. Ultimately, it is the fault of neither teacher nor pupil, elder nor novice, but the consequence of a collective crisis of confidence in our culture. The loss of respect for traditional values, the progressive relativisation of all canons and ethics, results in a conceptual miasma in which one television interviewee's opinion is as good as another. So far, all attempts to replace traditional procedures with pragmatic ones has met with little success, largely, I believe, because they are based on a shallow, one-sided and biologically ignorant view of human nature . . . they fail to take into account those fundamental archetypal determinants which demand that religious forms of experience, family integrity, stability, and continuity in relationships between the generations, hierarchical social structures, gender differences,

initiatory procedures, and so on, be respected and allowed expression.[20]

Such failure has resulted in a desperate search for replacements for ritual and initiation—thus, the specters of delinquency, teenage gangs, mall culture, rampant runawayism, drug and alcohol abuse, sexual promiscuity and unwanted pregnancies, involvement in cults, and other varieties of alienated experience. Indeed, perhaps the most tragic and irreversible form of alienation, that of suicide, can be seen as a negative rite of passage. I have found that whenever I have worked with high school counselors on this issue—helping them create powerful, meaningful night journeys and rites of passage containing elements of dying to the outmoded self and being reborn into the mature self—the incidence of suicide decreases dramatically.

Traditionally, puberty and adolescent rites of passage trained young people to survive the inevitable sense of alienation experienced by those who are betwixt and between, neither child nor adult. Initiatory rites and journeys served to carry them past these thresholds, luring them with mystery, while giving them practical knowledge in survival and in becoming full participants in the form and functioning of their society. With such experience, the adolescent would not have to act out his alienation and confusion in ways destructive to self or society. Thus, these initiatory events provided empowering experiences that gave the young person his or her own unique sense of valued identity, as well as full membership and continuity within the society.

The literature of adolescence is rich in the description of these initiations. Perhaps the best known of these are Huckleberry Finn's trip down the Mississippi and the runaway episode in *Tom Sawyer.* In recent years, some of the most loved literature of this genre has come from the pen of Madeleine L'Engle, especially her books *A Wrinkle in Time* and *A Wind in the Door.* In each, children and adolescents are called upon to discover within themselves remarkable capacities that they then use to serve the universe.[21]

We must remember that what we call modern life is but a thin crust over thousands of years of human experience and coding. Rituals practiced for so many thousands of years are apparently so deeply rooted in the human psyche that, when adapted again for contemporary use, we find that they have lost none of their power to help us make the needed transition to a mature, multidimensional life.[22]

TIME: For planning a night journey, count on one or two organizational meetings of several hours each. The time needed for the journey itself, however, will vary widely according to individual circumstances.

MATERIALS NEEDED: Writing and drawing materials, face paints. Costume elements for role playing. Tape recorders to record the process of initiation if desired. Sacred objects and special gifts for the initiate(s). Food for ceremonies and final celebrational feast.

MUSIC: Whatever music would provide a sensitive background accompaniment to the various phases of the night journey as you have planned it.

INSTRUCTIONS FOR SOLO VOYAGERS: You can certainly plan a night journey for a friend or relative—or for yourself! But the experience will be richer and more mysterious if you bring in other allies and elders to help in the final planning and execution.

In the planning stages, the chief organizer of the journey can run the meeting, or the meeting can govern itself. During the night journey, participants will have planned their roles, but an overall written agenda might be helpful. Again, there can be an overall guide or an unfolding process.

Following the four stages of the classical rite of passage as described in the chapter on Telemachus' night journey, the group's members should work to create a viable yet potent ritual employing these stages for a particular young person, or a group of them. Along with the preparation for the rite of passage, the stages include: the night journey; traveling to the sacred grounds to acquire special knowledge; the marking or "scarring"; and the revelation of sacred objects and beings.

Below, there are suggestions drawn from planning discussions by members of other Odyssey workshops. It was fascinating to note the thrill and shock of recognition that group members had in coming up with suggestions for each of the stages. It was as if they were "remembering" knowledge from long ago, as well as uncovering hidden reservoirs of the power of ritual structure.

Before the Journey Begins: The Preparation

The night journey itself is preceded by the preparation of the young by the old. An important part of the story, as told in *The Odyssey,* involves a deep conversation between Telemachus and Athena-Mentes. This conversation is critical because it reveals to the elder ally that the young person is ready to take the necessary steps involved in growing up. Some subtle and not-so-subtle hints about the next stages are given to the young one by the elder playing the role of Mentes. The essential instruction (or piece of advice) is to take a journey in order to discover what has happened to the missing parent. This elder must leave the young one feeling deeply empowered, ready for action, full of courage. An actual journey is required because time and place must be shifted and context changed so that life can be seen from a completely different viewpoint. The unfamiliar also provides a doorway for the Mysteries to enter. But besides all that, young people need to *move*!

SOME QUESTIONS FOR THE GROUP TO ASK: Who are the young ones needing to make the night journey? What is the stated purpose of the journey? Is a parent actually missing, or a parent-child relationship damaged? Or is the journey in fact a search for a sense of deep cultural parenting? How do we conduct the necessary conversations? How do we as Mentes determine what these adolescents need, and how do we leave them feeling empowered and ready to move?

An important step in the preparation is taken by Telemachus himself. He reveals some sense of his newfound courage and willingness to be seen during confrontations with his mother and with the suitors. Then his old nurse, Eurycleia, accompanies him to his chamber, sees to his needs there, and withdraws, leaving him to sit up all night thinking about his journey.

QUESTIONS FOR THE GROUP'S CONSIDERATION: What should the young persons do next? How should they prepare themselves and plan the rite of passage? Who takes the role of Eurycleia, the one who cares for the young person's immediate needs (food, and a comfortable room and clothes) while also witnessing the growth process taking place?

In the ritual structures, elders become deep allies. Often their function is to say literally: Get on with it! As mentor, counselor, or old family friend, they take on the role of those who give the young people impetus for journeying forth.

It may be useful to remember as you begin discussing these questions in this phase of preparation that there seem to be overt male mysteries and covert female mysteries. As it is important to consult the young people, it is also important to have a variety of different plans, especially if the journey includes people of different sexes.

A model for the female mystery may be found in the story of Demeter and Persephone. This drama was the subject of the Eleusinian Mysteries and can, to some degree at least, be seen as a counterpart to the story of Odysseus and Telemachus. Both young ones embark on dark journeys, but while Telemachus, the son, goes in search of his father and his family past, Demeter, the mother, goes in search of her lost daughter, knowing that the world and the future will die unless they are reunited. This union of the generations is required for both initiations and for all lives to move forward, but the mother is looking to the future in her daughter, while in the initiations of *The Odyssey* the son looks backward to the father.

The next part of the preparation, which Telemachus performs himself, is to call an assembly of the people of Ithaca as well as the suitors, the first to have been called since Odysseus left. There, he presents his case against the suitors as well as he can.

We are told that Zeus himself observes the Assembly and sends two fighting eagles directly over the meeting place as a portent of bloody doom for the suitors. Even when the local expert on bird lore interprets their appearance as presaging a great calamity coming for the suitors, they ignore the warning and blame Penelope for the general discord. Actually they may be right in ways that they have not considered, ways that reflect Homeric irony, for as one critic has suggested:

> Like Circe, Penelope has turned her guests into swine, into unmanly banqueters, lovers of dance and song rather than war, who are shown, in their failure to string the bow, to be no match for Odysseus. To keep open a place for Odysseus she has symbolically stopped change on Ithaka.[23]

But while Telemachus is attacked and humiliated by the suitors, there are also several old wise men who befriend him, most notably, of course, Mentor.

QUESTIONS FOR CONSIDERATION HERE INCLUDE: Is it appropriate for your young people to make a public statement of their personal intentions and needs from the adult community—and before whom? If so, how do we make sure that some representative of "Zeus" attends? Is a portent required? Who stands as Mentor, to offer public affirmation?

Telemachus then retires and prays to Athena. She appears as Mentor, encouraging him with hearty compliments and assurances, and offers to get the ship and outfit it with volunteers. His job is to provide the food and wine for the trip and stow it in the appropriate strong jars and skins.

Now we're down to the nitty-gritty of the journey. What's needed? Car or truck or hay wagon or bicycle or boat? Who provides it? What share in this plan does the initiate have? If it is indeed food, how much is necessary? The point is that assistance of every kind is given, but many details are left to the adolescent.

It happens that Telemachus gives the instructions about food to his old nurse, who remonstrates with him, saying there is no need for him to do this, none at all. He should stay home and guard his own property. Telemachus insists that he will go but begs her not to tell his mother that he is gone, lest her "tears spoil her lovely cheeks."

QUESTION: Is it required that someone try to persuade the initiates to remain children? In *The Odyssey,* we are presented with a model that leads us to believe that both affirmation and protest are useful in honing the initiates' belief in themselves.

The most intricate part of the preparation process is taken by the goddess Athena. Disguised as Telemachus himself, she begs the ship, picks the sailors, and commands the men to gather at the harbor at nightfall. Then she goes to the palace and lulls the suitors asleep. Transforming herself into Mentor again, she calls Telemachus forth. They stow the provisions in the boat and sail away, with Athena-Mentor and Telemachus sitting side by side. When they are well under way, they pull out bowls, fill them with wine, and pour libations to the gods, but especially to Athena, "Lady of the gleaming eyes."

How may these things be accomplished in modern times? What are the deeper meanings of these tasks filled by Athena? What may humans do in her stead? Who is the archetypal presence that will sit next to the initiate as the night journey gets under way? What is the equivalent today of pouring libations to the gods? What is the function of role-playing throughout this initiatory event?

At each level in the preparation, participants should be given a few minutes to think about a modern equivalent or corresponding event. Some of these have included: learning the sacred language (Hebrew for the Bar or Bat Mitzvah candidate); encouraging the young ones to speak their fears aloud; being sent out into the woods (with hidden protectors); being taken away from home during the night or having people come at an unexpected time and declare that it's time to go now (but having the choice of going or not going); focusing on parts of one's religious training, such as the flight into Egypt, or the days in the Wilderness; keeping part of the ceremony secret; going with adults to spend the night as a guardian at a shelter for the homeless; planning and providing, with adults or other initiates, a holiday trip for emotionally disturbed children or a campout for learning-disabled youngsters; volunteering for a night, or several nights, to sit by the side of someone in a nursing home and sing and read or tell stories.

Telling the New Myth: Creating Sacred Ground

When the ship and its sailors come to Sandy Pylos, home of old Nestor, they see people offering sacrifices on the shore to honor Poseidon. I believe this provides a hint about what the group who is waiting to welcome the initiate may be doing when the night travelers arrive. (I don't mean they should be slaughtering oxen!) There could perhaps be a ceremony or ritual in honor of the tribal archetypes as the journeyers progress and the creation of a sense of sacred ground that is dedicated to the memory of a people's past, a place of sourcing.

Other seminar participants have suggested that a corresponding action might be that of visiting other churches and synagogues, attending other people's religious services, or visiting another race's cemeteries. Enlisting the assistance of other elders to tell the stories of those races and religions from the inside is obviously important.

Certainly the young initiates are welcomed warmly to the place, as Telemachus and Athena-Mentor are welcomed to Sandy Pylos. First they are feasted, prayers are offered, then comes the formal questioning: Who are they and where did they come from? This gives the young Telemachus (and our adolescents) the opportunity to state clearly the answers to those questions and to reveal the purpose of coming to this place. I believe this exchange is as important to the adults as it is to the ones who are seeking admission into the adult world, for it will prove to the adults that their successors are worthy beings.

Of course, when Telemachus speaks of his father, old Nestor is reminded of the entire Trojan War and immediately begins to tell about it. He also fills us in on the trouble every one of the Achaeans encountered on their way home from the war. We are left with a very strong sense that though the war may be remembered by some as glorious, it was much too costly.

In this passage we receive hints about our own Night Journey. The young ones may need to hear the old stories of family and clan, church and country, but with adult consideration. This can be the creation of a new kind of myth in which one looks back at the ancient deeds and doings and speaks clearly of what went wrong. Thus the adolescents are granted understanding of the mistakes that all people make, even (or perhaps especially) adults. Like Telemachus, their counsel is sought as they learn of the actions of peers. Thus the adolescent is afforded mature respect in the community.

POINTS FOR DISCUSSION: In the rite of passage we are planning, what are the old stories that need telling and how do we tell of the mistakes we elders made—both in our personal lives and in the world at large? How do we give the young ones an understanding of what happened and the opportunity to create a new reality?

A parallel to the Trojan War may be our own development of atomic weapons and how that has a potential of absolute disaster. What actions may the initiates want to take, knowing that we live in a time when wars must be made impossible, lest all civilization be totally destroyed?

During this stage of the recognition or creation of family and clan grounds as sacred grounds, and the stories as sacred stories, secrets, sometimes family secrets, are revealed. And in this way the initiates are deeply affirmed as people worthy of carrying on the evolution of the family or clan (or species). This recognition is given by elders of both sexes, just as Telemachus is saluted and warmly received as an important person by Nestor and his family and later by Menelaus and Helen. These representatives of the traditional order see Telemachus in his full potential, something he never experienced at home, where he could not be seen as anything but a child.

One of the ways they show their respect and their delight in the young one is the giving of family treasures. Menelaus presents Telemachus with a beautiful bowl, made by the god Hephaestus, and Helen gives him a robe woven by her own hands and intended for his bride when he marries. Some thought should be given to very special and meaningful gifts for the initiates participating in the Night Journey. Perhaps there is some family treasure to be passed on, or some symbolic statement of recognition of their adulthood.

Secrets to be shared with the initiates may include a willing revelation of individual actions or milestones in their lives that adults may have taken unwittingly, or deep questions and concerns that trouble them. The initiate is thus taken into their confidence. The avowed purpose is to give the generations an opportunity to work together in meaningful ways to help cleanse and green the world.

Ritual Scarring

Many societies the world over have initiated their young into adult status by processes of ritual marking or scarring. In *The Odyssey* the wounding may be ritualistic, but it is also real. Telemachus fights at his father's side against the suitors and in the battle receives a slight wound on his wrist and a scratch on his shoulder. By the time this occurs we are nearing the end of the story, and this action completes the initiation of Telemachus into full adulthood.

QUESTIONS FOR DISCUSSION: What are the ways that young people today mark themselves to "prove" their adult status and to show that they are part of a tribe? Is there a way for these actions to take on deeper meaning in the course of carrying out a rite of passage such as the Night Journey?

Much of the scarring our young people experience today involves invisible wounding. One powerful process that honors that wounding and brings it into ritualized awareness includes the use of body paint. Working in pairs, one person describes the nature of the psychological (or perhaps even physical) wounding he or she has undergone, while the partner draws signs or scars with paint on the face or throat, hands or body in ways that poignantly illustrate the fact that genuine scarring has taken place. At such an event it is the task of the elders to stand in high witness to the scarring, and not to attempt therapy. If there are a number of young people involved, they can honor each other, realizing that in fact no one escapes such marking. Thus recognized and saluted, the scarred ones can find release from shame and see instead that suffering actually contains within it the power to open them up to the realm of the sacred.

Revelation of Sacred Objects—or Beings

This phase of the journey of initiation by Telemachus reaches its climax in the beautiful scene of recognition with Odysseus. This story shows us that the sacred object may be the father, or any dear and seemingly lost person.

For our work in today's world, it is vital to notice that for Telemachus this recognition implied partnership and a great deal of plotting, planning, and action in the kingdom. So it should be with our design for the Night Journey for our young friends, associates, and family members. We can reveal traditional sacred objects: the Torah, the Kabbalistic Tree of Life, prayer shawls, communion cups, Bibles, paintings and images of angels and saints—or we can invite the young ones to create their own. But whatever these sacred objects may be, they should imply the knowing that some great task is at hand to be performed.

It is told that in the Eleusinian Mysteries one of the sacred objects that was revealed at the propitious moment to awestricken viewers was a stalk of wheat, so it is possible to keep this part simple, yet provide a profound effect. With so much to be done in the way of cleansing our home planet and caring for her citizens and for all life, the display of something like a sheaf of wheat may once again evoke a powerful response and provide an incentive for committed, useful action in the world.

As a final stage of this Night Journey, there needs to be some form of public recognition and affirmation of this process of initiation. This includes the parents—as Penelope finally sees that her son is a grown and responsible man—and the local citizenry. A final celebratory feast, in true Odyssean style, would be a fitting end to this ritual of transformation.

CHAPTER 12

The Beggar and the Goddess

THE stage is set. Athena has brought the family of Odysseus into a state of readiness and what Homer refers to as like-mindedness *(homophrosyne)*. Penelope is as ready as she will ever be—aided by the dreams and omens sent by Athena. Telemachus has matured through his rite of passage and the experience of observing the well-functioning societies of Pylos and Sparta. He has also benefitted by having been nobly received there and treated like a grown man. Odysseus is wiser and deeper by virtue of his many experiences and initiations. He too has just enjoyed the virtues and delights of an ideal civilization during his stay with the Phaeacians, who see him as a man of culture and like-mindedness, a true peer and a natural for Phaeacian citizenship. Armed with these high standards then, the principal characters are now prepared to bring in a new order to counter and destroy the disorder and anarchy of Ithaca. In the unfolding of the Hero's Journey, the return often requires a magical flight. Otherwise one is tempted to stay in the rich realms of amplified power and never put one's gifts and teachings into practice in the ordinary world.

The Morning Star appears in the sky as the first sign of welcome to Odysseus, back on his home island after twenty years away. The Phaeacian sailors carry him gently, still sleeping, onto the shore and stow his many rich presents at a nearby olive tree before taking their silent departure.

When Odysseus wakes he does not know where he is, for Athena has covered the island in mist. She does this to give herself time to disguise Odysseus and make her plans. Naturally he is filled with anguish, thinking bad fortune has followed him as usual and that he has landed once more in some foreign place where he will have to start all over again. Back to square one. But no, not this time, for while he is checking his treasures, Athena comes toward him "in the shape of a young shepherd, with all the delicate beauty that marks the sons of kings. A handsome cloak was folded back across her shoulders, her feet shone white between the sandal straps. . . . She was a welcome sight to Odysseus."[1]

Odysseus kneels to the shepherd and, unaware of the irony of his words, says, "I pray to you as I should to a god . . . tell me exactly where I am." The "shepherd" tells him that he is indeed in Ithaca. Although his heart leaps for joy at this information, Odysseus is all too wise in the ways of the heroic world. So he spins a wild and woolly yarn, claiming to be a Cretan merchant. This is all of a piece for the man of many ways—another island, another character, another story. Through this initial encounter, both man and goddess mirror each other in pretense and play-acting. Finally Athena, smiling, reaches across the barrier of mutual illusion and caresses him. As she does so, she comes closer in appearance to who she is. Homer says, "Now she looked like a woman, tall, beautiful, and accomplished."[2]

And she speaks to the point: "What a cunning knave it would take to beat you at your tricks!" She admits, "Even a god would be hard put to it."[3] Then, in a remarkable speech, she honors him as her extension in the world of space and time. And she says:

"We are both adepts in chicane. For in the world of men you have no rival as statesman and orator, while I am pre-eminent among the gods for invention and resource.

"And yet you did not know me, Pallas Athena, daughter of Zeus, who always stands by your side and guards you through all your adventures."[4]

So, home at last after a twenty-year exile, Odysseus encounters his guardian face to face for the first time in a meeting in which she declares their bond and mutual identity. Odysseus responds quickly and with deep insight, "It is a difficult thing, Goddess, for a mortal man to know you at sight, even a man of experience; you turn yourself into all sorts of shapes."[5] By which he also implies, "Where the hell have you been?" And of course she replies that she has not been able to be with him in a form that he would recognize. Why not? Because he has angered Poseidon by blinding his son, Polyphemus. More profoundly, he has angered the deep world and, as the ideal representative of his culture, he has been in sore need of the training of that inner realm. Yet, she assures him that she has been there throughout it all, guiding, protecting, arranging, keeping him and his family alive. The archetypal protector, the ally of the soul, never really leaves us, though its calling card may only be discerned in other people, in jokes, voices in the dark, curious opportunities, and breathtaking synchronicities.

This is key to the whole epic, for the appearances and disappearances of the goddess in her different guises have actually shaped the poem. Odysseus soon learns that Athena has protected his son, Telemachus, and his wife, Penelope, from the start, as well as having always protected him. This is the classic mystery religion journey of a movement from masks, deception, and illusion to the transparency of epiphany, when the goddess is fully revealed.

Marina Warner, in her wonderful book *Monuments and Maidens: The Allegory of the Female Form,* has written several remarkable chapters about the place of Athena in Western imagination. Commenting on the relationship of Athena to

Odysseus, she writes, "The recognition of Athena by Odysseus brings to a climax of mutual respect and love the series of magical metamorphoses that the goddess of wisdom, daughter of Metis, has undertaken in order to accomplish Odysseus' homecoming."[6]

Now, as we know, Athena appears in many disguises and undergoes almost continual metamorphoses. Beginning as the aged Mentis, an old family friend, she comes to Telemachus, filling him full of spirit and daring before changing into a bird and flying up the chimney. Then as Mentor, another old man, she serves as guide to Telemachus in his journey as initiate to Pylos and King Nestor. Athena apparently likes the guise of old men. At Pylos, Athena-Mentor orders a sacrificial feast for the gods and then changes into a sea eagle and wings away. (She also enjoys her bird incarnations—always a good compromise form for a Heavens-coursing god.) She disguises herself as Telemachus himself in order to pick an efficient crew quickly and give them secret instructions so they can leave in the night to go off to Nestor at Pylos, and from there to Menelaus and Helen in Sparta. Returning as Mentor at the end, she helps Odysseus and Telemachus fight the suitors' relatives, and then also as Mentor arbitrates a new peace.

Athena is also adept at inner disguises. She changes the consciousness of her wards, coming to them in dreams and sleep, refreshing their souls, and filling them with spirit and heart and new enthusiasm. In both *The Iliad* and *The Odyssey,* she is definitely the goddess of altered states of consciousness. This dream inspiration is especially evident in her relationship to Penelope, who has the wiliness of Athena herself, as well as the quick-wittedness the goddess favors in her protégés. Athena enters Penelope's dreams a number of times in order to lull her fears and increase her beauty.

Like Athena, Penelope is a highly skilled weaver of wool (as well as of words) and has mastery of the weaver's requirements—agility and craft. Weaving is always the metaphor for Athena's wisdom and power over human possibilities. She weaves the various strands of the action to their successful conclusion, guiding the steps of the family of Odysseus, threading them through safe paths when they are in danger, and, above all, drawing the strands of their separate journeys closer together, until their very souls have been woven into one tapestry of accord and harmony.

Athena is supremely the goddess or archetype of those who would reorchestrate, those who take what is given and reweave it into new possibilities. *The Odyssey* itself is about the reweaving of the heroic mind into a consciousness prepared for the coming of a high civilization not very far removed from the one that Odysseus saw on Scheria, the Island of the Phaeacians.

Essential to the understanding of this tale is the revelation that occurs on the beach at Ithaca, that Athena and Odysseus are well matched. Athena, in a touching disclosure, tells him that she could never abandon him, for such is the mind within him, a mind so like her own that she will always be allied with him: "And that is why I cannot desert you in your misfortunes: you are so civilized, so intelligent, so self-possessed."[7]

Those are the sunny qualities that they share, but they are matched in shadowy ones as well. For example, they are both past masters of disguise and trickery. As Marina Warner says:

> . . . in loving collusion as they both change shape and assume differing personae to conceal their identities, Athena from mortals, including her beloved Odysseus, and Odysseus from other men and women. The essence of both their characters is to dissimulate. The masks that Odysseus assumes reflect his own Athena-like cleverness and adroitness; his transformations, within their earthly limits, have been learned in her mold, and are often achieved with her assistance. Athena's protection of Odysseus provides the poem with its main spiritual theme, and its own thematic imagery is of disguise.[8]

Where Marina Warner speaks of disguise, I prefer to speak of transformation. Consider again what the goddess does with Odysseus when he meets Nausicaa—making him appear taller and handsomer than he actually is. Throughout the poem she adds and subtracts height and beauty as it suits the occasion. He is in his glorious prime at one moment and a disreputable antique in the next. We are never quite sure what he actually looks like, but then, neither is he. In this he is made to emulate the goddess, whose own form changes at her whim.

Athena, as goddess of changes, inherits those traits from her mother, Metis, the Titaness, who herself was a shape-shifter. Until she was consumed by her husband, Zeus, Metis had the capacity to transform thought into many different forms; thus she is the first primal goddess of the transformation of mind and thought. Her daughter, Athena, more prudent and more political than her mother, functions in *The Odyssey* as a protean divine power. By comparison, Proteus himself, the god of shape-shifting, seems rather dull in *The Odyssey*. He turns into fish and seals. Athena, however, is a polished protean. She displays the full capacity for change that one must assume when engaging the ultimate game of co-creation—of a partnership between human beings and the gods, the higher principles.

This necessity for shape-shifting is consistent with my hypothesis that *The Odyssey*, in addition to being superb poetry and a consummate traveler's tale, is an epic about the initiation of consciousness for the purpose of creating a high civilization. This glorious work, which comes into its final form around 720 B.C., exerted a powerful influence upon that very consciousness that inaugurated the great Hellenic culture and civilization. This culture in turn became the inspiration for our own, especially in science, art, education, drama, language, politics, architecture, and philosophy. Even now the Homerically inspired Hellenic and Hellenistic cultures continue to inform our style of mind, our modes of seeing, our ways of being.

Yet today we have grown stalemated and inflexible in attitudes that are not unlike the old heroic patriarchal forms writ large. Rather than the Achaeans and the Trojans, the contenders until recently were the Soviets and the Americans. The Cyclops is not some one-eyed monster but our own limited vision. And, like Odysseus and his protector Athena, we are called again to a robustness of spirit joined to psychic agility that will let us play with tender brilliance in the drama of whole system transition our planet is undergoing. Like Odysseus and Athena, we are asked to become shape-shifters so that we may partner both evolutionary process and planetary governance.

Never before has the responsibility of the human being for the planetary process been greater. Never before have we gained power of such magnitude over the primordial issues of life and death. The density and intimacy of the global village, along with the staggering consequences of our new knowledge and technologies, make us directors of a world that up to now has mostly directed us.

This is a responsibility for which we are ill prepared and for which the usual formulas and stopgap solutions will not work. At a deeper level, however, many are discovering that in spite of themselves they have been surprisingly well prepared. Most of us have at least ten times the amount of life experience of our ancestors of a hundred years ago. And most of us have, psychologically at least, been far more sensitized to our woundings than they. The combination of this magnitude of experience, joined to the sensitivity and deepening that can come of our woundings, makes us not unlike Odysseus in what we have learned in the long voyage home to this moment.

Now we stand on the shores of our "Ithaca," knowing that we require a spiritual partnership, an "Athena" of the soul, to meet us so that we may do the work of rebuilding the Earth in whatever way is appropriate for us all. We need the knowledge and experience of the inner and outer worlds to join Great Mind in the higher responsibility of co-creation. But to learn the process of co-creation, or to be available for it, we have to become protean—able to transform and extend ourselves in body, mind, and spirit. Since the Absolute does not contract, we have to expand the relative, that is, ourselves. Thus, the guiding metaphor of *The Odyssey* speaks with stunning relevance to us and to our time. Perhaps this explains why Athena, the ruling force behind this epic of changes, has been the subject of growing interest since we have entered into protean times.

Athena lifts the mist, and Odysseus knows he is home. Harbor, haven, olive groves—all there. He is in sight of the Cave of the Nymphs where he has performed many ceremonies. He falls to the ground and kisses the generous soil. Then, arms raised in salutation, he invokes the Nymphs: "And I had thought, you Nymphs of the Springs, you Daughters of Zeus, that I should never set my eyes on you again! Accept my greetings and my loving prayers."[9]

With Athena's help, Odysseus stows his treasures far back in the Cave of the Nymphs, after which the goddess closes the cavern entrance with a stone. Then the two of them sit down cozily together by the trunk of a hallowed olive tree to plot the downfall of the suitors. Odysseus is deeply moved by her wise counsel and the tenor of her advice. It is so like his own! After she has given him the gist of the state of affairs in Ithaca, he exclaims:

> It seems to me that I should have come to the same miserable end as King Agamemnon directly I set foot in my home, if you, goddess, had not made all this clear to me. I beseech you to think of some way by which I could pay these miscreants out. And take your stand at my side, filling me with the spirit that dares all, as you did on the day when we pulled down Troy's shining diadem of towers. Ah, Lady of the bright eyes, if only you would aid me with such vehemence as you did, then, I could fight against three hundred, with you beside me, sovereign goddess, and with your whole-hearted help to count on![10]

Guided by Athena, Odysseus is encouraged to go humbly as a beggar to his home. Having survived the ultimate road of trials, Odysseus is now on the way to inner mastery in the realm of spirit. Thus, he must appear and pass through the most profound stage of humility. This is reminiscent of the first Beatitude of the Sermon on the Mount, which has been translated: "Blessed are the beggars for the spirit, for theirs is the kingdom of Heaven'' (Matt. 5:3). It is those who do not have the attachment to appearance who can go humbly, and being humble, they are capable of learning much. So Odysseus is transformed by his goddess into a withered, bald-headed old man in rags, a disreputable vagrant who will pass safely through his kingdom and his palace and search out the hearts of friends and foes.

Following the directives of Athena, Odysseus makes his way inland and meets the swineherd Eumaeus, the one of all Odysseus' servants who cares the most about him. It is the two old servants—Eumaeus among the swine, and Eurycleia in the palace—who have managed to keep some order in the face of widespread breakdown.

Within the palace, Eurycleia administers the household; Penelope is too emotionally spent to exert any authority. It is Eurycleia who keeps the stores, gives out the provisions, and assigns the tasks among the household staff. It is she who keeps the accounts and guards the family's possessions.

Her male counterpart, Eumaeus, manages his part of the estate with equal excellence. We are told that with no help from either Penelope or Laertes, Odysseus' father, he built a pen for the great numbers of pigs he now harbors. His hut, too, is a model of craft and symmetry. It has a court—''lofty and beautiful,'' says Homer—bounded by a wall of stones and wild pear trees. Outside the court there is an artfully fenced stockage, subdivided into twelve sties, each containing fifty sows and their litters, while the boars are penned outside. Additionally, he has four highly trained watchdogs and four assistants working for him. When we first see him he is making sandals.

Eumaeus sees his job as the preservation of his master's estate against the erosion of the suitors. Thus the rich details of his quarters and attitudes make an obvious contrast with the profligacy and general anarchy of the suitors. He is the last true guardian in Ithaca even though he exercises authority over only part of the estate. Still, he maintains the feelings and knowledge of a diligent overseer of the whole estate, as we see when he itemizes to the ''beggar'' his absent master's wealth in livestock, the twelve herds of cattle, twelve flocks of sheep, twelve of goats, and twelve of pigs on the mainland, and the eleven flocks of goats elsewhere on Ithaca.

This is considerable prosperity for an island king, and it is important that Odysseus learn the state of his own holdings from the swineherd. This wealth is joined to the theme of resurrection in a fascinating manner. We recall that the pig is associated in this ancient culture with the return of the soul and rebirth. Thus, the pig herder, keeper of order and overseer of his master's wealth, is the first agent for Odysseus' rebirth into the society of Ithaca.

So it will prove with Eurycleia, the keeper of order and wealth in the household. She will recognize her beloved master—and thus the resurrection of the hero—through the scar on his thigh made by a boar's tusk when Odysseus was quite young. Through these faithful servants, each associated in some way with the mystery of the pig, Odysseus will be reborn into the kingdom that once was his, and with their aid he will be able to restore and rebuild his society.

The swineherd, not recognizing his master, tells him the story of Odysseus' fate as it is known in Ithaca. Behind his beggarly mask, Odysseus discovers the strength of Eumaeus' feelings toward his master and is at the same time heartened by the kindness and generosity being offered an unknown guest. The two, Odysseus as beggar and the swineherd, take to each other in immediate friendship and like-mindedness, and Odysseus regales him with another wild and woolly tale of his life as a Cretan seafarer. Being a true protégé of Athena, he embroiders upon a set of nested pretenses—Odysseus, pretending to be a begger, pretending to be a Cretan merchant, pretending to have lost his wealth to pirates, pretending to have known Odysseus in Crete.

Eumaeus is greatly entertained, but maintains his skepticism when his guest tells him that he has actually seen Odysseus. Together they put away enormous amounts of pork and bread and wine, and when Odysseus offers a tale of how he once got another man's cloak to cover his body on the field at Troy, Eumaeus takes the hint and generously gives him his own, even though he will have to go without: "One man, one cloak, that's our rule hereabouts."

The next day, we see how impressed Eumaeus is by his strange guest when he tells Penelope, "My Queen . . . with the tales he can tell, the man would fascinate you. . . . To have that man by me at home with his enchanting tales was like sitting with one's eyes fixed on some bard inspired to melt one's heart with song, so that nothing matters but to listen as long as he will sing."[11]

It is in the swineherd's presence that Odysseus first meets his grown son, whom he has not seen since the boy was an infant. Telemachus has returned from his journey during the safety of the night. And he too was guided by Athena to the swineherd's hut. Odysseus, still incognito and perceived as a beggar, discovers how much he has been missed and mourned by his son, who also tells him that Laertes, his ancient father, grievously longs for Odysseus. A warm sympathy grows between the "beggar" and Telemachus, each deferring to the other in courtesies and mutual support. Odysseus declares himself entirely on the side of Telemachus in his complaints against the suitors. When Eumaeus leaves to tell Penelope of her son's return, Athena magically changes Odysseus into his own form (but, naturally, taller and more beautiful than he probably is). Looking thus like a god, Odysseus reveals his true identity to his son.

This is a meeting in the Mystery, and the meeting is a Mystery. Telemachus is now about twenty years old and, through his initiation and night journey, has come of age, both biologically and spiritually. Here is Odysseus returning to his kingdom after his own trials and initiations in the fullness of second maturity, greeting the son who has just come of age in his first maturity. With this meeting the two initiations are completed. The one who has entered the initiation of first maturity with a journey of breadth, and the one who has entered into the initiation of second maturity, the journey of depth; the two initiates meeting in the place of the keeper of the holy pigs. Clearly, we are participants in a Mystery play.

Indeed, the son, meeting Odysseus in his full splendor, states the wonder that first maturity must always feel before the mystery and awesomeness of fully realized second maturity, where the depths of existence match the breadth of experience. He says, "No, you are not Odysseus, my father, but some being more than man."

Odysseus replies with the critical words, "I am not a god. I am your father."

When Telemachus responds that no mortal man can perform what Odysseus has done, Odysseus replies, "My son, it is your own father at home once more . . . after many sufferings and many wanderings, returned after twenty long years to my native land. This is indeed the doing of Athena, the Queen of Victory; she has made me such as I am, for it is her will and she has the power. . . ."[12]

Here is Odysseus avowing publicly that his destiny and partnership are with the goddess—and that he is of the order of the initiates who have entered into divine partnership and spiritual alliance. This is perhaps another reason why, when he dies, he will be received as a demi-god himself. When the full impact of the revelation that this god-like stranger is truly Odysseus strikes Telemachus, he flings his arms around his father's neck and bursts into tears, and then in a mighty release of what had been stored for twenty years, the two of them sob without ceasing in each other's arms for hours on end. Father and son so poignantly reunited, Odysseus is now able to cross his own threshold. In the Hero's Journey this represents the great step across the threshold of one world into another.

Plotting together, they determine to stow away any weapons lying around in the hall of the palace, leaving only enough for themselves to use. Telemachus will go down and show himself as alive and well to the suitors who plotted to kill him; while Odysseus, disguised again as the wretched old beggar, will investigate the atrocious goings-on at first hand. With his hard-won genius for psychological detail, Odysseus warns his son not to overreact if he is maltreated by the suitors, but simply to hold fast to the thought that their day of judgment is at hand.

Returning to the palace, the now steely-willed Telemachus brushes off the blandishments and concerns of his mother and his nurse, Eurycleia, over his return. Penelope is stunned at his appearance and demeanor. A month ago a passive, disconsolate boy went on a journey. Now he has returned a man, filled with purpose and wearing an Athena-endowed magical grace that astonishes the suitors and all others who see him. Like a priest preparing an initiate to receive some sacred knowledge by requiring her to purify herself, he orders his mother to wash and dress herself to receive his news. No longer will he allow her to drag around in genteel unkemptness and unwashed misery.

When she has refreshed herself, he reveals the first stage of his sacred knowledge: describing selected details of what he learned on his visits to Nestor and to Menelaus and Helen. However, he does not disclose his meeting with his father. The resurrection of that sacred person to his earthly beloved requires still more preparation on all sides and by everyone. His tale to his mother is given further weight by a prophet, Theoclymenus. This man, rescued from certain death and brought back to Ithaca by Telemachus, assures Penelope that the omens declare that Odysseus is actually in Ithaca!

Signs, omens, and dreams proliferate as the poem draws to its close. As Odysseus returns from the depth world where he has lived for ten long years, he brings with him elements of that world, which break through into the local world of Ithaca. The atmosphere is thick with the conjunction of these two realities. True to the final arcing of the cycle of the Hero's Journey, the master of the island is about to become the master of two worlds in his return home. The traditions of myth and the traditions of Mystery are being woven together by the goddess of weaving herself.

Meanwhile, the still-disguised Odysseus and his friend the swineherd arrive in town. Their senses are immediately filled by the music of a lyre and the smell of an endless banquet. Odysseus looks at his rambling palace and declares to the swineherd that it must be the house of the king because of its many buildings, sturdy doors, court, and fine battlements.

Also the aristocratic coupling of music and banquets declares its royal nature. "This is not a house a man could storm from without,"[13] Odysseus declares, and we hear his inner thought that the house will have to be stormed from within.

As he speaks, an ancient dog lying abandoned on a dung heap lifts up his ears and painfully raises his head. It is Odysseus' old hound, Argos, who must now be around twenty-four years old. He has clung to life, waiting for the moment of his master's return. As soon as he becomes aware of Odysseus' presence he wags his tail in recognition, and then drops his head and dies in happiness. In this most poignant of meetings, Odysseus wipes away a tear and tries to hide his strong emotion from the swineherd.

In the meantime, within the palace, the suitors are debating the necessity of killing Telemachus to get him out of the way in order that one of them may marry Penelope and inherit Odysseus' lands and goods. They disagree about whether to divide the inheritance among them all or give it all to the one who marries Penelope. It is on this note of anarchy and disorder that Odysseus, the beggar, makes his entry into the palace. Athena appears before him and urges him to go around collecting dinner scraps from the suitors in order to distinguish the good from the bad. All but one are taken aback by his dreadful appearance and give him food out of pity. The exception is Antinous ("anti-mind"), who is incensed by his begging and yells, "What god has inflicted this plague on us to spoil our dinner?"[14] He then hurls a stool at Odysseus; it strikes him painfully on the right shoulder. To their credit, all of the suitors are indignant at this unkindness.

Upstairs, Penelope hears of the assault by Anti-mind on the one who is intelligence itself traveling incognito, and she utters a prefigurative curse, "Archer Apollo, strike him as he struck!" She then damns him for the scoundrel he is. From that moment, all her attention is focused on the stranger in her palace. She summons her trusty swineherd to her side and asks him to bring the stranger to her. It is then that Eumaeus tells her of his fascinating presence and bardic speech, as well as of his belief that Odysseus is near at hand. The wise queen becomes even more excited, for she, as lady of the depths and of other realms of consciousness, begins to sense that the man who has become the initiate of the depths is somehow near. She somehow links the stranger and his story with the coming of Odysseus, while continuing to curse the ruinous actions of the suitors and stating very strongly that, if only Odysseus would return, he and his son would soon purge the house of the disease of the suitors.

At that moment Penelope hears Telemachus give a loud sneeze that "echoed round the house in the most alarming fashion." She laughs at this, perhaps her first laugh in years, for she feels that this is an omen for good, and her son has just sneezed a blessing on all that she has said. Sneezing and laughing, the often involuntary reflexes of the autonomic system, mark an opening and an exchange between the inner and outer worlds. Thus when one sneezes, the ancient practice the world over is for someone else to hasten to say some variation of "God bless you." For the ancient wisdom has it that at that moment you are wide open to anything and anyone.

Similarly, laughter shakes up all our expectations. It is not just the coordinated contraction of fifteen facial muscles, accompanied by altered breathing. It is the universe itself flung into a kaleidoscope of new possibilities. Laughter can be an evolutionary event, giving us the impetus to break through the stalemates of our lives and open up to greater forms of knowing. In the parenthesis between Telemachus' sneeze and Penelope's laugh, a new order of blessed but unlikely events can unfold. The event is the essence of high comedy—the world turned upside down, resurrection, the return of the dead one.

Odysseus, however, will not reveal himself to Penelope immediately. In fact, the beggar suggests that they postpone their talk until later in the evening when they can have privacy. Penelope is delighted with the stranger's discretion and accounts him "no fool."

In the interim Irus, the town beggar, enters. This beggar, a notorious fellow of immense appetites, insults the new beggar for invading his territory and challenges him to a public fighting match to entertain the suitors. The point is well made here that being a beggar does not necessarily make one a holy man. This is another test of humiliation for Odysseus, and he handles the situation masterfully. However, poor Irus, after only one reasonably restrained punch from Odysseus, ends up much the worse for wear. Odysseus drags him out and props him up against the courtyard wall, telling him, "Drop the part of beggar-king; it doesn't suit the likes of you." He then addresses the cheering suitors with ominous warnings about their lawlessness and the coming vengeance of Odysseus. The thought must have carried upstairs, for Penelope is unaccountably filled with a strange idea. Let us turn to her now, for she is the focus and progenitor of the coming action.

Meetings with Remarkable Beings

TIME: Three hours.

MATERIALS NEEDED: Simple but effective costume paraphernalia—scarves, masks, hats, drapery, and so on, brought by all participants to allow them to quickly "disguise" themselves as yarn spinner and god. Writing materials and journals.

MUSIC: Very spirited music such as that found in the Hooked on Classics tapes for the first part of the exercise, in which you become another person. Then, for the second part of the process, as you experience the presence of the Great Friend and archetypal partner, the music should be something that inspires a sense of awe and majesty. Music from Area II would be appropriate here—such as passages from *Finlandia* by Sibelius, or Smetana's *My Country.* Also applicable would be "Eric's Theme" from Vangelis' *Chariots of Fire.* During the last section of the process, when one conducts a written dialogue with the Great Friend, it is helpful to use soft, evocative background music from Area I, or even the sounds of waves on a beach or other natural sounds.

INSTRUCTIONS FOR THE SOLO VOYAGER: In working alone you essentially follow the script given below, which you will record on tape, but you will work in front of a mirror. Therefore you dress up like the character you are claiming to be and tell your incredible story to the person in the mirror. After doing this, you walk around for a while away from the mirror, getting more and more into the character you are portraying, and then return again to the mirror to tell a still more embellished version of your wild tale. You repeat this process three or four times, getting more deeply into the character as you walk around, only to return to the mirror to tell a richer and more detailed version of who you claim to be. Finally, you stop telling the story and, looking closely into the mirror, begin to sense a shift in yourself as you become the goddess Athena, looking at your local self as your beloved friend in the human world. Then play the tape of the script and follow the directions. Then, when you are ready, pick up your journal and dialogue with the Odysseus part of yourself and the godly ally within.

SCRIPT FOR THE GUIDE: We begin with the magic and mystery of disguise and taking delight in the tall tale. Gather in groups of twos or threes. . . . Now, speaking one at a time, begin to spin a wild and woolly yarn about yourself, the way Odysseus did to the shepherd boy who was really Athena. Tell it with a straight face, but tell it outrageously. Something on the order of: "I was born in Turkey of a Gypsy mother and a Swedish father who was a giant. We traveled with a circus as my father was a trainer of elephants while my mother told fortunes. I was one of three sets of twins, each of whom hated the other. My own twin tried to push me into the tiger's cage, but I was safe for I knew how to think tiger thoughts. . . ."

As you tell your story, feel yourself becoming the person you're talking about. Take pieces of your clothing or costumes from the collection and adjust them so that you are also taking on a kind of disguise. For example, the person whose life is being described above might wrap a scarf around her or his head and speak with a peculiar accent. As the others listen, they nod sympathetically, and can even sketch quickly the character and story being told. Begin. [Ten minutes or more.]

[Play cheerful, spirited music throughout the tale telling. When all the participants have had time to spin a good yarn to their partner(s), the guide should say:]

Now that each of you has become someone else with an interesting history, please begin to stroll around the room, walking the way your character would walk, noticing things your character would notice. Leave your drawing and writing materials in a safe place at the side of the room and just wander around, looking at the world through the eyes of the character you have become. When the music stops, find someone nearby and introduce yourself, in your character. Tell your story—either the one you developed in the smaller group, or embroider on it, bringing in additions or complications—but do it in character. Introduce yourself as a remarkable being getting ready to hear about another remarkable being.

[Let the music continue until everyone seems in character and all are busy looking at each other as Odysseus in one of his disguises. Then let the music stop as the guide says:]

Stop now. Find yourself near a remarkable-looking person; introduce yourself, and tell your story. [This part of the process should take five to ten minutes.]

Now the music will start again and, still in disguise, begin to look for someone else to tell your story to. Notice if you have developed your yarn in a particular way. Are you telling it to get a result from the hearer; is it becoming more and more your own story in disguise, as Odysseus, the beggar in Ithaca, was really most truly himself in disguise, or when spinning a yarn for the goddess Athena? Begin to walk now, looking for another person to tell your story to. [Music plays several minutes and stops. The guide says:]

Find someone and share your stories, each listening deeply to the other, each trying to persuade the other that the story is true. [Five to ten minutes.]

Now as the music plays again, walk more slowly through the room, and when the music stops, find someone near you again, and begin once more to tell your story. [Music plays several moments, then stops, and the guide says:]

Find someone and look at this remarkable being with the costume and the disguise and feel yourself eager to share stories. [The group should barely have begun to talk when the music changes radically to an entirely different sound. The guide interrupts:]

Stop telling the story now, realize that the storytelling is done, is finished. The person in front of you is not at all the person you thought. Look very closely, look deeply at the face before you. As I talk, begin to sense the shift in yourself, begin to see and feel the shift that's taking place in the person facing you. Feel yourself becoming the goddess Athena. Feel yourself filled with laughter and delight at the Odysseus in front of you, this remarkable human who is a genius of disguise, and who tells the best stories in the world. Look at your beloved Odysseus standing there and realize what fun it is to have a human ally, what joy there is in knowing the person behind these incredible antic actions.

And begin gently to laugh. "I know you. I know you! You can't fool me. You're just like I am. And I am so fond of you. You wonderful, remarkable being! What pleasure you give me!" Begin to laugh in delight at this wonderful person in front of you. Both of you become the goddess Athena looking at Odysseus with such sheer joy in the *chutzpah,* the zest, the wiliness this Odysseus brings to life in the world. Reach out slowly and begin to remove the pieces of costume that have created the disguise. Take off the Gypsy scarf, the masks, the hats, and all the while your eyes are saying, "I know who you are in there. This disguise is no longer necessary. I know you, and I am so glad to see you. Welcome. Welcome. Welcome." [Allow time for the goddess to incarnate in each person and for the room to fill with laughter.]

Now let yourself begin to shift a bit. Allow your consciousness to open up. Let yourself be filled with whatever constitutes the goddess Athena for you. For Odysseus she was the Great Friend and ally, the Ever Near, the archetypal partner. Now, let yourself be filled with a sense of that being who is your version of the Ever Near, your Athena, your Great Friend and ally, your Ever Near one, your partner in the archetypal realms. Allow yourself to be filled now with that presence. [Majestic music plays for several minutes as the sense of identity with the god grows clearer. When the guide feels that the participants—at least most of them—have within them the sense of the presence of their great allies, the guide advises them:]

Go back now into your original groups, pick up your journals and writing materials. We are going to create a dialogue between the Odysseus part of yourself and the god or goddess ally within.

[The music changes to quiet, evocative mood sounds.]

Sitting quietly with your journal, remembering how it feels to be disguised and yet to be recognized for the remarkable being that you are, remembering how it feels to incarnate the great ally, and how it feels to be yourself as Odysseus, write the following question as Odysseus and allow the god/goddess to give the response. [Allow a few minutes for settling and letting the music work.]

The question you ask as Odysseus is: "Great Friend, who are you?" Write the question, "Great Friend, who are you?" Listen for the response as you shift into the sense of that great ally, and begin to write the answer. [Five minutes.]

Now, still as Odysseus, ask: "When and through whom have you appeared in disguise in my life?" Write the question, "When and through whom have you appeared in disguise in my life?" Let the archetypal friend begin to write an answer to the question. [Five minutes.]

Next question: "How can we work together? What would you like us to do together?" Write the question and let the god/goddess answer, in writing. [Five minutes.]

Next question: "How will I know that you are near me? Can you give me a sign?" Write the question, listen for the answer, and let your deep ally begin to write that answer. [Five minutes.]

These questions are just to get you started. Take the time now to think of your own questions and listen for the answers. Write both questions and answers. Let your hand write the questions and then write the answers. [Allow thirty to forty-five minutes for this extended process. The music should play throughout. At the end of this period the guide says:]

Now spend a few moments planning and plotting together, you and your great ally. Odysseus and Athena considered deeply the strategies they should use in order to accomplish the cleansing of the homeplace. What do you and your friend need to do in this world? How can you do it best? When will you meet again? How often should you meet and compare notes? What if any disguises do you each need to adopt? Take a few final moments now and make your plans together. [Ten to fifteen minutes.]

Realizing that this can be the beginning of a new or at least deeply renewed friendship, and that this dialogue can continue if you choose, begin now to bring to a close this session with your Great Friend; allow your sense of this presence to recede. Thank the ally for being with you. Release it now to the depth world, and shift your consciousness until you find yourself wholly in this room and with these friends. Stretch and breathe deeply. Clap your hands. Look at the remarkable beings in your group and see them for what they are—truly remarkable! Stretch out your hands and recognize each of them for the wonder they are, behind all disguises. And like the goddess Athena, who laughed with delight at her beloved Odysseus, join together in laughing at the incredible disguises we wear and stories we tell.

If you have drawings or notes that you took of your partners' stories or appearance while they were in disguise and spinning yarns, you may wish to share them now.

CHAPTER 13

Penelope

IT has been said of Penelope that she passes in and out of a scene "like a phrase of music or a gold thread in a woven texture."[1] From her first appearance in the Hall in Ithaca in Book One, as "exceedingly wise Penelope, the bright of women,"[2] to the final reunion at the end of the epic, we are deeply engaged by her. She is as rich, vital, and evocative a character as any in literature.

We know that she was married to Odysseus when she was very young. When the heroes sailed to Troy, she was still a teenager, left alone with in-laws and a baby in a large, strange household. She raised her child and developed her considerable skills in weaving and needlework, but remained terribly alone, with no one to talk to or challenge her. All her relatives, including her cousins Helen and Clytemnestra, lived far away. She emerges in the poem as the archetypal single parent. And yet she is described throughout as a woman of extraordinary skills and immense intellectual power. She must also be singularly attractive, for the suitors, many of whom are younger than she, want her almost as much as they want Odysseus' palace and lands.

When the suitors begin to pour in from all over Ithaca and the neighboring areas, treating her house as their own, emptying her larders and slaughtering her cattle for their daily feasts, making free with her maids, she has no one to champion her. Her mother-in-law has died of grief over her missing son, while her father-in-law, Laertes, has retired to a simple life of tending his vineyards up in the hills and wants no part of the disaster at the palace. Only a few old stalwart servants who had been devoted to Odysseus remain loyal to her. All the other war widows have either remarried or passed on their inheritance to their children. Penelope alone remains in an ambiguous state, the last one to hope for her husband's return in spite of all the evidence to the contrary.

The ambiguity of her state is furthered by the fact that she is the queen of an island that, until the time of Odysseus, had always been ruled by queens in matrilineal succession. Laertes, we gather, was never king of Ithaca, only the consort of Queen Anticleia and the respected father of the new patriarchal king. The fact that Penelope and Odysseus had no daughter further empowered the growing patriarchal inclinations of the region. But Odysseus simply wasn't around long enough to establish his position or the succession of his son.

In a world where, for time out of mind, the queen had been the principal ruler, Penelope was still viewed as the source of wealth and authority in Ithaca, as well as having the right to choose her next designated consort. She, however, "behaving as a good patrilineal wife (who nonetheless, by Odysseus' absence, has been handed all the trappings of matrilineal householder power), stands against them, wavering, and waits for the return of the husband she loves."[3] Thus, she neither marries nor hands on to Telemachus the kingdom she insists on keeping for his absent father. Sympathy for her has vanished. She is as alone as anyone could be.

On top of this, she is saddled with the old Greek laws of hospitality, which generally required that no guests be turned away, regardless of how disagreeable they might be or how much they might have outworn their welcome. And she has 108 of them—108 men who came to dinner—all taking advantage of her weakening position, all hoping to be the matrilineal king-designate. On the one hand, she manages to ward them off with her wit and cunning, but on the other, she is driven more and more into herself, into silence and brooding. But whenever she is kindled out of dull misery, her intellect rises, and she speaks a poetic language of extraordinary beauty:

> Artemis, goddess and queen, daughter of Zeus, how I wish
> that with the cast of your arrow you could take the life from inside
> my heart, this moment, or that soon the storm wind would snatch me away, and be gone, carrying me down misty pathways,
> and set me down where the recurrent Ocean empties his stream. . . .[4]

It is no wonder that she prays to Artemis, for the lonely goddess of the hunt and of wild things shares with Penelope a brooding solitude. Also, of all the Greek pantheon, Artemis is the goddess most devoted to chastity. Penelope, twenty years chaste, undoubtedly has a special introspective relationship to this goddess in her loneliness, although not the activating partnership and protection she has with Athena. Penelope broods with Artemis and acts with Athena.

There is tension between Penelope and her son in spite of their deep affection for each other. On the one hand, he strongly resembles his father, for whom she pines, and on the other, Telemachus is disappointed in her compromise policy with the suitors. When we meet them, the chill in their relationship is only too apparent. This friction is illustrated in almost the first words Telemachus speaks when Athena-Mentes asks him, "Are you really Odysseus' son?" He answers, "My mother says I am."

One thing seems clear: She has been trying to keep the place of master of the household open for Odysseus, and in so doing, she has perhaps allowed her son to be caught in immaturity or lost in the passivity of daydreaming. While the war with Troy continued, most of these things could be borne. But now as the postwar years drag on, and Odysseus is still gone, Penelope's life-deferred condition has resulted in a household filled with despair and frustration.

I once discussed the plight of Penelope with a group of working mothers, many of whom, it turned out, were single parents—either divorced or widowed. I was struck by their apparent empathy with Penelope. As they spoke of the pain and frustration of raising half-parented children, and the responsibilities of supporting and keeping their households together with little or no help, it seemed as if the chasm of three thousand years separating them from Penelope had vanished. For them, she became a living presence, radically present and contemporaneous in her problems and predicaments. They appreciated her intelligence and cunning as well as her brooding nature, and seemed to know more about her "inside story" than all the classical scholars who have written of her. After the meeting, a number of them formed a group called Penelope's Women, which continues to meet on a regular basis to sustain and support its members.

When we first see Penelope in the beginning of Book One, her position is worse than Odysseus'. He at least is caught between adventures, stuck on a beautiful island with a lovely, nurturing goddess. Penelope, however, is trapped in stagnation and hopelessness, with virtually no allies or sources of comfort. It is therefore necessary for Athena to reach her in a way that she can accept and understand. Given as she is to much grieving and quiet weeping in her room, she is naturally also given to much sleeping. And so, in Book Four, Athena comes to her in a dream, looking and speaking like her sister. In the dream the goddess tells her that her son is safe and under the guardianship of Pallas Athena. However, the goddess refuses to answer her questions about Odysseus, leading us to believe that a special grace is waiting for her, if only she can keep the faith.

Athena has a special relationship to Penelope, who, like the goddess, is a mistress of both weaving and cunning. With cunning Penelope weaves and unweaves to preserve her marriage. On the practical level she persuaded her suitors not to force her to choose a husband from among them until she could finish the shroud she was weaving for Laertes, Odysseus' father. They agreed. After all, they could play and feast and waste the kingdom while they waited. For the next three years she unraveled at night the work she had woven during the day, until some of her serving maids betrayed her secret and she was forced to complete the shroud. However, the metaphor is clear: It was not for Laertes but for Odysseus that the shroud was being woven. As Norman Austin suggests: "In weaving and unraveling the shroud Penelope lays her husband in his grave by day and raises him, Lazarus-like, from the dead by night."[5]

On the intellectual level she is indeed the brightest of women, and outclasses and outthinks the suitors on every possible occasion. (At the end of the poem, in the test of the bed, she will even outsmart Odysseus.) Morally, she is the most steadfast and loyal of women, ever near Odysseus in her mind and heart, as Athena is ever near him in spirit. In these qualities Penelope is, like her husband, an avatar as well as a deserving protégé of like-minded Athena.

The nearness of Odysseus in the palace in his disguise as a beggar excites some unconscious knowing in Penelope. After hearing about the beggar from Eumaeus, she cannot stop thinking about him. Odysseus, as the beggar, is now ruling both upstairs and downstairs—he has established territorial rights in the court of the suitors and in the mind of Penelope. But Odysseus cannot yet reveal his identity to Penelope, for early disclosure with its inevitable shock and unconstrained rapture might endanger all of them. This is evidently in keeping with Athena's master plan. The goddess is weaving a careful web both to protect her charges against unnecessary dangers and to prepare their minds for a proper meeting once the suitors have been vanquished.

Penelope suddenly receives an Athena-given insight: She is to appear before the suitors in the fullness of her beauty to fan their ardor and enhance her value to her husband and son. For the second time in the story we hear her laugh. The notion seems outrageous; she has never before wanted to appear desirable to the suitors. Quite the opposite. Even odder is the notion that filling the suitors with desire would please her angry son and her absent, if not dead, husband. The peculiarity of the idea belongs to the logic and candor of a god; a human would censor and revise and "make sense" of the plan.

Also, we could surmise that the goddess, maiden though she may be, knows perfectly well that any woman would want to look her very best if her husband were coming home from a journey—especially one that lasted twenty years! She would want to eradicate any signs of aging, and to look as much like the woman he last saw as she possibly could. This insight is a woman-to-woman gift from Athena to Penelope, who will remain unaware, on the conscious level at least, that Odysseus is present and viewing her for the first time with enormous pleasure.

Penelope obeys, telling her maid, "The spirit moves me, as it never has before, to pay these lovers of mine a visit—much as I detest them. I should also like to have a word with my son for his own benefit and warn him not to spend his whole time with these unruly young men, who may speak with him fair but whose intentions are evil."[6]

Athena enhances the scheme by making Penelope fall immediately into a deep sleep on the couch where she is sitting. With Penelope in this relaxed state, the goddess is able to endow her with superhuman beauty. When she descends the stairs, her appearance staggers the suitors: "Their hearts were melted by desire, and every man among them prayed that he might hold her in his arms."[7] Ignoring them, Penelope turns to Telemachus and scolds him in the way that mothers have been speaking to their adolescent children for millennia:

> Telemachus, your wits have deserted you. As a boy you used to have much more sense, but now that you are grown up and have entered on manhood . . . you no longer show the same judgment and tact. I am thinking of the scene that the house has just witnessed and of how you allowed this visitor of ours to be so shamefully treated. What if a guest sitting

quietly in our hall were to suffer some injury from such rough handling? It is on you that people would lay the blame and the disgrace.[8]

Telemachus responds with meekness and Penelope grows in the suitors' estimation. Indeed, they are still so bowled over by her ravishing beauty that one of them says to her, "Wise Penelope, if all the Achaeans in Ionian Argos could set eyes on you, these walls of yours would see an even greater gathering of lovers at tomorrow's feast, for in beauty, stature, and sense there is not a woman to touch you."[9]

Penelope's response to this gallantry is to declare that all her beauty and merit were destroyed when Odysseus embarked for Troy, and her continued troubles have wasted her further. She inveighs against the free meals she is forced to give to the suitors in spite of all traditions to the contrary, and reminds them of the fact that no one has ever given her the gifts that suitors are expected to bestow.

Meanwhile, over in the corner, the beggar Odysseus is delighted at this bewitching coquetry, understanding that all the time her heart and attention are set on quite other concerns. At this point, Odysseus and Penelope are united in mind and spirit and we know that their true meeting will come soon. This episode also heralds the beginning of other critical moments in the Mystery play. It corresponds to the highly charged point of the Mystery ceremonies when, as Norman Austin suggests, there occurs "the ritual cry for words of good omen only, which is to say for silence, stillness, and disciplined concentration on the epiphany about to take place. Penelope's seduction of the suitors is her distraction of the impious and stupid. While the initiates gather closer to participate in mind's discovery of mind."[10]

At nightfall, the suitors and the household staff leave. Only Odysseus remains in the great hall. Penelope enters, looking, Homer says, as lovely as Artemis or golden Aphrodite, and sits on a chair by the fire, chased in ivory and silver. The queen begins by asking the beggar, "Who are you and where do you hail from?"

Instead of answering her directly, he praises her wide renown and noble reputation extravagantly. She is clearly pleased to be addressed in so complimentary a fashion. By this we may imagine that she is used to hearing only her son's petulant criticisms and the suitors' bawdy and belligerent remarks. But she dismisses the praise and speaks again of how her beauty left with Odysseus, but would return manyfold if only he could return.

This sets the mood, and from this point the poet's double entendres move in fuguelike fashion throughout this glorious scene. As it is actually Odysseus she is speaking to, she is unknowingly acknowledging his compliments in a way that must please him deeply.

She then sums up her misery: the unwelcome suits, the plundering of her estate, the constant longing for Odysseus. She speaks too of the tricks and tactics that she has used to try to avoid marriage. We learn again of the famous delaying tactic of weaving the shroud for Laertes, the father of Odysseus. We see, as Odysseus does, the torchlit hours of nightly unweaving and the slow work by day. We feel with Odysseus the rage at her maids' betrayal.

She speaks despairingly of her hopeless present condition. Now, she says, she is without strategies:

> I can neither evade marriage with one of them nor think of any means of escape, particularly as my parents insist that I should take this step, while the sight of these people eating him out of house and home revolts my son, who realizes well enough what is happening, being a man by now and well qualified to look after a flourishing estate.[11]

Again she asks the beggar to tell her who he is, for surely he did not spring from a tree or a rock. Odysseus responds by telling her his made-up Cretan biography, as well as how he had met Odysseus on his way to Troy and how he had played host to him for twelve days. He even implies that her husband has undergone a rebirth while abroad, having put into a difficult harbor at a place where there is the Cave of Eileithuia, the goddess of childbirth. Is Odysseus telling his wife of his own initiatory experiences of renewal? Norman Austin suggests: "Odysseus, his ears full of Penelope's little parable on weaving and unweaving as a defensive tactic, proceeds to weave a piece of fabric himself."[12]

Penelope's response to this impressive weaving is to melt into tears the way "snow melts on the mountain tops when the warming spring brings the thawing winds."[13] Odysseus is so moved that he has to exert the utmost control to stop from crying himself and so keeps his eyes wide open and unblinking, like horn or iron.

But the weaving must be tested, and so Penelope asks the beggar to give her a full accounting of how Odysseus dressed and appeared. At first Odysseus demurs, claiming nineteen years of absence for a poor memory. But then he proceeds to give a richly detailed description, including the thick-folded purple cloak that he had worn, the sheathed golden brooch and its intricate workmanship of a hunting scene, the quality and texture of his tunic, and even the complexion and hair texture of his squire.

This disclosure, obviously accurate, moves Penelope to another fit of weeping, for the remembrance is acute, and she fears that the beloved may well be dead. She is extremely vulnerable now, and her feelings begin to move toward the stranger. "Sir, I pitied you before; but now you shall be a dear and honored guest in my house. For it was I who gave him those clothes just as you described them . . . and now I shall never welcome him home to the land he loved so well."[14]

The stranger proceeds to assure her that Odysseus is alive and well and will appear very soon. He even tells her something of the actual story, adding that Odysseus has lost all his company of men in a shipwreck off the island of Thrinakia. Using a pun, he tells her that Odysseus had been *odysseused* (given many troubles) by Zeus when his men ate the cattle of Helios. Saying nothing of the years with Calypso, the stranger refers only to his stay on the Isle of the Phaeacians. But then he adds a fiction to his travelogue. He tells Penelope that although Odysseus will return with rich treasures, he has presently gone to the oracle of Zeus at the sacred cult center of Dodona to ask the god whether he should approach Ithaca disguised or not.

Penelope's reply is an unconscious double entendre: "Sir, may what you say prove true! If it does, you shall learn from my liberality what my friendship means and the world will envy you your luck."[15] The word in Greek that she uses for friendship, *philotetes,* can mean either friendship or sexual relations. Then, already addressing him as "dear friend," she offers him the hospitality of the house: the maid will make up a bed for him, and he can have a bath, a rubdown with oil, good clothes, and a place beside Telemachus at breakfast. She justifies her lavish hospitality by saying, "For how are you, sir, to find out whether I really have more sense and fore-thought than other women, if you sit down to meals unkempt and ill-clad in my house."[16]

In other words, she is asking the stranger to enjoy her mental qualities—the same qualities that belonged to Odysseus as well. In his polite refusal of the bed, Odysseus shows a sensitive regard for her reputation. But he does accept the offer of a foot bath, though he requests that it be given only by some old and respectable woman who has had as much experience in life as he has had: "If there is such a one, I should not object to her handling my feet."

To which the enchanted Penelope replies,

> My dear friend—as I cannot help calling the wisest guest this house has ever welcomed from abroad, for you put everything so well and you talk so sensibly—I have just such an old woman, a decent soul who faithfully nursed my unhappy husband and brought him up; in fact she took him in her arms the moment he was born.[17]

It would seem that we have moved with Penelope from hospitality to active if unconscious courtship. In the space of a few minutes' conversation she has moved from feeling pity to sympathy, to admiration, to professions of love for the stranger now being referred to as "my dear friend" and then even as "the wisest guest this house has ever welcomed," which some translate as, "guest, dearer than any other."

She calls Eurycleia to do this service for one who is her master's peer in age. Noticing his feet, she also remarks to the nurse that her guest's hands and feet resemble those of Odysseus. There is an implied growing subjective recognition of Odysseus by Penelope, although her long years of waiting still shield her conscious mind from full recognition.

So now, Eurycleia, the woman who received Odysseus' head as it emerged from the womb, will now attend his resurrection by attending to his feet. In fact, Eurycleia immediately remarks on the strong resemblance between the stranger and Odysseus, especially his feet. This puts Odysseus on his guard, and he swings away from the hearth toward the darkness so that his old nurse will not notice a certain scar on his leg. Eurycleia, however, finds the well-remembered scar by touch as she washes his feet and limbs. This is a scar he had received in boyhood from a boar's tusk when hunting with his grandfather, Autolycus.

Now, Autolycus (Lone Wolf) had been the preeminent thief and liar of his day. When asked to name his baby grandson, he replied, "I have odysseused many in my time, up and down the wide world, men and women both; therefore let his name be Odysseus."[18] This great troubler, then, had meant for his grandson to be the cause of pain and trouble.

When Odysseus had grown sufficiently to receive his grandfather's promised gifts, he visited him and was almost immediately invited to join a boar hunt. The entire event proved an odysseusing one, with much pain given and received; as Odysseus is slashed at the knee by the boar's tusk. He then kills the boar, and the sons of Autolycus stanch his wound. Odysseus wins his grandfather's favor and is dispatched back to Ithaca loaded with presents and proud of his scar, the identifying initiatory mark of sacred kings and goddess consorts.

Delight and anguish course through the old woman as she feels the scar. Abruptly she lets go of Odysseus' foot and the basin hits the floor, spilling the water. Her voice is strangled by emotion and she says, "Of course, you are Odysseus, my dear child." She looks toward Penelope and tries to attract her attention. Penelope, however, is "away," lost in thought, Athena having distracted her mind with other things. Odysseus pulls his old nurse close and admonishes her not to let a soul in the house learn the truth.

After the bath, Odysseus and Penelope move closer together by the fireplace to continue their talk. She pours out her heart to the stranger with astonishing openness. Already, they are like the closest of friends or, dare we say, husband and wife talking with each other. She tells of her many sleepless nights in which her cares come to her with a thousand stings to prick her heart and turn her regular misery into torture. She tells too how she has been driven from one side to the other—trying to fathom whether she should stay with her son and wait for Odysseus or marry the best of the suitors.

Penelope's dilemma stems from the fact that Telemachus, now grown, wants her to leave so that he has some estate left to inherit. The situation grows even more ambiguous, for as we said earlier, Penelope lives in a country that until recently has been ruled by matrilineal succession. She still has the wealth as well as the power and the choice of designating her consort—and of choosing whether to pass on her estates to the new king or to leave them to her son. This ambiguity is the reason the suitors want to get rid of Telemachus, so that they may inherit the queen's lands and wealth entirely. None of the suitors, we gather, has anything like the wealth and lands held by Penelope, so marriage with her would make any of them king of Ithaca, where he would reside with the queen. However, if she leaves the estates to Telemachus, she would then move out of the palace and live with her new husband on his property. Thus, marriage would have gained him a beautiful but middle-aged woman as his wife, and not much else—a bad match in the patriarchal age.

In the light of this ambiguity, her words take on more and more symbolic content. She is speaking now from another realm. She projects her problem into the form of a complex image—the myth of the nightingale who sings in sorrow for her beloved son whom in careless folly she had killed. Will she too, the nightingale singer of exquisite speech, kill her son out of the folly of the wrong decision?

It is likely, however, that Penelope has another reason for her candor, one spawned by the recent flurry of prophecies and omens about the imminent return of Odysseus. Thus, she continues in this symbolic mode by asking the stranger to interpret a dream. Whether or not she actually dreamed this dream is not clear. Its purpose seems to be to provoke the stranger to give her yet another sign and confirm her own interpretation of the dream.

In the dream, she says, an eagle came swooping down from the hills and killed each one of her twenty geese who had just come in from the pond to pick up their grain. As she wept over the heap of dead geese, the eagle returned. Breaking into human speech, he told her to take heart, for this was not a dream but an image of reality soon to be fulfilled: "The geese were your lovers," says the prophetic bird, "and I that played the eagle's part am now your husband, home again and ready to deal out grim punishment to every man among them."[19]

Odysseus confirms the interpretation of the dream eagle, but Penelope still has her doubts for reasons that she gives in a justly famous metaphor:

> Dreams, sir, are awkward and confusing things: not all that people see in them comes true. For there are two gates through which these insubstantial visions reach us; one is of horn and the other of ivory. Those that come through the ivory gate cheat us with empty promises that never see fulfillment; while those that issue from the gate of burnished horn inform the dreamer what will really happen. But I fear it was not from this source that my own strange dream took wing, much as I and my son should rejoice if it proved so.[20]

Abruptly, she changes the subject and announces that she has come to a decision of a way to choose a husband. It refers to a powerful but magical bow that Odysseus had been given twenty-five years before by the son of Eurytus, whom Apollo himself had instructed in archery. So precious is the bow that it was safely left behind in the storeroom when Odysseus departed for Troy. Penelope says this bow will now provide the means by which she will propose a contest of strength matching one her husband used to perform. Setting up twelve axes in a row, one behind the other, he could, while standing a good way off, shoot an arrow through the holes in the heads of each of the axes. If any one of the suitors can string Odysseus' bow and replicate this performance, he will win her in marriage. This is both a brilliant and a mysterious device, for it evokes in an almost magical manner the uniqueness of Odysseus and his gifts of body, mind, and spirit. Only he who can most closely emulate Odysseus can be worthy of her. Such sympathetic magic might also serve to call the actual Odysseus home to the contest. The stranger naturally answers with enthusiasm and confirms her subjective feelings that Odysseus himself will be the winner.

Penelope of the depths, the dweller in subconscious realms and altered states of consciousness, is now able to act from this world with brilliant, intuitive knowing. I suspect that at some level Penelope has recognized Odysseus. Classical scholar Anne Amory asserts her sense that Penelope has by this time come to believe that the stranger is her husband: "But, because she has so strong a fear of making a mistake in just this situation, she cannot rationally accept her interior certainty, and her recognition therefore remains largely subconscious."[21] In telling the beggar her dream she is soliciting an omen from him, a further sign to prove or disprove his identity. If he discourages her from carrying out her plan, that may prove he is not Odysseus. But since his assurance that Odysseus will participate in the contest is so positive, Penelope must realize now at some level that it is Odysseus himself with whom she has been speaking.

And yet, at just that moment, she is overcome with sleepiness. The variety and intensity of emotions and ideas of that day have overwhelmed her. Her mind simply stops, and she cannot bring herself to the full recognition of Odysseus, which outer circumstances are announcing in a growing crescendo of signals. She has hoped so desperately for so long that the possibility of her hope becoming reality is more than she dares to believe. She has also lived too long in an inner world, has spent too much time in passive weeping. Thus, her instinctive reaction is to retreat to her rooms, to the comfort of her tears, till Athena brings her the sweet gift of sleep.

Downstairs in the portico Odysseus lies tossing on his bedroll, brewing trouble for the suitors and snarling in his mind. A party of maids passes by, giggling and joking on their way to amorous meetings with the suitors. This is almost too much for Odysseus. He forces himself to exercise his well-known self-control by reminding himself what he had to endure with far greater patience when the Cyclops was eating his men for dinner.

It is then that the goddess Athena puts in a bedside appearance in her preferred form as a majestic woman. Odysseus tells her of his perplexity. How is he to take on so large a crowd of suitors? And should he destroy them, what would be his place in Ithaca among the suitors' friends and relatives? He would have no safe refuge and would have to begin his troublesome odysseusing life all over again. Athena proclaims her understanding and her deep commitment to him in these sparkling words:

> "How hard you are to please!" explained the bright-eyed goddess. "Most people are content to put their trust in far less powerful allies, mere men, and not equipped with wisdom such as mine. But I that have never ceased to watch over you in all your adventures am a goddess. Will *this* make you understand? If you and I were surrounded by fifty companies of men-at-arms, all thirsting for your blood, you could drive away their cows and sheep beneath their very noses. Come now, give yourself up to sleep. It is mere vexation to lie awake and watch the whole night through; and presently you'll rise above your troubles," with which the lady goddess closed his eyes in sleep and withdrew to Olympus.[22]

As Odysseus falls asleep downstairs, upstairs Penelope comes awake. As she had done the previous day, she prays to Artemis for death. Would that the goddess pierce her heart and take away her spirit or cause her to vanish by being dropped into the circling sea. Would that she could die now with the image of Odysseus before her, rather than be forced to provide sexual pleasures for a lesser man. She had just dreamed that she had seen Odysseus by her side looking exactly as he looked when he sailed for Troy; and the dream was so real that she took it for fact and her heart knew exceeding joy. She would rather die now and enter into an everlasting dream than face the light of day and the probability of disappointment.

The psychological richness of this passage has confounded many a scholar. Why should she wish for death when the image of Odysseus is so clear to her? Perhaps it is because through all the signs and omens—and the actual odyssean reality that the stranger brings, soul recognizing soul, if not yet consciously—she cannot bear the great divide in which she finds herself. The bridging between the worlds is not yet complete. Her conscious self cannot yet accept what her subconscious knows, and thus the endless, infinite sea seems preferable to this chasm of unknowing.

Downstairs, her partner in the depths is also dreaming of reunion. The sounds of her prayers reach him, bringing him into a waking dream, and he sees her beside him with the light of recognition in her eyes. This image, so potent to his yearning heart, brings him wide awake and he prays to Zeus for an omen from someone in the house. Some signal that will give him a hint of what he is to do next. Within moments, thunder is heard. At that, a mill woman, slower in her work than the rest, stops her grinding of meal for the household bread and speaks:

> Zeus, lord of heaven and earth, what thunder from a starry sky! And nary a cloud in sight! You *must* have meant it for some lucky man. Listen to poor me too, and let my wish come true. Here 'tis; let this very day see the end of these junketings in the palace. Terrible work this, grinding the meal for the young lords. They've broken my back. May this be their last dinner, say I.[23]

The plan is now clearly confirmed by the gods, and Odysseus is a happy man. The omen of the mill woman, although not the most dramatic sign of the gods' involvement in *The Odyssey,* is perhaps the most humane. It is a statement, echoing down the millennia, of the protest of weaker folk who must do backbreaking labor to feed those whose apparent strength comes from arrogance in pride of birth and position. As Anne Amory has so poignantly reminded us: "Through our sympathy with the woman we see the suitors' behavior in a context wider than their relation to Odysseus and their punishment as more thoroughly deserved."[24]

As we observe this striking and now almost continuous weave of god-sent omens in the fabric of the final books of *The Odyssey,* it is important to reflect on the relationship of gods and humans, and the signals the gods can and cannot give. It is also useful to remind ourselves that ancient Greek consciousness understood these omens as confirmations of the order and justice of society. As Anne Amory explains:

> It must be borne in mind that the Greek gods are seldom omnipotent and arbitrary deities who manipulate men or impose an external fate upon them. Instead they are part of the natural fabric of men's lives and, even though presented as anthropomorphic beings who interact with men in a direct way, they reflect, rather than control, the forces which govern all men. In Homer, then, omens and dreams foretell only what can reasonably be expected to issue from the way in which "merit and fortune are interrelated." Thus the sequence of omens received by Odysseus in Books Twelve through Twenty . . . indicates that he will be victorious over the suitors because he is braver, more resourceful, and juster than they. The omens encourage him, similarly, because they reflect and confirm his own self-confidence.[25]

There is one final and overwhelming prophecy remaining. It occurs when one of the suitors, Ctesippus, an unruly spirit, hurls a cow's hoof at Odysseus. Telemachus rebukes him and the other suitors severely. Agelaus, another suitor, accepts the rebuke as just, but then strongly urges Telemachus to compel his mother to hurry up and choose one of them to marry. Telemachus replies that he has urged her to make her choice, but that his conscience forbids him to drive her from the house against her will. At these words, Athena deranges the suitors' wits to such an extent that they become hysterical with laughter. The hysteria continues until "their laughing faces took on a strained and alien look."[26] It seemed to them that blood spattered the food they ate and their hysteria turned to tears. It is then that the prophet Theoclymenus invokes their doom in a powerful voice and in words of ominous intensity:

> Unhappy men, what blight is this that has descended on you? Your heads, your faces, and your knees are veiled in night. There is a sound of mourning in the air; I see cheeks wet with tears. And look, the panels and the walls are splashed with blood. The porch is filled with ghosts. So is the court—ghosts hurrying down to darkness and to Hell. The sun is blotted out from heaven and a malignant mist has crept upon the world.[27]

The suitors' response is one of delighted giggles. "Throw him out," one exclaims. The prophet strides away in all dignity, but not before these final words: "I see advancing on you all catastrophe which you cannot hope to survive or shun, no, not a single one of you who spend your time insulting folk and running riot in King Odysseus' house."[28]

The suitors are growing less and less conscious as the family and friends of Odysseus are becoming more so. Even the best of them—Eurymachus and Agelaus—are becoming less human and more deranged. After all, they have spent years of doing nothing much but imbibing huge quantities of wine, eating enormous amounts of meat and bread, and occasionally interrupting their sodden pleasures with a game of quoits or the hurling of a javelin. They are men who have agreed to live in a parenthesis. Their lives have stopped for too long. There is no longer any impulse in any of them to do more than hope vaguely for some ultimate goal of marriage with Penelope.

She, on the other hand, has become exceedingly wise—mindful and crafty and cunning. In spite of all her words to the contrary, she has not decayed but rather gestated in the depths. Her unconscious moments have not been sodden but sourcing. Athena, her guardian, has been helping her to prepare her inner spirit for the outer events to come.

At this point in the poem we are faced with a contest between a crowd of boorish automatons and several highly enlightened humans championed by the goddess Athena. And there is no question of how it is all going to turn out. There is a contrast drawn here between the results of years of despair and longing focused on a worthy and steadfast love, and years spent in easygoing, thoughtless pleasure at another's expense. These years have been hard on everyone. But some have grown, while others have diminished themselves.

It could almost be said that the suitors represent the sounding of the death knell of the dark age of consciousness of Homer's time. They are not unlike the geometric stick figures that adorn the pots and vases of that period. And like those pots, they are about to be shattered so that other forms can emerge from the clay. Forms contained in the winged words of poets and bards but soon to be represented in plastic materials as human figures acquire a rare perfection of form and beauty. We see this bridging aesthetic between men and gods emerging in the family of Odysseus.

The right moment has come; Penelope has heard Theoclymenus' uncompromising prophecy. Telemachus looks to his father to give the sign to launch the attack. He does not do so. But Penelope follows her sense of *kairos,* of loaded time, and announces to the suitors the contest of the bow. She enters the storeroom and with much emotion takes down the mighty bow and its quiver of arrows. Ceremoniously, she brings them to the suitors, her ladies following with the twelve axes. She challenges them to end the empty pretext for their perpetual feasts—the eternal judgment of Mind before mindlessness—and come to the moment and contest of reckoning. Silently, she stands by while first one and then another try to string the bow and fail. "This bow will break apart and be the death of many a champion here,"[29] says one of the suitors prophetically.

As the hopeless contest continues, Odysseus slips out and reveals his true identity to his friends, the swineherd Eumaeus and the cowherd Philoetius, by showing them his scar. The men dissolve in tears of recognition and the three of them sob happily in each other's arms. Then Odysseus reminds himself and them of the business at hand, tells them the plan, and gives them explicit instructions about locking the doors and keeping the women in the other part of the house. Back inside the great hall, Odysseus asks to try the bow himself only to see if he has anything remaining of his old strength. The suitors are unhappy with this proposal, for they have seen the short work that he made of Irus and fear he might just succeed. Antinous, the acknowledged leader of the now mindless suitors, objects most vehemently. But Penelope sternly admonishes him:

> Antinous, it is neither good manners nor common decency to show such meanness to people who come to this house as Telemachus' guests. Do you imagine that if this stranger has enough faith in his own strength to bend the great bow of Odysseus he is going to carry me home with him and make me his wife? I don't believe he ever thought of such a thing himself.[30]

Eurymachus gives voice to their true fears—should the stranger be able to string the bow, the common folk will have a field day saying that what aristocrats can't do, a casual tramp can. What a blow to their reputations! Penelope shrewdly replies that their reputations are lost already because of their collective disgraceful behavior. Furthermore, the stranger is a big, well-built man and probably of noble birth. If he should win, she will give him fine clothes, shoes, and weapons and send him safely on his way.

The irony behind all this is delicious. Whether or not Penelope knows consciously the stranger is her husband, everything she says rings with truth. He will string the bow, but he will not wed her because he is already married to her. He will receive from her fine clothes and weapons because they are already his, and she will send him safely on his way wherever he wishes to go—to her own arms.

With that, it is time for Penelope to ascend the stairs. She is not to witness the forces she has set into motion. On her son's prompting, she goes up to attend to her weaving, but instead spends the time weeping for Odysseus. After all, her "weaving" is nearly finished. The full tapestry is about to be hung.

Weaving the World with Penelope

LET us recall the passage where Penelope talks about weaving and see what role her weaving plays in *The Odyssey.*

> But now I am in distress; see what trouble fate has poured upon me! All the chief men of the islands, from Dulichion and Same and woody Zacynthos, and all my neighbors in Ithaca, want to take me for a wife against my will, and they are wasting my house. So I take no heed of strangers or supplicants, or public heralds with their messages, but I pine away with longing for my husband.
>
> These men are in a great hurry, but I wind my schemes on my distaff. First there was the shroud. Some kind spirit put it into my head to set up a web on my loom, a great web of my finest thread. Then I said to them, "My good young men, you want me for a wife now Odysseus is dead, and you are in a hurry: but wait until I finish this cloth, for I don't want to waste the thread I have made

> for it. This is to be a shroud for my lord Laertes, when the fate of dolorous death shall take him off. I should be sorry to have a scandal among our women if he should lack a shroud, when he had all those great possessions."
>
> After that I used to weave the web in the daytime, but in the night I unravelled it by torchlight. For three years I kept up the pretence, and they believed it: but when the fourth year came round, the maids let out the secret, shameless things who cared nothing! and they came and caught me, and there was a great to-do. So I had to finish that, because I must, not because I would.
>
> And now I cannot avoid marriage, I cannot think of anything else to try . . . But never mind, tell me who you are and where you come from.[31]

In this wonderful passage, Penelope is unburdening herself to an unsightly old begger who, unknown to her, is actually her husband, Odysseus. Her tale of using the ruse of weaving to hold off a remarriage with one of the suitors offers a wonderful counterpoint to the ruse of disguise that Odysseus is using for the same purpose. Both are weaving realities as they see fit, guided by the goddess of weaving, Athena. The metaphor of weaving, used much in classical myth and literature, often had to do with the ways in which the world of givens and the world of grace could mesh and form a cloth of a better quality than the one that seemed inevitable. The warp and weft of human and divine threads tell the tale. When the weaving seems inadequate but finished—when Penelope is being forced to make a choice about the suitors, and Odysseus seems stuck forever, it seems, on Calypso's Isle—Athena inserts her shuttle of weft threads to reopen the weaving and extend the fabric.

In the process of weaving (see loom diagram and description on page 346), as the two sets of warp threads are separated on the loom, the shuttlecock, which carries the weft threads, is slipped between them—over the lying-down warp threads, and under the lifted-up warp threads. Just so do we hear of Penelope being made to lie down and sleep by Athena so that she may receive messages and courage from her dreams and have her beauty restored. Penelope clearly represents the lying-down threads.

Odysseus, on the other hand, is lifted up and forced by the

goddess to become active again, to resume his adventures. He thus represents the lifted-up warp threads on the goddess' loom of creation.

The warp threads must be strong enough to bear the tension of being strung upon the loom, to take the continual lifting and lowering, and to resist the abrasion of the weft threads being inserted and beaten into place to form the finished fabric. Thus does Athena strengthen and make more youthful both Penelope and Odysseus, as well as charge their resolve and give heart to their son, Telemachus.

The moment when the shuttle is passed through the opening in the warp threads is another instance of *kairos*, the potent time when things can happen, when the new fabric begins to take form. The goddess who bears the shuttle occasions these openings. She knows the right *kairos* for passing the weft threads through the warp. The whole of *The Odyssey* can be read as a narrative on using the right time to make time right. The metaphor is now apparent. Weaving is the work of sacred psychology.

Let us now begin to weave with Penelope.

TIME: One hour.

MATERIALS NEEDED: A room with a comfortable rug and pillows on which everyone can lie down if they wish.

MUSIC: This process can be done with or without music, at the discretion of the guide. If music is used, it should be used only during the induction of the dream. Choose a quiet, soothing selection from Area I.

INSTRUCTIONS FOR THE SOLO VOYAGER: This process can easily be done if you first record the script for the guide on tape. Be sure to allow long pauses in the appropriate places, and to follow the recommended times for reflection and dreaming.

SCRIPT FOR THE GUIDE: Let us begin by considering Penelope: brilliant, desirable, cunning, and valiant. The wise, but desperately worn and weary, wife of Odysseus. With this process we will enter her mind and gather a sense of weaving and unweaving and reweaving the world, as she did.

For much of the time that we have known her, Penelope has been sleeping, dreaming, or moving about in a waking dream that has been her only protection as she tries to keep her land and her heart open for Odysseus. It was while she was sleeping that the goddess Athena, in the guise of her sister, visited and gave her renewed hope for Odysseus' return and the courage to continue. Also during these many years, Penelope has been in a chronic state of mourning and tears. These factors all contribute to our uneasiness in taking on the Penelope role and its concomitant work. But we cannot complete our journey until all its parts have become our own and we have understood that weaving is part of our work in the world.

To begin, let us sit quietly in a circle.

[If the group is too large for one circle, break it into several smaller groups with no more than four to six people in each.]

Sit comfortably, on a bench or a chair if you are more comfortable that way. Let your eyes go soft, and begin to pay attention to your breathing. Have the sense that with each inhalation you are breathing all the way up from the Earth through your feet and legs . . . all the way up your spine . . . up and out through the crown of your head. Then, as you exhale, let your attention sink down through your body. Feel your outward breath flowing down the front of your body . . . down through your legs . . . down through your feet . . . and deep into the Earth.

Follow your breathing all the way in and up and all the way out and down. No effort. No strain. Just let your attention move from the Earth beneath you, all the way up your body with each inhalation, and then down from the crown all the way back to the Earth as you exhale. Continue breathing and letting your attention follow all the way up and all the way down. Just breathe easily. Long, slow breaths. . . .

[Music of a very quiet kind (Area I) should play through this centering and breathing time. When the group has become centered—after several minutes of the breathing exercise—the guide will say:]

Now, with our creative imaginations we're going to create our own versions of Penelope's loom in the center of each circle. We're going to weave ourselves into its threads and into the fabric we create with it. This loom will be absolutely unique to each group, which means it may look like no loom ever invented. You may have your eyes opened or closed, whichever you prefer, but do keep the muscles around them as relaxed as possible. Soft eyes. Soft eyes. The loom we want to create is for the purpose of weaving a net, a cloth of caring, a loose tapestry around the Earth, our homeplace. The cloth we create should be double layered. One layer will be above the Earth, perhaps in the energy fields surrounding the planet. And the second layer will be buried just beneath the Earth's surface. Together, the double-weave fabric will form a network of connection, weaving each of us into one another, and all of us into the Earth herself.

First, let us create our Earth-weaving loom. I'm passing out copies of a diagram that shows the kind of hand loom that may have been used by Penelope, and is still used by many weavers the world over. Look closely at its structure so that we can become familiar with its working parts even if we have never seen a loom, much less woven on one.

[The guide will want to photocopy page 346 and pass out copies to each of the participants at this point.]

On a hand loom, the longitudinally strung warp threads have an upper and lower section. The even numbered threads form the upper—or warp beam—part of the warp, and the odd-numbered threads form the lower—or web beam—part of the warp.

The weft threads, which are carried by the shuttlecock, are slipped laterally through the shed—the opening made by raising the warp beam and lowering the web beam of the two parts of the warp. The shed is usually controlled by foot pedals.

The shed is then closed, and the newly added line of warp thread is battened down. Depending on the loom, this is either done manually, by pulling the batten toward you, or mechanically, with another foot pedal. Battening the warp thread securely against the previous line of warp thread adds to the growing length of completed fabric, which is kept rolled up at the front end or bottom of the loom.

The weft thread in the shuttlecock is usually sent through from right to left first, the shed is closed, the thread is battened, the shed is reopened, and the shuttlecock is then sent back again from left to right, and so on throughout the weaving process.

Every time the shed is opened, the two sets of warp threads shift positions. The upper warp beam becomes the lower web beam and the lower warp becomes the upper, so that the weft thread, the filling yarn, is passed alternately over and under the warp threads, which is what binds them into "whole cloth."

A loom is a kind of frame for weaving; it has a beam on which warp threads are wound [A]; heddles (rods or cords), each with an eye through which a warp thread is drawn [B]; the harness, a frame which operates to form a shed for insertion of weft threads between warp threads [C]; the shuttle, which carries the weft threads through the shed [D]; the reed, which pushes each new weft row against the finished cloth [E]; and a beam to hold the roll of finished fabric [F].

In each group now, as you feel what is needed for the loom, speak that out. Will it be run by hand, or have you some other form of power to run it? What wood is it made from, or is it of some new material yet to be invented? Each group's loom may be made of many different things. And each person within the group will create his or her unique version of Penelope's loom. But we will all somehow work together to weave our cloth of caring for the Earth. Using your creative imagination, as you see or sense some part of the loom or what it needs, speak that out. [Allow several minutes for this to happen.]

Now, in the center of your group, within each circle, there stands a marvelous creation. A loom—our version of Penelope's loom. We have created it for the purpose of weaving a cloth of caring for our own lives and for the life of our homeplace, our own Ithaca.

Now we will begin to thread the loom, actually making threading movements with our hands and fingers. First, we will thread the warp yarn through the eyes of the heddle or rod. The warp threads stand for the cosmic forces, the energies and dimensions of Creation upon which our local lives are strung. Pay attention to the color and thickness of the yarn you are using. Describe it, say the words out loud. Say why you have chosen this yarn and what you want it to do. For example: "In my part of this loom I am threading a rich red silk yarn. It represents to me the power of the life force I would like to weave into my own life and into this cloth of caring for the Earth."

Thread the magic loom now. Make threading movements with your hands and fingers so that your body is involved in this creation. [Two to five minutes, depending on the size of the circle.]

The warp threads are in place. Let us now begin to weave the weft threads, the ones that are inserted between the two sets of warp threads to create the pattern and variety and strength we want for this cloth. In the passage about weaving we have just discussed, we learn that Athena holds the power of the weft threads in the story that is told in *The Odyssey.* What patterns do you want to include in this cloth for your life story, and for the Earth's life story? Who or what holds the power of the weft threads, the insertion threads?

Actually use your fingers to wind the weft yarn around your

shuttle now. Use an imaginary foot pedal to open the shed between the upper and lower warp threads and shoot your shuttle across the lower threads. Now, pull the batten tight, tight against the new row of weft threads. Use your foot pedal again to change sheds and separate the upper and lower warp threads again, and shoot your shuttle across from the other side. Once again pull the batten tight against the new row of weft threads. Begin to see the pattern and texture of your fabric grow with every movement of the shuttle carrying the weft through the warp.

Sense that you are weaving the patterns of your life—whether you think of them as negative or positive—into the Earth's pattern. Your whole life, consciously woven with all its parts, is adding richness, strength, variety, and interest to the pattern of the whole Earth. You are making the Earth stronger and healthier by your willingness to weave everything of your life into the whole.

What do you want in these weft threads? Who or what serves the Athena role for your story? Is there some deep part of you that feeds and seeds your yearning to know more and understand more, that keeps you studying and reading and participating in groups like this one? What else? Negative or positive, patterns of your life are now being woven into the loom. [Two to five minutes.]

The loom is threaded, the shuttle wound with weft threads, colors, and patterns. Now you are moving your body back and forth, your arms back and forth, in the process of weaving. We are weaving a net cloth that can gift the Earth, protect the Earth, seed the Earth, as it gifts, protects, and seeds our lives. And we are weaving it together. Each individual holds an important and unique part of pattern in the cloth. Move your body, your arms and hands now, as we weave the cloth.

At the same time let your senses meld with Penelope—the patient one, the loving one, holding the center. But she is also the one who lives in a state of mourning and grieving. So as you weave, remember what it is to be Penelope, the one who waits. Allow memories of sadness, reasons for grieving, to rise in you. Feel that you are weaving into this network the truth of those things in your life that you have feared were lost—your sense of frustration, perhaps, of not knowing how much longer you can go on trying to hold it all together.

Let the sense of Penelope, the brilliant one, but the one who waits and yearns and grieves, begin to express itself. Continue to make weaving motions with your arms and body, but allow what represents the Penelope in your life to find expression now. Perhaps it's in tears, or in cries of frustration and pain—however it wishes to come. Let all her pain rise in you. Feel all her weariness of waiting, of having to put people off, of having to look after a passive and depressed child, of being tired and unsure and unacknowledged and filled with dislike for the ones who besiege you. Feel how it is, having to keep it all together and make sense of it, of being so alone and lonely, so afraid that you will always be in just this exact state, that nothing good will ever come, that no change for the better will ever arrive. Let Penelope rise in your senses and, as she rises, express what she feels through your own life, your own story.

Continue to make the weaving motions and to know that Penelope's story—all the Penelope stories all over the world—are now being woven into this cloth of caring. The story of all the single parents is being woven into the cloth of caring. The story of all those waiting for loved ones who may never come home is being woven into this cloth of caring. The story of all those whose children are away from home and whose parents have no way of knowing whether they are alive or dead is being woven into this cloth. The story of all those whose loved ones are missing in action, or held hostage, or in comas, or bound in wasting diseases, or lost in Alzheimer's, is threading itself into the pattern. Continue to weave, speak or express now, either specifically or in general, the story of Penelope as you know it in your life. Let it be woven into the cloth you are creating together.

[Allow time for the mourning and frustration and loneliness to be expressed. When it has reached a peak, the guide says:]

Now that you are feeling something of what Penelope felt in her yearning and her sadness, begin to allow yourself to feel overcome by weariness and the need to sleep, as she so often does. If you feel a need to lie down, do so now. . . . As Penelope, you are utterly worn out, and you want to rest now. So let the weaving stop and close your eyes in sleep. Allow the sleepiness to wash through you and over you. . . . Sleep now. . . . Begin to feel so drowsy . . . so very drowsy . . . gentle . . . healing . . . sleep . . . that takes you away from all problems. . . . Sleep, gentle . . . lulling . . . sleep is coming now. Penelope has a chance to rest. . . . You are so weary. . . . It is time to rest now. . . . Feel comfortable . . . safe . . . relaxed . . . and . . . so . . . very . . . drowsy. Your eyelids are closing now if they have not already done so . . . your limbs relaxed . . . your muscles so very relaxed . . . entering sleep . . . sleep . . . sleep . . . sleep . . . sleep. A deep and contented sleep. . . . Stay alert to my voice, but still fall into sleep . . . sleep . . . a deep . . . deep . . . sleep.

[The guide can continue with these kinds of suggestions for a while until he or she decides that most participants are deeply relaxed and ready for the next part. The guide will then say:]

And in your sleep, your equivalent of the goddess Athena comes to you. She massages all your limbs and muscles, helping them relax, helping your muscles relax and be eased. Allow your Great Friend from the archetypal realm to come now and give you a gentle massage to help you rest more deeply. . . .

In this rest your Great Friend and ally is here to reweave your system so that new energy and strength will be there for you when you awaken. Let your friend work on your body now so that you are gaining new powers as you rest. . . . If there are places where you feel tight or tense, your friend will know those places and move to them with her hands and healing arts to release them, heal them. If there are places in your heart or brain that need healing or easing, she will do that work as well, reweaving your body and being as you sleep.

I will give you three minutes of clock time, which is equal subjectively to all the time you need for this to happen. So the three minutes may seem like a much longer time during which your Great Friend works to massage, to release, to heal and ease your body and mind. And your Great Friend is doing that now. [Three minutes.]

Now she begins to spread a special balm or cream all over your face so that your skin is renewed and given release from the tension of worry and despair. As the goddess Athena did for Penelope, your friend is making you younger and more beautiful than before. This is happening now. [Two to three minutes.]

At some point, but not for a while yet, I will ask you to begin to return to this room and this time. But for now I am asking you to allow your consciousness to shift a little so that you are more awake and aware than before, because it is time now to dream. . . . Penelope tells us that dreams emerge from the shadows through two different gates: one is a gate of horn and these dreams tell true; the other is a gate of ivory and dreams that come from that gate are always false.

Very easily now in your mind's eye, see a gate of horn, a spring of energy pointing upward but planted firmly in the horns of some sacred animal that represents the powers of Earth. A gate of horn; allow your mind to image it. And as you do so, notice that behind it is the great cavern of dreams. Emerging from the cavern of dreams and coming forth to the gate of horn is a dream for your life and your weaving. Allow the dream to come forward now, a dream of caring for your life and the life of your Ithaca. It's coming from the cavern of dreams through the gate of horn; a vision or sense or image or dream of hope and possibility. Let it come forward now, see it clearly in your mind's eye. You will have four minutes of clock time, equal subjectively to all the time you need—hours and even days—for this true dream to emerge through the gate of horn. [Four minutes.]

Now continue to sit or lie still in the same position, so it is easy to retain your dream image, and thank the giver of the dream, thank your Great Friend for reweaving you while you rested. And now, very gently begin to shift your consciousness into this place and time as I count from one to ten. You need not move your body. Only your awareness and focus will shift as I count slowly and bring you to waking awareness. You are returning deeply refreshed and rested, carrying with you an image or a full dream from the gate of horn that will be part of the new weaving of your life.

You need not move your body, but let your mind begin to come awake now. One . . . two . . . three . . . four . . . Remember how it felt to have your great ally work on your body and spread the balm of youth on your face. Five . . . Hold your image from the gate of horn. Six . . . Hold the image. Seven . . . Feel deeply refreshed and clear. Eight . . . Nearly awake now. Nine . . . Hold on to the dream image, hold on to the sense of reweaving. Ten! Fully awake now, remember your dream image or images, or some sense of knowing that came to you through the gate of horn. Hold on to that sense or memory and wait. Do you all have it still? Everyone still aware of that visit from the cave of dreams, of the images coming through the gate of horn? Everyone have it? Now, clap your hands and come completely into this place. Then you can begin to move, to stretch.

Just as Penelope told Odysseus her dream, please turn to someone in your weaving circle and relate what you saw or felt of the visit of your Great Friend and of your dream. Share together what you felt and saw. [Allow six to ten minutes for this sharing.]

INSTRUCTIONS FOR THE SOLO VOYAGER: Whenever there is a group sharing indicated, be sure to write down your impressions in your journal. Perhaps you might wish to have a written dialogue with your Great Friend, or even the Earth itself.

SCRIPT FOR THE GUIDE: Now please select what part of the dream or image or sensation you wish to weave into the cloth of caring for the Earth, and begin to weave again. All of you in the circle, move now back and forth with your bodies and your arms as you weave your dream image into the cloth of caring.

Begin to sing it in, or tone it in. Make a song or a chant of what you are including in the great weaving. [Allow time for the songs to build and peak.]

INSTRUCTIONS FOR THE SOLO VOYAGER: You might want to tape your weaving chant, then play it back and continue to chant with it, harmonizing or embellishing it as you weave your cloth of caring. You might also want to use this weaving chant later for meditation.

Come now to silence. Come to silence. And listen to the silence, feel the waves of resonance of the images that are now in the weaving. Reach out and pick up this net you have woven together. Actually have the sense that you are picking up a piece of woven cloth, all together. Looking at what you have created together, speak one at a time about what you feel is in the cloth—both for yourself and for the Earth.

For example, you may say something like, "I see in this cloth my first Sunday school dress and how pretty and alive I felt in it; I see the pain of all the children who do not have anything to eat, much less wear, and I feel the pain of their parents. I see in this cloth my renewed vow to give more of my income to Foster Parents and other organizations that care for children. I see in this cloth my vision of the principle of feminine wisdom flying over the Earth and touching with her fierce bright wings the lives of all Penelopes, of all lonely people everywhere." [Allow time for each person to speak.]

Now, stand up—still holding the cloth—and lifting it high, begin to waft it around the room. Let it touch and connect with other groups' cloths of caring. Wave it like a banner. Celebrate it. Now let the top layer float out to be joined by other people's cloths of caring, other kinds of beliefs and processes. Let it move out and out until it enters the resonant field around the whole Earth, adding our consciousness, our lives, our dreams to that field. Lift it out and let it go, watch it go, as if it were a magic carpet, available for us to see and feel connection to. Watch it go with our love and caring to cover the Earth.

Now, let us take the bottom layer of our magic weaving, our cloth of caring, and place it on the floor, having the sense that it can float through the floor and sink into the ground to create a field of dreams and caring, of love and empathy, that we can walk on and through each day. With each step we take, we can remember that our weaving is there in the Earth, enriching it, filling it and us with our lives and knowing. Plant this weaving deep in the Earth now so it can become part of a new seeding, of a new life for this Ithaca, this beloved homeplace of ours.

Now, we are thanking our fellow weavers, our Great Friends who came to help us reweave ourselves, and thanking the cave of dreams, the gate of horn, and the beautiful and brilliant Penelope herself. The weaving is accomplished. The gift is made.

CHAPTER 14

Revenge and Reunion

ODYSSEUS picks up the bow. The images surrounding him are not ones of death but of music.

> And now, as easily as a musician who knows his lyre strings the cord on a new peg after looping the twisted sheep-gut at both ends, he strung the great bow without effort or haste and with his right hand proved the string, which gave a lovely sound in answer like a swallow's note.[1]

The thunder rolls from Zeus, and the suitors' cheeks blanch as Odysseus looses a shaft dead center through the twelve axes. The solar king has returned on the day of the feast of Apollo, god of light, of cool intelligence.

With mordant wit Odysseus announces loudly to his son that the time has come to make ready the supper of the suitors while it is still light. After that they may enjoy the pleasures of music and dancing without which no feast is complete. Together they stand, Odysseus revealed for who he is, Telemachus resplendent in bronze and fully armed. On this day of Apollo, he calls on the god to help him and levels his second arrow at the throat of Antinous. Arrow after arrow speeds on its deadly way; one suitor after another falls to the bitter marriage with death foretold by Telemachus at the beginning of the epic. Telemachus fights with confidence and brilliance by his father's side; just before the arrows are spent, he brings up from the storerooms shields, spears, and helmets for his father and the two herders.

Melanthius, a surly goatherd who has taken sides with the suitors, slips into the storerooms, where he finds weapons and armor for the suitors who are still alive. But he is caught by the loyal herders, tied up, and suspended from a pillar.

When the battle seems lost to Odysseus and his allies because of the overwhelming odds, help appears in the form of Mentor. Odysseus hails "his old friend" with joy. The suitors, however, greet Athena-Mentor's appearance with a torrent of abuse. Athena taunts Odysseus with the remembrance of his bravery when fighting at Troy for Helen's sake. Where is his courage now when defending his own possessions? She herself withdraws for a few moments, flying up to the roof as a swallow, leaving Odysseus and his son on their own to test their courage.

The suitors rally at this sign of Mentor's desertion, and together six of them hurl their spears at Odysseus. But Athena makes their spears miscarry and Odysseus' men dispatch that group. Again the suitors hurl their spears but mostly in vain: Telemachus is lightly wounded on the wrist and Eumaeus receives a scratch on his shoulder.

Now, her fury up, Athena raises her fearful Gorgon-emblazoned aegis on high and the terrified suitors scatter through the halls like a herd of cattle driven to stampede by an attack of stinging gadflies. This is the only time in *The Odyssey* when Athena lets her old warlike character, so much in evidence in *The Iliad,* emerge. And this may well be the moment to reflect on our own tendency to revert to previous patterns under stress. Both Athena and Odysseus—and, to a lesser extent, Telemachus—have received much training in the depth world; all have grown deeply in their psyches. But when faced with the terrific challenge of the "real world" and its rank injustices, what emerges first is the old familiar imprinting. However, there is a difference now, for their actions are deeper and more reflective. Instead of bragging endlessly, as the old Odysseus would have done, the restored ruler of Ithaca will eventually make amends as gracefully and peaceably as he can.

Odysseus and his party follow the fleeing suitors in close pursuit. Skulls crack, the groans of the dying fill the air, and the entire floor runs with blood. Men beg for mercy. The minstrel, Phemius, who has served as an unwilling bard, pleads to be spared. Here, we hear Homer's own persona and persuasion coming through Phemius' lips:

> Respect and pity me, you will repent it later if you kill a minstrel like me, who sings for gods and men. I had no teacher but myself. All kinds of song spring unpremeditated to my lips; and I feel that I could sing for you as I could sing for a god. Think twice, therefore, before you cut my throat.[2]

Odysseus relents. And, on the prompting of his son, spares not only the bard but also Medon, the herald who had looked after Telemachus when he was a boy.

Eurycleia is the first to witness the grisly results, and the old lady responds in so primal a fashion she has to be stopped from howling in triumph over the phenomenal achievement she sees arrayed bloodily before her. Odysseus checks her exaltation:

> Restrain yourself, old dame, and gloat in silence. I'll have no jubilation here. It is an impious thing to exalt over the slain. These men fell victims to the hand of heaven and their own infamy. They paid respect to no one who came near them—good men and bad were all alike to them. And now their own insensate wickedness has brought them to this aweful end.[3]

Eurycleia is given compensation, however; she knows who among the fifty maids of Odysseus' household repeatedly consorted with the suitors, catching their plague of anarchy and becoming vicious to Penelope and the other members of the faithful staff. She calls them out and, in one of the most unsavory incidents of *The Odyssey*, they are forced to help clean up the results of the slaughter before Telemachus condemns them to death by hanging. The house is then fumigated with sulfur, and Odysseus asks Eurycleia to call in the faithful maids and tell Penelope of his presence. The maids enter and they and Odysseus greet each other with much teary-eyed affection.

When her nurse comes to awaken her, Penelope is in her usual state of deep sleep, the soundest since Odysseus left. This sleep has evidently restored her skeptical powers, because she greets the news that Eurycleia brings of Odysseus' return and the killing of the suitors with profound disbelief. The gods must have addled her old nurse's brains. But when Eurycleia tells her that Odysseus is the stranger, Penelope's heart leaps up and she clings to her nurse, tears streaming from her eyes. When she hears further details about how he managed the cleansing slaughter she falls again into doubt of his identity; only an immortal god could accomplish such a feat.

When Penelope descends to look at this "god," she enters into one of the most poignant scenes in all literature. It is nearly dark in the great hall. Penelope takes a seat by a wall in the firelight opposite Odysseus. He is some distance off, sitting by one of the pillars around the hearth. Both seem at a loss. What in the world do you do or say after twenty years of separation and constant yearning for each other? The man of the Sun and the woman of the Moon cast furtive glances at each other, and then stare at the ground. The silence goes on and on.

Finally, Telemachus cannot stand it any longer and he shouts:

> My mother—a devil of a mother you are, with your hard heart. Why do you keep all that way from father? Why won't you sit beside him and ask some question or say something?

> I'm sure no other woman could be so cold and keep her husband at a distance, now he has come home after twenty years and all those terrible dangers![4]

And she answers with those wonderful words:

> My boy, my heart is numbed. I cannot speak to him, or ask questions, or look into his face. If he is indeed Odysseus, and this is his house, we shall know each other well enough; there are secrets that we two know and no one else.[5]

Odysseus smiles at this; he answers at once simply and plainly:

> Leave your mother alone, Telemachus, and let her test me; she will soon know me better.[6]

It is up to Penelope to unmask the true man behind the many disguises he has worn for almost two decades. He then counsels his son to turn his mind instead to the problems they will soon face with the irate relatives of the suitors. Telemachus shrewdly returns the challenge to his father, saying everyone knows he has the best mind among men, no mortal can rival him. He leaves without seeing the exquisite yet homey ending of the heroic consciousness as the best mind among men is conquered by the best mind among women.[7]

However, Telemachus does put into action his father's plan of asking all the men and women in the house to put on their ceremonial clothes and dance heartily to the loud tunes of wedding songs. This serves as a decoy, another masking of reality, so that the neighbors will think someone is finally marrying the much-courted queen. News of the suitors' deaths will be delayed.

To the background sounds of wedding music, Odysseus and Penelope meet alone again. This time he comes as a bridegroom, freshly bathed and beautifully clothed, his looks and stature enhanced by Athena, in a reprise of the earlier encounter with Nausicaa. He looks like a god, but he sounds like a husband, complaining to his wife and calling her *daemonic*.

> Heaven made you as you are, but for sheer obstinacy you put all the rest of your sex in the shade. No other wife could

have steeled herself to keep so long out of the arms of a husband she had just got back after nineteen years of misadventure. Well, nurse, make a bed for me to sleep alone in. For my wife's heart is just about as hard as iron.[8]

Penelope's fascinating reply is to say that it is he who is *daemonic,* and then in ingenious but wifely fashion proceeds to weave words that answer him with the obverse of what he has just said.[9]

> I am not being haughty or indifferent. I am not even unduly surprised. But I have too clear a picture of you in my mind as you were when you sailed from Ithaca in your long-oared ship. Come, Eurycleia, make him a comfortable bed outside the bedroom that he built so well himself. Place the big bed out there, and make it up with rugs and blankets, and with laundered sheets.[10]

So one daemoniac tests the other. *Daemons,* in ancient Greek usage, serve as conduits between mortals and gods. To enter the ancient Mysteries, one had to be in touch with one's *daemon,* for only that aspect of one's character and destiny had the greater knowledge that allowed one to journey further than most ordinary mortals do. Socrates, that most extraordinary of mortals, never made any important decision without first consulting his *daemon*. The daemoniac therefore is not merely strange, but gifted with the capacity to see several worlds at the same time, and become, in the fulfillment of the Hero's Journey, master of both.

Both Odysseus and Penelope daemonically evoke and recognize signs from the depths and help them come to fruition. By naming each other "daemonic" they announce their remarriage at a deeper level, their sacred union corresponding to the true *Hieros Gamos,* the sacred marriage within the journey of the hero—Odysseus having consummated lesser and prefigurative forms of this union, first with Circe, and then Calypso. Now, in the fullness of the proper and long-awaited *Hieros Gamos,* the true partners in this sacred conjunction can serve as conduits for a new order of reality. But first Odysseus, the most cunning of men, must fall completely into the trap laid by Penelope, the most intelligent of women, and the mystery of the secret of their marriage bed revealed.

Odysseus, who has so often lied and deceived others, is utterly taken in by Penelope's test by deception, blows his daemonic cool, and explodes:

> Penelope, you exasperate me! . . . Short of a miracle, it would be hard even for a skilled workman to shift it somewhere else, and the strongest young fellow alive would have a job to budge it. For a great secret went into the making of that complicated bed; and it was my work and mine alone.[11]

He then proceeds to reveal the secret of the bed and how it was built into the organic structure of the palace:

> Inside the court there was a long-leaved olive-tree, which had grown to full height with a stem as thick as a pillar. Round this I built my room of close-set stonework, and when that was finished, I roofed it over thoroughly, and put in a solid, neatly fitted, double door. Next I lopped all the twigs off the olive, trimmed the stem from the root up, rounded it smoothly and carefully with my adze and trued it to the line, to make my bedpost. This I drilled through where necessary, and used as a basis for the bed itself, which I worked at till that too was done . . . there is our secret, and I have shown you that I know it.[12]

There is an even greater secret contained here. His identity is literally grounded in his marriage bed and Athena. The olive tree bedpost with its living root holds the bed of Odysseus and Penelope so that it cannot be moved, like their marriage. It was Athena, architect of the homecoming and special ally of both Odysseus and Penelope as well as their son, who gifted the land of Attica with the olive tree. The olive is her symbol, the announcement that she is present. Her ancient cult statue in the Parthenon was carved of olive wood and her victor at the Panathenaic Games was given a large amphora of olive oil as his prize. The secret of the living olive tree bed is the most precious mystery shared by Odysseus and Penelope and binds them together within the heart of the goddess. The importance of the bed to the poem and to Athena cannot be overestimated. As Marina Warner says in her interesting observation:

> It is the ultimate sign in an epic of altered and metamorphosing and deceiving appearances, expressing the centrality of Athena to the love of Penelope and Odysseus, and to chaste married fidelity for women. It is also Athena's final hiding place, a disguise that is not anthropomorphic or personified, but equally potent in a text pervaded throughout by praise of her wisdom, her care, her vigilance, her arts. The cunning that went into the contrivance of such a bed is her gift too, through her mother Metis, Cunning herself, to Odysseus *polymetis,* a craftsman like the men of her city Athens who gave her special tribute.[13]

By the sign of the secret of the bed, Penelope is released from all her years of doubt and despair. The poem states in multiple images the nature of this release: "her knees were loosened where she sat, and her heart melted . . . then with a burst of tears she ran straight toward him, and flung her arms about the neck of Odysseus and kissed his head and spoke."[14]

She asks him not to be angry over her initial reserve. She explains that she has lived for many years with the cold fear that a stranger would come and bewitch her with his talk. She has always had before her the example of Helen, whom Aphrodite had tempted to fall in love with a stranger.

Odysseus does not answer Penelope in words but in deeds: "Penelope's surrender melted Odysseus' heart, and he wept as he held his dear wife in his arms, so loyal and so true. . . . She kept her white arms round his neck and never quite let go."[15]

So now they are together unmasked and with no need for guile, able for the first time in twenty years to completely tell and be the truth. Well met and well mated by moonlight, they go to their olive tree bed and share much sweet loving and many truthful tales for as long as they need, for Athena stays the dawn.

And what of the dead suitors? Hermes, with his golden wand "that he can use at will to cast a spell on our eyes or wake us from soundest sleep,"[16] guides their shades down to the Underworld where they proceed, squeaking like bats. Once there, they meet Agamemnon and Achilles, who are comparing notes on their respective deaths and burials, still as bitter as when Odysseus met them on his own mortal journey to Hades. They are astonished at the large number of shades who have arrived, thinking that many ships must have been lost in a gale to account for so many newly arrived dead.

In response, one of the ghostly suitors gives them a short but accurate account of their misbehavior in the palace and the terrible consequences for them of the return of Odysseus. To this tale of horrors, the soul of Agamemnon responds by offering an encomium to Penelope. This is surprising, given his death at the hands of his own wife, which had caused him to warn Odysseus to distrust all women, even Penelope. Now he makes an exception and speaks the sentiments that will adorn Penelope for thousands of years to come:

> "Unconquerable Odysseus!" the soul of Agamemnon cried. "Ah happy prince, blessed in Icarius' daughter with a wife in whom all virtues meet, flawless Penelope, who has proved herself so good and wise, so faithful to her wedded love! Her glory will not fade with the years, but the deathless gods themselves will make a song for mortal ears, to grace Penelope the constant queen."[17]

Back in the world of the living, Odysseus goes to meet his father, Laertes, after advising Penelope to stay with her ladies in her room in the palace, seeing and speaking to no one. He goes fully armed and arranges for his son and the swineherd and cowman to be similarly prepared. He decides to try an experiment with his father to see if he will remember his son. Finding Laertes digging in his vineyard, Odysseus is at first shocked at his aged and ragged condition. His father, in his sorrow, has lost the gift for living, and is clearly just hanging on, waiting for death to deliver him. His lands, however, are well cared for, recalling the excellent husbandry of the swineherd Eumaeus. As Odysseus speaks with Laertes, he contrasts the well-tended lands with the ragged and parched look of the gardener, and observes that he does not look a slave but a king. Drawing him out with consummate skill, he gets Laertes to admit his belief that his beloved son is dead. Odysseus next conveys a story of having entertained his son five years before and given him opulent gifts. The omens were good when he left and he believed that he would see Laertes' son once again.

At this news the old man breaks down and in his misery scoops up black dust and pours it on his head. This is too much for Odysseus; "poignant compassion" forces its way through his nostrils. He seizes and kisses the old man, revealing who he really is, and tells him about the slaughter of the suitors at the palace. Laertes demands proof of his identity, and Odysseus rises to the occasion, not only showing his scar but giving an exact accounting of how many and what kinds of trees and vines Laertes had given him as a little boy.

At this, Laertes rises out of his lethargy to a kind of antique splendor. He even allows himself to be bathed, anointed, and decked out with a splendid mantle. Athena helps the process of rejuvenation by making him taller and more handsome than before, so that he seems to Odysseus like an immortal god. A splendid feast is had as Telemachus and the two followers of Odysseus join them, as do a faithful servant, Dolius, and his sons.

Before long, the relatives of the suitors are seen ascending the hill armed and ready for combat. With the help of their followers, the three generations of men, Laertes, Odysseus, and Telemachus, fight off the kinsmen. Against this unified family there is no hope for the enemy.

But there would have been much more bloodshed if it hadn't been for Athena, who ends the epic of homecoming as she had begun it—on Olympus, conferring with her father, Zeus, about the need for peace. With a terrifying cry from her goddess voice, she stops the fighting and sends the forces home. When Odysseus tries to follow after them, he is stopped by a flaming thunderbolt from Zeus himself, which lands in front of his bright-eyed daughter. Heaven has spoken; Earth must end its civil strife.

Athena, appearing again as Mentor, teaches the contending forces how to achieve a new peace. The warrior goddess at Troy has now evolved into the goddess of peaceful persuasion at Ithaca, and her human partner has also grown immeasurably in the course of the Mysteries and initiations she has laid out for him.

What began with tears of yearning ends in a peaceful persuasion, linked by a movement of consciousness into its deeper possibilities, and with it, the impetus for a new creation of consciousness and society. The Hero and the Goddess have come far together, and in succeeding centuries will travel further still.

Clearing the House of Death and the Meeting with the Beloved

IN many cultures, especially the Indo-European, the great bow carries profound significance. It represents the power of light from the Sun, the rays of Apollo the archer; it cleanses and purifies the world of corruption and evil doings; its presence states in no uncertain terms that a god-being has entered and will be reckoned with. We remember that Athena put the idea of the contest of the bow in Penelope's mind by way of a dream.

There is a similar bow in the great Indian epic *The Ramayana.* It originally belonged to the god Shiva, and the man who is able to string it will win the Princess Sita's hand in marriage. The hero,

Rama, is the only one who can handle the bow; thus he is the one to be united with this woman who represents all the powers of the Earth.

In *The Odyssey,* Odysseus' great bow once belonged to one of the most famous archers of the past, Eurytus, who had so much talent he had been coached by the god Apollo himself. It is therefore a very extraordinary bow, which is why Odysseus does not take it with him to Troy for the business of ordinary battling. It can be used only on sacred occasions having to do with his family's welfare. Not only can Odysseus—disguised as the beggar—string this bow, but he also makes it sing with a terrifying music, unleashing an arrow with devastating accuracy through the twelve ax heads. The number twelve carries so much power that one hesitates to choose its relevance for this passage: twelve constellations in the zodiac through which the Sun proceeds, twelve ships in Odysseus' fleet, twelve major gods. But the number twelve also signifies the solar king, Odysseus, who vanquishes the powers of darkness through an abundance of light. This he does on the feast day of Apollo, a solar god of light and enlightenment, whose symbols also include the bow and arrow.

Penelope has announced that she will marry anyone who can string the bow. Thus we see that the bow carries the power of union with the beloved as well as the power of cleansing light. Penelope, as keeper of the home, also represents, as does Sita, the great Earth herself. When we draw the bow to cleanse our house of death and darkness, we are also demonstrating again our willingness to partner the Earth in the deepest and most loving way possible.

TIME: Two hours, or more.

SUGGESTIONS: Participants might be invited to attend this final session wearing beautiful celebrational clothes under beggarly, disreputable garments.

MATERIALS NEEDED: A very long sheet or sheets of butcher paper, newsprint, or other kind of paper to be used to create a group mural of the hall in Ithaca. Crayons, Magic Markers, and a variety of other drawing and painting materials can be used.

Thumbtacks or some pins to hang the mural on the wall, if possible. A variety of small foam balls or sandbags will be helpful for throwing at the suitors in the mural. Candles to mark the line of demarcation between this realm and the world of the beloved, plus additional candles for each person to carry across the threshold.

MUSIC: For the drawing of the mural of the hall and the suitors use music with an ominous sound, such as Philip Glass' score for *Koyanisquaatsi.* If a more upbeat mood is desired, then any of the Hooked on Classics selections would work. During the stretching sequence, although no music is necessary, some people might prefer a background of unfolding cosmic sounds, especially during the period in which one is called to be filled with light. Then a selection like Michael Stearns' *Planetary Unfolding* would be appropriate. When hurling the balls and arrows, I recommend a highly energized and somewhat savage piece like Vangelis' *Heaven and Hell,* side 1, band 2. For the walk to the beloved, the first part of Vangelis' *Ignacio* is very beautiful.

INSTRUCTIONS FOR THE SOLO VOYAGER: This entire process is readily done alone by taping the script and following the instructions. During the part in which one works with a partner, just imagine that your partner is Odysseus himself standing by your side. Speak to him about what you are aiming at with your great bow of light, and sense him speaking with you in the same manner. When you cross the line of fire to the beloved within, have a sense of being suffused in the love and presence of the spiritual beloved. Most important of all for those who are working alone is to have some kind of celebration or party in your honor for having braved the Odyssean voyage all by yourself. If possible, tell some of your friends about what you have done during the weeks or months you have worked through this book and its processes. Let them plan a dinner or celebration for you at which time you can share with them your journey and discoveries.

SCRIPT FOR THE GUIDE: This first part of our final meeting together will be spent creating a group mural of the hall in Ithaca.

[If the group is small enough, everyone can work together on this creation but if there are more than twelve people, it may be advisable to split into smaller groups.]

Please take a long sheet of paper—at least six or eight feet long—for each set of six or seven people, and some drawing materials and colors. Begin to sketch in your ideas about how the great hall in Ithaca looked with all the suitors eating and drinking and creating a hideous and raucous mess. Have a really wild time of it. What did the hall look like to Odysseus? What is going on here? We're going for a Breughel effect, so really paint the excesses of each suitor and each suitor's actions. We're first going to draw the hall and then we're going to label the suitors, so we see what it is that needs to be cleared and cleansed and destroyed. Draw the hall now and all the suitors. [Allow thirty to forty-five minutes.]

Now we want to begin to identify the suitors and label what is going on in the painting, for this mural represents both our lives and our world. When we truly come home to ourselves we are able to see with blinding light the number of things that must be cleansed from the homeplace if we are to create the world anew.

Think now of some of the things in your life that are eating away at your substance, at your life force, at your energy. Are they habits? Are they fears? Do you find yourself so lacking in respect for your own life that you cannot bring yourself to take responsibility for it? Are they negative qualities that waste your powers and eat you alive? Things like envy and hate and rage that you cannot release appropriately.

Speak aloud as you begin to draw labels on these debilitating and ruinous suitors. Name them as you see them making demands on you that hurt you, as they drink and feast on your time and your heart.

Continue, if you wish, to draw other suitors, but focus on labeling them all over the mural. Go ahead and label suitors drawn by others, or even adding labels to other's labels if they speak to you. Notice how it is that the presence in your life of these lazy and insolent suitors also means that they are present in much magnified form in our mutual homeplace: the planet Earth. Envy and anger and defensiveness and sloth all make themselves devastating to the Earth, and all threaten her safety and sanity, as the suitors threaten the keeper of the homeplace, Penelope. Be very precise about what you are drawing, both for your own life and for the life of the planet. [Allow sufficient time for the drawing and labeling to be done, perhaps another twenty to thirty minutes.]

Now let us hang the mural. [If it needs to be patched together because it is in several pieces, then one piece after another should be tacked up.] And we want to spend some moments admiring our creation of this mural of the hall in Ithaca. [Five minutes or so while the group inspects the full panoply of this mural.]

So the hall has been established, and we have seen the nature of the suitors and what they will continue to do to waste and wreck our lives if they are not stopped. Now we will invite the strength of cleansing light to inform our being so that we may become the mighty bow of power and union itself.

Standing tall, with your feet a comfortable shoulder length apart, stretch your arms and hands above your head as high as you can. Breathe comfortably. Flex and wiggle your fingers, continuing to breathe easily. Now begin to make fists—close your hands to make fists, and open them again to stretch the fingers full out. Do this as quickly as you can, opening and closing the hands as rapidly as possible. Continue to breathe easily; open and close your hands. Open. Close. Open. Close. Open. Close. Now relax your arms and let them hang down at your sides.

Very slowly begin to bend forward from the waist, letting your arms hang forward and down as if you wanted to touch your toes. Do not lock your knees, let them be easy. Relax your shoulders and neck and just bend forward and down from the waist as far as you can comfortably go. Invite your lower back to release a little more if it will so that your hands are near the floor and you are bent nearly double. Remember to breathe easily. Swing the upper part of your body gently from side to side. Let your head hang down, relaxed.

Remain comfortably bent over from the waist, and once again open and close your hands. You are activating life energy in your hands. Open and close your hands as rapidly as possible. Open. Close. Open. Close. Continue that rapid opening and closing of your hands for a few more moments. . . .

Now stop. Very slowly, begin to raise your body as if the individual vertebrae of your spine were stacking themselves one at a time on top of each other. Let your head continue to stay relaxed and bent forward until the last moment, when the spine is straight and the neck vertebrae are ready to be stacked on top of the spine. Do this fluid movement very slowly and gently, and with full consciousness.

Now, once more, raise your arms above your head and this time stand on tiptoe for a moment as you stretch up. Open and close the hands rapidly. . . . Now, standing fully on both feet, come slowly down from tiptoe. Stretch up again, feeling your spine stretch and your arms stretch and your hands and fingers stretch. Very slowly, very gently, allow your spine to curve backward so that you are bending back as a bow would bend and you are stretching your body as if it were a bow. Bend back only as far as it feels completely comfortable. Do not strain. Do not push. Make sure you are continuing to breathe regularly and to open and close your hands. When you have stretched and bent backward as far and as long as you can, then relax and bring your hands and arms down to your sides. Notice how your spine feels. Scan the rest of your body and stretch anything that feels tight.

We are going to stretch up and back one more time, and this time we are going to invoke the light to fill our bodies so that they may become force fields of light to be used in our battle against those energies that devastate our lives.

Very mindfully and consciously, begin to raise your arms and stretch them above your head, breathing in easily and exhaling easily. . . . If you choose, you may now begin opening your hands to the sense of bright energy, feel sunlight entering your hands as you open and close them. . . . The power of the Sun and its cleansing energy is now bathing your hands and filling them with precision and strength, flexibility and skill for the tasks they must do. . . .

As you feel the light of the Sun entering your hands, begin to slowly, mindfully, and very gently bend backward so that your face and throat and heart are exposed to the light that is flowing into your hands, and pouring down your arms, and through your whole body. The Sun is also bathing your hair and face, neck and throat, high heart and central heart with its powerful light. Now it is activating its center in the body, the solar plexus, and the solar plexus in turn ignites, itself a miniature Sun, so that the entire front of your body is filled with light from inside and out. Your spine is stretching to open to the light of the Sun. The light is pouring from your heart and solar plexus, from your hands and from the Sun itself, in great jets down and up your spine, down and up your legs. You bend backward again—gently, gently—becoming a great bow of light, filled with the cleansing power of the Sun. . . . You are breathing easily and paying attention to your body as it forms this great bow.

Now slowly straighten your body again. Let yourself relax. Let your arms come slowly down to your sides. You may sit if you like, but keep remembering how it feels to be a bow of light. Feel your whole body filled with light. Feel this great surge of light pulsing through your entire being. Allow this feeling to grow and reverberate until you are totally light filled, until you know yourself to be a small sun pulsing with warmth and energy.

Filled with this intense sense of great light—of the Sun itself—pouring from each of us, let us now find appropriate arrows [the available little balls or sandbags] and perform Odysseus' task of cleansing the house of death in a way that is less bloody and more precise than he was able to be. Looking at your "arrows," decide which of the "suitors" in the mural you wish to annihilate or drive out of your life. Decide how your arrow is going to be used to accomplish that deed. It is relatively easy to throw the ball or bag at the mural, easy to hit what you're aiming at—but we need to go further. We need to identify precisely what it is we are going to do to cleanse this suitor from our lives.

Turn now to a partner and work in pairs, just as Odysseus and Telemachus worked together, as you set about cleansing the hall in Ithaca. [If you are voyaging solo, sense the presence of Odysseus by your side, working with you.] You may use an eraser, or a brighter color to wipe out the suitor, or you may throw a ball or a bag until you hit the suitor you want to knock out. But all the while you will be speaking in a stream-of-consciousness style to your partner [or to Odysseus or to your Great Friend if you are voyaging solo] about what you are doing with yourself as the bow of light. Speak of how your arrow is a weapon of precision, the perfect instrument for eliminating these unwanted suitors from your own personal Ithaca.

While you talk and throw, erase and blot out, fill the hall with cries of triumph. Feel that great sound that Odysseus made when he strung the bow. You are now that bow. Loosen your own great sound of release as you hurl your arrows at the suitors who are destroying life in your Ithaca.

Let the cleansing begin!

[Guide: allow ten to fifteen minutes, by which time the mural should be thoroughly destroyed by the onslaught. At the close of the process gather up the remaining fragments and give them to a participant who is willing to burn them ceremonially. If you are voyaging solo, gather up the fragments and create a burning and dispersing ritual of your own.]

The hall in Ithaca has been cleansed of darkness and debilitation. It is time to celebrate. It is time to enact the reunion of Odysseus and Penelope, the Sun's reunion with the Earth. Let the beggar be revealed as the true ruler of this Ithaca. Now as I place a line of candles across the center of this room I invite you to take off the top layer of beggarly clothes you've been wearing and reveal your celebrational clothes underneath.

[The guide or the solo reader places a line of lighted candles down the center of the room and then goes to the back of the room and lights as many individual candles as there are participants.]

Knowing yourself to be the true ruler of your own life—filled forever with the glorious light of the Sun, please come and pick up a candle that reflects in miniature the power of your light. There is a line of candles, a line of fiery light across the room, and we are going to move across that line of fire in order to move symbolically into the realm where we are one with the Beloved of our Souls, where Penelope and Odysseus, Sun and Earth, perpetually celebrate their union.

When we cross over that line we will feel ourselves to be in the force field of the love that Odysseus and Penelope feel for each other. And the love that Athena, the bright-eyed one, feels for them and for Homer—and, yes, for each of us. For we have lived again the great epic that celebrates Athena in all her appearances and disguises. We have helped her to understand how she too is changing and growing, just as she has helped us to understand how we are changing and growing, and how our work of transformation can bring new joy, new light, and new life to our homeplace, to the

Earth. We will be bathed in the light of that love and power and we will sit suffused by it and by the presence of our own inner Beloved Friend, whatever form he or she takes.

Let us now take up our lights, and, as the music plays, we will begin to walk *very, very slowly* until we approach and cross the line of light and find ourselves on the other side, in the Realm of All Light.

[The music begins—Vangelis' *Ignacio* or a similar piece. Allow time for each participant to enter the Realm of the Beloved and to sit there for a few minutes.]

We are sitting here now in this radiant field of love—a love that has been celebrated for thousands of years. It is here and now and very present with each of us. A love that brings us home to union at last with our own inner Beloved of the Soul. . . .

Knowing that this place is available to us each time we look at the light of a candle, or a star, or the Sun, let us release now the ones who have come here to be with us, to give us their love and light. And let us now join in joyous celebration of the journey of transformation we have made together.

[A party with food and dancing and singing should follow. Those who have worked to this point alone please remember the earlier instructions in this section where I suggest various ways of celebrating your triumphal journey.]

CHAPTER 15

Creating the New Myth

As long ago as 1948, Joseph Campbell noted that within "progressive societies" every vestige of the ancient heritage of ritual, morality, and art was in full decay. Today, the outward decay is decades worse, yet curiously there is new hope, for the decay commands us to become aware and conscious of our actions, and to seek new sources and resources for our lives. People can no longer bear the spiritual aridity and meaninglessness that come from living too long on the surface, even a successful surface. The trouble is that the lines of communication between the conscious and unconscious zones of the human psyche have been badly eroded by our concentration on external and superficial realities—and by our denial of the deeper inward worlds.

However, it is also possible to perceive the current breakdown of the membranes between cultures and ecologies—both inner and outer—as a sign that the depths are rising. And this is happening in ways that will allow us to build new bridges between these inner and outer worlds—even to make them stronger than they were when first forged in the childhood of humanity. For now that we have raised the stakes to almost unbearable heights, we know what we have to lose.

Although today the bridges between realities offered by the great religions may be in disrepair, these faiths are also seeding and cross-fertilizing each other. As the gods and guides of East, West, North, and South become available to us all—and to each other—this creates many fascinating new connections to the realms of Spirit. Athena and Spider Woman meet and compare notes. Isis and the Sophia, the feminine principle of wisdom, trace their common lineage. Apollo and Krishna play duets together on the lyre and the flute. Oya, the wild goddess of Africa, exchanges plants with Greek Demeter and tales of triumph with Indian Durga.

The growing threat of ecological disaster has, however, resulted in renewed appreciation of nature—of plants and animals, and the spellbinding Mystery of the movements of the Sun, the Moon, and the stars. Just as it did in ancient times, this fierce appreciation informs our knowings and provides the scaffolding for new bridges of communication and communion with Nature. Out of this has come a fervent revival of interest in archetypal realities, without which there can be no real comprehension of the nature and practice of myth. For archetypes are residents in the world of myth and great story. They may even be the creators of that world. Learning to become a partner, a "co-creator," with one or many archetypes means learning to build bridges to the source levels of our lives.

Searching out and testing these patterns of partnership from the places where we find them embedded and embodied in the great stories of humankind—waiting to usher evolutionary change into our lives—is the heart of the work of sacred psychology. And while it is work, because we use myth and story to anchor us and to provide the guidelines, it also becomes "play for mortal stakes," as Robert Frost reminds us: "for heaven and the future's sakes."

MYTH AS A MODEL FOR CREATING POSSIBLE WORLDS

In the most remarkable way, ancient myths—especially creation myths—prefigure some of the most exciting speculations on the frontiers of science today. The discoveries of the new physics and cosmology find their very lineaments in the myths of chaos and the making of the world. Marduk, the Babylonian storm god, blows his mighty winds into the body of Tiamat, the dragon goddess of chaos, and destroys her. But from her parts he creates the world and all its many creatures.

Similarly, modern chaos theory tells us that the raising of the vibrations, the winds, of energy upon the chaos of unstructured molecular particles is what lures pattern into weaving itself into matter. Just so, did the Yahweh of the Old Testament breathe upon the Deep, the Egyptian god Kheper speak his own name into the Void, and Earthmaker of the Winnebago Indians heat himself in a sweat lodge. Each of them sends a new vibration into the inchoate, and the world is called into being.

Myths of archetypes that are everywhere and all at once recall quantum physics' understanding of the ways in which everything is part of everything else. In the microcosm, every electron is aware of and influences every other electron, just as each one of us is ubiquitous throughout the great hologram, the macrocosm, that is our universe.

Today, we are at the brink of Second Genesis, soon to be able to create almost anything (and possibly anyone) we can imagine. Thus, we look to creator myths to discover what to do to re-create our world—and most important, what not to do to raise up monsters and aberrations. Just as Odysseus grew and deepened from his encounters with the Cyclops, Circe, and the Sirens on his mythic journey of self-renewal and the creation of a new society, so we return to the divine plays to discover the scenarios that await us in our mythic futures.

LIVING THE MYTHIC LIFE

Because of the acceleration of human experience in our time, each of us, in his or her own way, is becoming a mythic being. We have undergone as much unusual experience and suffered as many woundings as any mythic character. As in the Hero's Journey, we have heard and answered many calls, discovered remarkable allies, crossed and recrossed many thresholds of experience, found ourselves swallowed and re-gestated in the belly of the whale, entered upon a road of trials and high adventures, died many times to outworn and restrictive aspects of ourselves, and been chronically resurrected. We have fought with monsters of our own and others' making, tried to right wrongs or enhance the condition of life wherever we have found it, and even discovered a path to the beloved and marriage to the spiritual partner within. Our lives could hardly be called humdrum, but anytime they seemed dull, we went out and did something about it. Or, perhaps, some archetypal force entered and livened things up for us.

This is a phenomenon that is happening worldwide. We are all engaged in a mythic experiencing of the life of the soul and, by extension, of the Soul of the World. But what is unique about our time is that our lives are not amplified by reflection in the cultural mythic hero or heroine. Our lives are as mythic as theirs. We are direct participants in the story of the Soul in the World. We catch the evolutionary vibrations much more directly than we once did, which explains all the new emphasis on personal mythology. The most important event in this whole system transition is the radical incorporation of mythical and archetypal qualities in our lives. Whenever we study myth, it opens the gates to this disclosure. And we can begin to examine our own lives as mythic events—events that tell of the unfolding and uncoding of the Soul of the World.

The rise of the Goddess and of Gaia, as the personification of our planet, in our consciousness is part of that telling—the immanent image of our soul-directed living. At this point, the tension between soul and world, inner and outer, public and private, begins to disappear as we discover ourselves to be characters in the drama of the world soul, the *anima mundi*. In this mode, ego structures are seen as simply one aspect among the multiple aspects of the self. Indeed, the most accurate model of human existence will be able to account for its innate diversity, both among individuals and within each individual. The polyphrenic self is seen to be the healthy self. Spiritually, however, as mentioned earlier, James Hillman reminds us, "the soul's inherent multiplicity demands a theological fantasy of equal differentiation."[1] This means that now the gods too need to be polyphrenic, multifaceted images of the One.

In the state of partnership that blends into union, we are digested by God and re-formed by God. And in some sense, God becomes human for us. Thus, Meister Eckhart's great words that God says to us, "I became man for you. If you do not become God for me, you do me wrong." There is a transducing of substance and essence across transpersonal domains. Eckhart says, "If I am to know God directly, I must become completely God, and God I; so that this God and this I become one I."[2] We become part not just of a larger psychology of being, but of the secret life of God. It is no longer an intellectual or a speculative knowledge. It is entirely experiential.

And yet someone like Eckhart, one of the most powerful conceptual and experiential mystical theologians of the Christian Middle Ages, was clear in his statement that the mystical union is not the privilege of the few but the very vocation and ultimate realization of humanity. He says this because he believes that God is entirely immanent in us all, is in fact our very being.

The "archetype of partnership" is our very reason for being. Our limitations keep reducing this identity to merely a likeness. This is why we must expand our awareness into identity, while reducing our attachment to our local conditioning. The quality of our Selfhood depends on the presence of that divine image in us, on the degree of our own immanence in the archetype of God. Within the framework of a sacred psychology, the archetype of God can be experienced as the Beloved of the Soul. By becoming immersed in this archetypal and profoundly loving relationship, we can grow toward our true identity in God.

MYTHS TO COME

Finally, what is the point of it all? Why myth? Why sacred psychology? Why the journey of the soul? Where are we going and what will it be like when we get there? The point is that we are all becoming citizens of a universe larger than our aspirations, one that is infinitely richer and more complex than all our dreams. What this may well mean in our time is that this opening up, this expanding of our vision, is enabling us to co-create an entirely new order of being—a Type-One High Civilization. The best way I can describe this emergent civilization is to look at it in terms of its sensory, psychological, mythic, and spiritual requirements.

On the sensory and physical level it means we become responsive to the biological and ecological unfolding of the planet. To be able to do this, we must develop our own physical and sensory capacities so that we become capable of seeing the patterns in nature, capable of listening to the rhythms of awakening, and capable of recognizing our own bodies as reflections in miniature of the body of the Earth, so that we may give both our physical and planetary selves the appropriate nurturing and development.

On the psychological level we grow in kind, and educate ourselves to many different frames of mind and understandings. It means learning to think in images as well as in words. It also means learning to think kinesthetically, with subtle sensory knowing. It means harvesting the potentials developed in different cultures, and the stories of different cultures, and applying them to our own lives in ways that grant us access to intuitive and creative depths we rarely accessed before. It means too that the ecology of inner space becomes just as important as the ecology of our outer world.

In the sphere of relationships between people and cultures there will also be a considerable shift. Men and women will move more and more into full partnerships. There will have to be more emphasis on transformational friendships. We will come to view our life as an improvisation, since many of the traditional forms of family, social position, and profession can no longer be counted upon. Teaching-learning communities will spring up to serve both personal and societal growth. Cultures currently at war with each other, such as the Israelis and Palestinians, will go deeper and beyond their confrontation to look for their common story and its codings for reconciliation.

This leads us directly to myth, for every emerging society is only as good as the vitality of its myths and symbols. It is highly probable that in the next century we will be moving into a world myth—with Gaia as its focus. This does not mean the diminishment of traditional myths, but it does suggest that their archaic content that is no longer relevant will be lessened as their eternal and more universal structures come more into play. In the emerging mythos of this world civilization, the deeper stories inherent in our personal mythologies, coupled with those of the different cultural mythologies, will flow into an emerging planetary mythos. Thus the personal particulars of each of our stories will inform and evoke the personal universal of the cultural and planetary story, which will in turn lead to a richer play of archetypes. Maybe this is why in our time so many of us are finding our lives being lived mythically. It is no longer the "gods" who are numinous borderline persons. It is also ourselves. On a spiritual level all of this will require that more and more of us come to live our daily lives as a spiritual exercise.

In the next hundreds or thousands of years we may very well move into even higher orders of High Civilization, with greater responsibilities for world-making in a solar and galactic milieu. This will require a corresponding growth and deepening of our capacities in sensory, psychological, mythic, and spiritual domains. Perhaps this little corner of the galaxy is where They keep the school for budding Creators. Coded in myth perhaps, is the design of the larger story—who we really are, where we have come from, where we may hope to be. Part of the design is that our minds and souls must reach for this coding, test it fully, and even transcend it.

Toward the end of his life, after the storm and stress had cooled, D. H. Lawrence wrote a poem about the coming of a new spirit into time. This poem, rightly titled "Song of a Man Who Has Come Through," speaks to the issues of these pages and illumines them in images both potent and profound. For it is only in poetry that the news of the universe can be delivered fully, and heard with the wonder and astonishment it deserves.

SONG OF A MAN WHO HAS COME THROUGH

Not I, not I, but the wind that blows through me!
A fine wind is blowing the new direction of Time.
If only I let it bear me, carry me, if only it carry me!
If only I am sensitive, subtle, oh, delicate, a winged gift!
If only, most lovely of all, I yield myself and am
borrowed
By the fine, fine wind that takes its course through the
chaos of the world
Like a fine, an exquisite chisel, a wedge-blade inserted;
If only I am keen and hard like the sheer tip of a wedge
Driven by invisible blows,
The rock will split, we shall come at the wonder, we shall
find the Hesperides.

Oh for the wonder that bubbles into my soul,
I would be a good fountain, a good well-head,
Would blur no whisper, spoil no expression.

What is the knocking?
What is the knocking at the door in the night?
It is somebody wants to do us harm.

No, no, it is the three strange angels.
Admit them. Admit them.[3]

Epilogue

As I write these final words I have just come indoors from a beach in Florida where I witnessed the early morning launching of the space shuttle *Discovery* from Cape Kennedy. As we waited for the launch to happen, my students and I told ancient stories of the meeting of Heaven and Earth and whispered our wishes for the great voyage that was about to begin—this time a peace mission of seven civilians bringing telescopes into outer space with which to study other worlds.

Our eyes strained against the horizon as the minutes ticked by, past the announced launch time. There had been days of delays due to high winds, but this time *we are here,* singing the journey into being, drumming for the old gods of Earth and Heaven to show again their powers and quiet the winds.

Suddenly, the dark horizon blazes violet and orange. A giant Roman candle rises, alive and alight, lifted by fiery fingers against the gravity of Earth. Our jaws gape, the poetic words and high-sounding sentiments spoken in the previous moments gone. "Oh, boy," we exclaim. "Boy, oh, boy, oh, boy!" Our heads rise to the zenith of the sky as the thrusting rocket burns away and drops into the ocean and the capsule angles across the Heavens with great deliberation, a single fairy flame, a swiftly moving star, an atom in the night bearing a human nucleus.

A minute later, across the seas, a Russian satellite is launched bearing five passengers also on a mission of discovery.

Twelve people, the solar number, have flown to Heaven under the full Moon. Odysseus has set sail again, the whole Earth his Ithaca, the vastness of space waiting to reveal adventures and challenges that exceed all human knowing. This time, however, Penelope travels with him, the "brightest of women" carrying her loom of enchantments with which to weave together Heaven and Earth. As they sail past planet islands in the ocean of sky, what Sirens will call them to ecstatic or killing knowledge, what Cyclopean dangers threaten, what Circean transforming Mysteries will be imparted? How will they get past the asteroid belts of Scylla and the space warps of Charybdis?

Will some Poseidon of deep space resent and sabotage their efforts, and some cosmic Athena remain unseen but ever near to guide and protect their journey? Does she hope to draw them and others like them across the reaches of time and space to plant new civilizations bearing her spirit? Has she found new scope for her active nature in the galactic milieu?

And what of us on Earth? Do we try to make Paradise on Earth while some of us sail off to the Heavens? Has the three-thousand-year-long journey that separates us from the original journey of Odysseus given us learnings and initiations sufficient to entertain both ventures? Does Penelope's web connect the far-flung warp threads of our brains and bodies with the weft of a story so large that we cannot yet discern the pattern? Have we been unwoven like the shroud of Laertes in the long night of our century's disillusion that we may be re-made on the loom of day for a meeting so profound with the Beloved of the Soul that we have not dared believe it was possible?

You who have reached this page have lived the journey of

the soul and sensed its many turnings, its once and future truth. Write to me of what you have discovered that I may write of you and one day say:

> Sing in me, Muse, of the men and women of many many ways . . .

Notes

INTRODUCTION

1. Joseph Campbell, *The Hero with a Thousand Faces* (Princeton: Bollingen, 1972), pp. 3–4.

2. Joseph Campbell, *The Masks of God: Creative Mythology* (New York: The Viking Press, 1964), pp. 4–6 *passim*.

3. Campbell, *The Hero with a Thousand Faces,* p. 4.

4. Lawrence Cahoone, *The Dilemma of Modernity* (Albany, N.Y.: State University of New York Press, 1988), pp. 233–34.

5. Campbell, *The Hero with a Thousand Faces,* pp. 19–20.

6. *Ibid.* p. 17.

7. Thomas Hobbes, *Leviathan* (Oxford: Clarendon Press, 1929), Part I, chap. XIII. Hobbes is describing man in his imagined "natural state" living without political institutions or governance. He writes, "In such condition there is . . . no knowledge of the face of the earth; no account of time; no arts; no letters; no society; and which is worst of all, continual fear, and danger of violent death; and the life of man, solitary, poor, nasty, brutish, and short."

8. Rainer Maria Rilke, "Letter to Hulewicz." Quoted in Danah Zohar, *The Quantum Self* (New York: William Morrow, 1990), p. 188.

9. Evelyn Underhill, *Mysticism* (New York: Meridian Books, 1957,), p. 416.

CHAPTER ONE

1. Homer, *The Odyssey* 1. 1–10 (Lattimore translation), p. 27.

2. Some of these ideas of change and choice are discussed by Cedric Whitman in his essay "*The Odyssey* and Change," in *Twentieth Century Interpretations of The Odyssey,* ed. Howard W. Clarke (Englewood Cliffs, N.J: Prentice-Hall, 1983), pp. 80–81.

3. *Ibid.* p. 81.

4. The literature on the authorship of *The Iliad* and *The Odyssey* is as vast as it is contentious, the currents of scholarship following much the same rowdy, clinical, and diverse arguments as have attended questions as to the identity of Shakespeare and Christ. Until the 1930s there were few reputable modern scholars who thought that one person could have written either or both *The Iliad* and *The Odyssey.* This view of multiple authorship is well represented by Denys L. Page in *The Homeric Odyssey* (Oxford: The Clarendon Press, 1955). To Cedric Whitman, on the other hand, the unique personal vision and "ineradicable unity" of material in the Homeric epics attests to a probable single author who orchestrated the bardic lays of centuries into his own singular form. This perspective, especially as it applies to *The Iliad,* is found in Cedric H. Whitman, *Homer and the Heroic Tradition* (Cambridge, Mass: Harvard University Press, 1958). Whitman's argument takes into account the work of Milman Parry, who in the 1920s and 1930s demonstrated the prodigious epic-making capacity of Yugoslavian shepherds, who improvised stories for weeks on end using many of the same formulaic techniques as we find in Greek epic verse. See *The Making of Homeric Verse: The Collected Papers of Milman Parry.,* ed. with introduction by Adam Parry (Oxford: the Clarendon Press, 1971). However, as Whitman and literary critics like George Steiner have pointed out, there is an immense difference between the folk poetry of shepherds sitting in front of a recording device and the immensely complex style and formal artistic control that we find in the Homeric verse, suggesting one final author of genius, Homer.

5. Eric A. Havelock, *The Literate Revolution in Greece and Its Cultural Consequences* (Princeton: Princeton University Press, 1982).

6. George Steiner, "Introduction: Homer and the Scholars," in *Homer: A Collection of Critical Essays,* ed. George Steiner and Robert Fagles (Englewood Cliffs, N.J.: Prentice-Hall, 1962), pp. 6–7.

7. Julian Jaynes, *The Origins of Consciousness in the Breakdown of the*

Bicameral Mind (Princeton: Princeton University Press, 1978). I discuss this theory as it relates to the breakdown of the heroic age in my book *Life Force* (New York: Delta Books, 1980), pp. 71–80.

8. Jaynes begins to get fixated on his own hypothesis when he suggests that, with such a state of prevailing bicameral daze, we must read *The Iliad* as the tale of "noble automatons who knew not what they did." By this interpretation heroic Hector and wrathful Achilles muddled along in a fog, in which the left brain knew not what the right brain was doing. Thus, for example, there is a passage in *The Iliad* when Athena during a battle puts a triple portion of *menos,* a kind of vital life force, into the chest of her protégé Diomedes and he is able to feel such enormous energy and eagerness "thrusting up pungently into his nostrils" that he performs the most difficult feats with ease. With Jaynes' theory this *menos* would become an example of a gift of the right hemisphere to the left, with Athena set up as the avatar of the right brain.

9. Marija Gimbutas, *The Goddesses and Gods of Old Europe, 7000–3500 B.C.* (Berkeley and Los Angeles: University of California Press, 1982). See too the findings of James Mellaart in his work, *Çatal Huyuk* (New York: McGraw-Hill, 1967).

10. Marija Gimbutas, *The Early Civilization of Europe,* Monograph for Indo-European Studies 131 (Los Angeles: University of California, 1980), ch. 2, pp. 33–34.

11. An intense but considered description of this culture and its subsequent destruction is given in the remarkable study of Riane Eisler, *The Chalice and the Blade* (New York: Harper & Row, 1987).

12. For a critical discussion of archaeological findings and speculations that corroborate this view of ancient Cretan civilization, see the work of Nicolas Platon, *Crete* (Geneva: Nagel Publishers, 1966).

13. Spretnak, Charlene. *Lost Goddesses of Early Greece: A Collection of Pre-Hellenic Myths* (Boston: Beacon Press, 1984), pp. 99–101.

14. Still, as Kenneth Atchity and E. J. W. Barber point out, close study of the Homeric epics reveals many traces of an Indo-European "overlay" on the preexisting Aegean matriliny. The most balanced and harmonious "partnership" of the two cultures is revealed in the portrait of Phaeacian life. The considerable power of the women of *The Odyssey*—Helen, Penelope, and by rumor Clytemnestra—points to a pattern in southern Greece and Crete of the time of "influential daughters, daughters who inherit thrones, and sons who go away or are barely mentioned: in short, it seems, uxorilocal matriliny." As the authors further indicate, "Aegean princesses were not about to

see themselves so easily disenfranchised, as is obvious from the resulting history of marital, political, and theological spats which comprise so much of our corpus of Greek mythology and which dominate the consciousness of Homeric poems." Kenneth Atchity and E. J. W. Barber, "Greek Princes and Aegean Princesses: The Role of Women in the Homeric Poems," in *Critical Essays on Homer* (Boston: G. K. Hall & Co., 1987), pp. 17, 19.

15. Gregory Bateson, *Mind and Nature: A Necessary Unity* (New York: Bantam, 1980).

16. Rupert Sheldrake, *A New Science of Life: The Hypothesis of Formative Causation* (Los Angeles: J. P. Tarcher, 1981). For Sheldrake's more recent work see *The Presence of the Past* (New York: Times Books, 1989).

17. Ilya Prigogine, *From Being to Becoming: Time and Complexity in the Physical Sciences* (San Francisco: W. H. Freeman and Co., 1980).

18. This theory and its implications are discussed at length in James Gleick's remarkable book *Chaos* (New York: Penguin, 1988). An excellent discussion of chaos theory is also found in Anna F. Lemkow's excellent work, *The Wholeness Principle: Dynamics of Unity Within Science, Religion and Society* (Wheaton, Ill.: Quest Books, The Theosophical Publishing House, 1990), pp. 115–19. For a rigorous scientific treatment of the implications of chaos theory, see John Briggs and F. David Peat's masterful study, *Turbulent Mirror* (New York: Harper & Row, 1989).

19. Karl Pribram, *Languages of the Brain* (Englewood Cliffs, N. J.: Prentice-Hall, 1971), pp. 140–66. See also Karl Pribram, *Holonomy and Structure in the Organization of Perception*, reprint from the Department of Psychology, Stanford University (Stanford: Stanford University Press, 1974). For a fuller discussion of hologram theory, see my book, *The Possible Human* Los Angeles: J. P. Tarcher, 1982), pp. 182–200.

20. David Bohm, *Wholeness and the Implicate Order* (London: Routledge, Ark Paperbacks, 1973). See also David Bohm, "Quantum Theory as an Indication of a New Order in Physics, Part B," in *Implicate and Explicate Order in Physical Law* (Foundations of Physics), 3: 139, 1973.

21. For a fuller discussion of hologram theory, see my book *The Possible Human*, pp. 182–200.

22. Charles Hampden-Turner, *Maps of the Mind* (New York: Macmillan, 1981), p. 14.

CHAPTER TWO

1. C. P. Cavafy, "Ithaka," in *Collected Poems*, trans. Edmund Keeley and Philip Sherrad (Princeton: Princeton University Press, 1980), p. 35.

2. Plato's parable of the cave appears in Book VII of *The Republic*. There are many editions of this cornerstone of Western philosophy.

3. This diagram is found in Joseph Campbell's *The Hero with a Thousand Faces*, p. 241.

4. *Ibid.* pp. 245–46.

5. A good discussion of the mystery tradition in ancient Greece can be found in Walter Burkert's important work, *Greek Religion* (Cambridge: Harvard University Press, 1985), pp. 276–304 *passim.*

6. Joseph Campbell, *The Masks of God: Occidental Mythology* (New York: The Viking Press, 1964), p. 160.

7. Homer, *The Odyssey* 1. 1–10 (Fitzgerald translation), p. 1.

CHAPTER FOUR

1. Homer, *The Odyssey* 9. 193–96 (Butcher translation).

2. Joseph Campbell, *The Hero with a Thousand Faces* (Princeton: Princeton University Press, 1968), p. 97.

3. Homer, *The Odyssey* 9. 174–76 (Fitzgerald translation), p. 141.

4. *Ibid.* 9. 241–42 (Lattimore translation), p. 143.

5. *Ibid.* 9. 275–77 (Rouse translation), p. 104.

6. *Ibid.* 9. 375–402 (Rouse translation), pp. 107–8.

7. *Ibid.* 9. 404–12 (Rouse translation), p. 108.

8. *Ibid.* 9. 413–14 (Rouse translation), p. 108.

9. Joseph Campbell, *The Masks of God: Occidental Mythology* (New York: The Viking Press, 1964), p. 167.

10. Homer, *The Odyssey* 9. 501–05 (Rouse translation), p. 110

11. Similar points of correspondence are noted by Jenny Strauss Clay in *The Wrath of Athena: Gods and Men in The Odyssey* (Princeton: Princeton University Press, 1983), pp. 127–31.

12. *Ibid.* p. 129.

13. The basic exercise is to be found in the book by Robert Masters and myself, *Listening to the Body* (New York: Dell Publishing Company, Delta Books, 1978), pp. 169–81. Another version is found in my book *The Possible Human* (Los Angeles: J. P. Tarcher, Inc, 1982), pp. 63–71.

CHAPTER FIVE

1. Homer, *The Odyssey* 10. 39–45 (Lattimore translation), p. 153.
2. Joseph Campbell, *The Masks of God: Occidental Mythology* (New York: The Viking Press, 1964), p. 168.
3. James Hillman, *Archetypal Psychology: A Brief Account* (Dallas: Spring Publications, Inc., 1975), p. 33.
4. *Ibid.* pp. 51–52.
5. Campbell, *op. cit.*, p. 168.

CHAPTER SIX

1. J. G. Frazer, *Lectures on the Early History of Kingship* (London: 1905), pp. 291–92.
2. Quoted in Richard J. Sommer, "*The Odyssey* and Primitive Religion," in *Critical Essays on Homer*, ed. Kenneth Atchity et al. (Boston: G. K. Hall & Co, 1987), p. 189.
3. Homer, *The Odyssey* 10. 210–24 (Rouse translation), p. 116.
4. *Ibid.* 10. 294–301, p. 118.
5. *Ibid.* 10. 309–33 (Rieu translation), p. 164.
6. Jessie L. Weston, *From Ritual to Romance* (Garden City: Doubleday Anchor, 1957), p. 75.
7. Homer, *The Odyssey* 10. 392–95 (Rouse translation), p. 120.
8. Richard Sommer says of this incident that this "rejuvenation, we may suspect, is directly relatable both to the pattern of the original ritual whatever it may have been, and to the Homeric rearrangement of its details. Not only does Odysseus triumph over the tyrannical rite, but he makes use of its restorative magic as well, on his own terms. We need not suppose that Homer understood the meaning of the scene, or any of the others supplied to him by tradition, *as ritual*; the chances are slim, in fact, that he could have comprehended directly the foundation in cultic practice of the material which he altered. . . . The secondary growth of myth is speculative: each variation upon the ritually-oriented original pattern is a violation and an adventure in thinking beyond the limits of the collective tribal consciousness. The image of the Dying God is an assertion of that collective awareness, and Homer's Odysseus is a violation of it." Sommer, *op. cit.*, pp. 196–97.

I believe that this perspective is especially valuable in that it shows that the entire epic is a study in the consistency of deviation itself from all given traditions and expectations—both sacred and profane—as the principal form of the epic's action.

9. Paul D. MacLean, "On the Evolution of Three Mentalities," in *New Dimensions in Psychiatry: A World View,* Vol. 2., ed. Silvano Arieti and Gerard Chryanowski (New York: Wiley, 1977).

10. Jean Houston, *The Possible Human* (Los Angeles: J. P. Tarcher, 1982), p. 100.

11. Joseph Campbell, *The Masks of God: Primitive Mythology* (New York: Viking, 1962), pp. 170–202, 441–51; *The Masks of God: Occidental Mythology* (New York: Viking, 1964), pp. 154, 171.

12. Jane Ellen Harrison, *Prolegomena to the Study of Greek Religion,* (Cambridge: Cambridge University Press, 1922), pp. 14–15. This splendid book is a critical contribution from the early twentieth-century Cambridge school of mythologists. These scholars, including Gilbert Murray and F. M. Cornford, were influenced by anthropological data through Frazer and Tylor, which in turn profoundly extended their range of interpretation of Greek religion and literature by placing it into a cross-cultural and comparative framework. Jane Harrison's own breadth of vision and interdisciplinary studies allowed her to embrace both Jungian and Freudian perspectives to explore the roots of Greek myth and ritual. As can be imagined, at the time, this was not a popular approach.

13. Houston, *The Possible Human,* pp. 102–13.

CHAPTER SEVEN

1. Plato, *The Symposium,* trans. by Benjamin Jowett (New York: The Liberal Arts Press, 1957).

2. For a critical discussion of the theme of the androgyne, see Mircea Eliade's *The Two and the One* (Chicago: The University of Chicago Press, 1965). See also Wendy Doniger O'Flaherty's *Women, Androgynes, and Other Mythical Beasts* (Chicago: University of Chicago Press, 1980).

3. This point is well made by Teresa Carp in her fine discussion, "Teiresias, Samuel, and the Way Home," in *California Studies in Classical Antiquity,* vol. 12 (Berkeley: University of California Press, 1979), p. 71.

4. Heinrich Zimmer, *The King and the Corpse,* ed. Joseph Campbell, Bollingen Series XI (New York: Pantheon, 1948), pp. 67–95.

5. Homer, *The Odyssey* 11. 411–17 (Fitzgerald translation), p. 199.

6. *Ibid.* 11. 489–91 (Houston translation).

7. A fine treatment of Odysseus as the embodiment of pain and suffering is in George E. Dimock's essay "The Epic of Suffering and Fulfillment," in *Homer's Odyssey: A Critical Handbook,* ed. Connie Nelson (Belmont, Calif: Wadsworth Publishing Company, 1969), pp. 157–72.

CHAPTER EIGHT

1. Richard J. Sommer, "*The Odyssey* and Primitive Religion," *op. cit.*, p. 197.

2. Homer, *The Odyssey* 12. 188–89 (Houston translation).

3. *Ibid.* 12. 191 (Houston translation).

4. A searching discussion of the many meanings of "siren" in the ancient world is found in Gabriel Germain, "The Sirens and the Temptation of Knowledge," in *Homer: A Collection of Critical Essays,* ed. George Steiner and Robert Fagles (Englewood Cliffs, New Jersey: Prentice-Hall, 1962), pp. 91–97.

5. *Ibid.* pp. 95–6.

6. Homer, *The Odyssey* 12. 114–19, 122–4 (Rieu translation), p. 192.

7. *Ibid.* 12. 256–59 (Lattimore translation), pp. 191–92.

8. *Ibid.* 12. 277–93 (Rieu translation), pp. 196–97.

9. It is curious that the cattle are seen as the herd of Helios, a sun God, for in earlier times when the Mother Goddess was preeminent, cattle represented the lunar mysteries of the goddess. Thus the horns worn by many of the great goddesses like Isis and Hathor. This may be another aspect of Indo-Aryan invaders patriarchal theft of matrifocal mysteries. The goddess-nymphs who guard the cattle could be seen as the last remains of the memory that the herd once belonged to the Mother Goddess.

10. Homer, *The Odyssey* 12. 395–96 (Rieu translation), p. 199.

CHAPTER NINE

1. Charles H. Taylor, "The Obstacles to Odysseus' Return," in *Essays on The Odyssey: Selected Modern Criticism,* ed. Charles H. Taylor (Bloomington: Indiana University Press, 1963), p. 90. Taylor also echoes the frequently expressed fear that if Odysseus had stayed with

Calypso, "he would have no self, but would exist only as an appendage to the goddess, serving her desire." *Ibid.*

2. Hermann Guntert, *Kalypso,* quoted in William S. Anderson, "Calypso and Elysian," in *Essays on The Odyssey: Selected Modern Criticism,* ed. Charles H. Taylor, Jr. (Bloomington: Indiana University Press, 1963), p. 81.

3. Gilbert Murray, *Five Stages of Greek Religion* (London: Oxford University Press, 1935), p. 33.

4. Richard Sommer makes this point in his essay "*The Odyssey* and Primitive Religion," *op. cit.*, p. 203.

5. Homer, *The Odyssey* 1. 59–65 (Fitzgerald translation), p. 4.

6. *Ibid.* 5. 160–69 (Lattimore translation), p. 92.

7. *Ibid.* 5. 215–22, 225–27, p. 94.

CHAPTER TEN

1. Homer, *The Odyssey* 6. 149–61 (Lattimore translation), p. 106.

2. *Ibid.* 6. 180–82, p. 107.

3. *Ibid.* 6. 244–45, p. 108.

4. *Ibid.* 6. 276–79 (Houston translation).

5. George de F. Lord, "*The Odyssey* and the Western World" in *Essays on The Odyssey,* ed. Charles H. Taylor, Jr. (Bloomington: Indiana University Press, 1963), pp. 46–47.

6. Norman Austin, *Archery at the Dark of the Moon* (Berkeley: University of California Press, 1975), p. 156.

7. Kenneth Atchity and E. J. W. Barber, "Greek Princes and Aegean Princesses," *op. cit.*, pp. 18–19.

8. Homer, *The Odyssey* 8. 11–14 (Lattimore translation), p. 121.

9. Fifty-two rowers suggests, of course, the weeks in the year, symbolic of the cycle of completion which brings Odysseus, the solar hero, home at last to Ithaca.

10. Homer, *The Odyssey* 8. 120–23 (Lattimore translation), p. 125.

11. *Ibid.* 8. 246–49, p. 127.

12. *Ibid.* 8. 266–366, pp. 128–29.

13. Norman Austin makes this point. See Austin, *op. cit.*, p. 161.

14. Homer, *The Odyssey* 8. 457–65 (Lattimore translation), p. 133.

15. W. B. Stanford, "Personal Relationships," *Essays on The Odyssey,* ed. Taylor, *op cit.*, p. 23.

16. This perception of Nausicaa as the authoress of *The Odyssey* is found in Samuel Butler, *The Authoress of The Odyssey* (Chicago: University of Chicago Press, 1967). This is a reprint of the 2nd ed. (London,

1922). Robert Graves' novel is titled *Homer's Daughter* (New York: Doubleday & Co., Inc, 1955).

17. Homer, *The Odyssey* 8. 492–98, 514–20 (Lattimore translation), p. 134.

18. *Ibid.* 8. 523–31, pp. 134–35.

19. *Ibid.* 8. 539–541 (Houston translation).

20. *Ibid.* 8.

21. I describe this process in *The Possible Human,* pp. 54–57.

CHAPTER ELEVEN

1. The history of this argument is two hundred years old and is bound up with the ongoing debate between two camps of Homeric scholars, the "unitarians" or those who see the unity and integration of the entire poem; and the "analysts" who discern multiple hands and separate poems in the final assemblage. Denys Page offers a fine discussion as well as a selective bibliography around this debate in *The Homeric Odyssey* (Oxford: Clarendon Press, 1955), pp. 73–81, See also his Appendix on themes related to these discussions on pages 165 to 182.

2. Austin, *op. cit.,* p. 182.

3. Robert Masters and Jean Houston, *The Varieties of Psychedelic Experience* (New York: Holt, Rinehart and Winston, 1966).

4. This case is reported in *The Varieties of Psychedelic Experience* on pp. 220–21.

5. This research and its implications are reported in Robert Masters and Jean Houston, *Mind Games: A Guide to Inner Space* (New York: Viking, 1972); Robert Masters and Jean Houston, *Listening to the Body* (New York: Dell Publishing Co., 1978); Jean Houston, *Life Force: The Psycho-Historical Recovery of the Self* (New York: Delacorte, 1980); Jean Houston, *The Possible Human* (Los Angeles: J. P. Tarcher, 1982); Jean Houston, *The Search for the Beloved: Journeys in Sacred Psychology* (Los Angeles: J. P. Tarcher, 1987); Jean Houston, *Godseed: The Mythic Journey of Christ* (Wheaton, Ill.: Quest Books, 1992).

6. For an excellent treatment of the education of Telemachus, see the discussion by Werner Jaeger in *Paideia,* vol. 1. 2nd ed., trans. by Gilbert Highet (New York: Oxford University Press, 1945), pp. 29–34.

7. Austin, *op. cit.,* p. 163.

8. Homer, *The Odyssey* 1. 297–302 (Rieu translation), pp. 32–3.

9. Howard W. Clarke, "Telemachus" in *Homer's Odyssey: A Critical*

Handbook, ed. Connie Nelson (Belmont, Calif: Wadsworth Publishing Company, 1969), p. 30.

10. Homer, *The Odyssey* 2. 313–315 (Rieu translation), p. 46.

11. For some of the ideas in this chapter concerning the initiatory structure of the *Telemacheia* I am indebted to to Charles W. Eckert and his fine essay "Initiatory Motifs in the Story of Telemachus," in *Twentieth Century Interpretations of The Odyssey,* ed. Howard W. Clarke (Englewood Cliffs, N. J.: Prentice-Hall, 1983), pp. 38–51. Eckert writes about these boyhood rites of passage: "That such rituals were known to the Greeks in pre-Homeric times is highly probable, even if one argues only from the grounds that the vast majority of primitive societies employ initiation rites. This probability is increased by the fact that the Eleusiniana, the most popular cult of classical times, exhibits a clear initiatory structure: such rites as ablution and sacrifice, the journey from Athens to the sacred ground of the Telesterion at Eleusis in the company of a *mystagogos,* and the final *epopteia* or revelation of the sacred all have their analogues in social initiation. Greek education and the rearing of young men in general also recall initiatory practices at many points, especially in Sparta. But when we move from the social and religious spheres to those of myth and epic we move into a different dimension—one as large as the Near East itself, from which the early literature of the Greeks derives. It now seems an inescapable conclusion that the plot structures founded on the heroic quest, acts of purgation and regeneration, the slaying of chthonic demons, and the expiation of blood guilt are rooted in the sacred myths of the Near East and are disseminated and transformed by singers. To look in each society for a specific ritual which may have given rise to a myth known to that society is to ignore the cosmopolitan and itinerant nature of recited story" Eckert, *op. cit.,* p. 41.

12. Werner Jaeger, *op. cit.,* p. 34.

13. Homer, *The Odyssey* 3. 218–24 (Rieu translation), p. 56.

14. *Ibid.* 3. 230, p. 56.

15. Quoted in Sam D. Gill, "Disenchantment," in *Parabola,* Summer, 1976, p. 9.

16. *Ibid.* p. 9.

17. Homer, *The Odyssey* 4. 220–25 (Rieu translation), p. 70.

18. Anderson, *op. cit.,* p. 77.

19. Homer, *The Odyssey* 4. 611 (Rieu translation), p. 80.

20. Anthony Stevens, *Archetypes: A Natural History of the Self* (New York: William Morrow, 1982), p. 159.

21. See especially Madeleine L'Engle's remarkable study of adolescent "cosmic" initiation, *A Wrinkle in Time* (New York: Dell, 1980).

22. These rituals, their patterns, and contemporary as well as ancient use are discussed in a splendid volume of essays, *Betwixt and Between: Patterns of Masculine and Feminine Initiation,* ed. Louise Carus Mahdi, Steven Foster and Meredith Little (La Salle, Ill.: Open Court, 1987). See particularly the essays in Part Two, "The Initiation of Youth."

23. Helene P. Foley, "Reverse Similes and Sex Roles in the Odyssey" in *Homer's The Odyssey,* ed. Harold Bloom (New York: Chelsea House Publishers, 1988), p. 90.

CHAPTER TWELVE

1. Homer, *The Odyssey* 13. 221–26 (Rieu translation), p. 208.
2. *Ibid.* 13. 288–99, p. 209.
3. *Ibid.* 13. 291–92, pp. 209–10.
4. *Ibid.* 13. 296–302, p. 210.
5. *Ibid.* 13. 312–13 (Rouse translation), p. 154.
6. Marina Warner, *Monuments and Maidens: The Allegory of the Female Form* (New York: Atheneum, 1985), p. 92.
7. Homer, *The Odyssey* 13. 330–31 (Rieu translation), p. 211.
8. Warner, *op. cit.*, p. 96.
9. Homer, *The Odyssey* 13. 355–58 (Rieu translation), p. 211.
10. *Ibid.* 13. 382–91, p. 212.
11. *Ibid.* 17. 513–15, 518–22, p. 272.
12. *Ibid.* 16. 204–8 (Rouse translation), p. 184.
13. *Ibid.* 17. 268 (Houston translation).
14. *Ibid.* 17. 447 (Rieu translation), p. 270.

CHAPTER THIRTEEN

1. J. W. Mackail, "Penelope," in *Homer's Odyssey: A Critical Handbook,* ed. Connie Nelson (Belmont, Calif.: Wadsworth Publishing Co., 1969), p. 43.
2. Homer, *The Odyssey* 1. 332 (Houston translation).
3. Kenneth Atchity and E. J. W. Barber, "Greek Princes and Aegean Princesses: The Role of Women in the Homeric Poems," in

Critical Essays on Homer, ed. Kenneth Atchity (Boston: G. K. Hall and Co., 1987), p. 21. The authors illumine the Bronze Age tension between the increasingly powerful Indo-European patriarchy of the Achaean Greeks and the remaining matrilineal cultures as recorded in the Homeric epics. They see Penelope as the key figure in all of this. "*The Odyssey,* in fact, records the near-reversion, on Ithaka, to a fully matrilineal system. When Odysseus leaves for Troy, he leaves a father who is opposed to the matrilineal inclinations of the local populace and a son too young to retain effective patrilineal control over the island. It seems probable that the throne of Ithaka had been matrilineal before the coming of Laertes to the court of Antikleia. The marriage, apparently, was without female issue—which tipped the scales in favor of the patriliny. Odysseus, son of the matriarch, would become the next king. When Penelope and Odysseus were betrothed, Penelope must have agreed to allow the patrilineal system of Odysseus's family replace the matriliny still dominating the behavior of her cousins, Helen and Klytaimnestra." Atchity and Barber, *op. cit.,* p. 21.

4. Homer, *The Odyssey* 261–66 (Lattimore translation), pp. 299–300.

5. Austin, *op. cit.,* p. 253.

6. Homer, *The Odyssey* 18.165–69 (Rieu translation), p. 280.

7. *Ibid.* 18. 212–14, p. 281.

8. *Ibid.* 18. 215–17, 220–24, pp. 281–82.

9. *Ibid.* 18. 242–46, p. 282.

10. Austin, *op. cit.,* p. 213.

11. Homer, *The Odyssey* 19. 156–61 (Rieu translation), p. 292.

12. Austin, *op. cit.,* p. 215.

13. Homer, *The Odyssey* 19. 205–6 (Houston translation).

14. *Ibid.* 19. 290–92, 294–95 (Rieu translation), p. 294.

15. *Ibid.* 19. 306–8, p. 296.

16. *Ibid.* 19. 366–68, p. 296.

17. *Ibid.* 19. 350–55, p. 297.

18. *Ibid.* 19. 407–9. This is my literal translation of the Greek text. In his splendid new translation of *The Odyssey,* Allen Mandelbaum renders these lines as:

Because I come as one who, on his ways across the fertile earth, has been enraged by many men and women, let his name now be Odysseus, 'son of wrath and pain.' 19. 407–8, p. 401.

19. *Ibid.* 19. 548–50 (Rieu translation), p. 302.

20. *Ibid.* 19. 596–606, pp. 302–3.

21. Anne Amory, "The Reunion of Odysseus and Penelope," in *Essays on the Odyssey,* ed. Taylor, *op. cit.,* p. 105.
22. Homer, *The Odyssey* 20. 45–56 (Rieu translation), p. 305.
23. *Ibid.* 20. 111–19, p. 307.
24. Amory, *op. cit.,* p. 110.
25. *Ibid.* p. 112.
26. Homer, *The Odyssey* 20. 346–47 (Rieu translation), p. 313.
27. *Ibid.* 20. 351–57, pp. 313–14.
28. *Ibid.* 20. 366–69, p. 314.
29. *Ibid.* 20. 152–53, p. 320.
30. *Ibid.* 21. 311–17, p. 324.
31. *Ibid.* 19. 101–30 (Rouse translation), pp. 215–16.

CHAPTER FOURTEEN

1. Homer, *The Odyssey* 21. 403–8 (Rieu translation), p. 326.d.
2. *Ibid.* 22. 380–84, pp. 336–37.
3. *Ibid.* 22. 452–58, p. 338.
4. *Ibid.* 23. 97–103 (Rouse translation), p. 255.
5. *Ibid.* 23. 105–10, p. 255.
6. *Ibid.* 23. 113–14, p. 255.
7. On this point see Austin *op. cit.,* p. 237.
8. Homer, *The Odyssey* 22. 261–66 (Rieu translation), p. 345.
9. Norman Austin has noted how the extraordinary degree of rhetorical like-mindedness, *homophrosyne,* in these two speeches herald the final recognition of Odysseus and Penelope. He writes that "Odysseus' speech at 23. 166–72 and Penelope's reply vv. 174–80 are virtually the obverse and reverse of the same coin. At times the structure of their sentences runs parallel, at other times one is the reverse image of the other. Where Odysseus uses superlatives Penelope uses negatives, and she uses superlatives when he turns to negatives." Austin, *op. cit.,* p. 279, note 30.
10. Homer, *The Odyssey* 23, 176–82 (Rieu translation), p. 345.
11. *Ibid.* 23. 184–89, p. 345.
12. *Ibid.* 23. 190–99, pp. 345–46.
13. Warner, *op. cit.,* p. 100. *Polymetis* in this context refers to the great cunning and brilliance of Odysseus.
14. Homer, *The Odyssey* 23. 205–9 (Murray translation), p. 389.
15. *Ibid.* 23. 236–37, p. 346; 244–45 (Rieu translation), p. 347.
16. *Ibid.* 24. 2–4, p. 351.
17. *Ibid.* 24. 191–97, p. 356.

CHAPTER FIFTEEN

1. James Hillman, *Loose Ends* (Zurich: Spring Publications, 1975), p. 167.

2. Quoted in Evelyn Underhill, *Mysticism* (New York: Meridian Books, 1957), p. 420.

3. D. H. Lawrence, *Selected Poems* (New York: Viking Compass, 1959), p. 74.

Selected Bibliography

This bibliography represents books and articles quoted in *The Hero and The Goddess* plus a number of other suggested readings.

Atchity, Kenneth and E. J. W. Barber. "Greek Princes and Aegean Princesses: The Role of Women in the Homeric Poems." In *Critical Essays on Homer*. Boston: G. K. Hall & Co., 1987.

Amory, Anne. "The Reunion of Odysseus and Penelope." In *Essays on the Odyssey: Selected Modern Criticism*. Edited by Charles H. Taylor. Bloomington: Indiana University Press, 1963.

Austin, Norman. *Archery at the Dark of the Moon*. Berkeley: University of California Press, 1975.

Bateson, Gregory. *Mind and Nature: A Necessary Unity*. New York: Bantam, 1980.

Bloom, Harold, ed. *Modern Critical Interpretations: The Odyssey*. New York: Chelsea House Publishers, 1988.

Bohm, David. *Wholeness and the Implicate Order*. London: Routledge, Ark Paperbacks, 1973.

———. "Quantum Theory as an Indication of a New Order in Physics, Part B." *Implicate and Explicate Order in Physical Law, Foundations of Physics*. 1973.

Bradley, Edward M. "The Hubris of Odysseus." *Soundings* 51, 1968.

Briggs, John and F. David Peat. *Turbulent Mirror.* New York: Harper & Row, 1989.

Brisson, Luc. *Le Mythe de Tiresias.* Leiden, 1978.

Brown, C. S. "Odysseus and Polyphemus: The Name and the Curse." *Comparative Literature* 18, 1966.

Burkert, Walter. *Greek Religion.* Cambridge: Harvard University Press, 1985.

Butler, Samuel. *The Authoress of the Odyssey.* Chicago: University of Chicago Press, 1967.

Cahoone, Lawrence. *The Dilemma of Modernity.* Albany: State University of New York Press, 1988.

Carp, Teresa. "Teiresias, Samuel, and the Way Home." In *California Studies in Classical Antiquity,* vol. 12. Berkeley: University of California Press, 1979.

Carpenter, Rhys. *Folk Tale, Fiction and Saga in the Homeric Epics.* Sather Classical Lectures, vol. 20. Berkeley and Los Angeles: University of California Press, 1946.

Campbell, Joseph. *The Hero with a Thousand Faces.* Princeton: Bollingen, 1972.

———. *The Masks of God: Creative Mythology.* New York: Viking, 1964.

———. *The Masks of God: Occidental Mythology.* New York: Viking, 1964.

———. *The Masks of God: Primitive Mythology.* New York: Viking, 1962.

Cavafy, C. P. "Ithaka." From *Collected Poems.* Translated by Edmund Keeley and Philip Sherrad. Princeton: Princeton University Press, 1980.

Clarke, Howard W. "Telemachus." In *Homer's Odyssey: A Critical Handbook.* Edited by Connie Nelson. Belmont, California: Wadsworth Publishing Company, 1969.

Clay, Jenny Strauss. *The Wrath of Athena: Gods and Men in the Odyssey.* Princeton: Princeton University Press, 1983.

de F. Lord, George. "The Odyssey and the Western World." In *Essays on the Odyssey.* Edited by Charles H. Taylor, Jr. Bloomington: Indiana University Press, 1963.

Dimock, George E. "The Epic of Suffering and Fulfillment." In *Homer's Odyssey: A Critical Handbook.* Edited by Connie Nelson. Belmont, California: Wadsworth Publishing Company, 1969.

Eckert, Charles W. "Initiatory Motifs in the Story of Telemachus." In *Twentieth Century Interpretations of the Odyssey.* Edited by Howard W. Clarke. Englewood Cliffs: Prentice-Hall, 1983.

Eisler, Riane. *The Chalice and the Blade.* New York: Harper & Row, 1987.

Eliade, Mircea. *The Two and the One.* Chicago: The University of Chicago Press, 1965.

Finley, John H., Jr. *Homer's Odyssey.* Cambridge: Harvard University Press, 1978.

Finley, M. I. *The World of Odysseus.* New York: Viking, 1954.

Foley, Helene P. "Reverse Similes and Sex Roles in the Odyssey." In *Homer's The Odyssey.* Edited by Harold Bloom. New York: Chelsea House Publishers, 1988.

Frazer, J. G. *Lectures on the Early History of Kingship.* London: 1905.

Germain, Gabriel. "The Sirens and the Temptation of Knowledge." In *Homer: A Collection of Critical Essays.* Edited by George Steiner and Robert Fagles. Englewood Cliffs, New Jersey: Prentice-Hall, 1962.

Gill, Sam D. "Disenchantment," in *Parabola.* Summer, 1976.

Gimbutas, Marija. *The Early Civilization of Europe.* Los Angeles: University of California, 1980.

———. *The Goddesses and Gods of Old Europe, 7000–3500 B.C.* Berkeley and Los Angeles: University of California Press, 1982.

Gleick, James. *Chaos.* New York: Penguin, 1988.

Graves, Robert. *Homer's Daughter.* New York: Doubleday & Co., 1955.

Griffin, Jasper. *Homer on Life and Death.* Oxford: Clarendon, 1980.

Guntert, Hermann. *Kalypso* in William S. Anderson's "Calypso and Elysian." In *Essays on the Odyssey: Selected Modern Criticism.* Edited by Charles H. Taylor, Jr. Bloomington: Indiana University Press, 1963.

Hampden-Turner, Charles. *Maps of the Mind.* New York: Macmillan, 1981.

Harrison, Jane Ellen. *Prolegomena to the Study of Greek Religion.* Cambridge: Cambridge University Press, 1922.

Havelock, Eric A. *The Literate Revolution in Greece and its Cultural Consequences.* Princeton: Princeton University Press, 1982.

Heatherington, M. E. "Chaos, Order, and Cunning in the *Odyssey.*" *Studies in Philology* 83, 1976.

Hillman, James. *Archetypal Psychology: A Brief Account.* Dallas: Spring Publications, 1975.

———. *Loose Ends.* Zurich: Spring Publications, 1975.

Hobbes, Thomas. *Leviathan.* Oxford: Clarendon Press, 1929.

Holtsmark, E. B. "Spiritual Rebirth of the Hero: *Odyssey* V." *Classical Journal* 61, 1966.

Houston, Jean. *Life Force: The Psycho-Historical Recovery of the Self.* New York: Delta Books, 1980.

———. *Godseed: The Mythic Journey of Christ.* Warwick, New York: Amity House, 1988.

———. *The Possible Human.* Los Angeles: J. P. Tarcher, 1982.

———. *The Search for the Beloved: Journeys in Sacred Psychology.* Los Angeles: J. P. Tarcher, Inc., 1987.

Jaeger, Werner. *Paideia,* vol. 1. 2nd ed. Translated by Gilbert Highet. New York: Oxford University Press, 1945.

Jaynes, Julian. *The Origins of Consciousness in the Breakdown of the Bicameral Mind.* Princeton: Princeton University Press, 1978.

Kirk, G. S. *Homer and the Epic.* Cambridge: Cambridge University Press, 1965.

Lawrence, D. H. *Selected Poems.* New York: Viking Compass, 1959.

L'Engle, Madeleine. *A Wrinkle in Time.* New York: Dell, 1980.

Lemkow, Anna F. *The Wholeness Principle: Dynamics of Unity Within Science, Religion & Society.* Wheaton, Illinois: Quest Books: The Theosophical Publishing House, 1990.

Lord, A. B. *The Singer of Tales.* Harvard Studies in Comparative Literature, vol. 24. Cambridge: Harvard University Press, 1960.

Mackail, J. W. "Penelope" in *Homer's Odyssey: A Critical Handbook.* Edited by Connie Nelson. Belmont, California: Wadsworth Publishing Co., 1969.

MacLean, Paul D. "On the Evolution of Three Mentalities." In *New Dimensions in Psychiatry: A World View,* vol. 2. Edited by Silvano Arieti and Gerard Chryanowski. New York: Wiley, 1977.

Mahdi, Louise Carus, ed., Steven Foster and Meredith Little. *Betwixt and Between: Patterns of Masculine and Feminine Initiation.* La Salle, Illinois: Open Court, 1987.

Masters, Robert and Jean Houston, *Listening to the Body.* New York: Dell Publishing Co., 1978.

———. *Mind Games: A Guide to Inner Space.* New York: Viking, 1972.

———. *The Varieties of Psychedelic Experience.* New York: Holt, Rinehart and Winston, 1966.

Mellaart, James. *Çatal Huyuk.* New York: McGraw-Hill, 1967.

Murray, Gilbert. *Five Stages of Greek Religion.* London: 1935.

O'Flaherty, Wendy Doniger. *Women, Androgynes, and Other Mythical Beasts.* Chicago: University of Chicago Press, 1980.

Page, Denys. *The Homeric Odyssey.* Oxford: Clarendon Press, 1955.

Parry, Adam, ed. *The Making of Homeric Verse: The Collected Papers of Milman Parry.* Oxford: Clarendon Press, 1971.

Plato. *The Republic.* Book VII.

———. *The Symposium.* Translated by Benjamin Jowett. New York: The Liberal Arts Press, 1957.

Platon, Nicolas. *Crete.* Geneva: Nagel Publishers, 1966.

Pribram, Karl. *Languages of the Brain.* Englewood Cliffs, New Jersey: Prentice-Hall, 1971.

Prigogine, Ilya. *From Being to Becoming: Time and Complexity in the Physical Sciences.* San Francisco: W. H. Freeman and Co., 1980.

Rilke, Rainer Maria. "Letter to Hulewicz." In Danah Zohar, *The Quantum Self.* New York: William Morrow, 1990.

Sheldrake, Rupert. *A New Science of Life: The Hypothesis of Formative Causation.* Los Angeles: J. P. Tarcher, 1981.

———. *The Presence of the Past.* New York: Times Books, 1989.

Sommer, Richard J. "The Odyssey and Primitive Religion." In *Critical Essays on Homer.* Edited by Kenneth Atchity et al. Boston: G. K. Hall & Co.,

Stanford, W. B. *The Ulysses Theme.* 2nd ed. Oxford: Basil Blackwell and Mott, 1963.

———. "Personal Relationships." In *Essays on the Odyssey: Selected Modern Criticism.* Edited by Charles H. Taylor, Jr. Bloomington: Indiana University Press, 1963.

Spretnak, Charlene. *Lost Goddesses of Early Greece: A Collection of Pre-Hellenic Myths.* Boston: Beacon Press, 1984.

Steiner, George. "Introduction: Homer and the Scholars." In *Homer: A Collection of Critical Essays.* Edited by George Steiner and Robert Fagles. Englewood Cliffs, New Jersey: Prentice-Hall, 1962.

Stevens, Anthony. *Archetypes: A Natural History of the Self.* New York: William Morrow, 1982.

Taylor, Charles H. "The Obstacles to Odysseus' Return." In *Essays on the Odyssey: Selected Modern Criticism.* Edited by Charles H. Taylor, Jr. Bloomington: Indiana University Press, 1963.

Thornton, Agathe. *People and Themes in Homer's* Odyssey. London: Methuen, 1970.

Underhill, Evelyn. *Mysticism.* New York: Meridian Books, 1957.

Vivante, Paolo. *The Homeric Imagination.* Bloomington: Indiana University Press, 1970.

Warner, Marina. *Monuments and Maidens: The Allegory of the Female Form.* New York: Atheneum, 1985.

Webster, T. B. L. *From Mycenae to Homer.* London: Methuen, 1958.

Weston, Jessie L. *From Ritual to Romance.* Garden City: Doubleday Anchor, 1957.

Whitman, Cedric H. "The Odyssey and Change." In *Twentieth Century Interpretations of The Odyssey.* Englewood Cliffs, New Jersey: Prentice-Hall, 1983.

———. *Homer and the Heroic Tradition.* Cambridge, Massachusetts: Harvard University Press, 1958.

Zimmer, Heinrich. *The King and the Corpse.* Edited by Joseph Campbell. Bollingen Series XI. New York: Pantheon, 1948.

Zohar, Danah. *The Quantum Self.* New York: William Morrow, 1990.

A Guide to Translations of *The Odyssey*

There are numerous translations of *The Odyssey* spanning hundreds of years. The earlier ones such as those by George Chapman, William Cowper, and Alexander Pope, to name a few, are interesting for the style and language in which previous centuries have couched Homeric verse. Listed below are the more important modern translations. I provide a brief comment on each as well as indicating whether they are available in paperback. For the student of Greek who would care to read Homer in the original I refer you to:

ΟΜΗΡΟΥ ΟΔΥΣΣΕΙΑ *The Odyssey of Homer,* edited and with general and grammatical introduction, commentary, and indexes by W. B. Stanford, in two volumes. (London: Macmillan, 1974).

MODERN TRANSLATIONS

Andrews, S. O. (New York: Dutton, Everyman's Library, 1953.) Limping pentameters obscure the original Homeric vigor. Definitely not for every man or every woman either.

Butcher, Samuel and Andrew Lang. (New York: Random House, Modern Library, 1953.) Archaic style bores one to tears. Paperback.

Cook, Albert. (New York: Norton, 1967.) Now we're cooking! A beautiful translation in verse. It is especially notable in the way that it accurately reflects Homer's Greek, line for line, while keeping the power of the ancient oral style in English. Paperback.

Fitzgerald, Robert. (Garden City, N. Y.: Doubleday, 1961.) This is a brilliant piece of epic poetry, which undoubtedly gives the reader a wonderful sense of the energy and power of *The Odyssey*. However, it is also the freest of all the translations, Fitzgerald taking much poetic license with the original verse. Paperback.

Lattimore, Richmond. (New York: Harper & Row, 1967.) Lattimore is considered by many to be the finest translator of Greek poetry into English. His *Odyssey* is surely a masterpiece; eloquent, imaginative, and accurate, it is an achievement as poetically exciting as it is profound. Paperback.

Mandelbaum, Alan. (Berkeley: University of California Press, 1990.) A brand new verse translation by a poet who is noted for his splendid translations of Dante and Virgil. Mandelbaum has a remarkable ability to capture the innate music of Homer's epic in modern English. This translation truly sings.

Murray, A. T. (New York: G. P. Putnam's Sons, Loeb Classical Library, 2 vols., 1927.) Turgid and dull, but useful for the facing Greek text and references.

Palmer, George Herbert. (Boston: Houghton Mifflin, 1891.) A rather pedestrian and not very interesting prose translation. Paperback.

Rees, Ennis. (New York: Random House, 1961.) This verse translation has real merit to it but none of the fire and music of Lattimore, Fitzgerald, and Mandelbaum.

Rieu, E. V. (London: Penguin Books, 1987.) Perhaps the most useful of the prose translations. Clear and accurate in the telling, it serves the reader well in following the drama and plot lines of *The Odyssey* while marking with elegance and grace the psychological development of the characters. Paperback.

Rouse, W. H. D. (New York: Mentor Books, New American Library, 1937.) A wonderful rollicking prose translation much used in high school courses. A favorite of mine as it was my introduction to *The Odyssey*.

Shaw, T. E. (Lawrence of Arabia). (London: Oxford University Press, 1932.) You would think that Lawrence of Arabia, of all people, would have captured the spirit and flavor of Odysseus. But he didn't.

How to Pronounce the Names in *The Odyssey*

Achaeans: a-kē'ans
Acheron: ak'e-ron
Achilles: a-kil'ez
Agamemnon: ag-a-mem'non
Aeaea: ē-ē'a
Aegisthus: ē-jis'thus
Aeolia: ē-ō'li-a
Aeolus: ē'ō-lus, ē-ō'lus
Aetolia: e-tō'li-a
Aias: ā'as
Alcinous: al-sin'ō-us
Alcmene: alk-mē'nē
Alpheus: al-fē'us, al'fē-us
Amphimedon: am-fi'mē-don
Amphinomus: am-fin'ō-mus
Amphithea: am-fi'thē-a
Amphitryon: am-fit'ri-on
Anticlea: an-ti-klē'a
Antilochus: an-til'ō-kus
Antinous: an-tin'ō-us
Antiphates: an-tif'a-tēz
Antiphus: an'ti-fus
Aphrodite: af-rō-dī'tē
Apollo: a-pol'ō
Arcesius: är-ses'i-us
Ares: ãr'ēz
Arete: a-rē'te
Argives: är'jīvz, -givz
Argos: är'gōs
Argus: är'gus
Ariadne: ar-i-ad'nē
Artemis: är'te-mis
Athena: a-thē'na
Atreus: ā'trē-us, -trös
Autolycus: ô-tol'i-kus
Cadmus: kad'mus
Calypso: ka-lip'sō
Cephallenians: sef-a-lē'ni-uns
Charybdis: ka-rib'dis
Ciconians: si-kō'ni-anz
Cimmerians: si-mir'i-anz, ki-
Circe: sēr'sē
Clytemnestra: klī-tem-nes'tra
Cnossus: nos'us

Cocytus: kō-si'tus
Crete: krēt
Cronos: krō'nus
Ctesippus: te-sip'us
Cyclopes: sī-klō'pēz
Cyprus: sī'prus
Cythera: si-thir'a
Danaans: dan'ānz
Delos: dē'los
Demeter: dē-mē'ter
Demodocus: dē-mod'o-kus
Dionysus: dī-ō-nī'sus
Dodona: dō-dō'na
Dolius: dō'li-us
Dorians: dō'ri-anz
Dulichium: dū-lik'i-um
Elis: ē'lis
Elpenor: el-pē'nôr
Elysian Fields: ē-lizh'an
Erebus: er'ē-bus
Erechtheus: ē-rek'thūs
Erinys: e-rin'is, e-ri'nis
Euboea: ū-bē'a
Eumaeus: ū-mē'us
Eupeithes: ū-pē'thēz
Euryalus: ū-rī'a-lus
Eurybates: ū-rī'ba-tēz
Eurydamas: ū-rid'a-mas
Eurycleia: ū-rī'clē-a
Eurylochus: ū-ril'ō-kus
Eurymachus: ū-rim'a-kus
Eurynome: ū-rin'ō-mē
Gaia: jē'a
Halitherses: hal-i-ther'sēz
Hebe: hē'bē
Helius: hē'li-us
Hellespont: hel'es-pont
Hephaestus: hē-fes'tus
Hera: hēr'a
Heracles: her'a-klēz
Hermes: hėr'mēz
Icarius: ī-kār'i-us
Idomeneus: ī-dom'e-nus
Ilium: il'i-um
Irus: ī'rus
Ithaca: ith'a-ka
Lacedaemonia: las-e-dē-mo'ni-a
Laertes: lā-ėr'tēz
Laestrygones: les-trig'ō-nēz
Laodamas: lā-od'a-mas
Leda: lē'da
Lemnos: lem'nos
Lesbos: lez'bos
Leto: lē'tō
Leucothea: lö-koth'ē-a
Malea: ma-lē'a
Medon: mē'don
Melantheus: mē-lan'thus
Melantho: mē-lan'thō
Menelaus: men-e-lā'us
Mentor: men'tor
Mycenae: mī-sē'nē
Myrmidons: mėr'mi-dons
Nausicaa: nô-sik'ā-a
Neleus: nē'lus
Nestor: nes'tor
Odysseus: ō-dis'us, ō-dis'ē-us
Ogygia: ō-jij'i-a
Olympus: ō-lim'pus
Orestes: ō-res'tez
Ortygia: ôr-tij'i-a
Pallas: pal'as
Peisenor: pī-sē'nôr
Peisistratus: pī-sis'tra-tus
Peleus: pē'lūs, pē'lē-us
Penelope: pē-nel'ō-pē
Persephone: pėr-sef'ō-nē
Phaeacians: fē-ā'shanz
Phemius: fē'mi-us
Philoetius: fi-lē'shus
Phoenicia: fē-nish'a
Polybus: pol'i-bus
Polycaste: pol-i-kas'tē
Polyphemus: pol-i-fē'mus
Poseidon: po-sī'don
Priam: prī'am

Pylos: pī'lōs
Rhadamanthus: ra-ä-man'thus
Same: sā'mē
Scheria: shir'i-a
Sidon: sī'don
Sirens: sī'renz
Scylla: sil'a
Sparta: spär'ta
Styx: stiks
Tiresias: tī-rē'si-as
Telemachus: tē-lem'a-kus
Themis: thē'mis
Theoclymenus: thē''ō-klī'me-nus
Theseus: thē'sös, thē'sē-us
Tydeus: tī'dūs
Tyndareus: tin-dār'i-us
Zeus: zös

Musical Selections

The following listings are suggestions and are drawn from music that we have used successfully in the teaching and practice of this work. The reader should feel free to use his or her own favorites, while trying to keep within the mood of the applicable area. Some of the selections from one area can be used in the two other areas at the guide's discretion. Area I represents music that has been found to be particularly powerful as background music. It is also effective for guided imagery and meditation and during evocation of altered states of consciousness. Area II is evocative music and is meant to stimulate and enhance process itself. Area III represents music that has a celebratory character and is often used to accompany the conclusion of exercises and processes. The music listed below, as well as tapes of the exercises and processes in this book, taken from workshops by the author, are available from:

Wind Over the Earth, Inc.
1688 Redwood Avenue
Boulder, CO 80304
1 (800) 726-0847

AREA I: BACKGROUND MEDITATIVE MUSIC

Don G. Campbell, *Crystal Meditations* (Sound of Light).
Oldman Coyote, *Tear of the Moon* (Coyote Oldman).
Constance Demby, *Novus Magnificat* (Hearts of Space H5003).
Chaltanya Hari Deuter, *Land of Enchantment* (KUC 81).
Chaltanya Hari Deuter, *Ecstasy* (Kuckuck 044).
Kay Gardner, *A Rainbow Path* (Lady Slipper).
Gregorian Chants, *Officinum Tenebrarum* (Celestial Harmonies 13022-4).
Abbess Hildegard, *A Feather on the Breath of God, Sequences and Hymns by Abbess Hildegard of Bingen* (Hyperion Records).
Alan Hovhaness, *Mysterious Mountain* (RCA AGLI-4215).
Keith Jarrett, *Köln Concert* (POL 10067).
Georgia Kelly, *Ancient Echoes* (Heru Records).
Kitaro, *Silk Road* (Canyon 051-052).
Daniel Kobialka, *Dream Passage* (LiSem Enterprises OK 101).
Daniel Kobialka, *Timeless Motion* (LiSem Enterprises OK 102).
Ottmar Liebert, *Borrasca* (Higher Octave 7036).
Melissa Morgan, *Invocation to Isis*
R. Carlos Nakai, *Journeys: Native American Flute Music* (Canyon G13).
R. Carlos Nakai, *Sundance Season* (Celestial Harmonies 13024).
Vangelis Papathanassiou, *L'Apocalypse Now* (POL 31503).
Ottorino Respighi, *Ancient Dances and Airs* (Mercury 75009).
Mike Rowland, *The Fairy Ring* (Sona Gaia Productions).
Satsang Fellowship, *Song of the Golden Lotus: The Mantric Music of Swami Kriya Ramanada.*
Therese Schroeder-Sheker, *In Dulci Jubilo* (Celestial Harmonies 13039-2).
Therese Schroeder-Sheker, *Rosa-Mystica* (Celestial Harmonies 13034-2).
Tony Scott, *Music for Zen Mediation* (Verve V6-8634).
John Serrie, *And the Stars Go with You* (Mira Mar Images MPCD 2001).
Spiritual Environment, *Shamanic Dream* (Nightingale Records 321).
Michael Stearns, *Planetary Unfolding* (Sonic Atmospheres 307).
Michael Stearns, *Chronos* (Sonic Atmospheres 312).
Eric Tingstad/Nancy Rumbel, *Legends* (Narada NDA61022).
Eric Tingstad/Nancy Rumbel, *Homeland* (Narada NDA61026).
Rob Whitesides-Woo, *Heart to Crown* (Serenity 005).

Rob Whitesides-Woo, *Miracles* (Serenity 002).
Rob Whitesides-Woo, *Mountain Light* (Serenity 018).
Henry Wolff/Nancy Hemings, *Tibetan Bells II* (Serenity 006).

AREA II: EVOCATIVE MUSIC

J. S. Bach, *Brandenburg Concertos—Volumes I & II* (COL 42274 and COL 42275).
Samuel Barber, *Adagio for Strings* (RCA AGLI-3790).
Deuter, *Ecstasy* (Kuckuck 044).
Empire of the Sun (soundtrack) (Warner 25668-2).
Field of Dreams (soundtrack) (RCA 3060).
Kay Gardner, *Rainbow Path* (Lady Slipper).
Robert Gass and Wings of Song, *Extended Chant Series: Heart of Perfect Wisdom, Kalama, Shri Ram, Om Namah Shivaya, Alleluia* (Spring Hill Music 1012, 1011, 1013, 1005, 1006).
Al Gromer Khan, *Mahogany Nights* (Hearts of Space 11020).
Philip Glass, *Koyanisquaatsi* (POL 14042).
The Gyoto Monks, *Freedom Chants* (Rykodisc RCD 20113).
Mickey Hart, *At the Edge* (Rykodisc RCD 10124).
Hildegard of Bingen, *A Feather on the Breath of God* (Hyperion CDA 66039).
Jean Michel Jarre, *Oxygene* (NTI 824746).
Jean Michel Jarre, *Equinoxe* (Polydor 829456).
Magnum Mysterium, *Collection of Sacred Music* (Celestial Harmonies 18.45012).
The Mission (Virgin 90567-2).
Mendelssohn/Bruch, *Violin Concertos* (Capital 69003).
Nana Mouskouri, *Passport* (Philips 830764).
Nana Mouskouri, *Why Worry* (Philips 830492).
Nana Mouskouri, *Ma Verite* (POL 26391).
Nana Mouskouri, *Libertad* (POL 26799).
Nana Mouskouri, *Tierra Viva* (POL 32958).
NASA Voyager II Space Sounds, *Miranda* (Brain/Mind Research).
Olatunji, *Drums of Passion* (COL CK8210).
Carl Orff, *Carmina Burana* (COL 33172).
Francis Poulenc, *Concerto for Organ* (Angel S-35953).
The Rustavi Choir, *Georgian Voices* (Elektra/Nonesuch 79224).
Camille Saint-Saëns, *Symphony No. 3* (RCA ATLI-4039).
Jean Sibelius, *Finlandia* (Phillips 9500140).

Smetana, *My Country* (DGG 2707054).
Smetana, *The Moldau* (COL 36716).
Jeffrey Thompson, *Child of a Dream* (Brain/Mind Research).
Taise, *Wait for the Lord*
Tchaikovsky, *Violin Concerto in D* (Angel-EMI 32807).
Vangelis, *Heaven and Hell* (RCA 5110).
Vangelis, *Ignacio* (POL 13042).
Vangelis, *Odes* (POL 1473109).
Vangelis, *Opera Sauvage* (POL 29663).
Vangelis, *L'Apoloclypse Des Animaux* (POL 831503-2).
Vangelis, *Direct* (Arista 8545).
Vangelis, *Chariots of Fire* (POL 800020-2).
Vivaldi, *Gloria* (Elec. 45248).
Paul Winter, *Miss Gaia/Earth Mass* (Living Music LD0002).
Zuleika, *White Pavillion*

AREA III: CELEBRATORY MUSIC

Anugama, *Exotic Dance* (Nightingale Records NGH CD-311).
Enya, *Water Mark* (Geffen 24233).
Hooked on Classics, *Volumes I, II, III* (K-Tel NU 6113, NU 6893, NU 626).
Jean Houston/Howard Jerome, *You Are More* (Wind Over the Earth).
Nusrat Fateh Ali Khan, *Qawwal and Party* (Real World #991300-2).
Nusrat Fateh Ali Khan, *Mustt Mustt* (Real World #91630-2).
Daniel Kobialka, *Timeless Motion* (LiSem Enterprises DK 102).
Eric Kunzel and Cincinnati Pops Orchestra, *Pomp & Pizazz* (Telarc 80122).
La Bamba (soundtrack) (Warner 25605-2).
Brent Lewis, *Earth Tribe Rhythms* (COM 3300).
Perles Du Baroque (Arion Records ARN 436342).
Smetana, *The Moldau* (COL 36716).
Paul Simon, *Graceland* (Warner Bros. 9 25447-2).
Paul Simon, *The Rhythm of the Saints* (Warner Bros. 9 26098-2).

If you are interested in receiving information about seminars given by Jean Houston, please write to:

Jean Houston
Box 3300
Pomona, New York 10970

Index

About the Author

Jean Houston, internationally renowned philospher, human potential expert, and mythologist, is the author of the national bestsellers *The Possible Human* and *Search for the Beloved*, among many other books. Her pioneering work helping the indigenous peoples preserve their cultures while moving into the next millennium has earned her much acclaim. Additionally, Dr. Houston is codirector of the Foundation for Mind Research, and the founder and director of the Mystery School, a thirteen-year-old program of spiritual study and sacred psychology based on the principles of the ancient mystery traditions. Her intensive, high-energy workshops blend lectures and presentations on myth, history, and psychology with music, meditations, and dance.